The Basic Law and Hong Kong's Future

Edited by

PETER WESLEY-SMITH, BA, LLB (Adelaide), PhD (HK)
Professor, Department of Law, University of Hong Kong

ALBERT H Y CHEN, LLB, PCLL (HK), LLM (Harvard), Solicitor
Senior Lecturer, Department of Law, University of Hong Kong

Butterworths
Hong Kong – Singapore – Malaysia
1988

THE BUTTERWORTH GROUP OF COMPANIES

SINGAPORE   BUTTERWORTH & CO (ASIA) PTE LTD
                  30 Robinson Road #12-01 Tuan Sing Towers,
                  Singapore 0104

MALAYSIA   MALAYAN LAW JOURNAL SDN BHD
                  Kuala Lumpur

AUSTRALIA   BUTTERWORTHS PTY LTD
                  Sydney, Melbourne, Brisbane, Adelaide, Perth, Canberra
                  and Hobart

CANADA   BUTTERWORTHS CANADA LTD
                  Toronto and Vancouver

IRELAND   BUTTERWORTH (IRELAND) LTD
                  Dublin

NEW ZEALAND   BUTTERWORTHS OF NEW ZEALAND LTD
                  Wellington and Auckland

UK   BUTTERWORTH & CO (PUBLISHERS) LTD
                  London, Edinburgh

UNITED STATES   BUTTERWORTH LEGAL PUBLISHERS
OF AMERICA   St Paul, Minnesota
                  Seattle, Washington
                  Boston, Massachusetts
                  Austin, Texas
                  D & S PUBLISHING COMPANY
                  Clearwater, Florida

©
Butterworth & Co (Asia) Pte Ltd
1988

ISBN 0-409-99569-X
ISBN 0-409-99567-3 (pb)

Typeset in Singapore by Times Graphics and
printed in Hong Kong by Astros Printing Limited.

*The photograph on the cover is
reproduced by the kind permission of the
Information Services Department,
Government of Hong Kong.*

Preface

ONE of the mainland members of the Basic Law Drafting Committee, Mr Zhang Youyu, has recently strongly insisted that the Basic Law for the Hong Kong Special Administrative Region will not be a constitution. The Basic Law will certainly be subordinate to the constitution of China and be classified as a 'basic statute.' From Hong Kong's point of view, however, the draft Basic Law is definitely constitutional in character, just as the present Letters Patent and Royal Instructions can be said to comprise the written constitution of the colony. In this book the Basic Law is treated as a constitutional instrument in the sense that it lays down the structure and powers of government. To regard it in any other light would be seriously misleading.

It is no small task to expect of authors that they rush into book-bound print on so formidable a topic. We are grateful to all our contributors for completing their essays within the very short time-frame we allowed them. We are also grateful to the publishers for taking on a venture which must have considerably tested their resources. The General Office of the Faculty of Law, University of Hong Kong, coped admirably with the secretarial demands we made. We must finally express our appreciation to the inventors of STD services, word-processing packages, and fax machines, without whom this book could not have been published on schedule.

PETER WESLEY-SMITH and ALBERT H Y CHEN

August 1988, Hong Kong

Contents

References to the Basic Law

Abbreviations

BL	Basic Law
BLCC	Basic Law Consultative Committee
BLDC	Basic Law Drafting Committee
CBL	Committee for the Basic Law
CPG	Central People's Government
CPPCC	Chinese People's Political Consultative Conference
ExCo	Executive Council
JD	Joint Declaration on the Question of Hong Kong
LegCo	Legislative Council
LP	Letters Patent
NPC	National People's Congress
NPCSC	Standing Committee of the National People's Congress
PRC	People's Republic of China
RI	Royal Instructions
SAR	Special Administrative Region
UK	United Kingdom
UrbCo	Urban Council

Introduction

PETER WESLEY-SMITH AND ALBERT H Y CHEN

THE Draft Basic Law of the Hong Kong Special Administrative
Region of the People's Republic of China (For Solicitation of
Opinions)[1] was published at the end of April 1988. It is very
much a preliminary draft, but it contains enough of the proposed
constitution for Hong Kong in the 50-year period after 30 June
1997 to enable Hong Kong citizens to express their views. After
five months of 'consultation' with the public the Basic Law
Drafting Committee will reconsider the draft, choose between
the options in the annexes and elsewhere, and present a revised
draft to the Standing Committee of the National People's
Congress. In due course, subject to amendment by the Standing
Committee and following a further consultation process in 1989,
the final draft of the Basic Law will be submitted to and enacted
by the NPC and promulgated by the President of the People's
Republic of China. It will bear the status of a basic statute of the
state under article 62 of the Chinese constitution of 1982.

The purpose of this collection of essays is to provide the
historical and political background to the drafting of the Basic
Law and to subject the discussion draft to an immediate,
preliminary analysis. We hope that the discussion contained in
these pages will both inform and enlighten its readers on the
issues involved. As such it is intended to be a contribution to the
debate and a record of the views held by Hong Kong commentators in 1988. We do not claim to have provided an exhaustive
or authoritative exposition. Our contributors had too little time,
and in any event were requested to keep their documentation
and footnotes to a minimum. This was painful for the academics
amongst us, who are accustomed to leisurely research and
discussion with colleagues in the common room before commit-
ting themselves on paper. The editing was not as thorough as we
would have wished; our primary and rather modest function,
apart from chasing after tardy or recalcitrant authors, was to
ensure that the 'r' in 'draft Basic Law' invariably appeared.

1 Reproduced in the Appendix.

In planning and editing this book we did not attempt to achieve unanimity of approach or treatment from our essayists, who on some points disagree with each other, or to prevent occasional overlapping of topics within separate chapters. Part I covers background issues and discusses the context in which the Basic Law must be assessed. What are the principal characteristics of the present constitution of Hong Kong? Should they be carried forward into the SAR period? What attitudes towards political affairs are displayed by the people of Hong Kong? What approaches to constitutional matters are evident in the practice of mainland officials? What does 'one country, two systems' mean and what difficulties might be expected in its implementation? What course has the drafting process followed? How does Hong Kong's constitutional development in the transition to Chinese sovereignty compare with the manner in which other British colonies have been detached from the British empire? Parts II and III consist of responses to the Basic Law emerging from the seventh plenary session of the Basic Law Drafting Committee held on 26–28 April 1988. In Part II we seek to present a quite structured review of the principal provisions, whereas the contributors of the shorter commentaries in Part III were given a free hand to write on whatever aspects most appealed to them. Doubtless some important issues are ignored or receive only passing consideration. A truly comprehensive scrutiny of the Basic Law was not our objective.

We wish to make only one general comment by way of introduction, and this is that, in the main, our authors have responded to the draft Basic Law as *text*. Informed by awareness of such issues as are discussed in Part I, we have nevertheless concentrated on a critical appraisal of the actual words used in the document according to their ordinary meaning. In general, therefore, we have paid little attention to the ideological, practical, and personality factors which have been influential in the drafting process and which may inhibit substantial amendment of the present draft. This is partly because these are matters about which no detailed and reliable information is at this stage readily available, and partly because in the future the Basic Law is likely to be regarded and interpreted simply as a piece of legislation, albeit legislation of a fundamental kind. Lawyers and judges in the SAR will approach the Basic Law as they would any other written constitution in the common law world. In this they may differ from legal personnel in the PRC, and here may be the crucial dilemma: the more closely are the assumptions and techniques of the present judicial system observed, the less workable might be a constitution whose design and creation were dominated by persons schooled in a contrasting tradition.

What the fate of the final Basic Law will be — what role it will play in the Hong Kong SAR polity — is not something we would care to predict. But it must be remembered that 'law is not text, it is the use which is made of text. If there is a constitutional truth to be found it is not in the text of the constitution, but rather in the function of applying the text to the governance of a community.'[2] The author of this passage was concerned to promote, in Sir Owen Dixon's words, the 'deeper, more ordered, more philosophical and perhaps more enduring conceptions of justice'[3] upon which a constitution is erected and which ought to determine its meaning and effect. The actual document is not insignificant, but 'the point is to analyse the concepts which underlie it; not so much the meaning of its words, but the philosophical and logical meanings implicit in the process of applying its words'[4] in the political enterprise of governing the Special Administrative Region. Whether judges in the SAR will search for such meanings and apply the deep-seated values of the Hong Kong community in making the Basic Law work is a different question; whether they will be permitted to do so by the authorities in Beijing is yet another. It would be premature for this volume to attempt analysis of the draft Basic Law at this more profound level. Indeed the task of constitutional explication, and the practical activity of finding a meaningful and appropriate fundamental law for the future Hong Kong SAR, have only just begun.

2 M J Detmold, *The Australian Commonwealth: A Fundamental Analysis of its Constitution* (Sydney: Law Book Co Ltd, 1985) 5.
3 *Jesting Pilate* (Melbourne: Law Book Co Ltd, 1965) 165.
4 Detmold (n 1 above) 6; see also 262.

Contributors

Johannes Chan
Lecturer, Department of Law, University of Hong Kong

Denis Chang
Queen's Counsel, Member of the Executive Committee of the Basic
Law Consultative Committee

Albert H Y Chen
Senior Lecturer, Department of Law, University of Hong Kong

Joseph Y S Cheng
Senior Lecturer, Department of Government and Public
Administration, Chinese University of Hong Kong

Frank Ching
Journalist

Albert C Y Ho
Solicitor

Kuan Hsin-chi
Reader, Department of Government and Public Administration,
Chinese University of Hong Kong

Martin C M Lee
Queen's Counsel, Member of the Hong Kong Legislative Council,
Member of the Basic Law Drafting Committee

Nihal Jayawickrama
Senior Lecturer, Department of Law, University of Hong Kong

Emily Lau
Correspondent, Far Eastern Economic Review

Lau Siu-kai
Reader, Department of Sociology, Chinese University of
Hong Kong

Henry Litton
Queen's Counsel

Norman Miners
Senior Lecturer, Department of Political Science, University of
Hong Kong

Roda Mushkat
Senior Lecturer, Department of Law, University of Hong Kong

Byron S J Weng
Reader, Department of Government and Public Administration,
Chinese University of Hong Kong

Peter Wesley-Smith
Professor, Department of Law, University of Hong Kong

Part I

Background and Context

1 The Present Constitution of Hong Kong

PETER WESLEY-SMITH

WU TINGFANG, Chinese Minister to the United States of America 1897–1902, was a native son of Hong Kong. As Ng Choy, he was the first Chinese barrister in the colony, the first Chinese magistrate, and the first Chinese member of the Legislative Council. Many years after leaving Hong Kong he wrote a charming little book called *America through the Spectacles of an Oriental Diplomat*[1] in which he suggested that Britain's possession of Hong Kong was of small value to the British.

When Hongkong was ceded to Great Britain at the conclusion of a war in which China was defeated, it was a bare island containing only a few fishermen's huts. In order to make it a trading port and encourage people to live there, the British Government spent large sums of money year after year for its improvement and development, and through the wise administration of the local Government every facility was afforded for free trade. It is now a prosperous British colony with a population of nearly half a million. But what have been the advantages to Great Britain? Financially she has been a great loser, for the Island which she received at the close of her war with China was for many years a great drain on her national treasury. Now Hongkong is a self-supporting colony, but what benefits do the British enjoy there that do not belong to everyone else? The colony is open to all foreigners, and every right which a British merchant has is equally shared with everyone else. According to the census of 1911, out of a population of 456,739 only 12,075 were non-Chinese, of whom a small portion were British; the rest were Chinese. Thus the prosperity of that colony depends upon the Chinese who, it is needless to say, are in possession of all the privileges that are enjoyed by British residents. It should be noticed that the number of foreign firms and stores (ie non-British) have been and are increasing, while big British hongs are less numerous than before. Financially, the British people have certainly not been gainers by the acquisition of that colony. Of course I shall be told that it adds to the prestige of Great Britain, but this is an empty, bumptious boast dearly paid for by the British tax-payer.[2]

1 New York: Frederick A Stokes Co, 1914; republished in Taipei by Ch'eng-wen Publishing Co in 1968.
2 Ibid 174–176.

5

Those sentiments have probably not lost their accuracy in the years since they were first expressed. The British government, at least, has not recognised any over-riding interest in retaining its last economically significant colony, and Hong Kong's return to China has caused no anguish among British electors. But those who have considered the matter have believed that Hong Kong is an exemplar of something worth preserving. Wu Tingfang had no doubts about this:

> From an economic and moral point of view, however, I must admit that a great deal of good has been done by the British Government in Hongkong. It has provided the Chinese with an actual working model of a Western system of government which, notwithstanding many difficulties, has succeeded in transforming a barren island into a prosperous town, which is now the largest shipping port in China. The impartial administration of law and the humane treatment of criminals cannot but excite admiration and gain the confidence of the natives. If the British Government, in acquiring the desert island, had for its purpose the instruction of the natives in a modern system of government, she is to be sincerely congratulated, but it is feared that her motives were less altruistic.[3]

The impartial administration of law and a modern system of government: such were, in the eyes (or through the spectacles) of a man who had become a great Chinese reformer, the contribution which the colony made to political life in the Far East. They were, and are, prescribed in Hong Kong's constitution.

THE CONSTITUTION DESCRIBED[4]

A constitution enables us to discover how we are legitimately governed. It may be written, in the sense that one or a small number of fundamental documents sets out the principal institutions of government and defines their inter-relationships, or unwritten. The United Kingdom has an unwritten constitution: the rules identifying and limiting government agencies cannot be found in one authoritative source but must be gleaned from statutes, judicial decisions, practices, and deep-rooted ideas or philosophies. Hong Kong, however, has a written constitution, principally contained in the Letters Patent and Royal Instructions. These documents emanate from the Queen, whose authority to issue them derives from the legal principle that she

3 Ibid 176.
4 See generally Peter Wesley-Smith, *Constitutional and Administrative Law in Hong Kong* (Hong Kong: China & Hong Kong Law Studies Ltd, 1987–88) Vols I and II.

may govern ceded territories outside the United Kingdom in any way she — in reality, the executive government in Britain — sees fit. The Letters Patent establish the primary organs of government: the office of Governor, the Executive Council, and the Legislative Council; they also specify the main powers of government and restrictions on them. The Royal Instructions add further details. But this written or 'concrete' constitution does not tell us all we need to know about what government is and how it is to operate. It must be supplemented by other sources, and these are contained in the 'abstract' constitution, comprising every precept which is constitutional in nature. Legislation (both imperial and local, parliamentary and prerogative, primary and subsidiary), decisions by the courts, and conventions supply additional rules — and a complete understanding of the constitution requires recourse to all of its sources. Indeed, without an appreciation of the role played by conventions — practices expressing norms of proper political conduct — we would be seriously misled by the paper constitution. Some formal constitutional rules remain on the books only because they are never actually employed: if anyone dared to invoke them (if, for example, the Queen refused to assent to a bill passed by both houses of parliament) a constitutional crisis would ensue and the rules would be removed. Constitutional morality or propriety, as accepted by the principal actors in the system, is often a better guide to what is truly 'constitutional' than the precepts contained in the primary documents.

FUNCTIONS OF THE CONSTITUTION

Any constitution is, to a large degree, a rationalisation of politics: it represents the principles of government which citizens accept or political groups impose; it sanctifies an established political fact. Once announced, however, and implemented in a stable political environment, it usually plays a mediating role, determining the basic rules of the political game. Political, economic, and social action takes place within its confines. Ideas and circumstances are to a certain extent circumscribed by the constitution — but when they change, the constitution must eventually change with them or be replaced.

These rather elementary observations apply as well to the Hong Kong constitution as to any other. Hong Kong is a colony of the United Kingdom (though for public relations purposes nowadays called a territory) because it was acquired through the (reluctant) agreement of the government of dynastic China. The British government pronounced Hong Kong a colony and declared that it was to be governed according to the Letters

Patent and the Royal Instructions. Any Chinese disapproval was ineffective and, as a colony, the territory grew and prospered. Its officials, appointed by Britain, established a regime of law and order within the framework of the constitution, and most of its inhabitants, whether coerced by officialdom or willingly compliant, recognised and respected the new political reality. Life in the colony was directed by the government system created in Whitehall. The written constitution was amended many times over the years, but no radical change occurred because none was compelled by political forces. It was not until the 1980s that the need for a new constitutional order was acknowledged: hence the Joint Declaration signed in 1984.

The present constitution is entirely flexible: the basic documents can be amended by a simple legislative act requiring no arduous formalities, and the legislation, common law, and conventions of the abstract constitution can similarly adapt or be altered without difficulty. From the point of view of Hong Kong, the concrete constitution is, however, entirely rigid, in that no political process occurring within the colony can amend the Letters Patent or Royal Instructions. The proposed replacement of the concrete constitution will be achieved without Hong Kong's formal participation, in accordance with a treaty between the United Kingdom and the People's Republic of China and by virtue of a Basic Law in neither of which Hong Kong had a formal voice.

Constitutions, by their very nature, in some way limit or control the exercise of power within a territory. In Hong Kong the authority of the organs of government is defined and restricted; any excess of authority can be restrained by the courts and any attempted usurpation of power by individuals or groups can be lawfully prevented by government agencies. The constitution proclaims the principles by which power may be exercised. It is concerned with what *shall be*. Other constitutions — and in part the Chinese constitution of 1982 exemplifies this — may propagate political ideas and objectives. They declare what *will be*.

The broad notion of a constitution — the abstract constitution — encompasses not just institutional arrangements but fundamental principles for the exercise of political authority. The Hong Kong constitution, through the common law, assumes the predominance of law and its impartial administration. This is the ideal of the Rule of Law, with its corollary of an independent judicial branch of government.

This discussion supplies various criteria for analysing and assessing the existing and future Hong Kong constitutions. The constitutional lawyer is interested in such questions as:

(1) What are the sources of the constitution? Where do its rules and principles come from and how are they made?
(2) To what extent is the written, concrete constitution supplemented by the prescriptions of the abstract constitution?
(3) Can the written constitution be amended, and if so by whom? Is any special formality required? Is constitutional change difficult or easy to achieve?
(4) Is the constitution indigenous or is it imposed by an authority outside the territory?
(5) Does the constitution purport to reflect and determine the actual distribution of power within the territory or does it lay down ideals or guidelines for future developments?
(6) Are there underlying assumptions or principles upon which the constitution is predicated?

CONTENT OF THE CONSTITUTION

It is proposed to consider British Hong Kong's constitution in terms of three broad principles.

First, and most obviously, it is a colonial constitution; indeed it is typical of the constitutions of many dependent territories within the British empire prior to the mid-nineteenth century. It is old hat, with a couple of fresh plumes but no real concession to fashion. As such it reflects imperial supremacy and colonial subordinacy. The British government has complete authority over Hong Kong in the executive and legislative spheres. The constitution itself is promulgated by the Queen as advised by her ministers in Britain and it cannot be affected by events in the colony. In that sense Hong Kong has no formal autonomy. Executively, the Governor, in whom lies ultimately all significant (non-judicial) government power within the territory, is appointed by the Queen and holds office during her pleasure (that is, his commission can be withdrawn at any time and for any reason). He must loyally implement in Hong Kong the policies of Her Majesty's Government in the United Kingdom and he must accede to all instructions. Certain acts of the British government, called Acts of State, such as declarations of war or proclamations as to the extent of colonial territory, cannot be disputed by Hong Kong courts. Hong Kong has no independent treaty-making power or right of diplomatic representation in foreign countries, and arrangements for its defence are the responsibility of the United Kingdom authorities.

The imperial parliament may legislate for Hong Kong on any subject and its dictates must be obeyed as the highest source of legislative power. Apart from granting the constitution itself, the Queen has expressly reserved her general power to legislate under the prerogative. The Hong Kong legislature's activities are under strict control from London, not only by instructions to the Governor but by reservation and disallowance as well. Bills in certain categories must be reserved for the royal assent (although, if unconstitutionally assented to by the Governor, they will become law). Any ordinance properly passed in Hong Kong is subject to disallowance — in effect, repeal — by the Queen and thus to being deprived of all validity. Therefore from beginning to end the legislative process in Hong Kong may be interfered with and controlled by the imperial authorities.

Under Act of Parliament and prerogative legislation the Hong Kong courts are denied the power of final adjudication in important cases. The Judicial Committee of the Privy Council is the appeal court of last resort. It is not a servant of Her Majesty's Government, for it is a strictly judicial body, and when sitting on appeal from Hong Kong it may be considered in one sense a Hong Kong court — yet it operates in London, its composition is determined in London, it formally advises the Queen, and its jurisdiction cannot be removed by colonial legislation.

The second general principle is that the constitution implements a system of 'gubernatorial government'; that is, the ultimate responsibility within the colony for the performance of the government lies in the Governor and the Governor alone. The Governor is head of the executive branch. He makes policy, he directs its implementation, he is accountable for it to the Secretary of State for Foreign and Commonwealth Affairs. He is advised but not constrained by the Executive Council. He appoints officials. He is also the legislature, though he must act with the advice and consent of the Legislative Council, of which he is President. He may refuse to assent to bills passed by the Council. In the Executive Council he makes a great deal of the colony's subsidiary legislation. Subject to the law, he nevertheless controls much of the law-making process. While he may not interfere with the work of the courts, he may remit fines and pardon offenders and commute sentences of death. He appoints judges. The Governor is not only the focus of power, in charge of the 'efficient' (in Bagehot's term) part of the constitution, he also maintains the 'dignified' aspect: representing the Queen, he acts the role of local 'head of state' on ceremonial occasions. Pomp and circumstance are perquisites (or burdens) of his office.

This form of colonial government entails 'the four nots': in Hong Kong there is not responsible government, self-government, a representative legislature, or democracy.

(1) Responsible government has been defined by Roberts-Wray thus: 'In constitutional usage the expression may be said (briefly) to connote a system of government by or on the advice

of Ministers who are responsible to a legislature consisting wholly, or mainly, of elected members; and this responsibility implies an obligation to resign if they no longer have the confidence of the legislature.'[5] To some extent the Secretaries in Hong Kong resemble ministers responsible to the Legislative Council. They speak for the government, announce and defend policies relating to their 'portfolios,' and control the branches and departments beneath them. The triumvirate of Chief Secretary (who on occasions functions much like a prime minister), Financial Secretary, and Attorney General sit at the apex of the government apparatus — each is on the Executive Council, equivalent in some respects to Cabinet under the Westminster model — and are the Governor's principal advisers. Nevertheless the Governor is not obliged to accept their advice; the legislature is not wholly or mainly composed of elected members; the Secretaries cannot be forced to resign by Legislative Councillors. The Governor is not primarily a figurehead who merely ratifies decisions taken by others, and his own job security depends on the confidence of the Queen and her government in the United Kingdom, not of the Legislative Council.

(2) Self-government means control by the community within a territory of all aspects of government, including foreign affairs. The Hong Kong government has no authority over its foreign relations and the Governor, who invariably comes from the United Kingdom, is chosen without reference to the local community. While the legislature is chiefly composed of indigenous inhabitants, most of them are not elected by their fellow citizens but are selected and appointed by the Governor. Thus even in relation to internal affairs there is no self-government.

(3) A representative legislature is defined by the Colonial Laws Validity Act 1865 as 'any colonial legislature which shall comprise a legislative body of which one half are elected by inhabitants of the colony.' By section 5, every representative legislature 'shall, in respect to the colony under its jurisdiction, have, and be deemed at all times to have had, full power to make laws respecting the constitution, powers, and procedure of such legislature. . . . ' Hong Kong's legislature is not a representative legislature and has no power over its own constitution. Strictly, possession of a representative legislature is not incompatible with gubernatorial government, but it would cause great tensions to retain the Governor's full power while popularly electing the legislative body. Such a system prompted the disturbances in

5 Kenneth Roberts-Wray, *Commonwealth and Colonial Law* (London: Stevens & Sons, 1966) 64.

Canada leading to the Durham Report in 1839 which fore-shadowed the growth of responsible government, internal self-government, and eventual independence for the colonies.[6] Roberts-Wray comments that 'In the absence of abundant goodwill and mutual understanding, constant conflict is inevitable.'[7]

(4) Without the election of either the Legislative Council or the Governor there can be no democracy, at least as that term is usually understood. The Governor is selected by a government which is popularly elected in the United Kingdom, not in Hong Kong. Officials in the colony used to claim that a form of democracy — democracy by consultation — was in operation, but could only do so by employing a tendentious definition of democracy.[8] This claim was unfortunate, for if Hong Kong is now democratic there can be no reason to develop a more representative government system after (or before) 1997. Openness, consultation, sensitivity to public opinion, readiness to adopt policies popularly approved: these are all desirable attributes of government, but unless the Governor is accountable to the people of Hong Kong there is no democracy.

The third characteristic of the constitution is the limited legislative competence enjoyed by the legislature. Ordinances may not be repugnant to (or inconsistent with) Acts of Parliament applying to the colony, other than in certain limited categories (civil aviation, merchant shipping, and admiralty jurisdiction), or to the written constitution. Major prerogatives are free from interference by the local legislature, and prerogative legislation is possibly (the law is uncertain on this) also protected. Some kind of restriction exists in relation to laws with extraterritorial effect. The consequence is that judicial review of legislation operates in Hong Kong, unlike the United Kingdom where the doctrine of parliamentary supremacy prohibits the judges from considering whether primary legislation is ultra vires. This is significant because judicial review in some form seems to be inescapable if the spirit of the Joint Declaration on the Question of Hong Kong is observed. In the present constitution the function of judicial review is to uphold imperial dominance; in the Special Administrative Region the primary purpose will be to

6 See Miners' essay in this book, pp 44–45.
7 Roberts-Wray (n 5 above) 248.
8 John Rear, 'One Brand of Politics' in Keith Hopkins (ed), *Hong Kong: The Industrial Colony* (Hong Kong: Oxford University Press, 1971) 56. An Attorney General once claimed that Hong Kong had perfected its own version of Athenian democracy: see the government's annual report, *Hong Kong 1983: A Review of 1982* (Hong Kong: Government Printer, 1983) 5.

ensure respect for the Basic Law and thus, perhaps, to uphold the dominance of the Central People's Government and the exercise of sovereignty by China. Judicial review of *administrative* action is of course well established in the common law and will continue in the post-1997 period.

Colonial subordinacy, gubernatorial government, and limited legislative competence: these characterise Hong Kong's formal constitution in 1988. In addition there are the values expressed in the doctrine of the Rule of Law which Wu Tingfang admired and which are at least partially reflected in the design and functioning of the abstract constitution. These include the independence of the judiciary from interference by the executive branch of government.

OPERATION OF THE CONSTITUTION

The strict provisions of the written constitution are considerably modified in practice, and in some instances reliance on legal powers would be considered unconstitutional as being contrary to conventions contained in the abstract constitution. Gubernatorial authority, for example, would seem under the Letters Patent to include power to instruct the Attorney General on his discretion to prosecute; yet Attorneys General have frequently asserted their independence in this respect from any influence, even from directions by the Governor. The image of the Governor exercising total control, personally making all major decisions of government, is unrealistic. He must delegate extensively. In practice (though not in theory, as pointed out above) he operates a kind of ministerial system, leaving policy-formulation to the Secretaries and department heads as approved by the Executive Council. The relationship between Downing Street and Upper Albert Road allows for a high degree of colonial autonomy in fact. This has been recently studied by Norman Miners for the 1912-41 period. Up to 1939, Miners concludes, 'there were about 120 occasions when the Colonial Office refused to agree to a proposal put forward by the Governor of Hong Kong or instructed him to change his policy, an average of just over four rejections a year out of some 600 dispatches, telegrams, and reports that were sent to London annually.'[9]

In general a British Governor was allowed a very wide measure of discretion to rule his colony as he saw fit. Enquiries, suggestions, and occasional rebuffs from London were no more than a tiresome

9 *Hong Kong Under Imperial Rule, 1912–1941* (Hong Kong, Oxford, New York: Oxford University Press, 1987) 278.

irritant, and the authorities at home could normally be pacified by a soothing report composed of carefully selected facts which showed that all was well. The staff of the Colonial Office shared a common set of values and beliefs about the aims of imperial policy with the officers of the colonial administrative service and were normally content to trust the Governor's judgement as to what was necessary or practicable in existing circumstances. Officials were more often a Governor's allies in his attempts to persuade the Foreign Office of the need to modify British policy to suit the territory's interests than captious critics seeking to dictate to him how his colony should be run. Ministers were an unpredictable element: normally they were kept too busy to concern themselves with Hong Kong's affairs, but on rare occasions they could intervene with potentially devastating effects. However, such crises could normally be handled by a resourceful Governor, ministers passed on to other offices of state, and the even tenour of colonial administration could once more be resumed.[10]

Governors did of course bear in mind the interests of the Empire, and adapted policies in order to avoid interference by the Colonial Office, but they often identified themselves with what they perceived to be colonial interests and occasionally exhibited strikingly independent attitudes. (The relatively recent recruitment of governors whose loyalty is to the diplomatic corps rather than, as in the old days, to the colonial service, beginning with Sir Murray MacLehose, has apparently resulted in closer co-operation between Hong Kong and the United Kingdom, perhaps to the colony's detriment.) Reserved bills usually received the royal assent as a matter of course, and even on the last occasion when the disallowance power was exercised, in 1913, the Governor was first asked if he had any objections.[11] It seems reasonable to assume that the degree of colonial autonomy in practice has been enhanced since the Second World War. One Chief Secretary claimed a few years ago that in his experience the Hong Kong government had been overruled on only one issue (capital punishment). On a few matters, notably negotiation of the Joint Declaration, decision-making was taken out of the hands of the colonial authorities, but on purely local affairs the imperial connection has probably meant no more than paternal advice and consent. Even prerogative legislation and Acts of Parliament affecting Hong Kong have often been drafted in the territory.

Imperial supremacy, therefore, should not be taken to mean that the Hong Kong authorities are not largely in control of the colonial government: they possess at least quasi-autonomy. The

10 Ibid 284.
11 Ibid 75.

inhabitants of Hong Kong are in the main denied any formal participation in government and thus quasi-autonomy is not theirs. Nevertheless the system permits the vast majority of government decisions to be made locally by officials in close touch with local public opinion.

THE CONSTITUTION AS A MODEL FOR THE BASIC LAW

The paucity of instances of imperial interference in Hong Kong affairs arises from political considerations. The devices for asserting Whitehall's supremacy are still in place and resort to them would not be unconstitutional. Their retention in an anti-imperial age is primarily a result of two factors: China's concern lest internal self-government lead to demands for independence (or, at least, colonial apprehension that China would react in such a way), and fears by prominent citizens that representative government would encourage the formation of a welfare state in Hong Kong.[12] In the circumstances of the late 1980s neither factor is still relevant, for Hong Kong's post–1997 status as a region of China under the Central People's Government is proclaimed in the Joint Declaration and the draft Basic Law, while the slogan '*gangren zhigang*', and a genuine 'high degree of autonomy,' must depend on a significant element of control of the government of the Special Administrative Region by SAR citizens. There is thus no warrant for assuming that Hong Kong's subordinacy to Britain under one system ought necessarily to become subordinacy to China under another. Insofar as Hong Kong's stability and prosperity are thought to depend on the imperial connection — a dubious proposition — the present system works in practice because the UK authorities have no interest in exercising their powers over the colony. There is no guarantee, and not much likelihood, that PRC officials would be similarly circumspect if granted the same powers over the SAR. Further, the executive authorities in the SAR (including the Chief Executive) must be accountable to the legislature, as stated in section I of Annex I of the Joint Declaration, which the Governor presently is not (except in a very weak sense of 'accountable').

12 See Norman Miners, 'Plans for Constitutional Reform in Hong Kong, 1946–52' (1986) 107 *China Quarterly* 463 and, generally, Steve Tsang, *Democracy Shelved: Great Britain, China, and Attempts at Constitutional Reform in Hong Kong, 1945–1952* (Hong Kong, Oxford, New York: Oxford University Press, 1988).

Thus the first two general characteristics of the existing constitution cannot provide a satisfactory model for the constitution of the SAR. The third — restrictions on legislative competence — must, however, be preserved, in order to ensure the protection of rights and freedoms and the predominance of the Basic Law. The legislature must act lawfully, and the courts are the appropriate institutions to decide on matters of law. Judicial review is already part of the legal system which the Joint Declaration promises to maintain, it flows logically from our assumptions about legality and the legal process, and it provides some measure of protection for citizens against wayward government. Local judges, with their power of 'final adjudication,' are the best interpreters of the SAR constitution and, as judges, they can bring to their task the distinctive skills, assumptions, and techniques of their craft. Constitutional interpretation is now the exclusive preserve of judges. If, in the course of litigation, appeals on constitutional questions go to the Privy Council, the members of that tribunal remain judges independent of the executive authorities and sit as a court of final appeal for Hong Kong. This is not inconsistent with colonial subordinacy to the imperial government.

Hong Kong has not followed the usual path of British colonies towards responsible government and internal self-government. Under the existing system the ultimate remedy for unconstitutional behaviour by the Governor is dismissal from office. But in advanced dependent territories and independent countries which have Westminster-style governments there is a technique for preventing subversion of the constitution which can maintain the imperial connection while preserving a high degree of local autonomy. This is the use of 'reserve powers' by the Queen's representative, exercising his discretion without formal advice, including the ability to dismiss the chief executive and dissolve the legislature. The best-known recent example of this is the dismissal of the Prime Minister of Australia in 1975 by the Governor General. The constitution of Australia, as does the constitution of the United Kingdom, distinguishes between the head of state and the chief executive. The former has formal powers — issuing the writs for elections, appointing (but not selecting) the prime minister, signing bills into law, and so forth — and ceremonial duties while the latter effectively runs the government. In Hong Kong the Governor combines all functions. A better model for his ultimate control is the Westminster one: not only would a Hong Kong head of state relieve the chief executive from formal and ceremonial obligations and operate as a buffer between Hong Kong and China, he would be duty-bound to rescue the Basic Law from government sabotage in a manner which emphasised the SAR's high degree of autonomy. This would not jeopardise China's sovereignty. However, no such device appears in the draft Basic Law.

THE TRANSITION TO 1997

There have been a number of constitutional developments in the 1980s. Elections, through an electoral college and functional constituencies, have been introduced for 24 out of 56 members (excluding the Governor) of the Legislative Council, and changes have been made at the district and regional levels to increase representativeness. The Hong Kong Act 1985 has confirmed, for municipal law purposes, that as from 1 July 1997 Her Majesty will no longer have sovereignty or jurisdiction over Hong Kong, and an Order in Council has authorised the Hong Kong legislature to repeal or amend any enactment, including Acts of Parliament and prerogative legislation, so far as it is part of the law of Hong Kong, in relation to narrowly specified subjects, and to make laws on those subjects with extraterritorial operation. The Letters Patent and Royal Instructions have been amended a number of times.

The White Paper of February 1988 concludes that 'The aim of the Government in the period up to 1997 is that Hong Kong's system of representative government should be able to evolve gradually and progressively from the present system, in a manner that commands the full confidence of the people of Hong Kong, ensures that government remains both responsive and effective and provides for a smooth transfer of government in 1997 and a high degree of continuity thereafter.' The recommendations of the White Paper include reduction of the number of appointed members from 22 to 20, retention of the Governor as President of the Legislative Council, and in 1991 the direct election from geographic constituencies of ten Legislative Councillors. None of these will have any significant effect on the fundamental nature of the Hong Kong constitution, which continues to exhibit colonial subordinacy to the United Kingdom (the Joint Declaration, in article 4, affirms that until 1997 the government of the UK will be responsible for the administration of Hong Kong), gubernatorial government, and judicial review of legislation. In practice, however, there has been a major shift in the locus of power: no major change in Hong Kong is now contemplated by the government without China's clear approval. Whatever the spirit (and letter) of the Joint Declaration, the Central People's Government has already assumed a role unthinkable just a few years ago and which is an augury of post-1997 realities. No doubt on some matters, such as political censorship and the issuing of visas, the Hong Kong government has long been constrained by its relationship with the People's Republic of China, but the new relationship seems unprecedented in Hong Kong's history; until recent times, indeed, Hong Kong was adamant to resist the slightest suspicion of interference by Chinese officialdom.[13]

Further developments are on the agenda for constitutional reform during the transition to 1997. In particular, it will be necessary to localise the sources of law, to renegotiate treaties under which Hong Kong participates in the international arena, and to replace the jurisdiction of the Judicial Committee of the Privy Council by a local court of final appeal. A representative legislature is unlikely to be achieved and any diminution of imperial supremacy or gubernatorial power will be almost imperceptible. The values of the Rule of Law will continue to be proclaimed both before and after the terminal date of British administration. But innovations will be gradual and conservative, designed to converge with the system proposed in the Basic Law.

13 See Peter Wesley-Smith, 'The Proposed Establishment of a "China Office" in Hong Kong' (1981) 19 *Journal of Oriental Studies* 175.

2 The Political Values of the Hong Kong Chinese

LAU SIU-KAI*

POLITICAL values in traditional China revolved around two core ideas about political power. One was the supreme jurisdiction of the autonomous political order, centring upon the universal kingship, in all domains of social and cultural life. Theoretically, the state, as the embodiment of collective interests, was free to intervene in social and cultural affairs and to curb the power and autonomy of socio-cultural groups. The other idea, propagated by Confucianism, was that the state should exercise self-restraint in the application of political power. Active, unremitting interventionism by the state was frowned upon, and 'light' or 'limited' government was idealised.

This divergence between the de jure all-encompassing view of political power and the de facto expectation of its limitation was aptly described by Benjamin I Schwartz:

> The 'political culture' was indeed unambiguously authoritarian and based on a positive evaluation of hierarchy and status. There was nothing which precluded the ad hoc, arbitrary and often brutal intervention of state power in the lives of groups or individuals. Yet the dominant orientation did not ordinarily lead to unremitting intervention by organizational means for either 'good' or 'evil' goals.[1]

The explanation for this paradox in traditional political culture seems to lie in the very conception of the legitimacy of political power, which had been developed in China long before her unification in 221 BC. The Chinese emperor was considered to have 'no "right" to rule, but a "Heavenly Mandate" (*tianming*), ie a duty to fulfil. It was his duty to keep the human society in good order (*zhi*). The guidelines for this order had to correspond

*The author is grateful to the Hong Kong Television Broadcasts Limited and the Institute of Social Studies of the Chinese University of Hong Kong for generously funding the surveys on which this chapter is based.

1 Benjamin I Schwartz, 'The Primacy of the Political Order in East Asian Societies: Some Preliminary Generalizations' in Stuart R Schram (ed), *Foundations and Limits of State Power in China* (Hong Kong: Chinese University Press, 1987) 4.

19

to a cosmic order which was believed to include moral principles. They were written down in traditional texts commonly called books of rites (*li*). Their norms and principles were considered by the emperors as exemplary and binding. They limited his free will and his right (capacity) to take political decisions.'[2]

While it is true that in traditional Chinese political theory, and according to public opinion, the emperor was not considered to be an absolute ruler, the fact that political power was basically unchecked by institutional means or by social-economic power means that when self-imposed restraints broke down, society would be at the mercy of unremitting intervention by the state. It was only the limited nature of the actual capability of the state and of the resources at its disposal that could restrict arbitrary state interventionism.

Structurally speaking, the monocratic and bureaucratic colonial regime in Hong Kong bears striking resemblance to the imperial bureaucratic regime of traditional China. The authoritarian colonial system seems to provide fertile ground for the transplantation and perpetuation of traditional Chinese political culture in Hong Kong. The preservation of that culture might be even more complete, and individual elements of it even more accentuated, because of the 'closed' nature of alien colonial rule. Nevertheless, the very nature of colonial rule, its 'benign' character, its self-imposed limitation of governmental functions, its legalistic orientation, and its consultative mode of rule have not only considerably counteracted the negative impact of alien rule on the traditional political culture of the Hong Kong Chinese, but have also spawned a more sophisticated and differentiated political culture among them. The processes of economic development and Westernisation are undoubtedly of equal importance in selectively transforming 'old' political values and fostering 'new' ones.

The resulting political culture of the Hong Kong Chinese is an admixture of 'old' and 'new' elements. It may be reasonable to argue that the evolution of this political culture had not taken a smooth or gradual trajectory. In fact, it seems that the evolutionary process has speeded up since the late 1960s, with the increasing involvement of the government in the social, and, to a lesser extent, the economic spheres, and has further accelerated since the early 1980s with the onset of the Sino-British negotiation over the future of Hong Kong. The progressive political

2 Karl Bünger, 'Concluding Remarks on Two Aspects of the Chinese Unitary State as Compared with the European State System' in Schram (n 1 above) 316–317.

assertion of the activist segment of the populace and the accommodative stance taken by the government towards it also produce 'educative' effects on the political beliefs of the man in the street.

In this chapter four aspects relating to the conception of political power (attitude towards politics, conception of the political system, attitude towards government, and conception of governmental functions) in the political culture of the Hong Kong Chinese will be explored. The thrust of the findings is that the Hong Kong Chinese, compared to their traditional counterparts, espouse a more limited conception of the exercise of political power, while their support for the idea of the supreme, all-encompassing jurisdiction of the autonomous state is less obvious. In a certain sense, the political culture of the Hong Kong Chinese might be said to have 'progressed' to the stage that the political sector is seen as but one among several 'autonomous' sectors in society, albeit still the dominant one. In contrast to traditional China, the political culture of the Hong Kong Chinese would confer a much higher level of autonomy to society and the economy. The contraction of the role of the state as seen in the political culture of the Hong Kong Chinese thus constitutes the direction of political cultural development in one of the most modernised Chinese societies to date.

The data upon which this chapter is based were collected in two questionnaire surveys conducted in 1985 and 1986 respectively (see the Appendix to this chapter). As the 1985 survey provided the bulk of the data, figures presented in the following discussion pertain to that survey unless expressly specified. Even though both surveys were implemented in Kwun Tong, a residential-cum-industrial community in the eastern part of Kowloon, the fact that previous research experience shows that communities do not differ much in political culture should enable the findings there to be generalised to apply to the whole of the Chinese populace in Hong Kong.

ATTITUDE TOWARDS POLITICS

The term 'politics' in traditional China carried the negative meanings of pursuit of private interests to the detriment of public good, chicanery, violence, personal feuds, immorality, government harassment, corruption, ambitions of personal status, and others, which together constitute a form of indictment of the arbitrariness and rapaciousness of political power in the state-dominated traditional social order.

The political experience of the Hong Kong Chinese has mitigated the seriousness of anti-political feelings. Table 1 lists the distribution of responses to a series of probing questions in the 1985 survey, which were designed to throw light on the various facets of anti-political attitudes in Hong Kong. These findings present a complex attitudinal orientation which is ambivalent in substance.

It appears that unconditional abhorrence and fear of politics have abated among the Hong Kong Chinese. Anti-political sentiments, however, linger on as a plurality of respondents

Table 1
Attitudes towards politics
(figures in percent)

Statement	Agree very much	Agree	Disagree	Disagree very much	Don't Know	No Answer
1. Democratic politics will facilitate the appearance of dangerous careerists.	1.2	40.3	32.6	1.2		24.6
2. The purpose of political participation is to improve the livelihood of myself and my family. It is not for the sake of realising political ideals.	1.0	51.6	27.1	1.0		19.2
3. Even if many people vote blindly, their right to vote should not be denied.	0.9	43.4	44.2	2.6		8.9
4. 'Politics' means the oppression of a group of people by another group for the sake of the latter's self-interest.	1.4	31.4	43.3	2.9		21.0
5. Politics is dirty.	3.0	26.1	45.5	3.0		22.4
6. Politics is dangerous.	3.1	41.9	32.1	1.7		21.3
7. Political leaders are unworthy of trust.	2.6	27.0	42.5	1.3		26.6

(45%) agreed or strongly agreed that politics was dangerous and a similar proportion (41.5%) agreed or strongly agreed that 'democratic politics will facilitate the appearance of dangerous careerists.' Nevertheless, there seems to be improvements in other areas such as trust of political leaders, right to vote, perception of politics as dirty, and the oppressive possibilities of politics.

Unlike the moralistic conception of politics in traditional political doctrines, the attitude towards politics of the Hong Kong Chinese is primarily instrumental, as the majority of respondents related political participation to the enhancement of private interests. Despite reality to the contrary, political power was traditionally conceived as the means to promote both public ends (hence it should be controlled only by the government) and personal status (in this sense power was something to be enjoyed rather than deployed to achieve measurable results).[3] From the developmental perspective, the transition from a moralistic to an instrumental approach to politics represents a significant step in the transformation of a political culture. In order for this transition to occur, the relevance of government and politics to the people must have been greatly increased.

In Hong Kong, the increasing perception of government as the benefactor and the primary solver of social and even private problems is critical in the formation of an instrumental orientation towards politics on the part of the Hong Kong Chinese.[4] A growing sense of dependence on the government for a variety of things related to daily living makes it well-nigh impossible for people to 'avoid' politics. As this increased 'approach' stance towards politics by the Hong Kong Chinese has been reciprocated by the accommodationist position of the government in the past two decades, a more favourable attitude towards politics might thus result.

3 According to Lucian W Pye, *Asian Power and Politics: The Cultural Dimensions of Authority* (Cambridge, Mass: Harvard University Press, 1985), in Asian cultures 'people tend to see power as status, a tendency which even today many Asian rulers nostalgically wish to preserve. For when power implies the security of status there can be no political process. Contention and strife cease. All are expected to devote themselves to displaying the proper respect and honor for others, according to their station. Any criticism of leaders becomes an attack upon the social system. Hence to criticize is to display bad taste, to be less than worthy.' (p 22)

4 Lau Siu-kai and Kuan Hsin-chi, 'The Changing Political Culture of the Hong Kong Chinese' in Joseph Y S Cheng (ed), *Hong Kong in Transition* (Hong Kong: Oxford University Press, 1986) 30–35. In our 1985 survey, 74.3% of the respondents agreed and 4% strongly agreed with the statement that the work of the government was intimately related to daily living.

CONCEPTION OF POLITICAL SYSTEM

It is quite inconceivable that the common man has any idea about the abstract concept of 'political system.' Be that as it may, we still tried to fathom in a rough manner how the 'political system' appeared to the Hong Kong Chinese in our 1986 survey through a battery of test items. The findings are shown in Table 2.

Several observations can be drawn from the table. In the first place, there was overwhelming endorsement of the existing political system, whatever it meant to the respondents. This finding, however, is not surprising at all, as it falls into line with other similar findings.

Second, because of the general support for the existing political system, any drastic attempt to alter it would be opposed. Thus 79.3% of the respondents agreed and 7.2% strongly agreed that any political reform should be gradual and must not be hasty. The passive response of the Hong Kong Chinese to the call for 'democratisation' in Hong Kong by the democratic activists recently betokened their basically conservative orientation.

Third, there appears also a reformist or idealistic strand in the political ethos of the Hong Kong Chinese. Almost half of the respondents (49%) agreed or strongly agreed that political leaders elected by the people would perform a better job than the incumbent Hong Kong government, while only 24.5% disagreed or strongly disagreed. On another occasion, it was found that 55.7% of them thought that, in general, the people and social leaders in Hong Kong knew better than the government what was good and what was bad for Hong Kong. Moreover, as evidenced in Table 2, they were optimistic about the chance of success of democratic reform in Hong Kong, for 54.7% rated the chance as very good.

On the face of it, it is difficult to square the Hong Kong Chinese people's favourable reception of elections and optimism about democratic reform with their lukewarm response to concrete democratic appeals by activists. On closer scrutiny, however, the riddle is not difficult to explain, and the solution lies in the particular conception of 'democracy' in the mind of the Hong Kong Chinese. The answers of the respondents on what was a democratic government are revealing. A plurality of them (43.9%) would classify a government as democratic if it were willing to consult public opinion, without requiring that public opinion must be followed. A percentage of 23.2, the second largest proportion, considered democratic government as a government elected by the people. A percentage of 15.8 thought that a government that could lead the people was democratic, while 0.7% would deem a government democratic if it gave to the people whatever they wanted. In Western democratic theory,

Table 2
Conception of the political system
(figures in percent)

Statement	Agree very much	Agree	Disagree	Disagree very much	Don't Know / No Answer
1. I think the existing political system is good enough. If there is any problem, it is mainly because of the fault of some government officials.	1.3	51.0	31.4	0.7	15.6
2. The chance of success for democratic reform in Hong Kong is good.	2.3	52.4	15.5	0.5	29.2
3. The emergence of political parties will make the political system of Hong Kong better.	0.5	34.3	27.5	0.8	36.9
4. Political leaders elected by the people will perform better than the incumbent Hong Kong government.	3.4	45.6	24.0	0.5	26.5
5. Any political reform should be gradual; it must not be hasty.	7.2	79.3	1.0	0	7.2
6. It will be better for Hong Kong to be governed by a few capable men than to talk about political reform.	4.7	54.2	24.4	1.0	15.6
7. Whichever kind of government is immaterial, provided a minimum standard of living can be safeguarded for myself.	4.2	56.6	31.2	2.6	5.5
8. Although the political system of Hong Kong is not perfect, it is the best we can have under existing circumstances.	2.6	71.7	16.6	0	9.1

election is the sine qua non of democratic government, but it does not appear to be the crucial element in the mind of the Hong Kong Chinese. Since the Hong Kong government prides itself on its activeness in consulting public opinion, and since this self-proclaimed virtue of the Hong Kong government is to a certain extent recognised by the people, democratic reform, if it is phrased as refinements of the system of consultative government, would not constitute drastic institutional change in the mind of the respondents, and thus they would embrace it and be optimistic about its success. The validity of this argument can be borne out by the findings in Table 3.

Table 3
Probability of success of democratic reform by
selected conceptions of democratic government
(figures in percent)

High probability	Consultative government	Government that can lead	Elective government	Sub-total (N)
Strongly agree	61.1	5.6	27.8	94.5 (17)
Agree	50.9	17.3	29.1	97.3 (365)
Disagree	51.8	24.6	19.3	95.7 (109)
Strongly disagree	25.0	25.0	25.0	75.0 (3)

In Table 3, it appears that those who were more optimistic about the probability of success of democratic reform were more likely to define democratic government as consultative government.

The primordial importance of consultative government in the ethos of the Hong Kong Chinese can be examined from another angle. Our respondents were asked about the most important factor for social stability. A percentage of 14.5 picked the traditional virtues of *li yi lien chi* (rules of propriety, righteousness, modesty and sense of shame),[5] 37.5% law, 29.6% a sound political system, and 7.3% strong leaders. The fact that institutional factors such as law and political system were preferred should testify to the 'modernity' of the political values of the Hong Kong Chinese. Nonetheless, the preference for law and political system as the factors for social stability is fully compatible with the preference for consultative government as demo-

5 See generally Chang Wei Jen, 'Traditional Chinese Attitudes Toward Law and Authority' (unpublished conference paper, March 1986) 26–31.

cratic government. Surprisingly, it was those who rated strong leaders as most crucial to social stability who were more inclined to define democratic government as elective government. It might be that those who favoured election saw it as the vehicle to deliver to them strong leaders, whom they saw lacking in the faceless bureaucracy currently presiding over Hong Kong.

In fact, the preference for consultative government seems to camouflage a fear of politics. Hence it can be hypothesised that those who are less fearful of politics would place more emphasis on election as the criterion of democratic government. The data show that this seems to be in fact the case. Respondents who agreed that politics was repression of one group of people by another were more prone to define democratic government as consultative government, and vice versa for those who disagreed. This might provide a further clue for explaining the riddle of the apparent co-existence of political idealism and behavioural conservatism among the Hong Kong Chinese.

Our fourth observation about Table 2 is that the growing emphasis placed on law and institutions has not displaced the importance attached to good leaders, who were lauded as the linchpin of any political system in traditional political thought. According to Confucian teachings, '[f]or its governing, the state could not rely solely on a complete and perfect set of institutions.'[6] Morever, 'the administration of government lies in getting proper men. Such men are to be got by means of the ruler's own character. That character is to be cultivated by his treading in the ways of duty.'[7] But 'Confucius' stress on the "superior man" was not intended to substitute a government by men for government by laws, but rather to implant the concept of government by men within a system of government by law.'[8] Traditional China was often described as government by man instead of government by law and castigated as such, even though it had developed, among traditional societies, a set of relatively advanced rational-legal bureaucratic institutions — institutions that provided the stimulus to institutional changes in the modern West.[9] In view of the centuries-old valuation of good leaders in China and the tendency of Chinese to personify government and to identify government with prominent political

6 Hsiao Kung-chuan, *A History of Chinese Political Thought*, (Princeton, NJ: Princeton University Press, 1979) Vol 1 123.
7 Ibid.
8 Ibid 124.
9 See Ssu-yu Teng, 'Chinese Influence on the Western Examination System' in John L Bishop (ed), *Studies of Governmental Institutions in Chinese History* (Cambridge, Mass: Harvard University Press, 1968) 197–242.

figures, the emphasis on good leaders by the Hong Kong Chinese appears natural, and this emphasis might even have been further accentuated by the lack of identifiable leaders in Hong Kong in the first place.[10]

While it is incontrovertible that the importance of institutions and law is widely recognised by the Hong Kong Chinese, it is not possible to conclude that the importance of rule by (superior) man has thus been irreversibly displaced. It seems that whether rule by institutions or rule by man is more important to the Hong Kong Chinese is still a moot point. They obviously see the centrality of a good political system, but they are also fully aware that good institutions, in order to function well, have to be manned by good officials and leaders. Thus, more than half of our respondents (52.3%) agreed or strongly agreed with the following statement: 'I think the existing political system is good enough. If there is any problem, it is mainly because of the fault of some government officials.' On another occasion, they seemed to place more emphasis on rule by man than rule by institutions, as 58.9% of them agreed or strongly agreed that 'it will be better for Hong Kong to be governed by a few capable men than to talk about political reform.' In short, although the Hong Kong Chinese have embraced institutions as an integral part of the political system to an extent unknown in traditional and modern China, they have not yet 'progressed' to the stage where the concept of rule by man is relegated to oblivion.

Fifth, the 'progress' made by the Hong Kong Chinese in their political values can be measured by their attitude towards political parties. Since the appearance of political parties in the last decade or so of Manchu rule in China, the term political party has become a bête noire to the ordinary Chinese. This abhorrence of political parties might even have been exacerbated among the Hong Kong Chinese, since many of the more elderly of them fled to Hong Kong for political reasons. The term political party conjures up images of confrontation, factions, totalitarianism, corruption, political plots, ideological indoctrination, closed political arenas, and adversarial politics. The attitude towards political parties hence provides an acid test of the level of 'modernity' of the political values of the Hong Kong Chinese. In our 1985 survey, while less than half of the respondents (34.8%) agreed or agreed strongly that 'the emergence of political parties will make the political system of Hong

10 See Lau Siu-kai, 'Local Leaders and Local Politics in Hong Kong' in A Aoi et al (eds), *Family and Community Changes in East Asia* (Tokyo: Japan Sociological Society, 1985) 374–396.

Kong better,' they already formed a plurality of those who gave definite answers. Even though we lack previously collected data to serve as a reference point for comparative purposes, we feel that it might not be unjustified to conclude that the Hong Kong Chinese have formed a fairly favourable attitude towards political parties as an integral part of the political system. Nevertheless, since 36.9% of them either answered 'don't know' or gave no answers at all, one must say that the topic of political parties is still a very controversial subject to the Hong Kong Chinese and they have difficulty in arriving at a definite opinion on it. In this connection it is noteworthy that a higher percentage (57.6) of those who disagreed that political parties would improve Hong Kong's political system, compared to those who agreed (43.9%) defined democratic government as consultative government. Conversely, a higher proportion of those who agreed that political parties would make Hong Kong's political system better (35.1%) defined democratic government as government elected by the people than that (17.2%) of those who disagreed. In other words, those who were more favourably disposed towards consultative government were less receptive to political parties, while the reverse was true of those who preferred elective government.

Finally the instrumental orientation towards politics which we have mentioned in the previous section also colours people's conception of the political system. Thus 56.6% of the respondents agreed and 4.2% agreed very much (see Table 2) with this statement: 'whichever kind of government is immaterial, provided a minimum standard of living can be safeguarded for myself.' This finding qualifies the idealistic strands in the conception of the political system detected before. Accordingly, in the ethos of the Hong Kong Chinese, 'modern' democratic tenets have made their presence, but they seem to occupy a subsidiary position and fail to be synthesised with the traditional elements. Even so, their impact on other facets of the political ethos is palpable.

ATTITUDE TOWARDS GOVERNMENT

The complex attitudinal syndrome of the Hong Kong Chinese towards government is the result of a melange of conditioning factors — traditional political values, 'imported' Western political ideas, actual political experience, the behaviour of the Hong Kong and Chinese governments, the influence of political leaders and activists, and the less-than-given nature of the authority of the colonial regime. Consequently, the attitudinal syndrome is suffused with ambivalence and ambiguities, which not only fail to provide clear guides to political action, but also exert a dampening effect on political involvement. The overall impact of the largely 'unexpected' issue of 1997 on the attitude towards government is hard to ascertain at this stage, for its effects are diverse and multiple-edged. The 1997 malaise simultaneously gives an impetus to political participation, raises political fears, and instigates political withdrawal. Furthermore, it is not possible to predict in the meantime whether the present confused state of popular attitudes towards government represents a transitional state moving in a definite direction or a stable condition, because the future political development of Hong Kong is still fluid.

Table 4 presents the findings on various attitudes towards government by the respondents in the 1985 survey. The general picture arising from the seemingly contradictory findings is a favourable, yet cynical, orientation towards government in general, and the Hong Kong government in particular.

What is most remarkable in Table 4 is the finding that a plurality of the respondents were able to recognise an autonomous political institution embodied in the Hong Kong government which functioned in accordance with a distinctive set of principles. Thus, 47.1% of them disagreed or disagreed strongly with this statement: 'Managing government is akin to business management, as the most important thing is profit-making.' Given the traditional conception of government as the guardian of the public good and as a moraliser and the disdain for crass money-making behaviour, this ability to distinguish between political and economic institutions is understandable. It also shows that despite the pervasive penetration of economic reasoning in materialistic Hong Kong, the political sector and the government are still able to maintain a distinctive identity. This might be attributed to the fact that the colonial government, by virtue of its 'secluded' nature, has so far been able to maintain its institutional distinctiveness by minimising its entanglements with society and economy. Another piece of evidence also provides indirect testimony to the autonomy of the political sector. The number of respondents who disagreed or strongly disagreed with the statement that only those who had a prestigious occupation and had done well could make good (political) leaders amounted to 53.2%. Hence, even though the Hong Kong Chinese admire achievers in the social and economic spheres, they do not necessarily consider them as 'natural' political leaders. Apparently they are capable of distinguishing between political skills and non-political skills.

Table 4
Attitude towards government
(figures in percent)

Statement	Agree very much	Agree	Disagree	Disagree very much	Don't Know	No Answer
1. Managing government is akin to business management, as the most important thing is profit-making.	1.8	37.7	42.5	4.6		13.4
2. Government should treat the people like a father treats his children.	8.2	72.9	13.0	0.8		5.1
3. A good government should concentrate on improving the livelihood of the people. It should not pay too much attention to long-term political ideals or 'isms.'	5.9	65.3	16.9	0.4		11.5
4. Most of the time the Hong Kong government avows that it is the protector of public interests. In reality it always promotes its own interests.	5.7	55.3	23.5	0.5		15.0
5. There is an intimate relationship between the activities of the government and my daily living.	4.0	74.3	11.9	0.7		9.1
6. The Hong Kong government is a good government.	1.0	60.2	21.1	0.5		17.1
7. The Hong Kong government takes care mainly of the interests of the wealthy.	4.8	39.6	42.5	1.2		11.9

The ability to identify a separate and autonomous political sector is probably related to the acceptance of the idea of public interest. It should be noted that 62.6% of the respondents in the 1985 survey admitted the existence of the so-called public interest in society. Accordingly, autonomy of the government or the political sector will be granted and recognised by the people if it is seen to be pursuing public interest, in whatever ways public interests are defined by them. On the other hand, if the government is not seen as the guardian of public interests, a strong element of political cynicism towards it is unavoidable, even though a distinctive identity and institutional autonomy are still granted to it. On this point two pieces of evidence are revealing. The number of respondents who agreed and those who strongly agreed with the statement, 'Most of the time the Hong Kong government avows that it is the protector of public interests. In reality, it always promotes its own interests,' amounted to 65.3% and 5.9% respectively. In the same vein, a substantial proportion of respondents (44.4%) agreed or strongly agreed with the statement that the Hong Kong government takes care mainly of the interests of the wealthy (rather than public interests). Thus the Hong Kong government is either seen as but one of a multitude of self-regarding private interests or as the bulwark of the dominant private interest in Hong Kong. Because the Hong Kong government is not seen as representing public interests, the people are reluctant to offer automatic compliance with its wishes, even though for a variety of other reasons resistance to government action and violation of the law are comparatively rare in Hong Kong. Nonetheless, cynical and suspicious sentiments are palpable. For example, 55.7% of the respondents in the 1985 survey declared that the people and social leaders knew better than the government what was good or bad for Hong Kong, while only 21.5% demurred. And 52.9% rejected the prerogative of the government to compel people to do things against their wishes on the ground of 'public interest.' Thus while the ruling coalition in Hong Kong, dominated by the bureaucracy and supported by business elites, has provided the political infrastructure undergirding the post-war economic miracle, it has not been able to consign a high level of 'giveness' or 'naturalness' to the authority of the alien colonial government.

The less-than-given nature of the legitimacy of the colonial regime has not, however, thrown its rule into jeopardy. The performance of the bureaucracy, sheer habituation, and the lack of viable political alternatives, particularly the first factor, combine to give the Hong Kong government a secure legitimacy basis to exercise continued and unchallenged rule. The general acceptance of the Hong Kong government can be seen in Table 5,

Table 5

Trust in governments

(figures in percent)

Governments	Distrust very much	Distrust	Trust	Trust very much	Don't Know / No Answer
1. Hong Kong government	3.9	12.9	68.2	3.9	14.0
2. British government	3.5	30.9	37.8	1.7	26.1
3. Chinese government	8.1	34.8	29.7	1.8	25.6

which illustrates the different levels of trust in the Hong Kong, British, and Chinese governments according to the 1985 survey.

Similar findings were obtained in the 1986 survey, where 76.4% of the respondents trusted or trusted very much the Hong Kong government, 56.6% the British government, and only 31.8% the Chinese government. The crucial importance of government performance as a factor in political trust can be corroborated by several findings. In our study of four localities in 1982, 'the percentages of respondents who said that the government's performance was good or average were 15.2 and 59.1 in Kwun Tong, 18.4 and 52.1 in Tuen Mun, 22 and 50.5 in Tai Hang Tung, and 15.5 and 54.4 in Sai Ying Pun.'[11] In Table 4, 61.2% of the respondents agreed or strongly agreed that the Hong Kong government was a good government. Likewise, in the 1986 survey, 43.6% of respondents rated the performance of the government as good or very good, while 46.6% considered it as about average. Only a minuscule 9.5% thought that the government had done a poor or very poor job. Thus, despite the less-than-given character of colonial authority and suspicious and cynical feelings of the public, the linkage of the government with the economic success of Hong Kong and its efficient administration have nevertheless much improved the status of the government in the eyes of the people.

The intimate relationship between the Hong Kong government and the people began two decades ago with the growing dependence of the changing Chinese society on the government and the latter's increasing involvement in socio-economic affairs. The new slogan of the government, 'positive non-interventionism,' by adding the qualifier 'positive,' demonstrates that the government is prepared to intervene in society

11 Lau and Kuan (n 4 above) 29.

if the situation calls for it. This increasingly close relationship between the people and the government is also perceived by the Hong Kong Chinese, as 78.3% agreed or strongly agreed with the statement that 'there is an intimate relationship between the activities of the government and my daily living.' Needless to say there is a 'vicious circle' here in the sense that, once the government has started to intervene in society by providing various goods and services, it will stimulate rising expectations and also rising frustrations among the people.

The salience of the government in society as perceived by the Hong Kong Chinese can also be seen in an earlier study of ours:

> The increasing awareness of the relevance of the government to one's livelihood naturally fosters a sense of dependence on the government for the satisfaction of one's needs. If the emphasis on self-help and the avoidance of governmental contacts were the norms in the past, the findings of this survey seem to show that these norms are fading fast. Two types of problems were distinguished in this survey, community problems and personal or family problems, and the respondents were asked to identify the person or organization most responsible for their solution. In the replies, the prominence of the government as the primary problem-solver is astounding.
>
> [A table] shows, in no uncertain terms, that the government is the most frequently quoted agency responsible for solving community problems. [Another table] adds a further consideration. Not only is the government held to be responsible for the solution of community problems, but it is thought to be the most effective means of getting things done.
>
> Parallel with the dependence on the government as a problem-solver there is inevitably a sense of diffidence on the part of the people: they feel unable to solve local problems through their own initiative and efforts. And this is, in fact, the case here. What is even more surprising is that this sense of dependence on the government is extended to the realm of personal and family problems. The Chinese people have often been applauded for the resilience and resourceful-ness of their family and kinship network, and it is precisely these qualities of the Chinese family that enable it to distance itself from the potentially threatening political authorities. But . . . a significant proportion of the respondents held the government responsible for the solution of their personal and family problems, and the number of people replying that they themselves or their family were responsible was, in contrast, far from impressive. This finding is even more puzzling since the most important family problem named by respon-dents was a financial one, which on the face of it should have only an indirect relationship with the government. But that is not the end of the story. Compared with those who held the government responsible for the solution of personal and family problems, an even larger proportion claimed that only the government was capable of solving them. The percentages of those who strongly emphasized this capacity of the government and those who were less enthusiastic were 37.9 and

12.7 in Kwun Tong, 33.3 and 12.8 in Tuen Mun, 43.1 and 7.3 in Tai Hang Tung, and 30.1 and 8 in Sai Ying Pun.

In all, what transpires from the above findings is that the people of Hong Kong are fast adopting an active and even interventionist conception of government, and it is unavoidable that they should like to see the government measure up to their expectations. Such an expectation would severely tax the capabilities of a government which is used to basing its political legitimacy on its performance and would call for drastic revision of its cherished doctrine of limited government.[12]

But this increasingly close relationship between government and people is seen in an instrumental and pragmatic light. The government is perceived primarily as service deliverer and benefactor with 'unlimited' resources. At the very least, there is no manifest evidence to show that individuals and groups in Hong Kong, in their attempts to obtain benefits from the government, see themselves embroiled in a zero-sum-like game. The general impression would seem to be a group of non-competitive individuals and groups jointly making claims on the unlimited resources controlled by an alien entity, viz the colonial government. As a result, the vertical relationship between individuals or groups with the government is emphasised to the neglect of horizontal relationships among them. This condition of unaggregated demands enables the government, provided the total amount of demands does not become intractable, to deal with them separately without jeopardising colonial rule. However, at the same time the paucity of aggregating mechanisms also deprives the government of the leverage to contain, control, or manipulate demands from society, thus leaving the government vulnerable to incessant attacks by the aggrieved. Yet, large-scale political actions against the government are difficult to organise. They are even more difficult to sustain.

The instrumental and pragmatic conception of the government-people nexus can be seen in the fact that 65.3% of the respondents agreed and 5.7% strongly agreed with the following statement: 'A good government should concentrate on improving the livelihood of the people. It should not pay too much attention to long-term political ideals or "isms." ' Furthermore, this instrumentalism and pragmatism is reminiscent of traditional Chinese expectations of the government, which also carried a heavy paternalistic dimension. In fact, 72.9% of the respondents agreed and 8.2% agreed very much with the statement that the government should treat the people like a father

12 Ibid 31 and 34.

treats his children. Only a tiny 13.8% of them refuted the statement. Support for paternalism also implies that the claims of the people against the government are not rightful entitlements belonging to the people which the government has the duty to respect, but instead are pleas or petitions for governmental beneficence. The fact that many 'demands' on the government in Hong Kong take the form of petitions is a case in point, though this may not necessarily be seen as the most effective means of influence.

In the last section, we have shown that the Hong Kong Chinese are capable of differentiating between the political and economic spheres. They are also basically reluctant to condone direct government interference in the economy, particularly in the area of income redistribution, as mentioned later in this chapter. However, given the growing dependence of society on the government, the preparedness of the Hong Kong Chinese to seek government action in solving public and private problems and the importance attached to governmental paternalism, the general conception of government has to be an interventionist, activist, or expansive one. This orientation reflects the idea of the omnipotence of the state among traditional and modern Chinese. From previously reported findings, one might say that the perceived functions and powers of government might to an unknown extent be circumscribed by the demand for autonomy of the economy and the need to safeguard the cherished personal freedoms. But to what extent the economy or personal freedoms are seen as 'completely' outside of political intervention is difficult to determine. From the fact that the Hong Kong Chinese are not reluctant to deny rights to others if such rights are seen as posing a threat to social order, we might conclude that even personal freedoms are not immune from political onslaughts in situations popularly defined as 'threatening.' In the case of the economy, the staggering economic inequalities, the strong negative elements in the evaluation of the wealthy, and the perceived future economic difficulties in Hong Kong would dampen the subjective resistance of the Hong Kong Chinese to governmental interference in the economy. We might even venture to say that the limited economic functions of the Hong Kong government are only self-imposed by the very economic doctrine adopted by the government itself, which so far has been able to ward off demands on it to play a more interventionist role in the economy. A government without such restrictive economic doctrines or one without the necessary political autonomy might have to succumb to popular pressures to intervene.

What is more significant, however, is that governmental intervention in social affairs is not only condoned by the Hong Kong Chinese, but is actually demanded by them. Since social intervention on the part of the government perforce requires economic intervention in order to procure the necessary resources or provide the necessary conditions, to what extent social interventionism and economic laissez-faire can co-exist is still an insistent question which, however, has not yet taxed the mind of the Hong Kong Chinese.

FUNCTIONS OF THE GOVERNMENT

The role of the government in relation to law and order and in establishing and maintaining the physical infrastructures for economic and social development is widely internalised by the Hong Kong Chinese. And these functions enter into the definitions of economic laissez-faire and social non-interventionism which have been practised by the colonial government for a protracted period. Whether the Hong Kong Chinese, given their traditional heritage of an expansive and interventionist government, have really endorsed such limitations on the functions of the government is still not clearly known. Hence the extent to which the present limited government is supported by the values of the Hong Kong Chinese is still controversial. In the past two decades, the Hong Kong Chinese had clamoured for increased government facilities and services. It seems, however, that they still dislike the entry of the government into social and economic realms.

In order to tap into the Hong Kong Chinese conception of the social, economic, and cultural functions of government, a series of probing questions were asked of our respondents in the 1985 survey. The results are tabulated in Table 6.

Some astounding findings have been obtained, the most important of which is the acceptance of an influential role for the government in the moral sphere, though our respondents were careful to distinguish between public and private morals. The conclusion that can be drawn in this connection is that the moralising function of the government is still quite salient in the ethos of the Hong Kong Chinese.

An overwhelming majority of the respondents, 93%, agreed or strongly agreed that officials should set good examples and teach the people correct morals and behaviour. The shirking of such functions by the colonial government would obviously disappoint the people. In respect of the established, non-controversial moral norms, the responsibility of the government to enforce them is called for. For instance, filial piety has long been the central 'public' morality of China, hence 75.1% of the respondents agreed or strongly agreed that the government should enact a law to penalise those children who failed to take care of their

Table 6
Perception of the functions of government
(figures in percent)

Statement	Agree very much	Agree	Disagree	Disagree very much	Don't Know / No Answer
1. Government should enact a law to penalise those children who fail to take care of their elderly parents.	9.0	66.1	18.5	0.9	5.5
2. Officials should set good examples and teach the people correct morals and behaviour.	9.4	83.6	3.1	0.3	3.7
3. Government should use legal means to deter divorce.	0.7	22.3	62.8	4.6	9.6
4. The profusion of social problems is due to the fault of the government.	0.8	28.6	56.3	1.0	13.3
5. Government is primarily responsible for solving social problems.	9.0	80.2	6.0	0	4.8
6. Government should force the rich to become more charitable.	3.1	35.3	53.2	2.6	5.7
7. Government should find a job for everyone, so that no one will be unemployed.	9.0	67.3	18.6	1.0	4.0
8. Government should provide a place to live for all the people of Hong Kong.	17.9	75.1	4.8	0.5	1.7

elderly parents. But there is a limit to the moralising role of the government. For the private or relatively controversial moral norms of recent origin, the responsibility of the government to enforce them is only dimly recognised. The issue of divorce provides a test case. Divorce poses a threat to the cherished family ideal, hence it was frowned upon and severely discouraged in traditional China. Modernisation nevertheless has gradually changed popular attitudes towards divorce in Hong Kong, but it is still a controversial topic which divides the populace. In the 1986 survey, 37.6% of the respondents refused to accept divorce while 41.4% accepted it. However, it appears that divorce is also largely seen as a private affair which is beyond the reach of society, not to say the government. Therefore, the government is not given the 'right' to interfere with divorce between people. Thus 67.4% of the respondents in the 1985 survey disagreed or strongly disagreed that the government should use legal means to deter divorce. In conclusion, as in the case of the traditional and modern Chinese, the moralising role of the government is generally accepted by the Hong Kong Chinese. However, such a role is restricted to the established public moral realm, which seems to be a shrinking realm when, with the rise of individualism, an increasing number of previously public moral norms will be transformed into private moral norms, though undoubtedly some moral norms (eg smoking in public places) hitherto considered as private will be progressively transformed into public moral norms.

While the interventionist role of the government in the moral sphere is generally condoned, intervention in the economic sphere fails to receive ardent support. Despite the strand of egalitarianism in traditional Chinese economic thought and in traditional norms to obligate the wealthy to be philanthropic as a means of reducing economic inequalities, the Hong Kong Chinese are nevertheless reluctant to resort to administrative means to redistribute income. Thus less than half (38.4%) of the respondents agreed or strongly agreed with the statement that the government should force the rich to become more charitable. This finding is consonant with the general picture of economic autonomy from politics in the mind of the Hong Kong Chinese.

Support for non-interventionism in the economic sphere, however, stands in stark contrast to calls for interventionism in social problems and public services. There is evidence that if the Hong Kong Chinese are given a choice between help from government and help from family, the latter will be chosen. But the complexity of the modern Hong Kong society has already reached a point where the government has to assume responsibility for a lot of public concerns, and the people basically have to depend on it for many aspects of their well-being. The involvement of the government in many public and social services since the late 1960s has already rendered anachronistic its vaunted doctrine of social non-interventionism, leaving a gap between ideology and reality, which continues to infuse elements of inconsistency and hesitancy into the government's social and welfare policies as it wavers between the poles of social self-dependence and governmental engagement.

The Hong Kong Chinese, despite their inexorable dependence on the public sector for their well-being, are nevertheless still capable of making a distinction between society and polity. Social problems and shortfalls in public services are explained largely in terms of endogenous societal factors. The responsibility for them is not shifted to the political sector as a ploy to demand public action. In Table 6, 57.4% of the respondents disagreed or strongly disagreed with the argument that the profusion of social problems was due to the fault of the government. This line of reasoning echoes that of the traditional Chinese, and it reflects, just as in traditional China, a distinct demarcation between civil society and government in Hong Kong. Unlike the case of traditional China, the distinctness of the demarcation in Hong Kong should be even greater because of the self-imposed limits on the functions of political power by the colonial government.

Absolving the government of responsibility for social problems, however, does not relieve it of the obligation to solve them. Hence, fully 89.2% of the respondents attributed to the government the primary responsibility for solving social problems. Implicit in this finding obviously is a lack of confidence in self-help or in social efficacy on the part of the Hong Kong Chinese. As the emergence of social problems is related to deficiencies in public and social services, it logically follows that the government should make provisions for them. Not surprisingly, 78.3% of the respondents agreed or strongly agreed that the government should find a job for everyone so that no one would be left unemployed. In a similar vein, 93% felt that the government should provide a place to live for all the people.

Simultaneous support for social and moral interventionism and economic non-interventionism on the part of the Hong Kong Chinese is intrinsically contradictory, and the contradiction will be sharpened when a choice has to be made between the two. This contradiction will be intensified under certain conditions: decreasing availability of resources with a slowdown in economic growth, a faster increase in the demand for social and public services than the speed of economic growth, more emphasis on social well-being or economic equity than on economic growth, and a more 'integralist' view of the government as part of the social order rather than as an outside benefactor with a bottomless reservoir of resources. In the last situation, when social actors are perceived as competing among themselves for a limited pool of resources rather than fighting separately against a resourceful government, people will be forced to choose explicitly between priorities. However, up to now these conditions have not matured to the point of compelling people to choose between social and moral interventionism and economic non-interventionism, or of raising in their mind the need for political equality (equitable distribution of political power) to mitigate economic inequalities and make available more social and public services. In short, there is as yet no conclusive evidence to indicate whether economic non-interventionism or social/moral interventionism is more important in the ethos of the Hong Kong Chinese. There is, however, a hint that when a critical choice has to be made between the two, economic non-interventionism might be relegated to lesser importance. In the 1986 survey, the respondents were asked to choose between two arguments about social welfare. The first stated that existing social welfare was inadequate for it did not make it possible for people and families who are suffering to improve their living conditions. The other argument countered the first by saying that too much or too comprehensive social welfare would lead many self-reliant people into indolence and dependence on welfare. The percentage of respondents who agreed with the first argument was 52.3% while those who endorsed the second one was only 29.7%. This finding definitely cannot furnish evidence that economic non-interventionism will be in jeopardy when the hard choice between social well-being and economic freedom has to be made. But it seems to indicate that the support for the free capitalist economy might not be absolute or unconditional. The traditional Chinese tendency to put social (and political) interests over and above economic interests seems to have a residual influence even in a free-for-all capitalist system.

CONCLUSION

While still maintaining a largely anti-political or apolitical predisposition, the Hong Kong Chinese are somehow able in their values to lessen subscription to traditional ideas of political omnipotence, political omniscience, and political omnipresence. While still recognising the wide domain of political power, the Hong Kong Chinese have installed some restraints on its jurisdiction and penetration. The economic realm is basically considered as beyond political interference, so are private moral norms. Public interests are recognised, but they are no longer solely defined by the government, nor are governmental interests equated with them. Compared with the traditional Chinese, the Hong Kong Chinese are more prepared to grant legitimacy to private interests and confer upon them an autonomous status, provided they are not detrimental to public interests, however defined. The social realm, in contrast, is still vulnerable to political intervention, and the government's performance in this sphere is critical to its overall appraisal by the people.

Popular acceptance of the existing political system is widespread, and the performance of the Hong Kong government is rated favourably. This is apparently related to the practice of 'limited' government on the part of the colonial regime. In this connection, it is important to point out that the laissez-faire orientation of the government is more in line with the political values of the Hong Kong Chinese than its deliberate detachment from an active social and moral role. On the other hand, the less-than-given nature of the authority of the colonial government, and its impersonal, faceless, and 'secluded' nature, also detract from popular attachment to it. Consequently, the government is accepted, but not loved, by the people. The strands of alienation, cynicism, and suspicion towards the Hong Kong government, amid high regard for its performance, provide the context for the general ambivalence towards the government and the political system of Hong Kong.

More importantly, the greater primacy placed on the limitation of political power than on political participation in the political culture of the Hong Kong Chinese might have something to do with the limited popular appeal of the democratic rhetoric articulated by the small-scale democratic movement in Hong Kong. It appears that the central concern of the Hong Kong Chinese is to establish 'negative' democracy by restricting the jurisdiction of political power. They are much less interested in pursuing the 'positive' democracy of participation in the sharing of political power.

Appendix
The 1985 and 1986 Surveys

A survey was conducted in the summer and autumn of 1985 in Kwun Tong. The district of Kwun Tong was selected as the research site because its nature as a heterogeneous industrial-cum-residential community makes it most representative of Hong Kong as a whole. The sampling frame used was based on a 2% sample of the complete household list prepared by the Census and Statistics Department for 1981 Census. The size of the systematic sample was 1,687. In all, 792 interviews had been successfully completed, yielding a response rate of 46.9%, which was fairly satisfactory, considering the increasing difficulty of getting access to respondents. After further checking, 767 relatively error-free cases could be used for quantitative analysis.

The locale of the second survey was also Kwun Tong, thus allowing more valid comparisons between the findings in the two surveys. It was implemented in the summer and autumn of 1986. The sampling frame, which was furnished by the Census and Statistics Department in April 1986, consisted of 175,138 households. The final systematic sample composed of 800 households. At the end of the exercise, 539 completed interviews were obtained.

In both surveys, only persons 18 years old or over were interviewed.

3 The Normal Pattern of Decolonisation of British Dependent Territories

NORMAN MINERS

EVER since the first British colonial settlement was founded four hundred years ago the area of the British empire has been subject to periodic expansion and contraction. Territories have been gained as a result of new settlements, annexations, and victories in war, and have been lost by defeat, rebellions, and treaties with foreign powers. But up to 1920, when the British empire reached its largest extent as a result of victory in the First World War, very few colonies had been voluntarily surrendered. Boundary adjustments were negotiated with other colonial powers, and one colony might be exchanged for another, as when Britain acquired Malacca in 1824 in exchange for Bengkulen, and Zanzibar in 1890 in exchange for Heligoland. But these and other cessions of territory were motivated by calculations of imperial self-interest, when it seemed that the economic or strategic advantages in retaining an area were outweighed by the diplomatic or financial costs. In such withdrawals no heed was paid to the wishes of the native inhabitants who were transferred from the sovereignty of one European power to another, though in a few cases some safeguards as to their treatment and the preservation of certain institutions were inserted in the treaty.

These examples of decolonisation were fundamentally different from the process whereby the inhabitants of a colony were advanced along the road to self-government and were finally established as independent states, free to choose for themselves whether to continue their association with Britain as a member of the Commonwealth or to cut all links with the former imperial power. The stages of this progression from colonial control to sovereign independence were first traced out in the nineteenth and early twentieth century in the colonies which had been largely populated by settlers from Britain. The change from representative government, where the legislature was composed of a majority of elected members but the administration remained in the hands of the Governor and his officials, to responsible government under ministers chosen from the colonial parliament first took place in 1839 when rebellions in the colonies of Upper and Lower Canada persuaded the British government to send out the Earl of Durham to conduct an inquiry. His report recommended that in future the Governor should be required to select as members of his Executive Council men who had the support of the majority in the legislature, and that these ministers should be free to decide all questions of internal policy except for matters concerning the constitution, foreign relations, external trade, and the disposal of public lands. This constitutional innovation in Canada was soon followed by similar developments in the Australian and New Zealand colonies, and later in South Africa. The limitations on the powers of the colonial governments laid down in the Durham Report were gradually removed over the following 90 years, and the complete freedom of the Dominions (as they were then called) to manage their own internal and external affairs was formally acknowledged by the Statute of Westminster passed by the imperial parliament in 1931. The Dominions were defined at that time as 'autonomous communities within the British Empire, equal in status, in no way subordinate one to another in any aspect of their domestic and external affairs, though united by a common allegiance to the Crown, and freely associated as members of the British Commonwealth of Nations.'[1]

A similar progression to eventual Dominion status was promised to the rest of the colonial empire at various times, but the timescale envisaged for this transformation was exceedingly vague. In 1938 the Secretary of State for the Colonies suggested that some territories might take centuries to achieve self-government.[2] Before the outbreak of the Second World War it was only in India, Burma, and Ceylon that any real progress along this road had been made. During the war the British government, under pressure from its ally, the United States of America, and needing to harness the goodwill of its colonial subjects for the prosecution of the war, felt obliged to make much more specific promises to the colonies of future self-government. After the war, in 1947 and 1948, five dependencies were set free from imperial control. Three of these, India, Pakistan, and Ceylon, chose to remain within the Commonwealth, but Burma decided to sever all links with the British Crown, and in Palestine the British administration walked out, abandoning the country to chaos and civil war between the Arabs and the Jews. Of these five cases only Ceylon attained independence without bloodshed and violence as the culmination of a deliberately phased handover of power from the colonial government to local ministers.

1 *Imperial Conference, 1926. Summary of Proceedings* (Cmd 2768) 14.
2 *House of Commons Debates* (7 December 1938) 1247.

Meanwhile in the other colonies governors were instructed by the Secretary of State to take immediate steps to give the population a greater voice in the management of local affairs, in the hope that the prospect of constitutional progress would forestall outbreaks of violence. By the end of 1966 all the larger colonies except Rhodesia and South Arabia had attained independence within the Commonwealth. This unexpectedly speedy dissolution of the colonial empire was in the main a deliberate process of withdrawal in which Britain retained control of the successive moves towards independence and moderated every change by appropriate amendments to the constitutional documents of the colony concerned.

A precise specification of the stages by which a colony should advance from undiluted autocratic rule by the Governor and his officials to self-government was never laid down in any official document.[3] Every colony had its own peculiar problems and moved at its own pace towards independence with its progress punctuated by crises, commissions of inquiry sent out from London, and conferences with local politicians. The account which follows sets out the stages through which most of the colonial territories passed. Under the earliest form of crown colony government the Governor ruled the territory acting on the advice of an Executive Council consisting entirely of his own officials, and laws were made by a Legislative Council where officials held a majority of the seats, though it also included a number of representatives of local commercial interests, usually Europeans, who were chosen by the Governor. They could make known their grievances and express their opinions on proposed legislation, but were always certain to be outvoted by the official majority. In a few colonies the frustration of the unofficial members was relieved by creating committees of the Council on which unofficial members were allowed to be in a majority. This was done in Hong Kong, where the unofficial members had a majority on the Finance Committee of the Legislative Council from 1920.[4]

The next move forward was the addition of elected members to the Legislative Council. These might be selected by important interests within the colony such as the Chamber of Commerce, the Chamber of Mines, the university, or the trade unions, by

3 A tentative plan for the stages by which the African colonies might advance to self-government was set out in the unpublished report of a departmental committee in the Colonial Office under Andrew Cohen, which reported on 22 May 1947. See the papers in CO847/36/47238(47).

4 See N J Miners, *Hong Kong Under Imperial Rule, 1912–1941* (Hong Kong, Oxford, New York: Oxford University Press, 1987) 65.

communal groups, or were indirectly chosen by local district or regional councils. Members directly elected from territorial constituencies were rare at this stage of development, and where they were present the franchise was limited to property owners or those who had completed several years of education. The number of unofficial members selected in these various ways was then successively increased until, together with the nominated unofficial members, they outnumbered the officials on the Council. This was the stage of 'semi-representative government' where the nominated unofficial, members held the balance between the officials and the elected unofficial members.[5] The Governor ceased to preside over the legislature, which elected its own Speaker on the model of the parliament at Westminster.

Later still the number of elected members was increased until they held more than half the seats, when the Legislative Council became a 'representative legislature.' Some of these members were directly elected by territorial constituencies, though the right to vote was still restricted to those qualified by income, age, or education.

Meanwhile changes took place in the Executive Council. The first was the addition of a few nominated unofficial members to join the officials. This occured comparatively early in Hong Kong with the appointment of two European unofficial members in 1896. At the time when a representative legislature was formed, or sometimes earlier, the Governor was instructed to add to his Executive Council a number of members who had the support of the elected majority in the legislature. In some colonies they were actually elected by the Legislative Council. These members were given responsibility for certain areas of policy such as transport, education, or medical matters, but they were not put in charge of any particular department. Their responsibility extended to initiating discussions on their subject in the Executive Council, answering questions in and overseeing the passage of legislation through the Legislative Council, and working with the head of a department to see that the policy decided in the Executive Council was implemented. But the civil servants remained under the Governor who continued to preside over the Executive Council which still comprised nominated official and unofficial members as well as the elected members, and policy decisions were taken by a majority vote. This stage of 'semi-responsible government' was sometimes very short. The

5 The terms 'semi-representative government' and 'semi-responsible government' are taken from Martin Wight, *The Development of the Legislative Council 1606–1945* (London: Faber & Faber, 1946). The term 'representative legislature' is defined in the Colonial Laws Validity Act 1865. (see p 11 above).

elected members of the Executive Council were not satisfied with quasi-ministerial status and insisted on being given full responsibility for their departments with the right to issue instructions to the civil service. So the members became full ministers with one of them being appointed as 'Leader of Government Business,' or later as Prime Minister. The Executive Council was renamed the Council of Ministers. But certain departments continued to remain outside the ministerial system under the control of officials directly responsible to the Governor. These usually included defence, police, external affairs, and sometimes finance.

The scene was now set for the final moves towards independence. Usually a conference was convened including if possible all significant political groups within the colony to secure agreement on the form of the independence constitution. The legislature was reconstituted so that it was elected by territorial constituencies on the basis of one person, one vote, on the model of the House of Commons. All official and nominated unofficial members lost their seats in it, but sometimes a few places were reserved to ensure the representation of particular minority groups. A final general election was then held to determine which political party should form the government which would take the country into independence. Once this was settled a date was fixed for the ending of colonial rule, and amid scenes of festive jubilation the Union Jack was lowered at midnight and the new national flag was raised. The new government took over complete responsibility for all departments of the state. If the country decided to become a member of the Commonwealth, as was normally the case, the former colonial Governor remained for a short period filling the ceremonial office of Governor-General before the position was filled by some local dignitary.

During the years leading up to independence efforts were made to accelerate the appointment of local people to all vacancies in the civil service and to promote them to the highest posts wherever possible. But most expatriate officers chose to remain until the date of independence when they became entitled on resignation to large sums in compensation for loss of career. Their sudden departure left large gaps in the civil service and often some of the departing expatriates had to be re-engaged on contract to avoid an unacceptable decline in the efficiency of the administration, since it was difficult to find local replacements. Localisation of the defence forces caused particular problems. The military units in a colony were normally made up of soldiers and non-commissioned officers from the local population with the officer ranks being filled by expatriates. In some colonies there were also units of the British army which were entirely composed of British troops. The local forces were transferred under the control of the new government at independence, but often localisation of the officer corps had been much less rapid than in the civil service and some armies had hardly any indigenous officers at all. In a few African states the slow pace of localisation led to army mutinies after independence. The units of the British army in the territory were always withdrawn at or before the date of independence. If the government wished to retain any of them to help in the defence of the new state or in internal security operations, as happened in Ceylon and Malaya, a defence treaty was signed between the new government and Britain after independence.

The successive constitutional changes at each stage leading up to independence and the final constitution of the new state were drafted in proper legal terminology by British lawyers and embodied in Orders in Council which were formally assented to by the Queen at a meeting of her Privy Council. Most new governments considered that such a constitutional instrument made in Britain was incompatible with their dignity as sovereign states. So some time after independence steps were taken to draft a new and truly autochthonous constitution.[6] At the same time the opportunity was often taken to alter the form of government from a monarchy to a republic within the Commonwealth. The Governor-General representing the Queen was replaced by an elected President, and other changes in the constitution might also be made. In some states, such as Ghana, Kenya, and Malawi, the Prime Minister chose to step up to become President. Under the new constitution this office more closely resembled the President of the United States, who is head of the executive branch, than the ceremonial presidency, which exists in India.

Though such changes might take place after independence, the constitutions of all the new states which emerged from the colonial empire closely followed the pattern of the British system of government. The main difference from the Westminster model was that the legislature of the new state was not sovereign like the British parliament, but was limited in its power by a written constitution which could be interpreted and enforced by the judges of the new Supreme Court. But in other respects the British system was closely followed and a number of the

6 See K C Wheare, *Constitutional Structure of the Commonwealth* (Oxford: Clarendon Press, 1960) 89–113 and K Robinson, 'Constitutional Autochthony in Ghana' (1961) 1 *Journal of Commonwealth Political Studies* 41–55.

unwritten rules of political practice in Britain, such as the conventions of ministerial responsibility and the role of the prime minister, were codified and set down in detail in the new constitutions to avoid any doubts as to the way in which the system should be operated.[7] This copying of the Westminster model was not imposed upon the new nations of the Commonwealth by Britain. It was the system of government demanded by the new nationalist leaders many of whom had had legal training and who believed, perhaps mistakenly, that the British system was best.

Their preference is not altogether surprising since the normal pattern of decolonisation sketched out above bears some resemblance to the stages by which parliamentary government was established in Britain itself. Indeed, the powers of the Governor in a crown colony before 1939 have been compared to those of a mediaeval king. In the normal process of decolonisation the Governor first loses his power to pass whatever laws he pleases when the elected element in the legislature approaches a majority. Then he is compelled to share his executive power with ministers who owe their position to the choice of the electorate and are responsible to the legislature. Finally at independence he is stripped of all real power in every sphere of government and becomes a ceremonial figure acting entirely at the prompting of his ministers, much like the British monarch. The crucial stage in this transformation is the step from semi-responsible to responsible government, when the civil service comes directly under the control of elected ministers. Once this watershed is passed imperial control is effectively at an end and the pace of the final advance to sovereign independence is entirely in the hands of local ministers. This stage may be taken at a rush in a few months, as happened in Zimbabwe, or it may be delayed almost indefinitely, as happened in the case of the Dominions in the nineteenth century, and in the colonies of Bermuda and the Cayman Islands today.

Hong Kong is unique in that it has never advanced further than the first steps along the road to responsible government which has been followed by every other British colony. There have been two occasions in Hong Kong's history when it seemed possible that Hong Kong might make the first moves to self-government while remaining under British rule. The first was in the period 1946 to 1952 when a number of different proposals for constitutional change were put forward which were in line

7 Some independence constitutions provided for a federal system of government, unlike the unitary system in Britain. Such complications have been omitted from the account given in the text.

with the moves being made in the rest of the colonial empire in the aftermath of the Second World War. In 1947 the Secretary of State for the Colonies, Creech Jones, suggested to the Governor that the Legislative Council should be reconstituted to comprise seven official members, seven unofficial members directly elected by the Hong Kong people, and four nominated unofficial members; and that some of the unofficial members should be invited to join the Executive Council where they should be associated with the work of particular departments and gradually assume some responsibility for executive policy.[8] This was a proposal to set up a semi-representative legislature and a quasi-ministerial system. But the Governor, Sir Mark Young, completely rejected these ideas, preferring to continue with the plans which he had already drawn up to establish a powerful municipal council. Two years later the nominated unofficial members of the existing legislature voted unanimously against the proposed municipal council and themselves proposed a reform of the Legislative Council so that it would consist of six official members, five nominated unofficial, and six elected unofficial members. No mention was made of changes in the Executive Council. This was a new proposal for a semi-representative legislature, and on this occasion the Governor, Sir Alexander Grantham, was prepared to accept it, provided that the right to vote was confined to British subjects who were literate and over 25 years old. But action to implement the scheme was deferred in view of the victory of the communists in the Chinese civil war and the establishment of the People's Republic of China across the border. In 1950 and 1952 Grantham put forward modified proposals to the Colonial Office, suggesting that there should be no direct elections, for fear that communist candidates might be preferred by the Hong Kong electorate, but that instead the six elected members should be chosen by various groups and institutions (what would now be called 'functional constituencies'). However, these plans were also abandoned, principally because it was feared that their announcement might provoke an adverse reaction from China.

Over the next 32 years there were no significant constitutional changes except for successive increases in the number of nominated unofficial members in the Legislative Council. These were always counterbalanced by a corresponding increase in the

8 Colonial Office to Sir Mark Young, telegram, 25 January 1947: CO537/1651. This and subsequent events are documented in N J Miners, 'Plans for Constitutional Reform in Hong Kong, 1946–52' (1986) 107 *China Quarterly* 463.

number of official members to preserve the official majority, though after 1976 the full number of official members was not in fact appointed. Then in 1984, when the negotiations with China on the future of Hong Kong after 1997 were in their closing stages, the Hong Kong government issued a Green Paper entitled *The Further Development of Representative Government in Hong Kong.* This laid out a programme for political change which was remarkably close to the traditional British programme for decolonisation. The Legislative Council was to be enlarged in 1988 by the addition of 24 members, 12 elected by functional constituencies and 12 by an electoral college consisting of members of District Boards and the Urban and Regional Councils. These elected members, together with the reduced number of nominated officials remaining on the Council, would transform the Council into a semi-representative legislature. This new legislature would elect four of its members to the Executive Council in 1988 and eight in 1991, and these members might possibly assume ministerial functions some time in the future. Finally it was suggested that a future Governor might be selected by an electoral college composed of all the unofficial members of the Executive and Legislative Councils. This last was the only really novel proposal in the Green Paper. In the normal process of decolonisation the Governor is gradually stripped of his executive powers which pass to the Prime Minister and other ministers chosen by the legislature; the Green Paper envisaged that the Governor should retain his full powers (except that he would lose the right to act contrary to the majority view of the Executive Council), but should be transformed into an elected chief executive. If all these plans were implemented they would indeed fulfil the professed aim of the Green Paper which was stated to be 'to develop progressively a system of government the authority for which is firmly rooted in Hong Kong, which is able to represent authoritatively the views of the people of Hong Kong, and which is more directly accountable to the people of Hong Kong.'

Regrettably it does not seem that this is going to happen, apart from the changes in the composition of the Legislative Council. These were rapidly implemented in 1985 without the two-stage phasing of the change which had been recommended in the Green Paper. When introducing the Green Paper the Governor, Sir Edward Youde, told the Legislative Council: 'We have done our utmost in framing these proposals to ensure that there need be no conflict with the principle of continuity between the systems in force both before and after 1997.'[9] Though the Green

9 *Hong Kong Hansard 1983–84* (18 July 1984) 1214.

Paper proposals were put forward in July 1984, two months before the Joint Declaration on the Question of Hong Kong was published in September, they were generally compatible with the rather imprecise delineation of the system of government of the future Special Administration Region set out in Annex 1 of that document. It would appear that at the time the Hong Kong government may have hoped to establish an institutional framework during the terminal years of British rule which the Chinese authorities would find difficult to dismantle, and so predetermine the form of the Basic Law of the future SAR. If this was indeed the authorities' intention, it has not been fulfilled. Representatives of the Chinese government soon informed Hong Kong of their abhorrence of the 1984 Green Paper and made their view clear in private and public communications that there should be no further changes in the system of government until the Basic Law was published, and that any institutional changes before 1997 must follow the pattern laid down in the Basic Law. In consequence of this intervention the 1987 Green Paper, *Review of Developments in Representative Government*, confined itself in the main to discussing trivial changes in the District Boards and Urban Council. Some possible changes in the Legislative Council were adumbrated, but with an obvious lack of enthusiasm. There was no mention of elections to the Executive Council, nor of members with quasi-ministerial function, nor of the method of selecting a future Governor; it was not even suggested that a few seats should be added to the Legislative Council to enable it to move from the status of a semi-representative legislature to a representative legislature with more than half the members having to be elected. The wording of the 1988 White Paper clearly showed that there was no longer any possibility of Hong Kong following the normal pattern of decolonisation by the institutionalisation of responsible government. The initiative of the Hong Kong government in 1984 had petered out, just as had happened with the earlier proposals put forward in the period 1947–52.

The decolonisation of Hong Kong will be totally different from the normal post-war pattern, and will more closely resemble the transfers of territory without the consent of the inhabitants which took place between the imperial powers in the nineteenth century. The nearest recent parallel is the return of the British leased territory of Weihaiwei to China in 1930. This small area at the end of Shandong province had remained politically undeveloped during the 32 years of British rule. It did not even possess Executive or Legislative Councils: the Commissioner was the sole executive and was authorised to make and proclaim such ordinances as he chose. When the British government decided to transfer the territory back to China in 1930 the Commissioner did no more than hand over the keys of the government offices to the incoming Chinese Commissioner, attend the formal celebrations, and depart on the next ship. The only element of institutional continuity between the British and Chinese administrations was provided by the civil service clerks, who were rehired by the new Chinese Commissioner.[10] The changeover from British colonial rule to the Special Administrative Region of the People's Republic of China will not be as abrupt as occurred at Weihaiwei but it cannot be as smooth a transition as has occurred in other British colonies since the essential element, the emergence of responsible government by ministers accountable to the legislature who take over the full management of public affairs at independence, will not have taken place.

---

10 See Pamela Atwell, *British Mandarins and Chinese Reformers* (Hong Kong: Oxford University Press, 1985) 164–172.

4 Chinese Constitutional Practice

KUAN HSIN-CHI

THE Basic Law will be promulgated under the authority of the Chinese constitution. The status of article 31 of the constitution, which provides the legal basis for the Basic Law, and its relations to the other articles are not as yet of great interest to lawyers in China. In their writings they are more concerned with how to justify the government policy of permitting a capitalist system to persist within China for a guaranteed period of time. Article 31 is held to be a legal expression of the concept of 'one country, two systems.' The legal theory that Chinese lawyers are trying to establish is as follows: the constitution is the mother law while the Basic Law is a local one; 'one country, two systems' does not mean that the two systems are united under federalism; the socialist system is the foundation for 'one country, two systems'; there must not be equal status between the 'two systems.'

Both in Chinese legal theory and in political practice, the future of the Basic Law cannot therefore be insulated from the future of the Chinese constitution. This is why Hong Kong people should be interested in constitutional development in China.

Behind the discussions of the ways by which the Basic Law may guarantee 'no fundamental changes in the social, economic and legal systems' in Hong Kong after 1997 there lies a deep concern with Chinese constitutional practice in past decades. If the Chinese constitution has meant very little to Chinese leaders, will the Basic Law be taken seriously? Can it be relied upon as a set of norms governing the interactions between Hong Kong and state organs of China? Can it effectively protect the legitimate though minority interests of Hong Kong in China? These are fundamental questions that loom large in sceptical minds. For the optimist, however, the past need not repeat itself, especially as a new trend seems to have set in.

The People's Republic of China has had five constitutions, including the Common Programme of 1949 which served as the basic law for the transitional period until 1954. Among these five constitutions, three, viz the common programme of 1949, the constitution of 1975, and the constitution of 1978, can be regarded as revolutionary constitutions. They meant no more than another tool for class struggle, for the radical transformation of society, rather than for the establishment of the rule of law.

In comparison, the constitution of 1954 did get rid of the revolutionary mandate, but failed to establish constitutionalism, if that is defined as the limitation of government powers in the interest of individual liberties. Many provisions were still declarative in intent. The constitution stressed the protection of revolutionary achievements and proclaimed socialist policies to be pursued. It recognised the leadership of the Chinese Communist Party in 'a broad people's democratic united front,' without at the same time requiring the Party to observe the constitution.

As a result of various forces, the supremacy of the constitution was in practice suppressed by the leadership of the Party. It has been reported that, even during the so-called 'constitutional era' of 1954–57, members of the Chinese Communist Party did not pay attention to the law of the state.[1] The situation must have been much worse during the periods when politics had to take command. In 1958, for instance, the absolute leadership of the Party was proclaimed as follows:

> [t]he policy of the Party is the soul of the people's democratic legal system; the people's democratic legal system is the instrument for implementing the Party policy. This is to say, the Party policy commands legal work and legal work can never be separated from the Party policy. Legal work can only serve as a tool for the Party policy and cannot be above or beyond politics . . . . Without the leadership of the Party there would not be the people's democratic legal system. Therefore, legislative and judicial activities as well as other forms of legal work must all be under the absolute leadership of the Party.[2]

THE CONSTITUTION OF 1982

The present constitution was enacted in 1982. It was preceded by the trial of the Gang of Four and was surrounded by widespread public discussions and speeches of political leaders. It seemed

1 Johnson Chalmers, 'The Changing Nature and Locus of Authority in Communist China' in J M H Lindbeck (ed), *China: Management of a Revolutionary Society* (Seattle: University of Washington Press, 1971) 57.
2 New China News Agency (28 August 1958), as quoted in Lee Shane Rong, *The Legal System and Political Development in Communist China, 1949–69* (PhD dissertation, North Texas State University, 1973; University Microfilms, 1973) 82.

that the political leadership took great care to impress upon the public that they had begun to subscribe to the idea of law. Peng Zhen, the then Chairman of the Standing Committee of the National People's Congress, went so far as to announce repeatedly the superiority of the constitution over the Party. All these developments were further buttressed by the rehabilitation of thousands of victims of the 'Great Proletarian Cultural Revolution.' The official press in China sang a eulogy to usher in the beginning of a new era, the era of the Rule of Law.

Subsequent developments in society followed a similar path. The scope of open discussion on a larger number of public issues expanded. Law curricula were revived in academic institutions. An open policy was adopted and special economic zones established. Citizens resorted for the first time to petitions and complaints to the government and the people's courts (article 41 of the constitution). And there were many other changes. In terms of textual analysis, the constitution calls for quite a few important new departures, such as the replacement of class struggle by modernisation as the priority task of the state, the deconcentration of political powers, and the obligation of the Communist Party to abide by the constitution.

Thus, the constitution has been described as an 'inclusion constitution' meaning that the ruling party attempted to do the following:

> ... integrate itself with its society, rather than insulate itself from it. The watershed for the transformation lies in the official verdict proclaiming the end of the class struggle. There follows a series of structural and behavioral changes, including the upgrading of the status of the state and the replacement of the command, arbitrary and dogmatic modes of action and organization by a manipulative, procedural and empirically oriented mode.[3]

In other words, the constitution of 1982 offers fresh hopes for the development of the Rule of Law. Is there any reason for Hong Kong to worry?

MEANINGS OF CONSTITUTIONAL PRACTICE

An answer to this question depends on an objective evaluation of constitutional practice within a short time-span. Problems of methodology and data abound.

---

3 Kuan Hsin-chi, 'New Departures in China's Constitution' (1984) 17 *Studies in Comparative Communism* 53–68.

To a Western lawyer, constitutional practice means the activities by which constitutional norms are elucidated and upheld, especially against the politically powerful. Constitutional review by the courts then occupies a central place in the process. For the Chinese leadership, however, constitutional practice means the implementation of Party policy. In 1983, when Peng Zhen spoke of the implementation of the constitution on the anniversary of its promulgation, he meant 'the insistence on the socialist road, the insistence on the socialist system of public property, and the development of socialist democracy.'[4] At about the same time, Yang Shang-kun presented a version of 'constitutional practice' in his Report on the Work of the Standing Committee of the People's National Congress to the effect that 'we must first do well our propaganda and education work and prevent any unconstitutional activities from occurring and correct them if they do occur.'[5]

Apart from those who concur with the political leadership that the four fundamental principles are the guiding principles for the implementation of the constitution, there has been controversy among lawyers in China on the practical status of the constitution. Some of them regard it as the fundamental law of the country and as having normative force. Others believe that unconstitutionality is not a breach of law, since the constitution is 'too vague' and does not provide for sanctions, as generally required by a legal norm; even if it does, the same sanctions are already contained in statutes and regulations. Thus for many Chinese, the perception of constitutional practice differs from the perception shared by Western scholars.

A more common-sense understanding of the concept refers to the extent of compliance with constitutional norms in general activities. Furthermore, the general public tends to be interested more in the behaviour of political leaders and organisations than in the behaviour of the common people. This chapter will then address the issue of compliance on the part of political leaders or organisations, but leave the extent unmeasured. There are reports of compliance as well as of breaches. The extent of behaviour in either direction is hard to measure accurately. Of greater significance in our context are questions such as whether the constitution is taken seriously, how effective the constitutional norms are controlled and by whom.

4 (1983) 5 *Quanguo Renmin Daibiao Dahui Changwu Weiyuanhui Gongbao (Bulletin of the Standing Committee of the National People's Congress* [henceforth *SCNPC Bulletin*]) 3–8.
5 (1983) 3 *SCNPC Bulletin* 51–52.

TYPES OF NORM

The initial trouble with an analysis of constitutional practice in our sense is that not all provisions in the Chinese constitution are normative in nature. It is characteristic of the Chinese constitution that many provisions are declarative of policy without necessarily establishing any pattern of rights and obligations. For instance, article 14 declares that the '[t]he state continuously raises labour productivity, improves economic results and develops the productive forces by enhancing the enthusiasm of the working people. . . .' However, nobody can sue the state for a breach of the constitution, should an annual survey report a decline in labour productivity in China.

Normative provisions in the constitution are basically of two kinds: the first establishes primary rules of just conduct and the other articulates secondary rules to confer and distribute powers to respective organs.

The primary rules include, first, general principles governing the political system, and second, civic rights and duties of citizens. The general principles tend to favour the state over individuals and the public interest over other claims. Moreover, the vagueness of some fundamental provisions provides politicians acting in the name of the state with immense power against individuals and social organisations. In such a context, constitutional practice may turn out to be an enforcement of constitutional norms against relatively powerless citizens. For example, article 1 of the constitution declares that '[s]abotage of the socialist system by any organisation or individual is prohibited.' In the absence of rigorous interpretation of the key words 'sabotage' and 'socialist system,' this provision can easily be used against innocent people.

In the constitution, the enumeration of civic rights as primary rules is impressive. Many rights common to Western constitutions, such as freedom of speech, are included. There are, however, two major differences. First, emphasis is given to social and economic rights rather than civil liberties. The former category of rights is elaborated in greater detail than is the latter. In addition, the unity of rights and duties has always been stressed in constitutional theory in China. Certain rights that reflect the bad experiences of the Cultural Revolution, such as the inviolability of the personal dignity of citizens, may be assumed to command more sympathy on the part of the political leadership.

The secondary rules governing distribution of powers to the state organs are more concrete and elaborate. According to these rules, the Chinese state is unitarily organised, in both the horizontal and the vertical sense. At any horizontal level, the people's congress is 'the highest organ of state power' to which the executive and the judiciary are responsible. Vertically, a state organ supervises the corresponding work of the next lower level organs. Thus, the State Council exercises 'unified leadership' over the work of the local organs of state administration at the lower levels. Similarly, local governments at and above the county level direct the work of government at lower levels. In the same vein, the Supreme People's Court supervises the administration of justice by the local people's courts at different levels and by the special people's courts; people's courts at higher levels supervise the administration of justice by those at lower levels. The same principle of organisation applies to the system of the people's procuratorates.

In comparison with the executive and the judiciary, the principle of unified leadership is less straightforward with regard to the system of the people's congresses. The constitution does not expressly confer on the National People's Congress or its Standing Committee any right to supervise the work, especially activities other than legislation, of local people's congresses. It may even be argued that no clear-cut authority relationship exists between the different levels. The people's congresses of the provinces are empowered to adopt local regulations, which must not contravene the constitution, etc, and are required only to report them to the Standing Committee of the National People's Congress for the record. The Standing Committee of a local people's congress at and above the county level may on the other hand annul 'inappropriate resolutions' of the people's congress at the next lower level.

Although the organisational principle for the state structure sounds simple, there are ambiguities in a number of provisions. Theoretically speaking, there are bound to be conflicts and controversies over the nature and the distribution of jurisdictions. But no report has been published so far in this regard.

ARE RIGHTS TAKEN SERIOUSLY?

Violations of the civic rights of citizens or of human rights are said to be prevalent in China, especially during the Cultural Revolution, when about one million people were killed, 20 million people were arrested for 'revisionist' or 'counter-revolutionary' crimes, and 100 million people suffered politically.[6] And it is

---

6 Weggel Oskar, 'Gesetzgebung und Rechtspraxis im Nachmaoistischen China, Teil III: Das Öffentliche Recht-Verfassingsrecht (Ohne Organisationsrecht)' (December 1986) *China Aktuell* (Hamburg) 781–792.

precisely because of this track record that the people of Hong Kong are concerned about the worth of a Chinese constitution. Today, similar accounts are given from time to time by the Chinese and foreign press as well as by Amnesty International.

On the other hand, there are official and academic publications which report on how violations have been 'looked into.' The People's Publishing Company of Beijing, for instance, has published a series called *Explain the Law by Cases*, edited by Xin De-li and others in 1986, which tries to bring home the message that justice has been done at the end of the day.

The upholding of the constitutional norms of rights and freedoms is a difficult and complicated task. China has simply not yet established constitutionalism, whereby justice may prevail over political authority. The issue of religious freedom is an interesting example. Of all civil liberties, religious freedom is probably the most complicated one, since it involves first, constant challenge from the official ideology of atheism; second, in the case of Christianity, the bitter legacy of the church's former partnership with imperialism; third, the cultural-political problem of ethnic minorities; and finally, the countervailing threat of potential political power by organised religion. Therefore, practice in regard to religious freedom can be used to test the development of civic rights after 1982.

Freedom of religious belief is guaranteed by article 36 of the constitution. Coercion to belief or disbelief is prohibited and no discrimination against believers or non-believers is allowed. The state pledges to protect 'normal religious activities.' Finally, 'religious bodies and religious affairs are not subject to any foreign domination.' The provisions regarding freedom of 'normal religious activities' and freedom from 'any foreign domination' constitute the most important limitations on religious freedom. The right to religious belief is further reinforced by article 147 of the Criminal Code, which states that any person who unlawfully deprives citizens of their 'legitimate' freedom of religious belief and infringes the customs and habits of minority ethnic groups is, under serious circumstances, to be sentenced to not more than two years of fixed-term imprisonment or criminal detention.

It cannot be disputed that, as compared with the situation prevailing during the Cultural Revolution, the extent of religious freedom that Chinese citizens now enjoy has been much widened. The government has made efforts to meet the demands of believers and ethnic minorities in religious and cultural areas. Churches, temples, mosques, and monasteries have been restored, educational institutions for monks, seminarians, mullahs, and nuns reopened. Believers are no longer afraid of being known as such. Talking about their beliefs, displaying religious objects at home, attending religious classes, etc is no longer dangerous. In other words, simple worship is quite free nowadays.

Religious activities beyond simple worship, such as propagation, however, are still subject to limitations. The general policy of the Party is that such activities should follow a patriotic direction and must be carried out in designated places and under the supervision of the Department for Religious Affairs. In practice, activities sponsored by the Patriotic Religious Associations are legitimate, whereas others, such as preaching by itinerant priests, are not. There is therefore room for argument that this general policy has gone beyond the limitations imposed by the constitution. A more important point is, however, that practice varies from place to place. One crucial factor affecting the implementation of the constitutional clause on religious freedom is the openness of the cadres of the local Religious Affairs Bureau and Patriotic Religious Associations.[7] Jean Charbonnier[8] has reported the arrest of some itinerant preachers in recent years and surveillance of the movements of priests and militant Christians.

One final caveat about religious freedom is in order. If we take constitutional practice to mean 'taking rights seriously,' China still has a long way to go. The present extent of religious freedom is not grounded on the Chinese leaders' belief in civic rights. Rather, it is based, as revealed by Document No 19 of 1982 of the Central Committee of the Communist Party, on the policy of the united front in the new era of the four modernisations which demands the unifying of all vital forces in the country, despite ideological differences.

ARE PROCEDURAL NORMS IMPORTANT?

With regard to rules governing distribution of powers and jurisdictions, we are interested in the degree of importance Chinese leaders give to due procedures. It seems that the National People's Congress is particularly keen on this aspect. Constitutional practices pertaining to the civic rights of citizens have never been reported, unlike the issue of proper procedures regarding the structure of the state. This emphasis may, as shall

7 'Religion in the People's Republic' in 1349 *China News Analysis* (Hong Kong) (15 December 1987) 1–7.
8 Jean Charbonnier, 'Church and State in China Today' in 33 *Tripod* (Hong Kong) (June 1986) 61.

become evident, be due to the fact that, in most cases, the authority of the National People's Congress has been challenged.

The reported violations of constitutional norms have heavily centred on two types of activity.[9] The first type is encroachment on the prerogatives of the legislature by the executive. For example, duly promulgated provincial statutes were nullified by a provincial government, in violation of article 100 of the constitution. There are repeated reports of the violation of proper procedures governing the election and appointment of functionaries for local state organs. For instance, according to article 104, heads of counties, townships, and towns should be elected by the people's congresses at the corresponding levels. There were cases where they were in fact unilaterally appointed or reshuffled by the people's governments of the next higher levels. The majority of these cases reveal the weaker power position of the people's congresses vis-à-vis the people's government. The second type of constitutional breach concerns the exercise of jurisdiction by the wrong level of a people's congress. Thus, in contravention of article 101, the people's congress of a city elected the president of the people's court and the chief procurator for a city district.

STRUCTURAL HURDLES TO CONSTITUTIONALITY

The above examples indicate that constitutional practice in China still leaves much to be desired. There are basically two dimensions to the issue, one situational and the other structural. The situational dimension refers to the atmosphere of a specific era, while the structural aspects are common to all stages of development. In situational terms, there have been ups and downs in constitutional practice in China, with the years from 1954 to 1957 as the highest peak and the decade of the Cultural Revolution as the deepest abyss. The circumstances were determined by the prevailing coalition of leaders, the requirements of basic policy goals, and to a lesser extent the international environment. Only structural issues will be discussed in this chapter.

Three structural issues emerge from the above discussion. They are the relationship between the constitution and the Party, the conduct of local cadres, and the role of the National People's Congress as the guardian of the constitution.

9 Reports can be found in the *SCNPC Bulletins.*

Party and constitution

Political parties are significant players in the political process of many countries today. As a result, increasing numbers of countries have tried to regulate political parties, either by virtue of the constitution, a party law, electoral law, or a combination of them. The formation, operation, finance, and many other aspects of political parties are then subject to the control of legal norms.

In the Federal Republic of Germany, the rights and duties of political parties are regulated by article 21 of its Basic Law. The important and innovative idea there exhibited is the constitutionality of a political party, which shall be further regulated by federal laws and decided upon by the Federal Constitutional Court. The regulation of political parties is important for a divided nation, because the platform of a ruling party or even the combined platform of all parties in one part of the nation can under all circumstances only be 'partisan' to the question of national integration.

The impact of the Communist Party on social, political, and economic life in China certainly exceeds that of its counterparts in many countries. However, its rights and duties have never been clearly spelled out in Chinese constitutions except, in a very elementary way, in the constitutions of 1975 and 1978. Although these two constitutions have been ridiculed as unworthy, they are at least frank as to the de facto status of the Party in the Chinese political system when they declare that the state is led by the Party and the citizens are obliged to obey its leadership. The deplorable part of these two constitutions, in the context of the present discussion, is the absence of any duty imposed on the Party.

Under the present constitution, the Communist Party of China is expressly mentioned only in the preamble and is indirectly referred to in article 5. At best, the constitutional right of the Party to lead can be inferred from the following passage in the preamble of the constitution:

> Under the leadership of the Communist Party of China and the guidance of Marxism-Leninism and Mao Zedong Thought, the Chinese people of all nationalities will continue to adhere to the people's democratic dictatorship and follow the socialist road. . . .

Provided that the Party can be accepted as the sole representative of the working class, the leadership of the Party can be lawfully grounded on article 1 which proclaims China as a socialist state under the people's democratic dictatorship *led* by the working class.

The above discussion is academic, insofar as the Party does not believe and will certainly not accept that its leadership needs to be established by virtue of the law, rather than by its own fiat. Nevertheless, given that the Party does actually lead, the absence of constitutional provisions governing the scope and meaning of this leadership and providing remedial or compensational measures in case of negligent or faulty leadership hampers the development of the Rule of Law.

In view of the legal uncertainties concerning the leadership of the Party and in the spirit of the policy of economic reform, the political leadership of the day has enacted subsidiary regulations aiming at a delineation of powers. One case in point concerns the reorganisation of industrial enterprises owned by the whole people. To simplify the discussion, only the respective functions and powers of the plant director and the Party will be covered, while the role of the workers' congress, the union, and the relevant government departments will be omitted.

The Working Regulations Governing the Industrial Enterprises Owned by the Whole People (1986) stipulate that the director of the enterprise concerned is 'fully responsible for and assumes unified leadership with respect to work relating to direction of production and to business management.' They further stipulate that the director shall 'regularly report to and be supervised by the basic organisation of the Party within the enterprise.' Supervision is further defined by the Party's own Working Regulations Governing the Works of Basic Organisations in Industrial Enterprises Owned by the Whole People as ensuring that '[t]he enterprise and the director correctly carry out the guidelines and policies of the Party.'[10]

The above regulations are expected to be superseded by the draft Law on State-Owned Enterprises,[11] dated 9 January 1988. According to the draft law an enterprise 'operates under the sponsorship of its director' who 'exercises his authority in accordance with the law' and 'is protected by law' (article 6). It is further stipulated that the director is 'the legal representative of an enterprise' (article 42) and 'legally responsible for the enterprise's operations in all areas' (article 43). However, it seems that only in two areas, namely, 'production, management and spiritual construction' and 'establishment of organs,' does the plant director have independent and exclusive jurisdiction. In all other areas he is checked by many other organs, such as the State Council with respect to projects, the relevant 'government-authorised departments' regarding personnel policy and administration, and the workers' congress on issues of wages, bonuses,

---

10 [1987] 1 *Guowu Yuan Gongbao (Bulletin of the State Council)* (30 January) 5–11 (Regulations), 11–15 (Party Regulations).
11 English text in BBC, *Service of World Broadcast,* No FE/0052 B2/1 (19 January 1988).

rules and regulations, and welfare funds and services. In the provisions about balancing the power of the plant director, no mention is made of the leadership of the Party.

The leadership of the Party is stipulated in article 7 in very ambiguous and sparse terms:

> The basic organisation of the Chinese Communist Party in an enterprise ensures and oversees the implementation of general and specific policies of the Party and the state in that enterprise. It supports the director in discharging his authority in accordance with the law.

This article was later adopted as an amendment to article 33 of the charter of the Chinese Communist Party, as approved by the 13th congress of the Party in November 1987. An additional clause was added to that article which may clarify the emphasis on the leadership of the Party. The relevant clause stipulates that the basic organisations of the Party 'shall devote their major efforts to strengthen the development of the Party and to carry out ideological work and work with the people.' This clause can be interpreted to mean that the leadership of the Party in a state-owned enterprise shall be limited to Party and ideological affairs.

In the absence of an amendment to the constitution, legislation on the distribution of jurisdictions among the Party and other social, economic, or political organs in different contexts and areas is appropriate. The Chinese leadership has taken a bold and commendable step, because the Party has never been regulated before in any communist country. Yet more needs to be done in this direction.

The duty of the Party to obey the constitution was for the first time laid down, albeit indirectly, in the constitution of 1982. In the last paragraph of the preamble it is stipulated that 'all political parties . . . must take the Constitution as the basic norm of conduct, and they have the duty to uphold the dignity of the Constitution and ensure its implementation.' In addition, article 5 of the constitution stipulates that all political parties must abide by the constitution and the law.

Putting the Party under the law is a crucial step forward on the road to the Rule of Law. To what extent this can be realised in practice depends very much on the cadres of the Party.

Conduct of local cadres

We have referred above (see pp 61-62) to the importance of the openness of local cadres in safeguarding constitutional norms with regard to religious freedom. In this section, we shall concentrate on the intervention of Party cadres in the independence of the courts.[12]

A case revealing the powers of Party secretaries was reported as follows. Of all judicial decisions made in a certain county in 1985, those made by the Party committee amounted to 44%. Court decisions which were subsequently revised by the Party committee made up 10% of the total. Upon disagreement with the judges, some Party secretaries boasted that 'I may be unable to meddle in your right to adjudicate, I am still able to decide on your Party membership and promotion.'[13]

A similar case reported in the same source has this to tell. The head of the construction bureau of a county was served by the people's court a writ of summons, demanding an answer within 15 days. He complained to the Party Secretary of the county, who in turn reprimanded the President of the people's court to the effect that 'The court is led by the Party. How dare you summon a Party cadre. From now on, no summons is allowed without prior approval of the Party committee.'

Another case on the ignorance of local cadres was reported in 1985. A Party Secretary wanted to compel the court to decide on an unwarranted verdict of guilt and specifically asked for a punishment of eight years' imprisonment. The court was reluctant to comply, pointing out the absence of legal grounds for so doing. The Party Secretary angrily questioned the cadre of the court, saying that 'our state has promulgated so many laws. How come you can't find any that can be applied?'[14]

These are by no means isolated cases. There are plenty of similar cases reported in the Chinese newspapers. They reveal the typical attitudes and behaviour of some Party cadres who are still lagging behind. At the same time, they are also suggestive of the fact that formal separation between the Party and the state

---

12 For an official acknowledgment of the problem see, eg [1986] 2 *Zhonghua Renmin Gonghequo Zuigao Remin Fayuan Gongbao (Bulletin of the Supreme People's Court of the People's Republic of China)* (20 June) 11.

13 In-house commentator, '*Lingdao Ganbu Buneng Chaoyue Xianfa Xinshi Zhiquan* (Leading Cadres may not Contravene the Constitution when Exercising their Powers)' (1985) 12 *Faxue (Jurisprudence)* 1–2.

14 In-house commentator, '*Ping Lingdao Ganbu Daiou Xue Fa* (On Leading Cadres Setting Examples in Learning Laws)' (1985) 9 *Faxue (Jurisprudence)* 3–5. Two cases of successful intervention are reported in No 7 (1987) of the same journal (retitled *Law Science* since 1987). See Wu Yi, '*Yige Shengwei Shuji Di Fansi* (Reflections of a Deputy Secretary of a Provincial Party Committee)' at 46 and Fang Xie, '*Fa Da Haishi "Pishi" Da?* (Law or "Instruction": Which is Superior?)' at 47.

organs alone cannot completely eliminate the sources of unconstitutional acts. It is no wonder that in 1985 the Standing Committee of the National People's Congress found it necessary to launch a five-year legal education programme aimed at government and Party cadres at all levels. Apart from the optimistic reports of the Standing Committee of the National People's Congress in subsequent years, no independent assessment of the programme is yet available to the outside world. Even when educational work is beyond doubt, in the final analysis it is important to institutionalise arrangements whereby unconstitutional acts can be ascertained and corresponding judgments enforced.

Guardian of the constitution

Where does the responsibility to review unconstitutionality lie? Is such review enforceable? Has this responsibility been taken seriously?

The constitution of 1982 promises to 'look into' all violations of the constitution (article 5). This is a novel provision without precedent in the previous constitutions. If it were taken seriously, a major weakness of constitutional development in China might be somewhat remedied. This weakness refers to the absence of a specialised institution and a set of specified procedures for constitutional review. In other words, it amounts to the absence of a guardian of the constitution, whose authoritative judgment regarding breaches can be enforced.

According to articles 62 and 67, both the National People's Congress and its Standing Committee are empowered to 'supervise the enforcement of the Constitution.' The Standing Committee is further equipped with the power of interpretation. It is further stipulated in article 98 that the local people's congresses at different levels 'ensure the observance and implementation of the Constitution.' It can therefore be concluded that the *whole* system of the people's congresses is the guardian of the constitution. If this were truly the case, the system for upholding the constitutional norms must be very complicated. Surprisingly, however, neither the constitution nor any subsidiary legislation specifies how the system is to work or whether appeals against decisions of local congresses are permitted. Many other issues are ignored, and there is no reported precedent of constitutional review or academic discussion in China on the operation of the system.

According to the constitution, the objects of review are of two types, namely, laws which include national statutes, and other normative documents and behaviour. With respect to laws, the constitution provides for both pre-enactment and post-enactment review. For instance article 116, which deals with the enactment of regulations on self-government of autonomous areas, belongs to the first type, whereas articles 62, 67, 99, and 104 dealing with 'inappropriate' or 'unconstitutional' decisions, administrative and local regulations, and administrative orders are of the second type. Needless to say, review with respect to unconstitutional behaviour can only be ex post facto.

For ex post facto review of unconstitutionality (especially with regard to acts rather than laws), the absence of a set of specified procedures (or subsidiary legislation) renders ineffective the system of the people's congresses. It is not at all clear who (person, legal person, organisation) has the right to apply for a review by any people's congress, according to what procedures, within how long a period after the allegedly unconstitutional act has taken place, and so on. The delay in the enactment of subsidiary legislation renders empty the third paragraph of article 41 which provides:

> Citizens who have suffered losses through infringement of their civic rights by any state organ or functionary have the right to compensation in accordance with the law.

The right to review unconstitutionality with regard to infringement of civic rights clearly rests with the system of the people's congresses which, however, are not equipped to resolve problems involving the right to compensation. The people's courts, on the other hand, may be in a better position to administer the right to compensation but are not empowered to review unconstitutional acts.

Regardless of the procedural defects, it is from a political perspective very doubtful that the local people's congresses as they are can be effective guardians of the constitution. Although they are, on paper, 'local organs of state power' (article 96), they have been put under the leadership of the Party and have become sanatoriums for retired cadres or mere incidents of united front policy. Deputies to the local congresses have neither the legal competence nor the political power to live up to the expectation of the constitution. Thus, constitutional review simply does not constitute a significant part of the normal activities of the local congresses.

It is noted above that the Standing Committee of the National People's Congress stands out as the only organ in the whole system of the people's congresses that is equipped by the constitution with the power of interpretation. By virtue of this interpretative power, the Standing Committee must be regarded as the only possibly effective guardian of the constitution. The regrettable fact, however, is that it is not created solely for the purpose of reviewing constitutionality. Available data reveal that constitutional interpretation and review are not priority tasks among its many responsibilities.

In actual operation, it seems that the NPC Work Committee on the Legal System (*Fazhi Gongzuo Weiyuanhui*) bears the burden of law-related work. Again, this committee is by no means a specialised organ for constitutional review. It is a working group whose advice carries weight. Decisions lie officially with the Standing Committee and, ultimately, the National People's Congress.

The author has no access to information as to how the committee functions. There are no specialised publications, such as law reports or academic monographs, on constitutional interpretation and review. The Standing Committee does provide in its annual reports to the National People's Congress some information on constitutional interpretation and practice. The information given there is highly condensed, is couched in standard format and official jargon, and tends to focus on the prerogatives of the National People's Congress. Constitutional practice relating to other issues, especially the civic rights of the citizens, is never mentioned. A few typical cases of constitutional violations and 'remedial' actions taken by the Standing Committee are allegedly reported in the *Working Bulletin of the General Office of the Standing Committee*, which is not available to the public. None of this suggests that constitutional review is taken seriously.

CONCLUDING REMARKS

The period since 1982 can be characterised as activism in legislation with a lag in practice. Commendable are the efforts of the National People's Congress and the State Council in having promulgated over 60 statutes and 500 administrative regulations respectively. In terms of constitutional practice, however, more words (such as propaganda and education with respect to the constitution) than deeds (such as constitutional review) are seen.

There have even been moments when expediency seems to have prevailed over the requirements of the Rule of Law. The policy of dealing with serious economic crimes in 1982 and 1983, for instance, led to a massive campaign the operation of which did not always accord with legal procedures. It was the Party committee at different levels which organised a working group to fight against serious economic crimes. The legal basis for the concerted action led by the Party was the 'Urgent Notice' of the Central Committee of the Party and the respective Resolutions on Heavy Punishments for Criminals who Seriously Destroy the Economy adopted by the Central Committee, the State Council, and the Standing Committee of the National People's Congress. As compared with the past, the fact that normative documents were enacted before measures were undertaken can be regarded as an improvement. On the other hand, the fact that the Standing Committee can add the death penalty to the catalogue of allowable punishments under the Criminal Law (articles 117 and 118) simply through a 'resolution' also suggests that rights (the right to life) are not always adequately respected.

There is then no denial that the constitution is taken more seriously than ever before, although not seriously enough. Today, people at least argue openly and seriously whether certain acts are constitutional or not. If an act is found to be incompatible with a constitutional norm but is judged to be beneficial to the four modernisations, constitutional amendment is proposed. A pertinent case refers to the issue of transfer of the right of land use for a consideration. Such an act is impermissible under paragraph 4 of article 10. Since it has become prevalent in recent years and judged to be conducive to modernisation, it has to be legalised. The episode thus summarises in a succinct way how a constitution fares in today's China. Chinese constitutional thinking is still caught between the dilemma of whether a constitution should 'reflect the results of development' or 'provide norms governing development.' As a compromise constitution containing orthodox and progressive elements, but not necessarily a consensus about lasting values, the constitution of 1982 is subject to periodic demands for adjustment as social, political, and economic reforms deepen. Nevertheless, the demand for amendment itself is more superior than bypassing or white-washing unconstitutional acts.

Yet constitutional activism is still expressed in legislative amendment rather than in concern with enforcement. Constitutional practice amounts to frequent revisions. The fate of constitutional practice in terms of norms controlled by an effective institution can be even more uncertain. The tension between the necessity for control by norms and the desirability of policy discretion in rapid socio-economic change cannot be easily solved. Ways must be found and then institutionalised.

What is the prospect for the development of constitutional practice? In an earlier study, the author warned against optimism regarding the Rule of Law in China. Constitutional development hinges on the extent of self-restraint of the Party. The principle of socialism is both conceptually and in practice superior to the principle of justice. The Party seems to be increasingly prepared to abide by the constitution. It will act according to the existing law before its revision and observe the procedure for revision.[15] This assessment is still applicable today. There is, however, one new development of importance.

The most important development in China since 1982 is the legislation on the Party, as alluded to above (see pp 64–66). Although it is but a small dose of legislation, as only the basic organisations of the Party in an enterprise are affected, it has created a precedent in the communist world. It also represents a possible step towards a socialist *Rechtsstaat*. Further developments in this direction depend on more legislation along the same lines and whether or not there is actual conformity to the spirit of the legislation concerned. Again there is the issue of behavioural lag vis-à-vis legislative activism.

To shorten the behavioural lag, it is important to establish an effective mechanism for the enforcement of constitutional norms. From a comparative perspective, China is very under-developed indeed. Yugoslavia has since 1974 had a constitutional court which is independent of the executive and the legislature. In 1984 Hungary established a constitutional committee under the parliament. Then Poland followed suit in 1985 with the introduction of a more powerful organ in the form of a constitutional tribunal under the legislature. In Hungary, legislation in now underway to make their constitutional committee more effective and independent of the parliament. All these socialist countries are also undergoing rapid economic and political change. They have undertaken measures to improve the mechanism of constitutional review. How much longer has China to wait?[16]

15 Kuan Hsin-chi, 'Socialist Constitutions in Comparative Perspective' (1983) 16 *Chinese Law and Government* (Nos 2–3) 12–44.
16 Hu Jin Guang advocates the setting up of a constitutional committee under the National People's Congress in 'A Prolegomenon to Methods and Process of Constitutional Review in Our Country' in (1984) 3 *Studies and Research on Jurisprudence* (Beijing) 13–18, reprinted in (1987) 9 *Faxue* (Newspaper and Periodical Materials Reprints, published by The People's University, Beijing) 29–34.

5   The Hong Kong Model of 'One Country, Two Systems': Promises and Problems*

BYRON S J WENG

ON 28 April 1988, the Basic Law Drafting Committee of the Hong Kong Special Administrative Region of the People's Republic of China[1] concluded its seventh plenary session. The draft Basic Law of the Hong Kong Special Administrative Region of the People's Republic of China (For Solicitation of Opinions)[2] was released to the public and a process of consultation was launched. By the schedule previously announced, the law will not be formally enacted until early 1990.[3] However, from the Basic Law, one can already discern much about the legal arrangements of Beijing's 'one country, two systems' formula[4] as it is applied to Hong Kong. This formula was originally proposed

* An earlier version of this paper, prepared at the request of the organisers of a panel discussion for delivery at the 29th annual meeting of the American Association of Chinese Studies, 23–26 October 1987, Washington, DC, was published in (1987–88) 14(4) *Asian Affairs — An American Review* 193–209. Readers interested in a fuller analysis with pertinent factual details may want to consult another paper by the author entitled ' "One Country, Two Systems" and the Prospects of China's Reunification,' given at Grinnell College, Iowa, 4 September 1987.

1 For a shrewd early observation of the SAR Basic Law drafting process, see He Li, 'Contradictions between "one country" and "two systems" — on the Basic Law amidst stormy exchanges' *Jiushi Niandai* 14–20 (August 1985). See also W S Clarke, 'The Constitution of Hong Kong and 1997' in Y C Yao, et al, *Hong Kong and 1997: Strategies for the Future* (Hong Kong: Centre of Asian Studies, University of Hong Kong, 1985) 215–233.

2 The full text of the document was published in most of the major newspapers in Chinese and English in Hong Kong and in *Renmin Ribao* and *China Daily* on 29 April 1988. A pamphlet entitled *The Draft Basic Law of the Hong Kong Special Administrative Region of the People's Republic of China (for Solicitation of Opinions) with Introduction and Summary* (the introduction and summary being compiled by the Secretariat of the Basic Law Consultative Committee) was released in both Chinese and English free of charge to the Hong Kong public on the same day (See Appendix).

3 See *Ta Kung Pao* 2 July 1985, p 2 (text of Ji Pengfei's speech).

4 See Deng Xiaoping, 'One Country, Two Systems' in *Jianshe You Zhongguo Teshe de Shehui Zhuyi (Building Socialism with Chinese Characteristics)* (Beijing: Renmin Chubanshe, enlarged ed 1987) 41–44.

with Taiwan in mind but has been applied to Hong Kong first because of the 1997 question. According to Deng Xiaoping, the Hong Kong experience will eventually be a model for Taiwan.[5]

To gain an understanding of the Hong Kong model, one needs to examine not only the Basic Law but also the existing systems of Hong Kong, the Sino-British Joint Declaration on the Question of Hong Kong,[6] and the attitudes of the key players, ie the PRC, the UK, and the people of Hong Kong, whose actions will no doubt help shape the said model. In a sense, the Basic Law seeks to translate the promises of the Joint Declaration into a blueprint for Hong Kong's future. The challenge is to design a scheme which will enable China to resume sovereignty over the territory while keeping the present capitalist system basically unchanged. Understandably, to the extent that their envisaged futures differ, the key players will engage in political struggles in order to make their constituency's view prevail. A systematic and comprehensive study of all these factors — a voluminous task — will be undertaken at a later date. This chapter is only an attempt to examine the promises and problems of Beijing's 'one country, two systems' policy as manifested in the Hong Kong experience up to the time when the Basic Law was released.

The questions to be addressed here are the following: What are the essential features of the Hong Kong model as promised? What problems and difficulties have surfaced so far? Is Beijing likely to be successful in applying the Hong Kong model to Taiwan? Why or why not?

THE HONG KONG MODEL OF REUNIFICATION

In essence, the Hong Kong model prescribes that the way to peaceful reunification is through negotiation, consultation, legislation, and implementation.

First, *negotiations* are to be carried out between Beijing and the controlling government of the territory to be reunited regarding the terms for accepting Beijing's 'one country, two systems' scheme, now incorporated implicitly in article 31 of the 1982 constitution of the PRC.[7] The Joint Declaration, which

5 See *Wen Wei Po*, 17 April 1987, p 2.
6 See Government of Hong Kong White Paper, *A Draft Agreement Between the Government of the United Kingdom of Great Britain and Northern Ireland and the Government of the People's Republic of China on the Question of Hong Kong*, 26 September 1984 (Hong Kong: Government Printer, 1984).
7 Article 31 of the 1982 constitution of the PRC provides: 'The state may establish special administrative regions when necessary. The systems to be instituted in special administrative regions shall be prescribed by law enacted by the NPC in the light of specific conditions.'

entails the creation of a highly autonomous SAR upon China's resumption of the exercise of sovereignty over the territory wherein the existing capitalist system will remain unchanged for at least 50 years, represents the result of such negotiations in the case of Hong Kong.

Consultation refers to the follow-up negotiations of a less formal and more routine nature. Pending the final implementation of all the terms of the negotiated agreement, one or more joint liaison bodies made up of representatives from Beijing and the controlling government of the territory concerned are set up, so that outstanding problems or new difficulties can be dealt with through mutual consultation. Now a Sino-British Joint Liaison Group and a Land Commission are meeting regularly to discuss the case of Hong Kong.

Meanwhile, the NPC is enacting a basic law of the SAR which will become a kind of constitutional document for the territory during a specified period. The power of *legislation* is exclusively the NPC's, although some limited roles may be granted to a few of the territory's people, and public input, including dissident views, are generally tolerated and sometimes solicited. For Hong Kong, the BLDC was formally appointed by the NPC in 1985. It consists of 58 members, 23 of whom are prominent Hong Kong residents and the rest are mainlanders (one of the original 59 members is deceased). The BLDC in turn organised a 180-member Consultative Committee for the purpose of canvassing public opinion on the SAR Basic Law. Intensive debates on key issues have taken place within and without these committees during the drafting process.

Both consultation and the enactment of the Basic Law are preparatory steps leading towards the eventual *implementation* of the negotiated agreement. Conceivably, there are other transitional measures as well. When all the transitional measures have been implemented and the necessary preparations completed, reunification will be effectuated.[8] Sovereignty over the territory will be formally transferred. A new SAR government will be established in accordance with the Basic Law and the scheme of 'one country, two systems' will become a reality. With regard to Hong Kong, this is scheduled for 1 July 1997.

As described so far, it appears that the Hong Kong model is workable and has been working, but is this true? The answer to

8 Among the preparatory measures, the establishment of the first administration of the SAR has been considered by the BLDC. This was hotly debated by people with different views. The questions were: Should this first government be established before or after 30 June 1997 and should the British Hong Kong government have any role in it? See BL171, 172 and Annex 3.

this question depends on where one stands and whether one is concerned with only formal claims or with the substantive outcome as well. For instance, the PRC leaders' views may not be shared by the people of Hong Kong and the assessment of the situation by Taipei will differ from that of Beijing. An analyst concerned with the stability and prosperity of the territory will have more to consider than one who wants sovereign control at any cost. And a resident who wants his and his descendants' rights and freedoms assured will have even more to think about than the analyst.

PROBLEMS AND DIFFICULTIES

Up to the end of April 1988, the Hong Kong experience may be said to contain three main parts, namely, the Sino-British negotiations, the drafting of the SAR Basic Law, and the events associated with the British Hong Kong government's efforts to introduce a more representative government in the territory. The first is a matter of international diplomacy while the last two are domestic affairs within the jurisdiction of the PRC government and the British Hong Kong government respectively. Pertinent problems and difficulties that have surfaced include the following.

In the beginning, many observers discovered that few Beijing leaders had a realistic and accurate understanding of Hong Kong. Those accustomed to viewing the world from the perspective of the Chinese middle kingdom or Marxist philosophy seemed to be equally ignorant and self-righteous in their opinions about how a capitalist colony like Hong Kong could best be governed. This scared quite a number of the Hong Kong elite. There was much anxiety, and remedial lobbying (or educating) efforts were undertaken by leading figures in the early stage of the negotiations. Fortunately, the leaders in Beijing were wise enough to put those in the know in key positions to deal with the British and Hong Kong representatives so that the damage was not too great.

Next, the people of Hong Kong were frustrated because they could not take part in the negotiations which were to decide their own fate.[9] Both the British and the Chinese claimed that they

---

9 Some people in Hong Kong put forward the 'three-legged stool' argument. Some also argued that 'residual power' should rest in the Hong Kong people. Both groups were frustrated. For a summary of public opinion polls and representative samples of the views of major groups and the media in Hong Kong during the Sino-British negotiations, see Joseph Y S Cheng (ed), *Hong Kong in Search of a Future* (Hong Kong: Oxford University Press, 1984).

represented the interests of the Hong Kong people, but in fact the last were over-represented in some areas and inadequately represented in others. Throughout the whole process, they could only traverse the halls in Beijing and London to lobby the two negotiating parties. This they did to their own potential peril since such actions reflected their locus of loyalty and could affect their future careers. Had Hong Kong been negotiating for post-colonial arrangements on its own as many former British colonies have done, the situation would certainly have been different.

The Hong Kong people would later be reminded time and again by mainland sources that the British would return sovereign authority over Hong Kong to the PRC, not to them. The future government of the SAR would be directly under the Central People's Government. Its power would come from the NPC, not from the people of Hong Kong. Hence, whatever the NPC chose not to authorise, the SAR government could not do. The people of Hong Kong are not sovereign and therefore enjoy no legal powers other than those granted to them by the Basic Law.

Third, the Joint Declaration, with its 12-point statement and 14 items of concrete explanations, constitutes Beijing's new Hong Kong policy.[10] It has been welcomed by the people of Hong Kong. Yet, the people of Hong Kong have also learnt that the said document is somewhat less than the international guarantee that they had hoped for. A joint declaration is more an announcement of intention rather than a binding treaty with provisions of clear obligations that the parties must perform. However, that is not the real problem. What is pivotal is that the document amounts to a mere unilateral declaration of policy by the PRC towards the Hong Kong people. In the words of a Beijing legal authority,[11] 'the British pledged to return Hong Kong to the PRC, but the PRC made no pledge to the British.' Should Beijing renege on its promises later, the British government would be in no position to help the people of Hong Kong other than to give moral support.

Fourth, Beijing has promised, among other things, a highly autonomous SAR in which Hong Kong people will rule over Hong Kong. However, the drafting process and the provisions of the Basic Law have shown that Beijing's rulers have no intention of creating a truly autonomous Hong Kong-run SAR. The BLDC membership is predominantly mainland Chinese. Even the Consultative Committee, which is meant to be representative of the Hong Kong public, operates under the control of an

10 See n 6 above.
11 See *Kuai Bao*, 25 September 1984.

Executive Committee 'elected' in a forced, clearly undemocratic fashion amidst loud protests.[12] There has been no lack of debates. Dissident opinions are allowed an airing but there is no doubt as to the outcome regarding an issue where Beijing has expressed a clear view.

As to the articles of the Basic Law, the following points obviously indicate potential central control or interference in the affairs of the SAR, contrary to the promise of a high level of autonomy.[13]

(1) The governmental design clearly favours a strong Chief Executive who will dominate the other branches of the SAR government but who will be under the control of Beijing. The CE, as he or she appears in the Basic Law, resembles the powerful British colonial Governor of Hong Kong who is by law accountable only to London, not to anyone in Hong Kong.

The CE shall be appointed by the CPG on the basis of the results of elections or consultations to be held locally. Beijing, with the co-operation of some Hong Kong business elite, will be able to manipulate and to control the process of producing the CE. His or her appointment by the CPG is not likely to be just a pro forma exercise (BL14, 45 and Annex I, BL).

There will be an Executive Council to assist the CE in policy-making. Its members are appointed by and responsible only to him or her (BL54–56).

The principal officials of the various departments of the SAR executive authorities shall be appointed by the CPG upon nomination by the CE. Some critics are asking whether the scope of 'principal officials' designated in the Basic Law has expanded beyond what is described in the Joint Declaration (BL48 (5)).

(2) The CE shall be 'responsible to the Central People's Government and the HKSAR.' (In that order?) The question is raised as to why the CE is made responsible to the 'HKSAR' and not to its Legislative Council (BL43).

Among other duties, the CE is 'to execute the directives given by the CPG in respect of matters provided by this law' (BL48 (8)). Presumably, he or she is to do so without questioning them on any ground.

(3) The CE shall have the power to return a bill passed by the Legislative Council for reconsideration. Furthermore, he or she can dissolve the legislature with the approval of the CPG (BL49, 50).

---

12 See Yu Jiwen, 'Consultative Committee: Established to Control the Popular Will?' 192 *Jiushi Niandai* 46–49 (January 1986).

13 The following points have all been derived from the Basic Law of the SAR.

It is also proposed to give the CE the power to control the introduction of bills by members of the Legislative Council (BL73, alternative 1).

(4) The SAR legislature can move to impeach the CE only on two grounds: serious breach of law or dereliction of duty. The impeachment procedures require one-fourth of all members to move it and two-thirds of all members to agree to it. Even then, such a proposal 'shall be reported to the Central People's Government for decision' (BL72 (9)).

Under certain circumstances, the Legislative Council can also force the CE to resign. But this is possible only when he or she has dissolved the Legislative Council, and the newly elected legislature (a) still passes the original bill, which the CE had refused to sign twice, with a two-thirds majority; or (b) still refuses to approve the budget or to pass an important bill proposed by the CE (BL52 (2), (3)).

(5) The question whether the CE should be the presiding officer of the legislature is still to be decided (BL70). However, the President of the Legislative Council shall be vested with the power to 'announce that a member of the Legislative Council will no longer be qualified for such an office' under certain conditions. Such conditions include the member's inability to discharge the functions of his or her office due to serious illness 'or other reasons' (BL78).

The proposed system, in spite of its checks-and-balance mechanisms, clearly subordinates the Legislative Council, which is more likely to be Hong Kong-oriented, to the CE, who is likely to be Beijing-oriented, in terms of their power relationships.

(6) Laws enacted by the SAR legislature shall be reported to the Standing Committee of the National People's Congress for the record, and if the latter considers that such laws are 'not in conformity with this Law or legal procedures,' it may return them for reconsideration or revoke them (BL16).

(7) The power of interpretation of the Basic Law shall be vested in the NPCSC. Such interpretations are binding on the SAR courts. These courts may interpret only those articles of the Basic Law which are within the scope of the SAR's autonomy and only when they are adjudicating cases (BL169). Furthermore, these courts are required:

(a) to consult the CE 'where a question relating to defence, foreign affairs, or the executive acts of the CPG arises in any proceeding before the courts of the HKSAR,' whereupon the CE shall issue a binding certificate regarding such a question after obtaining a written statement from either the NPCSC or the State Council (BL18); and

(b) to 'seek an interpretation' from the NPCSC 'when a case involves the interpretation of a provision of this Law' concerning defence, foreign affairs, and 'other affairs which are the responsibilities of the Central People's Government' (BL169).

(8) Three bodies — the NPCSC, the State Council, and the SAR — shall have the power to propose amendments to the Basic Law. 'Amendment proposals from the HKSAR shall be submitted to the NPC by the HKSAR's delegation to the NPC after obtaining the consent of a two-thirds majority of the HKSAR's deputies to the NPC, a two-thirds majority of members of the HKSAR legislature and the Chief Executive of the HKSAR' (BL170). It is to be noted that the selection of the SAR's delegates to the NPC is a matter completely in the hands of the Central Government.

(9) It has been proposed that a Basic Law Committee of the SAR comprising both Hong Kong and mainland members should be set up under the NPCSC. It will study any proposal for amending the Basic Law, assist in the determination of the validity of SAR legislation, and be ready for consultation (a) by the NPCSC before the latter gives an interpretation of the Basic Law, or (b) by the State Council before it issues a directive to have a national law applied to the SAR (BL17, 169, 170). The composition and operating rules of such a committee are yet to be worked out.

(10) The Joint Declaration specifies that 'the laws of the HKSAR shall be the Basic Law, and the laws previously in force in Hong Kong and laws enacted by the HKSAR legislature' (Annex I, section II). Yet the Basic Law has now added not only a new category of laws enacted by the NPC and its Standing Committee relating to defence and foreign affairs, but also 'other laws which relate to the expression of national unity and territorial integrity and which, in accordance with the provisions of this Law, are not within the scope of the high degree of autonomy of the HKSAR' (BL17). The State Council has the power to apply such laws by proclamation. One may say that the SAR's legislative power is to be shared between the SAR Legislative Council and the Central Government organs, ie the NPC, the NPCSC, and the State Council.

(11) There is a provision that the SAR shall prohibit by law any acts that would undermine national unity or 'subvert the Central People's Government' (BL22).

(12) Departments under the CPG and provincial units of the PRC are prohibited from interfering in the affairs of the autonomous SAR. But the NPC, its Standing Committee, the State Council, and possibly the other organs of the Central Government are, by implication, not so prohibited (BL21).

(13) The CPG shall be responsible for the foreign affairs and the defence of the SAR and shall establish the necessary offices and send troops to the SAR. The SAR government shall have limited powers in external affairs of an economic and cultural nature as defined by the Basic Law (BL12, 13, and chapter 7). This in itself is not to be faulted. However, because the power of interpretation about what constitutes defence, foreign affairs, national unity, etc is held exclusively by Beijing, this too may become an avenue for Beijing to take away what it has given to the SAR whenever it is found desirable and convenient to do so.

It seems from the above that while the SAR will no doubt enjoy a higher level of autonomy when compared to the other local governments of China, any idea that the Hong Kong people shall have it their way is perhaps illusory.

Fifth, many Hong Kong people were misled by words such as 'autonomy' and 'elections' in the Joint Declaration and thought that a democratic system of government independent from that of the PRC could be developed for the SAR. They have now learnt that 'one country, two systems' does not go that far. What Beijing wants is a stable and prosperous Hong Kong under its rule, not a run-away Hong Kong that may become an anti-communist or anti-Beijing bastion. This has become quite clear both in the Basic Law drafting process and during the 1987 review of the British Hong Kong government's efforts to introduce a more representative government. Using dubious arguments (eg that Hong Kong people are as yet not politically mature enough, that no direct election should be introduced until the Basic Law is enacted, etc) and without overtly opposing democracy per se, a collusion of the rich (Hong Kong capitalists) and the powerful (Beijing and pro-Beijing forces) has practically forestalled any efforts to institute any effective Western-style democratic mechanism in Hong Kong.

Sixth, the Hong Kong experience has proven beyond any shadow of doubt that communist leaders and capitalist tycoons can make interesting political bed-fellows. Communist leaders are masters of united-front tactics; to them any potential enemy of the enemy is a friend until the enemy is eliminated. Capitalist tycoons of Hong Kong have the tradition of compradores; they are, by necessity or by choice, co-optees of the reigning force from whom they reap bountiful rewards for co-operating. This ironic relationship must make the true believers in both camps puzzled and angry. Gone are the Cold War days and with them the Cold War mentality. Still, one is not certain whether this is possible only where the communists are in charge of the government; the reverse seems not plausible. Even in the Hong Kong case, one suspects that both sides are aware of their marriage of convenience. The capitalists will probably flee if things turn sour or if business is no longer profitable. The communists may yet turn against the 'exploitative class' if the latter's services are no longer needed.

Seventh, there is a problem of semantics which reflects different political philosophies and suggests profound difficulties regarding the 'two systems.' Differences in perceptions of key words such as 'elections,' 'democracy,' 'democratic consultation,' 'democratic centralism,' 'representative,' 'accountable,' 'confidential,' etc crop up, sometimes unexpectedly. At times, such differences are calculated and intentional, like the interpretations given to 'elections' and 'one country, two systems.' The rich and the powerful say that 'elections' need not mean direct election by the general populace; controlled indirect elections will do just fine. The intellectuals and the masses say that is not so; 'elections' must mean first and foremost direct elections based on general franchise. When referring to the 'one country, two systems' concept, the mainlanders emphasise 'one country,' while Hong Kong people stress 'two systems.' At other times, the gaps come from varied experiences and habits of thinking, like the meanings associated with the terms 'democratic consultation' and 'confidential.' The Hong Kong people just cannot quite accept that a pre-vote agreement sought by the superior or the official in charge can be considered in any way 'democratic,' nor can they understand why everything said in a meeting must be kept confidential. Undoubtedly, there needs to be a good deal of learning on both sides.

Eighth, the Hong Kong experience drives home the point that individuals in an open and free society can be quite easily manipulated and subjugated by organised and purposeful groups. Even when faced with an important question like 'Hong Kong 1997' the Hong Kong people cannot present a united front. Even if they did initially, they would not stay united. Organisation and discipline, as seen in well developed political parties, do not come on their own without conscious efforts on the part of a leadership over a period of time. So far, the democratic advocates of Hong Kong have been out–manoeuvred by the rich and the powerful in practically every round — the selection of the executive personnel for the Consultative Committee of the Basic Law, the Daya Bay episode,[14] the debate over the selection of the

14 The Daya Bay nuclear plant issue kept the Hong Kong media busy for the summer months of 1986. Representative summaries of the episode can be found in the August 1986 issue of *Jiushi Niandai*, the 1 October 1986 issue of *Pai Shing Semi-monthly*, and the August and September 1986 issues of *Jing Bao*.

Chief Executive,[15] and the 1987 Green Paper debate regarding possible direct election in 1988 of some legislative councillors.[16] In political games, the idealistic and theory-peddling intellectuals and their associates are more often than not proven no match for the seasoned practitioners.

Ninth, the rumour mills have been unusually active in Hong Kong these past few years. People are puzzled and want to hear explanations for the continuing success of the Hong Kong economy. The 'vote with your feet' phenomenon has been given a lot of play. Refugees come and go, that is to say, many from Vietnam and from mainland China would risk their lives to come to Hong Kong while many in Hong Kong are leaving or trying to emigrate before this territory comes under communist rule. One indicator can be found in the rising number of applications for a 'Good Citizen Certificate' which is often required by immigration authorities in other countries. The figures for such applications in the last eight years are as follows:

1980	16,273
1981	17,521
1982	20,683
1983	20,477
1984	23,002
1985	23,063
1986	38,200*
1987	53,500*

*estimated figures

On the surface, Hong Kong still enjoys a net capital inflow but it has been observed that the in-coming capital tends to be foreign (American, Japanese, and Southeast Asian) and out-going capital has been largely local. Local capitalists are normally rooted in Hong Kong and are less likely to do well elsewhere; they pull out of this place reluctantly but when they do, they take with them many associated talents and a tradition. By contrast, the former sources of capital are purely profit-oriented and are more likely to leave quickly.

15 See Consultative Committee Discussion Papers CCBL-SG/POS-06-AP01-860804 and CCBL-SG/POS-00-PR02-860910 and Byron S J Weng, 'The Status of the Chief Executive of the HKSAR,' *Jingji yu Falu* (Hong Kong), February 1987, 58–65.
16 See Hong Kong Government Green Paper, *The 1987 Review of Developments in Representative Government*, May 1987.

These problems and difficulties will probably be solved and overcome in due course, especially if the PRC continues on its present course of internal reforms and modernisation and opening to the outside world. On the other hand, any threat in the PRC of a repetition of the Cultural Revolution or a stepped up campaign to stop 'bourgeois liberalisation' or 'spiritual pollution' from the West will probably exacerbate such problems and difficulties.

RELEVANCE TO TAIWAN

Having closely observed 'Hong Kong 1997' developments since the question was first mooted in 1982, the author has no doubt that China will successfully regain Hong Kong and is cautiously optimistic about the probability that Beijing will manage to maintain the relative stability and prosperity of the territory for a period. However, the author is rather sceptical about the applicability of the Hong Kong model of national unification to Taiwan. This is so mainly because (1) the Hong Kong experience itself contains many problems which may serve to discourage rather than entice Taiwan to accept the Hong Kong model, and (2) there are significant differences between Hong Kong and Taiwan so that what works for one may not work for the other.

The problems and difficulties discussed in the previous section must be seen at least as delaying factors. These problems and difficulties experienced in Hong Kong may not be entirely pertinent to Taiwan but they are food for thought for anyone in Taiwan who is considering the Beijing overtures.

If the mainlanders seem to lack a realistic and accurate understanding of the Hong Kong system, their ignorance about Taiwan must be even more pronounced. After all, Hong Kong has always been accessible to them but Taiwan has been cut off since 1949. Indeed, this is one of the impressions of the two trail-blazing reporters from Taipei's *Independent Evening Post* who visited the mainland in September 1987 for two weeks.[17] Efforts being made on the mainland to bridge the gaps in this regard are noted but the Taiwan people's confidence in Beijing can hardly be counted upon in the present situation.

Negotiations for reunification or co-operation between Beijing and Taipei, if they take place, will be direct and will not involve a foreign government. One might expect that the frustration of the Hong Kong people — being left out of the negotiation process — would not be repeated. And yet, the people of Taiwan are anxious

17 See *The Independent Evening Post*, 16 September 1987, p 2.

just the same. One needs only to point out that Taipei authorities have tried to suppress the right of "residents' self-determination" advocated by Taiwan's new Democratic Progressive Party in its platform;[18] and that Beijing authorities have pigeon-holed the slogan 'Taiwan ruled by Taiwan people'[19] even though a similar slogan, 'Hong Kong ruled by Hong Kong people,' was widely propagated by its media.

With regard to the nature of the Joint Declaration, Taiwan's reaction is a little surprising. On the one hand, the Taipei government denounced the Joint Declaration as invalid (since one of the concluding parties is its rival, 'the PRC Government') and warned that the Communist Party of China ('CPC') had a poor record of honouring its commitments. On the other hand, a view has been voiced to the effect that, should there be a negotiated agreement between Beijing and Taipei, it would not be an international treaty and Taiwan would not enjoy the benefit of international safeguards.[20] If there appears to be an inconsistency here, it only proves that Taipei still has little confidence in negotiations with Beijing.

As to the way in which Beijing seems to have reneged on its promise for a high level of autonomy in Hong Kong, surely it cannot have escaped Taiwan's attention. The draft articles discussed in the previous section are telling evidence that Beijing will take steps to regain tighter control over a territory after it has secured an agreement on reunification. Repeatedly, Beijing has said the terms for Taiwan will be even more generous than those promised to Hong Kong. Nonetheless, probably Taipei will not voluntarily take up Beijing's offers once it has studied the Hong Kong model in actuality. The story of refugees coming into and leaving Hong Kong carries the same kind of message for Taiwan.

In some respects, Taiwan would be even more difficult for Beijing to crack than Hong Kong. The Taiwan public have for decades been guided by the ruling Kuomintang ('KMT') and have been indoctrinated with patriotism and anti-communist

18 See *'Minzhu Jinbudang Zhenggang'* (The Platform of the Democratic Progressive Party), 6 November 1986, section 5, 'Peaceful and Independent National Defence and Diplomacy,' paragraphs 3 and 4. See also Nan Min, 'The Debates over Unification, Independence and Self-determination in Taiwan' 209 *Jiushi Niandai* 58–61 (June 1987).

19 See Zeng Yi, 'One Country, Two Systems, Taiwan Ruled by Taiwan People' 13 *Tai Sheng* (1985 No 1); Lin Chengzhi, 'The CPC Sets the KMT's Mind at Ease?' 20 *Taiwan yu Shijie* 10–11 (April 1985).

20 See 'Statement of the Ministry of Foreign Affairs of the Republic of China' 26 September 1984; Hungdah Chiu, 'The Re-Unification of China: Perspectives from Taiwan,' a paper delivered at the International Conference on the Re-Unification of China, 31 August–3 September 1987, Grinnell College, Iowa, section 4.

sentiments. They are probably less vulnerable to the 'divide and rule' tactics of the highly organised and purposeful CPC functionaries than their Hong Kong counterparts. It is also less likely that Taiwan's capitalists or other ruling elites would end up becoming strange political bed-fellows of the communist leaders, since they do not share the background of the Hong Kong capitalists who may think that there is a future for them in collaborating with the new rulers as they did with the British colonial authorities. And, as in the case of Hong Kong, there are bound to be semantic problems between the Taiwanese and the mainlanders. The Taiwanese would also emphasise 'two systems' rather than 'one country' if and when the 'one country, two systems' scheme becomes relevant.

All told, in the present conditions there are probably too many obstacles that Beijing must overcome to make the Hong Kong model applicable to Taiwan. This point can be further explained by examining the differences between the two territories and the attitudes of the government and the people in Taiwan. Both of these areas have already received considerable attention from other observers. We need only to highlight them to prove the point.

Taiwan differs from Hong Kong in the following significant ways:

(1) It is considerably larger in size and population, and therefore carries a much greater weight in the eyes of the PRC government, the USA government, and other relevant parties.

(2) It is an island geographically separated from the mainland of China by the Taiwan Straits, and therefore easier to defend against military invasion.

(3) Unlike Hong Kong, the island of Taiwan does not in any way depend on the mainland for water, food, and other basic supplies.

(4) The island is not a colony 'occupied' by a foreign government. In fact, it is an international personality[21] still recognised by 24 countries as the Republic of China ('ROC'), and it also maintains substantive relations with some 140 countries around the world.

(5) The KMT regime in Taipei is a long-standing rival of the CPC regime in Beijing in a conflict going back half a century. It used to be effective government of the whole of China to which CPC leaders actually pledged allegiance at one time.

---

21 See Chinese Society of International Law and Editorial Committee for the Chinese Yearbook on International Law and Affairs (eds) *Zhongguo Guojifa yu Guoji Shiwu Nianbao (Chinese Yearbook on International Law and Affairs)* vol 1 (1985–86) (Taipei: Taiwan Commercial Press, 1987) 485 ff.

(6) There is a well-trained modern army of about 500,000 men under the KMT's control. Its air force contingent has proven itself more than a match for the PRC.

(7) The government in Taiwan subscribes to the 'Three Principles of the People,' an ideology with a significant following among all classes of Chinese people.

(8) Not only have the people of Taiwan been long taught to despise the communists, an overwhelming majority of them have never set foot on the mainland and do not have personal memories or any real emotional attachment to the mainland.

From these differences, it is not difficult to see that Taiwan is in a much stronger position vis-à-vis the PRC than Hong Kong. In the final analysis, Hong Kong really has no choice but to comply with Beijing's wishes, be they generous or severe, but the same cannot be said about Taiwan.

The attitudes of both the government and the people in Taiwan show that the previous assessment is accurate. As Professor Hungdah Chiu explained at a recent conference held at Grinnell College, Iowa,[22] the ROC government's response to the PRC's overtures, stated on 10 June 1982 by the then Premier Sun Yun-suan and reiterated on 29 March 1986 by former President Chiang Ching-kuo, can be summarised as follows: The way to China's reunification is by the implementation of the Three Principles of the People and the ROC constitution on the mainland of China, and not by the 'nine-point proposal' or the 'one country, two systems' scheme; Beijing must abandon its so-called 'four principles' and renounce communism; negotiations will be possible only when Beijing accepts the principles of human dignity, democracy, and free enterprise; and, in Premier Sun's words:[23]

> If the political, economic, social and cultural gaps between the Chinese mainland and Free China continue to narrow, the conditions for peaceful reunification can gradually mature. The obstacles to reunification will be reduced naturally with the passage of time.

In Taiwan, there are now opposition parties purporting to represent views different from those of the KMT government which Beijing can ill afford to ignore. However, the draft platform issued by the new Democratic Progressive Party ('DPP') on 6 November 1986 offered Beijing little encouragement. While opposed to the KMT's "three no's" policy towards

22 See Hungdah Chiu (n 20 above).
23 See *The China Issue and China's Reunification* (Taipei: Government Information Office, 1982).

the mainland,[24] and being in favour of ending hostilities and increasing contact between the two parties across the Taiwan Straits, the people who drafted the policy statement stressed that the new party would oppose any negotiation between the CPC and the KMT in violation of 'the principle of self determination by the residents' of Taiwan. A leading moderate member of the DPP, legislator Kang Ning-hsiang, said in an interview with a Japanese correspondent in late 1985[25] that, in his view, there could be negotiations with the mainland authorities only if Beijing accepted four conditions. The four conditions were: (1) that Taiwan be allowed to purchase the defensive weapons it needs; (2) that Beijing stop the practice of ostracising Taiwan from the international community; (3) that economic linkages not be used as the means to promote Beijing's united-front tactics; and (4) that the extant democratic practices in Taiwan be affirmed and maintained.

Readers are reminded that Beijing's current policy towards Taiwan has its soft and hard components. It is a carrots-and-stick approach, so to speak. The hard part, primarily a matter of foreign policy, aims to deprive Taiwan of its international personality. The soft part is the domestic policy of 'one country, two systems' which is designed to reduce Taiwan to provincial status, with a seemingly generous promise of maintaining the status quo. When Beijing's envoys are bent on pushing their Taiwan colleagues out of every international organisation and inter-governmental conference, the soft overtures would not be regarded as trustworthy or palatable to Taipei. On this point the KMT and the DPP apparently concur.

CONCLUSION

Recent developments in all four Chinese territories — the mainland, Taiwan, Hong Kong, and Macau — are noteworthy. There has been ample discussion about the future Hong Kong SAR and Macau SAR governments which, though heated and polemical at times, promises to help usher into these areas more

24 In response to Beijing's call for 'three links,' ie the development of postal, trade, and aviation and shipping relations, the ROC government's policy towards the mainland has been one of 'no contact, no negotiation, no compromise.' Recently, Taipei announced a new policy to allow some categories of residents to visit the mainland with another set of "no's" attached to it, namely, 'no encouragement, no assistance, but no ban.'

25 See Huzhang Dongfu (Haruo Tobari), 'An Interview with Kang Ning-hsiang on the Question of China's Reunification' 111 Pai Shing Semi-monthly 33–35 (1 January 1986).

representative, if not completely democratic, post-colonial governments. With luck, reunification of these two territories with the PRC will be achieved without sacrificing the stability and prosperity of these thriving communities. On the mainland, recent reforms of the economic and political systems have already brought significant transformations to China's country-side, and further reforms are anticipated in the foreseeable future. The road ahead will have its twists and turns and some setbacks may yet come, but there is also hope that the ultimate effect will mean cumulative progress. In Taiwan, the changes in 1986 and 1987 have been nothing less than spectacular. It now appears that democracy on the island is a distinct prospect, even if there are still black spots here and there. With martial law lifted and some people being allowed to visit relatives on the mainland, expectations among the people are great.[26] Undoubtedly, other similar developments will follow in the months and years to come. Encouraged by these developments, Beijing's assessors would probably say that the 'one country, two systems' policy, put into motion shortly after January 1979, has had some significant effects, notably in the reduction of hostility and increase in non-governmental contact and trade across the Taiwan Straits.

However, this 'one country, two systems' policy, conceptually bold and creative though it is, is ultimately contradictory, overbearing, and transitional in nature.[27] Contradictory because it proposes to have a capitalist local system operating under the administration of a communist central government. Overbearing because the two systems are unequal in status and size, so that one side is likely to be overwhelmed by the other in the normal course of development. And transitional because the lifetime for the survival of the capitalist system is limited and its future adaptation to socialism more or less predestined. Hence, although the policy may have worked for the purpose of recovering Hong Kong from the British, it is unacceptable to Taiwan as the basis for reunification.

26 The policy was announced on 14 October 1987 and detailed regulations were disclosed the next day. Beijing's response was a positive seven-point policy made public on 16 October. All of these were well covered in the press in Hong Kong. See also a pamphlet distributed at the Double-Tenth celebration in Hong Kong, *Zhonghua Minguo Maixiang Minzhu Kaifang* (*The ROC Marches toward Democracy and Open Policy*) (October, 1987); and the topical coverage on this subject in 213 *Jiushi Niandai* 67 ff (October 1987).

27 See Byron S J Weng, 'A Rustic Discourse on "One Country, Two Systems" — its Concept, Nature, Content, Difficulties and Prospects' in F Q Quo and Zhao Fusan (eds), *Dierjie 'Taiwan zhi Jianglai' Xueshu Taolunhui Lunwenji* (*Proceedings of the Second Conference on 'Taiwan's Future'*) (Beijing: China Friendship Publishing Co, 1985) 349–384.

6 The Early History of the Drafting Process

EMILY LAU

HOW IT ALL BEGAN

PREPARATIONS for the formation of the Basic Law Drafting Committee got under way immediately after the signing of the Sino-British Joint Declaration on the Question of Hong Kong in December 1984. The BLDC is a working group under the Chinese National People's Congress responsible for writing a mini-constitution for the Hong Kong Special Administrative Region when the British colony reverts to Chinese sovereignty in 1997.

Beijing's original intention was probably to draft the Basic Law with minimum participation by the people of Hong Kong. But when demands for more Hong Kong involvement grew, Beijing decided to allow Hong Kong people to make up one-third of the BLDC. Beijing formally announced the appointment of the BLDC in June 1985. Of the 59 members, 23 are from Hong Kong. The rest are from the mainland. One mainland member, Kuo Dihuo, 81, a member of the National Committee of the Chinese People's Political Consultative Conference, passed away in 1986. Hong Kong member Fei Yimin died in 1988.

Five sub-groups were formed under the BLDC to examine five areas of the mini-constitution and each sub-group has two co-convenors, one from the mainland and one from Hong Kong. The five areas are: the relationship between the central government and the SAR; the political system; the economy; the rights and duties of the SAR inhabitants; and education, science, technology, culture, sports, and religion.

MAINLAND BLDC MEMBERS

The Chairman of the BLDC is Ji Pengfei, 77, Director of the State Council's Hong Kong and Macau Affairs Office. Under Ji, there are eight vice-chairmen, four from the mainland and four from Hong Kong. The four mainland vice-chairmen are Xu Jiatun, 71, Director of the Xinhua News Agency Hong Kong branch; Wang Hanbin, 61, Secretary General of the NPC

Standing Committee and Director of the NPC Work Committee on the Legal System; Hu Sheng, 69, President of the All-China Society for Research of Party History and Director of the Party History Research Centre of the Chinese Communist Party Central Committee; and Fei Xiaotong, 77, CPPCC Vice-Chairman and internationally known anthropologist.

According to an analysis in the local communist organ *Wen Wei Po* on 19 June 1985, the BLDC is directly under the leadership of the NPC Standing Committee. More than ten of the mainland members are from the ranks of vice minister and above and nearly ten are from the ranks of deputy professor and above.

Wen Wei Po said several of the mainland members took part in the drafting of the 1982 Chinese constitution. Zhang Youyu, 88, a member of the NPC Standing Committee and Deputy Director of the NPC Law Committee, and Hu Sheng both served on the Constitution Amendment Committee. Xiao Weiyun, 63, Assistant Professor of Law at Peking University and Xu Chongde, 58, Assistant Professor of Law at The People's University of China, both worked in the Secretariat of the Constitution Amendment Committee. All four members are said to be familiar with the historical background to article 31 of the Chinese constitution, which provides the raison d'être for Deng Xiaoping's concept of 'one country, two systems':

> The state may establish special administrative regions when necessary. The systems to be instituted in special administrative regions shall be prescribed by law enacted by the National People's Congress in the light of the specific conditions.

Some members took part, directly or indirectly, in the Sino-British negotiations which led to the Sino-British Joint Declaration on the Question of Hong Kong. Those directly involved in the talks included Zhou Nan, 60, Deputy Foreign Minister; Lu Ping, 60, Deputy Director of the Hong Kong and Macau Affairs Office under the State Council; Ke Zaishuo, 63, Director of the Hong Kong and Macau Affairs Office under the Foreign Ministry; and Shao Tianren, 73, adviser to the NPC Foreign Affairs Committee.

Those who took part in the negotiations indirectly were Li Hou, 64, Deputy Director of the Hong Kong and Macau Affairs Office under the State Council; Yong Longgui, 70, adviser to the NPC Finance and Economic Committee; Li Yumin, 57, Vice-President of the Bank of China; Jia Shi, 68, Vice-Minister of Foreign Economic Relations and Trade; and Wang Tieya, 74, Professor of Law at Peking University. *Wen Wei Po* said these people were very familiar with the negotiations and the meaning behind every provision in the Joint Declaration. Their participation would ensure that the Basic Law would be in line with the spirit of the Joint Declaration, the newspaper said.

There were also those from the official Xinhua News Agency Hong Kong branch, which is Beijing's chief representative in the colony. They included Xinhua Director Xu Jiatun, 71, and Deputy Secretary General Mao Junnian, 50, who was last year promoted Vice Director.

The last category of mainland members were the 'famous personalities' who were included to ensure broad political support for the Basic Law, *Wen Wei Po* said. These] eople included Rong Yiren, 71, a leading ed capitalist and head of the rich and influential Rong clan with relatives scattered all over the world. Rong is a Vice-Chairman of the NPC Standing Committee and Director of the China International Trust and Investment Corporation (CITIC); Fei Xiaotong; Qian Changzhao, 88, Vice-Chairman of the Revolutionary Committee of the Chinese Kuomintang and CPPCC Vice-Chairman; and Qian Weichang, 75, a Hong Kong University graduate and a member of the CPPCC National Committee and Chancellor of Shanghai Polytechnic University.

Since the mainland members came from different departments with different power bases, they did not act as a monolithic block, although they did not like to disagree in public. Power is concentrated in the hands of the officials. Xinhua was said to be directly answerable to the Chinese Communist Party Central Committee, while the Hong Kong and Macau Affairs Office and the Foreign Ministry are under the State Council.

It was evident that the Hong Kong and Macau Affairs Office took a tougher line whereas the Foreign Ministry tended to be more diplomatic and conciliatory. This divergence of views was highlighted in the sixth plenary BLDC meeting in Guangzhou in December 1987 at which Ke Zaishuo spoke of co-operation between Britain and China to ensure a smooth transition. He was contradicted by Ji Pengfei who spoke at length about his mistrust of the British.

Ji said Hong Kong could not have elections before 1997 to select the Chief Executive because China could not trust Britain to carry out fair elections. He also ruled out the 'through-train' proposal for the transition, an idea supported by some Hong Kong businessmen and the Hong Kong government. Under such a concept, people who are serving in the government before 1997 would continue to serve beyond 1997 after some formality to signify the change of sovereignty. Ji said that was unacceptable to China.

HONG KONG BLDC MEMBERS

Of the 23 Hong Kong BLDC members, the majority are from big business. Some are prominent professionals closely related to the business community. Nine are serving or former members of the Hong Kong government's Executive Council and Legislative Council. ExCo is the highest policy-making body in the colony and all its members are appointed by the government. LegCo is the law-making body with a largely advisory function. Since 1985, 24 of the 56 LegCo members are elected, half from electoral colleges and half from functional constituencies. The rest, including ten officials, are appointed by the government.

Four of the eight BLDC vice-chairmen are from Hong Kong. They are business tycoon Sir Yue-kong Pao, 68; industrialist Ann Tse-kai, 77, a member of the CPPCC Standing Committee and a former ExCo and LegCo member. Ann is also Chairman of the Basic Law Consultative Committee, a body of 180 Hong Kong members set up by the Chinese to collect and collate Hong Kong public opinion on the Basic Law.

Although the Chinese publicly stated that the BLDC would not lead the BLCC and that both the BLDC and the BLCC are of equal status, it was obvious from the start that the BLDC has a superior role. To ensure BLDC leadership of the BLCC, seven BLDC members were appointed to the BLCC. Besides making Ann chairman, former Hong Kong University Vice-Chancellor Rayson Huang, a former LegCo member, was made one of the five BLCC vice-chairmen. Huang is also a co-convenor of the BLDC sub-group on the relationship between the SAR and the Central Government.

Three other Hong Kong BLDC members were put on the BLCC Executive Committee: *Ming Pao Daily News* publisher Louis Cha, 63, who is also the co-convenor of the BLDC political sub-group; LegCo member and industrialist Wong Po-yan, 64, who is the co-convenor of the economic sub-group; and Anglican Bishop Peter Kwong, 49. BLDC Deputy Secretary General Mao Junnian was made BLCC Secretary General. Mao relinquished his BLCC post after he was promoted and was replaced by surveyor Leung Chun-ying. Another BLDC member on the BLCC is Raymond Wu, 49, former President of the Hong Kong Medical Association.

Another BLDC vice-chairman is the chief manager of the Bank of East Asia, David Li, 48, an elected member of LegCo representing the banks. The appointment of Li from relative obscurity to such an important position sparked off rumours that he was earmarked to become the first SAR Chief Executive. Of all the vice-chairmen, he is the youngest, the only Cantonese, and he comes from a well-known and influential family.

David Li's uncle Simon Li, 65, a Supreme Court judge who retired in 1987, was appointed co-convenor of the BLDC sub-group on SAR citizens' rights and obligations. His mainland counterpart is Wang Shuwen, 60, Director of the Institute of Legal Research at the Chinese Academy of Social Sciences.

Simon Li told some BLDC Hong Kong members he thought the Chinese government had at one stage intended to groom David Li to be the Chief Executive. Simon Li said that while his favourite nephew appeared to be acceptable to the Chinese and British governments, he did not seem acceptable to the Hong Kong people. Another vice-chairman from Hong Kong was the publisher of the communist organ *Ta Kung Pao*, Fei Yimin, 79 (recently deceased). Fei was also an NPC Standing Committee member.

Other businessmen on the BLDC include property and business magnate Li Ka-shing, 58; Cha Chi-ming, 71; Chairman of the pro-Beijing Hong Kong Chinese General Chamber of Commerce Henry Fok, 64, who is a member of the CPPCC Standing Committee and was made an NPC delegate in January 1988; accountant Sanford Yung, 60; Chairman of the New Territories interest group Heung Yee Kuk; Lau Wong-fat, 52, who is an indirectly elected member of LegCo representing the Regional Council; and Graham Cheng, 51.

Professionals on the BLDC include the former Vice-Chancellor of the Chinese University, Ma Lin, 63. Ma is the co-convenor of the sub-group on education, science, technology, culture, sports, labour, and religion. His mainland counterpart is Qian Wei-chang, 75, Chancellor of the Shanghai Polytechnic University. Another is Szeto Wah, 56, a LegCo member representing the teaching profession and President of the 30,000-strong Hong Kong Professional Teachers' Union.

Besides Simon Li, there are three lawyers on the BLDC. They include ExCo and LegCo member Maria Tam, 41, a barrister who has given up her practice to become a full-time politician. Another barrister is Martin Lee, 49, a Queen's Counsel who was elected to LegCo as the representative of lawyers. Another lawyer is Liu Yiu-chu, 52, a generally pro-Beijing solicitor who was made an NPC delegate in January 1988.

A number of the 23 Hong Kong BLDC members hold foreign passports. Under the Chinese Nationality Law, they should be regarded as 'foreigners.' Those who hold full British passports are Sir Yue-kong Pao, Simon Li, David Li, Maria Tam, Sanford Yung, and Graham Cheng. Rayson Huang holds a Singaporean passport. Ann Tse-kai and Liu Yiu-chu are evasive about what passports they hold but Liu stresses she can get out of Hong Kong at any time. The same applies to many of the Hong Kong members.

Controversy in the drafting process has been sharpened by personality conflicts among some Hong Kong members, the most obvious being Liu Yiu-chu's apparent antagonism towards Martin Lee and Maria Tam. However, politics makes strange bedfellows, and Liu and Tam seem to have formed an alliance in countering Lee's attempts to secure a more democratic political structure in the Basic Law. Lee's ally is fellow LegCo member Szeto Wah, a seasoned trade unionist who has clashed with Liu on several television debates.

Liu and Tam's loose alliance also has the support of Simon Li, Cha Chi-ming, Raymond Wu, and Wong Po-yan. They favour a more conservative approach in political reforms. Personality conflicts sometimes resulted in disputes in which members attacked the character and integrity of each other rather than discussed the issues involved. Some of the attacks were extremely acrimonious and have appalled and shocked the Hong Kong journalists who covered the BLDC meetings.

Conflicts and differences of opinion among Hong Kong BLDC members have been seen as a major weakness undermining Hong Kong's ability to secure an acceptable Basic Law. It is probably true to say that when Beijing first appointed the Hong Kong BLDC members, it did not expect some of them to be so argumentative and unco-operative. However, viewed in the wider context, the disagreements are but minor impediments and should not affect Beijing's grand scheme of drafting a Basic Law according to its own desire.

During the drafting process, Martin Lee and Szeto Wah have emerged as the champions of the democratic cause. Lee entered politics only a few years ago, following a successful and lucrative legal career. In May 1983 he joined a Hong Kong delegation to Beijing led by LegCo member Allen Lee to tell Chinese leaders that many Hong Kong people had no confidence in China's proposal of Hong Kong people ruling Hong Kong. The delegation said the idea could not preserve stability and prosperity because it was conceptually difficult to understand and impossible to practise, since socialism and capitalism were basically incompatible.

Martin Lee was quite highly regarded by the Chinese and was appointed to the BLDC in May 1985. In September of the same year he was elected as the constituency's legal representative to LegCo in the colony's first-ever LegCo elections. Since then he has become one of the most outspoken politicians, questioning

Beijing's sincerity in giving the SAR a high degree of autonomy and accusing the British and Hong Kong governments of breaking their promise of democracy and of selling the Hong Kong people down the river.

His confrontational tactics shocked and outraged the Chinese officials who had recommended his appointment to the BLDC and angered the pro-establishment councillors and some people in the business community, who regarded his calls for democracy as an attempt to destabilise the community and upset the economic applecart. While he commands wide support for his courage to speak frankly, some professionals criticise his arrogance and naivete and wonder how long he will be around. Others question his motives, saying he wants to be the future Chief Executive.

Szeto Wah is a veteran pressure group leader and union president. His cousin, Szeto Keung, is the deputy head of the foreign affairs department at the Xinhua News Agency Hong Kong branch. Unlike some BLDC members who do not have a strong sense of cultural identity, Szeto Wah takes great pride in being Chinese. During his previous confrontations with the government he was branded a pro-communist. In 1985 he was appointed to the BLDC and elected to LegCo as the teaching profession's representative. Because of his past involvement in pressure-group politics and his participation in demonstrations and rallies, he is regarded by the establishment as a radical and a troublemaker. Although he is the teachers' LegCo representative, the government refused to appoint him to the Board of Education or the Education Commission. Although an advocate of democracy, Szeto has been criticised as an authoritarian leader who does not tolerate dissent.

A very influential member is BLDC vice-chairman Sir Yue-kong Pao, shipping and business magnate. A fast mover in the world of high finance and diplomacy, Pao makes a career of being photographed with international dignitaries. Like other refugees from Shanghai, Pao fled to Hong Kong in 1949 when the communists came to power. Since then he has amassed a substantial fortune.

Other business magnates on the BLDC are Li Ka-shing and Cha Chi-ming, regarded as two of the richest people in Hong Kong. Pao has publicly stated that Hong Kong should be ruled by a handful of people who have made the colony prosperous. Pao, Li, and Cha are archetypal Hong Kong conservatives who have no time for representative government and who are determined not to let what they see as democratic nonsense get in the way of making money.

During the first BLDC plenary meeting in Beijing in June 1985, Cha tabled a proposal outlining the shape of the SAR government. Intensely political, Cha was one of the key supporters of Maria Tam's political group, the Progressive Hong Kong Society. His former daughter-in-law, Veronica Wu, was also deeply involved. Cha's proposal was said to be drafted with the help of, among other people, retired senior Hong Kong civil servant Denis Bray, who had been the Secretary for Home Affairs. It was said that Cha had business interests in Nigeria and had witnessed how democracy had failed to work in a newly independent country and was worried about political developments in Hong Kong. The proposal was also supported by the former Chief Secretary Sir David Akers-Jones.

The most controversial part of Cha's proposal dealt with the setting up of an advisory council, with no limit on the number of members, who would be appointed by the Chief Executive and who would serve for life. The members would be chosen from retired members of the Executive and Legislative Councils, businessmen, industrialists, and other prominent citizens. The council would elect from among its members one-third of LegCo. One-third would be elected by functional constituencies and one-third by an electoral college. The advisory council would also nominate the Chief Executive.

Another influential Hong Kong member is Louis Cha, the wealthy publisher of the Chinese language *Ming Pao Daily News*. In the past few years, *Ming Pao* had taken a pro-Beijing line and Louis Cha had also spoken out against democracy, saying it would invite Beijing's interference. Like many Hong Kong people, Louis Cha did not have much faith in the communists and felt uncertain about the long-term future. He said the freedom of the press would definitely diminish after 1997, but he hoped the situation would be tolerable. He said he has no foreign bolt-hole but admitted that that was not a problem. He said he might retire in Singapore or Taiwan. His compromising stance had been criticised as bending with the wind and lacking in principles and personal conviction. In early 1988, he was said to have been offered a seat on the NPC but he declined. Given his influential position in the media and his wavering position, he would continue to be a prime target of the united front.

Another very ambitious person on the BLDC is Maria Tam. The daughter of a retired police station sergeant who has emigrated to Canada, Tam formally entered politics in 1979 when she was elected to the Urban Council (UrbCo), a municipal body responsible for hygiene, culture, and the environment. Tam was a protégé of Akers-Jones who was chiefly responsible for her meteoric rise.

In 1981 she was appointed to LegCo and two years later to ExCo as someone with grassroots connections. For three years, Tam was the only person who sat on ExCo, LegCo, UrbCo, and a district board. Her rapid rise has attracted a lot of criticism and jealousy from her colleagues, but have not dampened her enthusiasm for politics. In May 1985 she was appointed to the BLDC. The following month she announced the formation of the Progressive Hong Kong Society with herself as Chairman. Tam had wanted to form a political party, but the group was told by Xu Jiatun that China only wanted to see groups promoting economic prosperity. Tam took the hint and said her group had no political ambitions.

In the past few years, Tam's public image has been dented by the controversy over the Legislative Council (Powers and Privileges) Bill and the building of the Daya Bay nuclear power plant. She has been described as trying to please both London and Beijing. Some of her ExCo colleagues said they did not trust her at all, implying she might act as an informer for the Chinese. Some observers said Tam was hanging onto power with the help of the British while also trying to carve out a political career for herself after 1997.

CONTROVERSY OVER THE FORMATION OF THE BLCC

After the formation of the BLDC, those of the BLDC members who were in Hong Kong were given the task of forming the BLCC. Controversy arose over the methods for selecting the BLCC. Some members wanted the BLCC to be democratically elected, others wanted it to be nominated by the powers that be. There was a strong indication that Beijing only wanted it to be a show-case for consulting Hong Kong people and did not intend to give it real influence.

The idea of selecting the BLCC by 'democratic consultation' was proposed. This was immediately criticised by Liu Yiu-chu, who said it was a communist united front code-word and should not be introduced into Hong Kong. Although regarded by Xinhua as pro-Beijing, Liu has been branded the 'unguided missile' by a Xinhua official because she sometimes aimed her attacks at Beijing as well. During one of the meetings of the Hong Kong BLDC members in August 1985 to approve the BLCC constitution, Xu Jiatun sternly rejected Liu's protestations about 'democratic consultation,' saying it was coined by the Kuomintang and was not a communist invention. He also expressed displeasure over criticism of the draft constitution. He said the Hong Kong people probably did not understand that Britain would be transferring sovereignty and administration to China, not to the people of Hong Kong; so there was no question of self-rule. Whatever right of self-government that Hong Kong people might get, they would have to get it from Beijing.

A senior Hong Kong government official later said the Chinese regarded the concept of 'returning the administration to the people' as almost equivalent to giving Hong Kong independence. Sensing China's sensitivity, many groups stopped using the phrase.

OVERT CHINESE INTERFERENCE IN HONG KONG AFFAIRS

The formation of the BLCC coincided with Beijing's mounting pressure to stop the progress of democratic reforms until the Basic Law has been promulgated by the National People's Congress in 1990. In October 1985, China openly expressed anxiety and unease with the pace of political reforms in the colony.

When receiving a delegation of Hong Kong architects in Beijing, Ji Pengfei used the opportunity to deliver a blunt warning against radical changes in order to avoid unnecessary chaos. He said the political system for Hong Kong after 1997 would be decided by the Basic Law and political reforms in the transition period must 'converge' with the Basic Law. Ji's remarks were deeply unnerving for the Hong Kong people, particularly businessmen and professionals. 'What are the Chinese trying to do? Do they not know they are undermining confidence by making so much noise?' asked one lawyer.

OUSTING OF LAU CHIN-SHEK

During this time, discussion on the formation of the BLCC reached its final stage, in time for Ji Pengfei's historic visit to the colony in December 1985 to inaugurate the BLCC's first meeting. A row broke out over attempts to exclude an independent labour leader, Director of the active Christian Industrial Committee (CIC), Lau Chin-shek, from the BLCC. Lau was one of the nominees for the seven seats allotted to a joint labour conference, which was dominated by pro-communist unions.

The CIC is an independent body which has long been in the forefront of demands for increased rights for workers and has helped in the formation of unions. Shortly before the joint labour conference election on 18 October 1985, Lau was asked by pro-Beijing trade unionist Tam Yiu-chung, a BLDC and LegCo member, to withdraw from the race. Without the pro-communist unions' support, it was unlikely that Lau would be elected. Lau refused to pull out.

As a result of the incident, over 20 independent labour and civil service unions withdrew from the conference. CIC Chairman Ding Lik-kiu was invited to join the BLCC but he also refused. It is understood that some pro-communist unionists disliked Lau for what they saw as his militancy in fighting for labour rights. Lau was said to be named in a Beijing meeting between independent labour leaders and officials of the Hong Kong and Macau Affairs Office. One official reportedly said Lau made too many demands for workers' benefits and might scare away investors.

Although Lau has been said to have some Taiwan links, he was not a bona fide rightwing representative; hence he was not of much value to the united front campaign, which wanted the involvement of pro-Taiwan people in the Basic Law process. Lau was also thought to be unpopular with big business leaders whom China was keen to please.

ACCUSATIONS OF DEVIATING FROM THE ACCORD

On 21 November 1985, in the most serious confrontation since the signing of the Joint Declaration in December 1984, China publicly accused Britain of 'deviating' from the accord. In an unprecedented news conference held at the Xinhua News Agency, Xu Jiatun said, 'China cannot help but notice there has been deviation from the Joint Declaration and there was a tendency to deviate from the Joint Declaration.' He warned that such deviation would have a negative and destructive effect but his failure to specify the nature of the alleged deviation led to allegations that he was indulging in what one lawyer called 'a clear case of intimidation.' The stock market's Hang Seng Index, a barometer of local confidence, dropped 50 points.

Xu said the political system of the SAR was China's business and would be clearly stated in the Basic Law. He said if the political reforms being carried out by the British in Hong Kong were incompatible with the Basic Law, it would be a misfortune for Hong Kong, China, and Britain. His remarks implied in no uncertain terms that the Chinese leadership would like the Hong Kong government to halt all political reforms until 1990 when the Basic Law is promulgated.

Some people in Hong Kong felt that rather than Britain deviating from the Joint Declaration, Xu's remarks constituted a breach of the accord, which said the British government 'will be responsible for the administration of Hong Kong with the object of maintaining and preserving its economic prosperity and social stability' and China will give its co-operation.

Xu's remarks caused reactions ranging from surprise through consternation to anger among Hong Kong people and British officials. 'A bombshell' was the general opinion regarding Xu's remarks. Although there were reports that the British government privately protested to the Chinese, there was a distinct unwillingness to confront the remarks head on, as though accommodation with Beijing's top official in Hong Kong was necessary for a quiet life.

British silence was seen by some as particularly disturbing. Failure on the part of either London or the Governor of Hong Kong to respond to a serious accusation relating to Britain's adherence to an international agreement suggested to some that London would not stand up to pressure from Beijing. This was later proven to be the case in the debate over introducing some elements of direct elections to LegCo in 1988. Up to that stage, the British had consistently maintained they would resist Chinese interference and would not be mere caretakers during the transition period. But it was rapidly becoming apparent in late 1985 that the British had little political will to confront the Chinese. Hence they urged the Hong Kong people to express their views and fend for themselves.

ROW OVER THE BLCC 'ELECTION'

Another row erupted on 6 December 1985 during the formation of the BLCC and its Standing Committee. The controversy came just one week after Xu's remarks on deviation from the Joint Declaration. The row blew up on the eve of Ji Pengfei's 12-day visit to Hong Kong to attend the BLCC inaugural meeting.

Many of the 180 people asked to join the BLCC were given only a day to decide whether to accept. The announcement of the BLCC formation, the election of the 19-member Standing Committee, later called Executive Committee so as to lessen the communist flavour, and the selection of the seven office bearers were completed in 11 days. Although the BLDC and BLCC were supposed to have equal status, five BLDC vice-chairmen turned up to preside over the BLCC Standing Committee election. Before the casting of votes, Sir Yue-kong Pao gave the members this directive: the committee should consist of people who love China and love Hong Kong and there should be both men and women on the committee, which should also include industrialists. Nineteen people were duly elected, with Lo Tak-shing, a former ExCo and LegCo member and founder of a company which helps Hong Kong people to emigrate, polling the highest number of votes. According to the BLCC constitution, the seven office bearers 'shall be elected from among members of the Standing Committee.'

However, immediately after the election of the Standing Committee Pao and three other BLDC vice-chairmen, Xu Jiatun, David Li, and Fei Yimin, proposed seven names to fill the seven posts. They named BLDC vice-chairman Ann Tse-kai to be BLCC Chairman. The five BLCC vice-chairmen were: BLDC member Rayson Huang, Supreme Court judge Ti-liang Yang, pro-Beijing businessman Wong Kwan-cheng, Urban Councillor Philip Kwok, and trade unionist Li Kai-ming. Mao Junnian, Xinhua Deputy Secretary General, was named BLCC Secretary General. Yang 'seconded' the motion. Nobody objected and the seven were installed without further ado. No election was held. In 1988 Yang resigned when he was made the Chief Justice; Wong had passed away.

The proceedings were immediately branded as a breach of the BLCC constitution. Critics said the BLDC vice-chairmen had no mandate to propose the candidates. The office bearers should be nominated and elected by the committee members themselves. Defending the action, Xu said the seven office bearers were selected 'by election through consultation,' arguing that consultation was a form of election. Mao said the Standing Committee has only 19 members and there was no need for one man, one vote. He said that during the drafting of the BLCC constitution the draftsmen had wanted to use the term 'consultation' instead of 'election' but since some members had objected, they replaced it with 'election.' However, he said that the term 'election' encompassed the idea of consultation and that BLDC members had never considered elections on a one man, one vote basis.

Standing Committee member Anglican Bishop Peter Kwong said that the term 'election' did not necessarily mean marking names on ballots: 'It was up to the 19 of us to choose the officers. If we did not object to the recommendations, it's completely constitutional for us to accept the suggested name list.'

BLCC vice-chairman Li Kai-ming said the nominations happened so quickly that they caught him completely unawares. He said the BLDC vice-chairmen probably wanted to get their nominees into office quickly to avoid the possibility of others winning the posts in a proper election at a later date. There was speculation that the Chinese wanted to prevent Lo Tak-shing from being elected BLCC chairman, since it would be embarrassing to have as BLCC chairman the head of an emigration company.

Another Standing Committee member Denis Chang, the then Chairman of the Hong Kong Bar Association, said he did not raise any objection at the time because it all happened so fast. After the nominations, some people applauded and the motion was considered passed, Chang said.

The fiasco was discussed at what Ti-liang Yang called the 'proper' BLCC Standing Committee meeting on 11 December. It was agreed that everything that happened at the 6 December meeting had contravened the BLCC constitution because the committee was not given seven days' notice of the meeting. Fresh elections were held to choose the seven office bearers and the original seven names were nominated. Lo Tak-shing was also nominated for the office of chairman, but he refused to stand for the elections. Four others were also nominated: Denis Chang, BLDC members Wong Po-yan and Louis Cha, and former LegCo member Ko Siu-wah. They all refused the nominations. The original seven were re-elected by a show of hands. Chang abstained from voting.

The massive climb-down was a response to the huge public outcry, but the damage had been done and the fresh elections with the same results showed how ready the BLCC members were to bend to Beijing's will. The election fiasco highlighted not only China's mistrust for democracy but also its lack of respect for the Rule of Law.

Public reaction to the breach of the BLCC constitution was swift but restrained. Many criticised the Standing Committee's failure to hold a proper election but few questioned the seven names put forward by the BLDC vice-chairmen. One exception was Hong Kong University Professor Edward Chen, himself a BLCC member. Chen said Ann Tse-kai should not be BLCC Chairman because that would affect the independence of the BLCC. Replacing Ann, Chen said, would allay fears that the Standing Committee was dominated by Beijing interests.

Political groups said they did not wish to go all out to confront the communists because they wanted to maintain a dialogue with them. They agreed they tended to be much harder with the colonial government. 'We dare not push the communists too hard because they will remember us for a long time and may take revenge, but the Hong Kong government will not do a thing like that,' one political activist said.

The incident was a blow to confidence and reinforced sus-picion that the whole Basic Law exercise was probably some kind of window-dressing. Those fears were borne out in the following two years when the BLDC proceeded with the drafting and largely ignored the views and opinions of the BLCC. Many BLCC members failed to turn up at meetings. Some commentators said that the BLCC existed only in name, but the committee did manage to compile and submit to the BLDC extensive reports, available also to the public in Hong Kong, on various issues to be covered in the Basic Law.

With the publication of the first draft of the Basic Law in April 1988, there are signs that the BLCC wants to exert its influence in the opinion-gathering exercise. There was worry that it might be a repeat performance of the Green Paper exercise conducted by the Hong Kong government in 1987 over the development of representative government, in which it decided to postpone the introduction of direct elections to LegCo until 1991, a year after the Basic Law is promulgated.

It remains to be seen how the Hong Kong people will react to the draft Basic Law, which is a very complicated and dry document. Many will not understand it, others may not even bother to read it because they do not think the Chinese will keep whatever promises they make. The experience of the three-year drafting process has led many to suspect that Beijing may not be so keen to listen to the wishes of Hong Kong people, particularly those who are neither rich nor powerful.

Part II

Textual Analysis

7 The Relationship Between the Central Government and the SAR

ALBERT H Y CHEN

As a constitutional instrument, a major function of the Basic Law is to design and erect an institutional framework for the operation of political forces participating in the governing of the Special Administrative Region. The politics of the SAR consist of at least two dimensions. First, there are the domestic politics of the SAR generated by interaction among political forces within the SAR and the possible conflict of interests between the different sectors and strata of Hong Kong society. Second, there are the politics of the division of power between the Central Government of the PRC and the SAR government. These two kinds of politics are not independent but related and mutually interactive. A major challenge for the drafters of the Basic Law is to create a structure of institutional arrangements within which conflicts arising from both types of politics of the SAR can be resolved without jeopardising the stability and prosperity of Hong Kong, and without undue damage to the national interests of China as perceived by the Central Government.

The same perspective can be derived from an analysis of the concept of 'one country, two systems' which inspired the Joint Declaration on the Question of Hong Kong. If the Basic Law is to make constitutional and legal provision for the implementation of that concept, then it is necessary for it both to provide for the nature and principles of the system to be practised in the SAR, and to regulate the relationship between that system and the system in force in mainland China. For the two systems are not to be completely separate and independent; they are to be united as parts of one country and to be subject to one sovereignty. To define the relationship between the two systems is, inter alia, to delineate the extent to which they are separate from each other as well as the extent to which they are integrated with each other.

The subject of this chapter is this relationship between the two systems. How should an appropriate balance between the principles of separation and the principles of integration be struck in the context of the SAR as part of the PRC? What are the constitutional issues arising from this exercise? To what extent does the Basic Law resolve these issues satisfactorily?

This chapter is divided into five parts. Section I is a general theoretical inquiry into the concept of autonomy, a key concept under the JD, which provides that the SAR will enjoy 'a high degree of autonomy.'[1] The relevant provisions of the JD, and the exact degree of autonomy it provides for, will be examined in section II. Section III is a commentary on those articles of the Basic Law which have a direct bearing on the scope of the SAR's autonomy and thus on the constitutional relationship between the SAR and the Central Government. Section IV considers the matter from an institutional rather than textual perspective, and investigates the institutional arrangements facilitating the interaction between the SAR and the central authorities. Finally, section V surveys other issues concerning the central-SAR relationship but not directly dealt with in the previous parts of this chapter.

I GENERAL THEORETICAL CONSIDERATIONS

The concept of autonomy refers to a particular form of distribution of governmental power within a sovereign state. It may be explained as follows. Suppose there is a sovereign state X, and a part of the territory of X is Y. The people of Y can be said to exercise a power of autonomy within the state X if they — usually through their representatives — are empowered to govern themselves in respect of certain affairs. (Examples of 'affairs' in this context are housing, education, transport, social welfare, environmental hygiene, medical services, taxation, etc.) The more extensive the kinds of affairs over which they are self-governing, the higher is their degree of autonomy. The idea of autonomy, however, presupposes that there are at least some governmental affairs over which the people of Y have no ultimate control. For if the people of Y, through their representatives, have complete control over every aspect of their existence and operation as a community, then they are not merely autonomous but constitute an independent nation-state.

In the above example, there are at least two kinds of government in state X. The first is the national or central government of state X, representing, exercising power on behalf of, and having authority over all the citizens of X. Second, there is a local government, or autonomous government, of area Y, representing, exercising power on behalf of, and having authority over the people of Y. Of course, insofar as the people of Y are also citizens of X, they can also participate in the formation and operation of the national government. But the fact would probably remain

1 JD3(2).

that the local government of Y will be able to represent their interests more directly and effectively than the national government, at least where the 'autonomous affairs' (ie affairs specified as the local autonomous government's responsibilities) are involved. For otherwise the people of Y will not derive any substantial benefit from the arrangement of autonomy.

The above analysis illustrates another possible way of defining the concept of autonomy: the people of Y are said to be exercising autonomy within the state of X (Y being part of X) if there exists a division of governmental powers between the local or regional government of Y and the central or national government of X. This division is based on classification of governmental affairs into different types, and the allocation of power over certain types of affairs (eg housing, education, etc as mentioned above) to one government, and of power over other types of affairs to the other government. Under this arrangement, the local government[2] will exercise various powers, such as policy-making powers, legislative powers and judicial powers, over certain designated types of affairs, and the national government will exercise governmental powers over other affairs. The more extensive the powers of the local government, the higher is the degree of autonomy, and vice versa.

If the concept of autonomy is understood as explained above, then it follows that autonomy is in fact a fairly widespread phenomenon in the nations of the contemporary world. Every regional or provincial government, every city council or local authority, exercises some powers of autonomy. The difference among them lies mainly in the degree of autonomy. If a particular authority has autonomous power only over relatively trivial affairs in a small area, then according to the ordinary usage of language, it can hardly deserve the title 'autonomous government,' although in theory the general concept of autonomy may still be applicable and relevant to it.

The scope of autonomy which is desirable or appropriate in any particular context usually depends on a complex of political, economic, social, cultural, and even racial, linguistic, and religious factors.[3] Where the population in a particular area of a nation-state is sharply distinguishable from those in other areas by reason of some of these factors, it may demand a high degree of autonomy for the purpose of protecting certain basic interests or values against encroachment by the nation-state as a whole. Even where no such considerations are involved, some lower

---

2 The word 'government' is used here in its wide sense, which embraces the executive, legislative as well as judicial branches of government.

3 See generally Yoram Dinstein (ed), *Models of Autonomy* (New Brunswick: Transaction Books, 1981).

levels of autonomy may be advantageous in the operation of certain levels of local government to stimulate local initiative, interest, and participation, and thus to promote efficiency and democracy.[4]

Although the policy to be adopted in any historical situation regarding whether and what degree of autonomy for an area within a state should exist is almost always determined by extra-legal considerations, technical constitutional devices do need to be examined in the process of the creative design of autonomous arrangements in any given set of circumstances. In particular, the following issues are likely to command the attention of consti-tutional and legal experts advising politicians on the construc-tion of models of autonomy:

(1) *Method by which the local government is to be formed.* For the advocates of local autonomy, the problem here is to ensure that the government of the autonomous region will truly rep-resent the interests of the people of that region.

(2) *Division of powers, in the legislative, executive, and judicial spheres, between the central government and the local govern-ment.* The challenge here is to draw a line between the domain of the local government and that of the central government, a line which is rational and reasonable in theory and practicable in reality.

(3) *Mechanisms for rectification of errors and resolution of disputes.* What institutional devices are to be established to ensure, on the one hand, that the local government will not exceed the scope of its autonomy, and, on the other hand, that the central government will not infringe upon the scope of such autonomy? Where such errors have indeed occurred, how are they to be rectified? Where conflicts of opinion regarding these matters arise between the two sides, how are they to be resolved?

Here it may be useful to compare the solutions to some of these problems afforded respectively by federal and non-federal models of autonomy. A federal state is formed by the union of more than one member state or province. There is a division of power between the federal government and the state (or provin-cial) governments. Thus the former will have exclusive jurisdic-tion over certain affairs; each of the state governments has exclusive jurisdiction over other affairs within its territory; and over some affairs, the federal and state governments have 'concurrent powers.' Concurrent powers exist where, for

4　See, eg, John Stuart Mill, *Considerations on Representative Government* (South Bend, Indiana: Gateway Editions, 1962, original edition published in London in 1861) especially ch XV.

example, both the federal legislature and a state legislature may be able to make law on a particular matter, but if there is a conflict between a relevant federal law and a state law, the former will prevail.

The division of power between the federal government and the state governments in a federal state is almost invariably set out in a written constitution which forms the constitutional and legal foundation of the federal state.[5] In some federal states, the state governments possess 'residuary powers,' which means that any power which has not been expressly assigned to the federal government by the constitution remains vested in the state government. This principle may be regarded as a reflection of the fact that each member state of the federal state had originally been a full sovereign state, or at least a separately governed entity, before the federation was formed. However, the reservation of residuary powers by the states is by no means a necessary feature of a federal state. It is perfectly possible and proper for the federal constitution to allocate such residuary powers to the federal government.

A most fundamental legal characteristic of the federal state is that the federal constitution, in which the division of powers is, inter alia, set out, is binding not only on the state governments but also on the federal government. The supremacy of this constitutional division of powers over the federal government means that the latter may not unilaterally upset the original division of powers by expanding its actions and activities beyond their constitutional limit, thus infringing the autonomy of the member states. The original division of powers can only be altered by amendment of the constitution, which usually requires the overwhelming support not only of the federal legislature but also of the legislatures of most of the states, or even of the people of the states themselves voting in a referendum.

Since the federal constitution limits the power of both the federal government and state governments, it is necessary to provide in its design a mechanism for interpreting and enforcing these constitutional limits on power and for imposing legal sanctions where such limits have been exceeded. In many states, this mechanism exists in the form of either a constitutional tribunal or the ordinary courts, which may, for example, declare as invalid federal laws touching upon a matter within the exclusive jurisdiction of a state and thus trespassing upon the state's autonomy, or conversely, a state law which deals with a matter within the exclusive jurisdiction of the federal

5 See generally K C Wheare, *Federal Government* (London: Oxford University Press, 4th ed 1963) especially 11–13, 79–80.

government. Thus conflicts or disputes between the federal and state governments arising from the constitutional division of power are resolved in this judicial forum.

The autonomy of a state as a member state of a federal state is, however, not the sole model of autonomy. Even in a unitary state, it is possible to have an autonomous area practising genuine autonomy. And it is possible for such an autonomous area to exercise a degree of autonomy higher than that of a member state of a federation. As explained above, the degree of autonomy depends primarily on the range of subject matters the governing power over which is assigned to the local autonomous government, and not on whether the arrangement is federal or not. What, then, is the essential difference between autonomy in a federation and that in a unitary state?

The main point here is that the power of an autonomous government in an area forming part of a unitary state is usually derived not from the constitution of the unitary state but from a law enacted by the legislature of the state. While a constitution is supreme over and binding on the national legislature, a law enacted by it is not. Thus while, in a federal state, the autonomy of each member state is constitutionally guaranteed by the provisions regarding division of power in the federal constitution, the autonomy of an area within a unitary state is not directly protected by the constitution. It is derived from ordinary national legislation and, at least in constitutional theory, may be withdrawn by legislative amendment without the need for constitutional amendment. Thus from the point of view of the constitutional theorist, the autonomy of a local government in a unitary state is less securely guaranteed or entrenched than the autonomy of a member state in a federation.

The difference may also be presented by analysing the delegation of governmental power from historical and logical points of view. In the process of the formation of a federal state, sovereign powers which were originally vested in the states are relinquished subject to the condition of having a fundamental constitutional guarantee of the division of power securing certain powers for the member states. On the other hand, the autonomy enjoyed by the people of an autonomous region of a unitary state does not logically exist prior to, but is the direct result of, a voluntary delegation of power by the national authority. In this situation, the granting of autonomy to the region is a concession by the fully sovereign nation-state, whereas in the federal situation, the autonomy of the member state is a reserved right of a community which once possessed sovereignty but voluntarily decided to transfer it to a new federal state subject to the reservation of rights and division of powers set out in the new federal constitution.

Typical examples of federal states include the USA, Canada, Australia, and India. It is noteworthy that in these countries, the ultimate forum for settling disputes regarding the interpretation and enforcement of the constitutional division of power between national and state authorities is the federal supreme court.[6] Examples of autonomy within a unitary state include the case of Greenland under the sovereignty of Denmark,[7] the devolution proposal for Scotland and Wales in 1975,[8] and the case of the SAR under the JD.[9] The case of Greenland is particularly instructive in relation to the mechanism for resolution of disputes between the central authority and the autonomous region. Since the constitutional structure is not federal, there is no federal supreme court which can serve as a forum for such dispute resolution. In theory, two alternative options are to designate either a supreme court of the national legal system or the local supreme court of the autonomous region as the forum for this purpose.[10] However, both solutions are not completely fair: the national supreme court might be perceived as biased in favour of the central authority, and a local court of the autonomous region in favour of the autonomous authority. A fairly ingenious solution in this regard is provided by section 18 of the Greenland Home Rule Act 1978:[11]

---

6 See generally Wheare (n 5 above) ch IV. See also R E Johnston, *The Effect of Judicial Review on Federal-State Relations in Australia, Canada and the United States* (Baton Rouge: Louisiana State University Press, 1969).

7 See Isi Foighel, 'A Framework for Local Autonomy: The Greenland Case' in Dinstein (n 3 above) 31.

8 See generally Harry Calvert (ed), *Devolution* (London: Professional Books, 1975); *Our Changing Democracy: Devolution to Scotland and Wales* (London: cmnd 6348, 1975). The proposals were not, however, implemented.

9 Two additional examples are Puerto Rico under the USA (see Natan Lerner, 'Puerto Rico: Autonomy, Statehood, Independence?' in Dinstein (n 3 above) 125) and the Cook Islands under New Zealand (see the materials on Cook Islands in Albert P Blaustein and Eric B Blaustein (eds), *Constitutions of Dependencies and Special Sovereignties* (Dobbs Ferry, New York: Oceana Publications, 1985). These two cases are not so typical as the three examples referred to in the text because, in the former cases, the autonomous entity has the right to terminate autonomy under the sovereign power and to become an independent nation-state instead.

10 Note, however, that in most non-federal arrangements for autonomy, the autonomous entity is subject to the ultimate judicial authority of the Central Government through appeals from the local courts to the highest court of the national judiciary on matters such as the constitutionality of local enactments, or challenges that local actions are beyond the permitted scope of autonomy under the constitutional documents defining the relationship between the autonomous and principal entities: Hurst Hannum and Richard B Lillich, 'The Concept of Autonomy in International Law' in Dinstein (n 3 above) 231–232.

11 For the text of the Act, see the section on Greenland in Blaustein and Blaustein (n 9 above).

18 (1) Should any doubt arise between the central authorities [of Denmark] and the home rule authorities [of Greenland] concerning their respective jurisdictions, the question shall be laid before a board consisting of two members nominated by the Government [of Denmark], two members nominated by the home rule authorities and three judges of the Supreme Court [of Denmark] nominated by its President, one of whom shall be nominated as Chairman.

(2) If the four members nominated by the Government and the home rule authorities reach agreement the question shall be considered settled. If these four fail to reach agreement the question shall be decided by the three Supreme Court judges.

(3) The Government may suspend an enactment or decision of the home rule authorities which has been placed before the board until such time as the board's decision is taken.

It may be seen that the essence of the arrangement is a preference for dispute settlement by a non-judicial mode of negotiation and consultation among, or mediation by, the four lay members of the board, failing which a judicial decision will be rendered by the three judges on the board.

II RELEVANT PROVISIONS IN THE JOINT DECLARATION

Paragraph 3(2) of the JD provides:

> The HKSAR will be directly under the authority of the Central People's Government of the PRC. The HKSAR will enjoy a high degree of autonomy, except in foreign and defence affairs which are the responsibilities of the CPG.

Some might think that the general phrase 'high degree of autonomy' is too vague: how high is this high degree of autonomy? Others might believe that the degree of autonomy is defined by the simple principle that the SAR will govern itself in respect of all political, social, economic and other matters except foreign and defence affairs. It is submitted here that both points of view are not justified if the whole of the JD and its Annexes are properly examined and assessed. In fact, a large proportion of the document consists precisely of provisions designed to give concrete substance to the phrase 'high degree of autonomy' as used in JD3(2). The following points may be noted in this regard.

(1) The SAR's autonomous powers not only include 'executive, legislative and independent judicial powers' (JD3(2)) but also extend to some external affairs such as the establishment of 'mutually beneficial economic relations with the UK and other countries' (JD3(9)), the maintenance and development of economic and cultural relations and the conclusion of relevant agreements with other countries and international organisations, using the name of 'Hong Kong, China' (JD3(10)), and the issue of

travel documents for entry into and exit from Hong Kong (JD3(10)).

(2) The degree of Hong Kong's autonomy and the exact relationship between the central authority and the SAR in relation to various matters is elaborated in different sections of Annex I of the JD as follows:

Matters	*Section no of Annex I*
Formation and operation of the SAR government	I, IV
Sources of law	II
Courts and the judiciary	III
Financial and fiscal matters	V
Economic and commercial matters	VI
Monetary matters	VII
Shipping	VIII
Civil aviation	IX
Cultural, educational, and other matters	X
External relations	XI
Defence, security, and public order	XII
Travel and immigration matters	XIV

Take, for example, the subject of civil aviation. What is the extent of the SAR's autonomy in relation to this matter? The answer is provided in detail by Annex I, section IX, JD.

(3) The SAR's powers over external affairs are conferred and regulated not only by section XI of Annex I, but also by relevant provisions in sections III, VI, VIII, IX and XIV thereof.

It is interesting to compare the proposed autonomy of the SAR under the JD with autonomous entities in other countries. The long list of items over which the SAR has autonomous control, and the inclusion in the list of many critically important powers, suggest that the SAR's autonomy is very high indeed from the comparative perspective. The significant fact in this regard is that almost no member states of federal states or autonomous governments in unitary states exercise complete autonomous powers over all of the following crucial matters of government — finance and taxation, monetary affairs, the issue of currency, customs, entry and exit controls, external trade relations, basic areas of law such as criminal law, criminal procedure, civil law, and civil procedure — whereas the SAR will exercise full autonomy over all these under the JD. The reservation to the national government of powers over defence and foreign affairs is of a minimal nature: if even these are not reserved, then the SAR will be an independent state and no longer an autonomous region within the PRC. No autonomous but non-independent entities in the world exercise full powers over defence and foreign affairs, although a few highly autonomous governments are actually authorised by their relevant central governments to enter into treaties and agreements relating to cultural and economic matters with other nations or regions.[12]

In one important respect, however, the autonomy of the SAR will be less than that enjoyed by some autonomous entities in other parts of the world. In many member states of federal states and some autonomous regions within unitary states, the Chief Executive and other leading members of the autonomous government are chosen by election by the people of the autonomous unit.[13] On the other hand, JD3(4) and Annex I, section I, JD require both the Chief Executive and principal officials of the SAR to be appointed by the CPG, although the appointment of the former will be 'on the basis of the results of elections or consultations to be held locally,' and the appointment of the latter on the basis of nominations by the CE.

It is not clear from the JD whether such appointment is a mere procedural formality or will be the occasion for the exercise of a substantive choice. On the one hand, it is possible that a constitutional convention will develop whereby the appointment procedure will be reduced to a mere formality for the purpose of confirming the result of the relevant election, consultation, or nomination exercise. This line of development will be conducive to political stability and local confidence. On the other hand, the express reservation of the power of appointment of both the CE and principal officials to the CPG is a constant reminder that the SAR's autonomy is clearly circumscribed. The CPG is not constitutionally bound to accede to the wishes, even if unequivocally expressed, of the people of Hong Kong as regards whom the latter want to be their CE and principal officials.

From this perspective, it seems that the extensive autonomous powers — of an extremely high degree when compared to other autonomous entities — of the SAR mentioned above might be rendered illusory given the possibly tight central control on the selection of leaders of the SAR government. Viewing the matter from a slightly different angle, one might say that the strict central control on the appointment of personnel was considered necessary precisely because the autonomous powers entrusted to these personnel are so great. In other autonomous arrangements, the powers of the autonomous unit are so limited that the threat to the central national authority is not significant even if the people of the autonomous entity are given a completely free hand in the selection of their CE and principal officials.

12 Hannum and Lillich (n 10 above) 234, 250; S A de Smith, *The New Commonwealth and its Constitutions* (London: Stevens & Sons, 1964) 57.
13 Hannum and Lillich (n 10 above) 219–222.

III RELEVANT PROVISIONS IN THE BASIC LAW

One of the achievements of the Basic Law is that it has set out most of the major issues to be addressed in translating the JD into a mini-constitution for Hong Kong, although not all such issues have been satisfactorily resolved by the provisions of the draft document. It is now therefore possible to discuss the main issues pertaining to the constitutional relationship between the Central Government and the SAR by examining and commenting on various relevant provisions in the Basic Law.

Although there is a chapter in the Basic Law, viz chapter II, which is expressly entitled the 'relationship between the central authorities and the HKSAR,' other relevant provisions may also be found in other parts of the Basic Law. For example, chapters V, VI, and VII provide for, inter alia, the extent to which Hong Kong is autonomous and free from central control as regards various economic, social, cultural, and external affairs. As these chapters form the subjects of other chapters in this book, this chapter will not consider them directly. We shall instead focus on the general provisions touching upon the central-SAR relationship in the preamble and chapters I, II, and IX.

The preamble

The preamble begins by stating that 'Hong Kong has been part of China's territory since ancient times, but it was occupied by Britain after the Opium War in 1840.' Hence 1 July 1997 will not be a day of transfer of sovereignty over Hong Kong, but a day on which (as stated in the preamble of the Basic Law) 'the government of the PRC will resume the exercise of sovereignty over Hong Kong.' Similar wording is found in China's declaration in JD1. From this point of view, any autonomous powers exercised by the Hong Kong community after July 1997 are not inherited or developed from the colonial government but are derived from the government of the PRC. This point has been repeatedly stressed in writings reflecting Chinese official thinking published in the Hong Kong press.[14]

Given this emphasis on the concept of Chinese sovereignty, it is not surprising that the will or wishes of the people of Hong Kong are not recognised in the preamble. It is the state, and not the people of Hong Kong, which 'has decided that upon China's resumption of the exercise of sovereignty over Hong Kong, a HKSAR will be established in accordance with the provisions of

---

14 See, eg Xin Weisi, *Political Commentaries by Xin Weisi* (Hong Kong: Ming Pao Publishers, 1987) (collection of newspaper articles in Chinese) especially 21–26, 148–158.

Article 31 of the Constitution of the PRC.' And according to the last paragraph of the preamble, the Basic Law is enacted by the National People's Congress in accordance with the Chinese constitution. It is not mentioned that the Basic Law is being enacted in consultation with the people of Hong Kong.

Another point to note about the preamble is that it expressly refers to the JD, in which 'the basic policies of the PRC regarding Hong Kong have been elaborated by our government.' Moreover, the principle of 'one country, two systems' is also expressly mentioned. This is noteworthy in the light of the fact that the phrase was not used in the JD itself. Originated by Deng Xiaoping, the phrase carries much ideological and political significance, and is considered in another chapter of this book.

Chapter I

Chapter I is entitled 'general principles,' and it includes, inter alia, general principles governing the central-SAR relationship. For example, it is emphasised that 'the HKSAR is an inalienable part of the PRC,' authorised by the NPC 'to exercise a high degree of autonomy in accordance with the provisions of this Law.' BL7 provides that land and natural resources in the SAR are PRC state property but are to be managed by the SAR government. Under BL8 and 10, any existing or future law which contravenes the Basic Law cannot be valid. The exact mechanism by which such validity is to be determined is governed by more detailed provisions in chapters II and X.

Chapter II

As the title of chapter II indicates, this chapter of the Basic Law addresses specifically the issue of the relationship between the central authorities and the SAR. Although the multiple facets of the question are not exhaustively covered by the provisions of chapter II, it does attempt to propose solutions to the following critical issues relevant to the central-SAR relationship.

(1) *Constitutional link between the Central Government and the SAR government.* BL11 provides that although the SAR 'enjoys a high degree of autonomy,' it is constitutionally a 'local administrative region of the PRC' and 'comes directly under the CPG.' There is an apparent contradiction between autonomy and direct subordination to the CPG, but it should be noted that BL11 is in fact based on Annex I, section I, JD, which provides that 'the HKSAR shall be directly under the authority of the CPG and shall enjoy a high degree of autonomy.' The provision is probably designed to state the point that the SAR, though physically located in the Guangdong province, is not under the authority of

Guangdong, but has, like the municipalities of Shanghai, Tian-jin, and Beijing, direct access in the government apparatus to and is administratively directly accountable to the CPG.

(2) *Stationing of military forces in the SAR.* This is provided for in BL13, which amplifies the relevant provisions in Annex I, section XII, JD. For example, the third paragraph of BL13 goes further than the JD provisions by requiring members of the garrison to abide by both 'nation-wide laws' and 'the laws of the HKSAR.' The application of this provision to criminal law matters and to other matters can be considered separately.

As far as the criminal law is concerned, the provision means that PRC soldiers in Hong Kong should be careful so as not to commit any offence under either PRC national law or SAR law. They are subject to the former because they are members of the national military; they are also made subject to the latter because they are physically in Hong Kong and should not be above or im-mune from the local law. However, the question is still unre-solved as regards whether the ordinary courts of the SAR, or the ordinary courts of the PRC, or special military courts will have jurisdiction to try a PRC soldier who is suspected of having committed in Hong Kong a criminal offence under either PRC national law or SAR law. In this regard it should be noted that at present, the jurisdiction of the Hong Kong courts over offences against the ordinary criminal law of Hong Kong committed by members of the British forces in Hong Kong is limited and does not extend to certain types of situation.[15]

The provision requiring the military to abide by both national and SAR laws may cause further complications if it is intended to cover non-criminal law situations. In Hong Kong's existing legal system, rules of conflict of laws apply to determine, in cases involving elements of different legal systems, the law of which legal system should be applied to govern any point which arises. In such cases, the effect of the third paragraph of BL13 might be to confuse the situation and disturb the normal operation of conflict of laws rules. For example, as regards the capacity to marry and the minimum age for a person to enter into marriage, should a PRC soldier be governed by PRC national law or Hong Kong law? Common law conflict of laws principles would give a

15 In which jurisdiction is exercised by the court-martial. See the United Kingdom Forces (Jurisdiction of Colonial Courts) Order 1965 (1965 SI No 1203, Laws of Hong Kong). See generally Harry Street and Rodney Brazier, *de Smith's Constitutional and Administrative Law* (Harmondsworths: Penguin Books, 5th ed 1985) ch 10; 41 *Halsbury's Laws of England* (4th ed); Albert H Y Chen and Johannes M M Chan, *Human Rights and the Rule of Law: The Challenges of Hong Kong's Transition* (Hong Kong: Wide Angle Press, 1987) 51–52 (in Chinese).

clear answer here, but the position is now rendered uncertain by the third paragraph of BL13.

(3) *SAR's executive powers.* These are dealt with in BL15, which apparently attempts to transcend the debate concerning 'residuary powers' which dominated the early stage of the drafting of the Basic Law.[16] In that debate, advocates of Hong Kong's interests argued that the division of powers between the central authority and the SAR under the Basic Law should be formulated in such a way that residuary powers vest in the SAR. In other words, any powers which are neither expressly reserved to the Central Government nor expressly delegated to the SAR government should belong to the SAR.

As a drafting technique, this proposal is probably right and rational. The degree of autonomy to be enjoyed by the SAR contemplated in the JD is so high that it would be difficult to enumerate specifically each and every matter over which the SAR should have jurisdiction, whereas it would be simple and easy to identify the few powers reserved to the Central Government and to provide in a sweep-all manner that all other powers vest in the SAR. Indeed, this approach seems to derive support from the following provisions in the JD:

> The HKSAR will enjoy a high degree of autonomy, except in foreign and defence affairs which are the responsibilities of the Central People's Government. [JD3(2)]
>
> Except for foreign and defence affairs which are the responsibilities of the Central People's Government, the HKSAR shall be vested with executive, legislative and independent judicial power, including that of final adjudication. [Annex I, section I, JD]

The very employment of the concept of residuary powers was opposed by mainland members of the Basic Law Drafting Committee. In their opinion, the idea is only relevant to a federal constitution; any suggestion that the federal model is applicable to the relationship between Hong Kong and China is to be firmly rejected. Their line of thought seems to be as follows. In the creation of a federal state, states which were originally sovereign states surrender their sovereignty and become members of the federal union. In such a situation, any reservation under the new federal constitution of residuary powers to the member states themselves is only natural.[17] Hong Kong, however, is not and has

---

16 See, eg Chen and Chan (n 15 above) 21–22.

17 Note, however, that it is by no means an invariable rule that residuary powers vest in the member states of a federal state. There exist federal constitutions which expressly assign residuary powers to the federal government. The constitution of Canada is an example. See n 5 above.

never been a sovereign state; sovereignty over it has always vested and will always vest in China. Any autonomy which it is to exercise in the future is not the result of a reservation of rights by the people of Hong Kong upon incorporation into China, but is the consequence of a voluntary act of delegation of power on the part of the national government of China. According to this scheme of thinking, the sharp and highly significant distinction between the nature of Hong Kong and of member states of federal unions makes it totally inappropriate to employ the concept of residuary powers in the Hong Kong situation.

BL15 as it stands represents an interesting compromise between ideological opposition to the federal approach and the practical need to enshrine a high degree of autonomy for the SAR. It provides a fairly long list[18] of subject matters over which the SAR is to have executive powers, followed by the general phrase 'and other administrative matters.' It is not clear whether and to what extent the ejusdem generis rule can apply to BL15. However, the existence of the catch-all phrase, and the supplementary provision in BL19 that the SAR may enjoy 'other powers granted to it by the National People's Congress, the Standing Committee of the NPC or the State Council,' show that the list of specific items in BL15 is not intended to be exhaustive.

(4) *SAR's legislative powers.* Compared to BL15, the first paragraph of BL16 is surprisingly simple. No attempt is made here to describe and delineate the scope of the SAR's legislative power by setting out the subject matters on which the SAR may legislate. Such listing of relevant subject matters is the normal practice in the drafting of federal constitutions as well as constitutional instruments for autonomous arrangements within a unitary state. And considerations of the locus of residuary power mentioned above are as relevant to legislative affairs as they are to executive affairs. It is therefore at first sight difficult to understand why the first paragraph of BL16 does not follow the format and style of BL15.

There are two possible explanations. First, it might have been the drafters' intention that the list of subject matters provided by BL15 is also applicable to legislative powers, although this has not been expressly stated. Second, the drafters might have considered it unnecessary to define the scope of the SAR's legislative power in BL16, given the existence already of the general requirement in BL10 that the SAR may not make any law contravening the Basic Law. Hence in a sense the whole of the Basic

---

18 The list is, however, not too long if one compares it with, say, the provisions on division of powers in the constitutions of Canada, Australia, India and Malaysia.

Law, and each provision in it, are concerned with and constitute a limitation on the scope of the law-making power of the SAR.

Paragraph 2 of BL16 requires all laws enacted by the SAR legislature to be reported to the NPCSC 'for the record.' This requirement can be traced back to Annex I, section II, JD, which also provides that '[l]aws enacted by the legislature which are in accordance with the Basic Law and legal procedures shall be regarded as valid.' However, the JD omitted to deal with the procedural mechanism to be adopted in determining whether a particular piece of SAR legislation is consistent with the BL and therefore valid. This gap in the JD is filled by the third paragraph of BL16, which is somewhat controversial.

This third paragraph in effect empowers the NPCSC to review each SAR enactment and to nullify any which it determines, after consultation with the 'Committee for the Basic Law of the HKSAR', to be inconsistent with the Basic Law. The CBL is apparently intended to be a mediating and arbitral organ for resolving differences of opinion between the central authority and the SAR. It will be considered in greater detail in section IV of this chapter. At this stage, several comments on other aspects of the third paragraph of BL16 may be made.

First, it is submitted that the vesting of a power of review of or supervision over SAR legislative activities in a body other than the SAR courts is not in itself unreasonable or objectionable. In any arrangement for autonomy, there must be mechanisms for ensuring that the autonomous entity does not exceed the permitted scope of its autonomy. In other words, the central or national authority needs to, in the design of the constitutional framework for autonomy, ensure that any trespass on the limits of autonomy by the autonomous entity can be effectively checked and rectified. The question then is by whom and according to what procedure is the power of review and supervision to be exercised.

In this regard, a survey of arrangements of autonomy in various parts of the world would reveal that it is not unnatural or unusual for such review and supervisory powers to be vested in a branch or organ of the national or central authority. Thus in most federal states, these powers are exercised by the judicial branch of the federal government, viz the federal supreme court, which is thus responsible for interpreting and enforcing the federal constitution, and for determining whether any state law is contrary to the federal constitution and hence invalid. In the case of Greenland discussed above, which is an example of autonomy under a non-federal framework, the review power lies in the last resort in the hands of three supreme court judges appointed by the Denmark government.

It is therefore difficult to sustain any argument that the power of reviewing whether a legislative act of the SAR has gone beyond the permitted scope of its autonomy under the BL should be vested exclusively in the SAR courts. This arrangement would be similar to one under which a state court of a member state of a federal state has exclusive jurisdiction (and the federal court has no jurisdiction) in determining whether a state law has violated the federal constitution, or one under which, taking again the example of Greenland, the Greenland courts have exclusive jurisdiction (and judges of the central Denmark authority have no jurisdiction) to decide whether an act enacted by the Greenland legislature is ultra vires the relevant law on autonomy for Greenland.

But to argue that the final review and supervisory powers over the exercise of legislative autonomy by the SAR cannot vest exclusively in the SAR courts does not necessarily mean that they should be vested in the NPCSC. The question still remains as to whether the NPCSC, or some other body specially created for this purpose, is the more appropriate forum for deciding whether the SAR has exceeded its autonomy. This issue will be explored in section IV of this chapter.

Assuming that we accept the vesting of review and supervisory powers in the NPCSC, our second comment on the third paragraph of BL16 is that the present procedure for the exercise of this power leaves much to be desired. Under the draft provision as it stands, the NPCSC may invalidate an SAR enactment at any time after it has been passed and without giving reasons. Prescription of a time limit for the exercise of the power of invalidation and a requirement that reasons for the decision should be given would be improvements upon the present draft.

Third, the provision in the last sentence of BL16 that the cessation of any law returned for reconsideration or revoked by the NPCSC shall not have retroactive effect is not without difficulties. The intention behind the provision is probably to minimise the effect of the NPCSC's invalidation of the enactment, and, in particular, disturbance to rights, obligations, and settled expectations which have arisen since the enactment came into existence. Although this objective is laudable, the drafters have probably overlooked the fact that making an enactment void ab initio might be in the interest of justice in some situations. Take, for example, the case of an enactment in criminal law which creates new criminal offences or provides for heavier penalties for existing offences. A finding that the enactment contravenes the Basic Law will not help persons undergoing imprisonment pursuant to the enactment unless the invalidation of the enactment operates retrospectively. It is in the interest of the liberty of subjects that the invalidation of laws restricting or otherwise prejudicing liberty be retroactive in effect.

Finally, it is noteworthy that while BL16 makes express provision for the NPCSC's power of review of SAR legislation, the power of the SAR courts to do the same is nowhere stipulated directly in the Basic Law. The lack of an express provision on the latter does not necessarily mean that there will be no judicial review of legislation in the SAR. An activist court will no doubt be able to assert this power and justify it by reference to Basic Law provisions,[19] common law principles,[20] as well as the practice in Hong Kong's present legal system.[21] On the other hand, it is not inconceivable that a politically timid court might abdicate the power and shirk the responsibility of judicial review by holding that the existence of BL16 and the absence of any provision in the Basic Law on the review of SAR legislation by the courts imply that such review power is exclusively vested in the NPCSC, and that any legislation not vetoed under BL16 must be conclusively presumed to be consistent with the Basic Law and enforced by the SAR courts.

(5) *Legislative powers of the national authorities in relation to Hong Kong.* These are covered in BL17, probably one of the most controversial articles in the Basic Law. The point arousing most concern is that the State Council may, after consultation with the CBL (except in 'cases of emergency' where such consultation is

19 BL10 provides that no law enacted by the SAR legislature shall contravene the Basic Law. BL169 empowers the SAR courts to interpret the Basic Law (except provisions therein on defence, foreign affairs and other affairs which are the responsibility of the CPG.) Thus it can be argued that after an SAR court has interpreted a Basic Law provision and a provision in an SAR enactment and found that they are in conflict with each other, the court should refuse to give effect to the latter provision. See also the discussion in ch 9 of this book, at p 184.

20 It is a basic principle in a common law legal system that it is for the courts of law (and for them alone) to interpret and enforce both the constitution and the law. It follows logically that where they find that a law is inconsistent with the constitution, they must refuse to recognise and enforce it. This is the type of argument used by the United States Supreme Court in *Marbury v Madison*, 1 Craunch 137, 2 L Ed 60 (1803), when it first asserted the power of judicial review of federal legislation. It should be noted that the US constitution does not have any express provision regarding the power of judicial review of legislation. See generally M Cappelletti, *Judicial Review in the Contemporary World* (Indianapolis: The Bobbs-Merrill Co Inc, 1971); Michael C Davis, 'A Common Law Court in a Marxist Country: The Case for Judicial Review in the Hong Kong Special Administrative Region' (1987–88) 16 Denver Journal of International Law and Policy (fall issue); Charles L Black, Jr, *The People and the Court: Judicial Review in a Democracy* (New York: Macmillan, 1960).

21 At present, the courts of Hong Kong can review whether an ordinance passed by the legislature is valid or outside its legislative competence. Thus the courts are bound not to enforce any ordinance which contravenes, say, an Act of Parliament applicable to Hong Kong or the Letters Patent. See ch 1 of this book, at p 12.

not necessary), apply (either by way of directives to the SAR or by direct decree) to the SAR 'laws enacted by the NPC or NPCSC which relate to defence and foreign affairs as well as other laws which give expression to national unity and territorial integrity and which, in accordance with the provisions of this Law, are outside the limits of the high degree of autonomy of the HKSAR.'

The first issue is whether BL17 is fully in accord with the JD. Annex I, section II, JD provides, inter alia, that '[t]he laws of the HKSAR shall be this Law, and the laws previously in force in Hong Kong and laws enacted by the HKSAR legislature as above.'[22] On the face of it, it seems to suggest that laws enacted by the national legislature of China will (with the exception of the BL) not apply in the SAR. At least, there is nothing in the JD which corresponds to the third paragraph of BL17 regarding the application of certain categories of PRC national laws to the SAR.

It might, however, be too hasty to conclude at this point that the existence of the third paragraph of BL17 contravenes the JD. JD3(2) provides: 'The HKSAR will enjoy a high degree of autonomy, except in foreign and defence affairs which are the responsibilities of the Central People's Government.' And Annex I, section I elaborates as follows: 'Except for foreign and defence affairs which are the responsibilities of the Central People's Government, the HKSAR shall be vested with executive, legislative and independent judicial power, including that of final adjudication. The Central People's Government shall authorise the HKSAR to conduct on its own those external affairs specified in section XI of this Annex.' The JD therefore seems to imply that the SAR has no policy-making and law-making powers with regard to defence and foreign affairs (except certain external affairs).

The JD is not a perfect and water-tight document; relevant issues which were overlooked in the drafting of the JD must nevertheless be resolved in the Basic Law. The problem of legislation on defence and foreign affairs serves as a good illustration of this point. If the division of powers between the Central Government and the SAR is such that foreign and defence affairs are assigned to the former, it cannot be right that the Central Government should have no power to apply, or to compel the application of, relevant centrally made laws on foreign and defence affairs to the SAR.

Hence the third paragraph of BL17 is not unreasonable insofar as it relates to defence and foreign affairs. However, the

22 This provision has now been set out as the first paragraph of BL17.

application to the SAR of the third category of national laws — 'other laws which give expression to national unity and territorial integrity and which, in accordance with the provisions of this Law, are outside the limits of the high degree of autonomy of the HKSAR' — is indeed worrying. The phrase is vague and people in Hong Kong fear that concepts such as 'national unity' and 'territorial integrity' may be widely interpreted by the mainland government, so that an uncertain but potentially large number of mainland laws may become applicable in the SAR. This constitutes a considerable threat to the SAR's autonomy.

The 'Summary' of the Basic Law compiled by the Secretariat of the Consultative Committee for the Basic Law states that the national laws which will be applied in the SAR under BL17 'include the Nationality Law of the PRC, the Organic Law of the NPC, the Statement of the Government of the PRC on Territorial Sea, etc.' If these are the types of law which the draftsmen had in mind when BL17 was formulated, one way to improve the present draft and to allay the fears of the people of Hong Kong would be to provide in a schedule to the Basic Law a complete list of relevant national laws which are to be applied in the SAR. Alternatively, if it is thought too difficult to compile an exhaustive list or too inconvenient to allow for frequent amendment of the list, a list of various types of national law to be applied in Hong Kong should at least be provided, together with a fairly detailed description of the nature of each type of law.

Another area of concern is the relationship between BL17 and BL22, which requires the SAR to 'prohibit by law any act designed to undermine national unity or subvert the Central People's Government.' As a matter of principle, BL22 is perhaps unquestionable, since every government needs to secure its power against treason and its own overthrow. The original intention behind BL22 is also laudable: recognising that the PRC law on treason and related crimes, which is contained in the chapter on counter-revolutionary crimes in the PRC Criminal Law, is probably inappropriate for direct application to Hong Kong, it was decided to instruct the SAR to make its own laws on treason and related activities. However, the question left unanswered is: what is to happen if, in the opinion of the Central Government, the SAR is in breach of its obligation under BL22 because, for example, the laws on treason made by the SAR do not meet the requirements of the Central Government? Would the latter than resort to its powers under BL17 to legislate directly for the SAR? If this is the intended design, would this not contravene the spirit of BL22? These are difficult points, and they need to be carefully examined.

(6) *Judicial power of the SAR.* Although the structure of the future judicial system is covered by section 4 of chapter IV of the Basic Law, BL18 deals with the question of the limit of the SAR's judicial power in relation to the central authority. In this regard, the JD provision about the vesting of judicial (as well as executive and legislative) power in the SAR being subject to the exceptions for defence and foreign affairs has already been quoted above. Moreover, even under Hong Kong's existing legal system, the jurisdiction of the courts is limited in various ways.[23] Such existing limitations are preserved by the second paragrah of BL18. The relationship between the second and third paragraphs of BL18 is not, however, clear. The second paragraph seems to confirm that the jurisdiction of the SAR courts will be no less than that of the existing Hong Kong courts, whereas the third paragraph probably has the effect of introducing *additional* restrictions on the jurisdiction of the post-1997 courts in Hong Kong.

The relationship between the first and second sentences of the third paragraph is also ambiguous. There are at least two possible interpretations of their relationship. The *first* interpretation is that the first and second sentences cover different types of case. The first sentence is concerned with cases where the subject of defence, foreign affairs, or executive acts of the CPG is a dominant element. The SAR courts will not hear these cases at all. And the second sentence covers cases in which the subject of defence, foreign affairs etc is not a dominant feature and which the court does proceed to hear, but in the course of the hearing a question relating to defence, foreign affairs, etc arises. For example, is a particular person — a foreign diplomat — entitled to diplomatic immunity? Is a foreign government recognised by China? Does a state of war exist between China and a particular country? The court will not attempt to answer these questions itself, but will seek the advice of the CE, whose certificate on the question would be binding. This, then, is the first possible interpretation of the third paragraph of BL18.

The *second* possible interpretation is that the first and second sentences of the third paragraph do not deal with mutually exclusive types of situation, but the second sentence is in fact an elaboration of the procedure to be adopted in implementing the

23 See Chen and Chan (n 15 above) 40–41, 51. For example, the courts' jurisdiction in respect of actions in personam is governed by, inter alia, the rules on service of process outside the jurisdiction contained in O 11 of the Rules of the Supreme Court, and their criminal jurisdiction is, subject to certain statutory exceptions, confined to offences committed in Hong Kong.

principle stated by the first sentence. In other words, whenever any party argues that, or the court itself suspects that, the case might be one relating to defence, foreign affairs, etc the CE must be consulted as regards whether the case does relate to such matters. If the CE certifies that it does, then the case is taken out of the hands of the court. According to this interpretation, the content of the certificate to be issued by the CE will invariably relate to the 'classification' question of whether the case is one relating to defence, foreign affairs, etc in the terms of the first sentence of the third paragraph of BL18, and the certificate is not to be used to answer substantive questions of defence, foreign affairs, etc as suggested in the above paragraph.

It is submitted that the first interpretation is the only sensible one and that appropriate amendment should be made to the third paragraph of BL18 to confirm this interpretation and to rule out the possibility of the second interpretation. The latter is dangerous and unacceptable because it would mean that the extent of the courts' jurisdiction would be determined by the CE (following the directions of the NPCSC or the State Council in accordance with the fourth paragraph of BL18), which would be a direct violation of a fundamental principle of Hong Kong's existing legal system.[24] On the other hand, the first interpretation fits in well with the existing common law practice concerning Acts of State and facts of state.[25]

A final point to note about BL18 is that the jurisdiction of the SAR courts is restricted thereunder not only as regards defence and foreign affairs — which restriction is not inconsistent with the JD and is also based on the existing law — but also as regards 'the executive acts of the CPG.' This phrase causes some difficulty and uncertainty because, under the existing law, there is no corresponding rule directly excluding the jurisdiction of the Hong Kong courts as regards the 'executive acts' of the UK government.[26] Executive acts of the Hong Kong government may

24 That is, the common law principle that the jurisdiction of the courts is limited by law and only by law, and that it is for the courts to interpret and enforce the law, including the legal rules regarding the limits of the courts' jurisdiction.
25 See generally 18 *Halsbury's Laws of England* (4th ed) 725–730, and the discussion in ch 9 of this book at pp 181–184 and ch 12 at p 260.
26 See, however, s 34 of the Crown Proceedings Ordinance (Cap 300, LHK 1964 ed). The ordinance provides for the civil liabilities and rights of the Crown and civil proceedings by and against the Crown. Section 34(2)(b) provides that nothing in the ordinance shall authorise proceedings to be taken against the Crown under the ordinance in respect of any alleged liability of the Crown arising otherwise than in respect of Her Majesty's Government in Hong Kong. A certificate of the Chief Secretary to the effect that any alleged liability of the Crown arises otherwise than in respect of Her Majesty's Government in Hong Kong shall be conclusive as to the matter so certified (s 34(3)). Note also

of course be challenged in the Hong Kong courts under the law on judicial review of administrative action. The JD provides in Annex I, section XIII that '[e]very person shall have the right to challenge the actions of the executive in the courts,' and this statement has now been incorporated as part of BL34. The combined effect of this and BL18 is apparently that the Hong Kong courts may review the legality of executive acts of the SAR government but not of the Central Government.

This principle might be acceptable insofar as it means that the Central Government may not be sued in an SAR court, which would be consistent with the present rule protecting the Crown from being sued in Hong Kong in its capacity as the government of the UK.[27] But if it means that a claim that an act committed by any individual in Hong Kong is authorised by the Central Government is a defence to criminal prosecution or civil action in Hong Kong in respect of that act, then it is definitely objectionable and totally inconsistent with the spirit of the Rule of Law. For the Rule of Law requires that any government official or agent be subject to the law and answerable in law for his or her conduct; orders from superiors in the government are no defence if the act ordered to be done and actually done is not authorised by law. It is therefore submitted that the third paragraph of BL18 should also be amended so as to define more carefully and restrictively the scope of the exclusion of jurisdiction as regards 'executive acts of the CPG.'

Chapter IX

The interpretation and amendment of the Basic Law, which are critical issues in the central-SAR relationship, are dealt with in chapter IX of the Basic Law. The chapter contains only two articles, which will now be separately considered.

In examining BL169, several crucial differences between the systems of constitutional and legal interpretation in the Chinese legal system and in a common law system need to be borne in mind.[28] First, the PRC constitution empowers the NPCSC to

that s 34(2)(c) provides that nothing in the ordinance shall authorise proceedings to be taken against the Crown in respect of any act, neglect, or default of any officer or agent of the Crown unless such officer was at the material time paid wholly out of revenues of Hong Kong. For the common law restrictions on proceedings against the Crown, see 11 *Halsbury's Laws of England* (4th ed) para 1401.

27 See n 26 above.

28 See generally Albert H Y Chen, *Hong Kong's Legal System and the Basic Law* (Hong Kong: Wide Angle Press, 1986) 196–206 (in Chinese).

'interpret laws,'[29] whereas in Hong Kong's common law system, it is a natural and basic presupposition that all laws are to be interpreted by the courts. This difference can be traced back to a difference in political ideology: the common law system emphasises the separation of legislative, executive, and judicial functions and powers, but in socialist Chinese constitutional thinking, the NPC system is not only a legislative organ but also the supreme 'organ of state power' exercising unified political power on behalf of the people, and executive, judicial, and procuratorial organs are all derived from and accountable to the NPC system.[30]

Second, while in Hong Kong the law may only be authoritatively interpreted when a court is deciding a case before it, the Chinese system is such that the NPCSC can give a binding interpretation of a law at any time, even if no case has arisen requiring the determination of the point. Hence 'interpretation' of a law by the NPCSC is more akin to legislative amendment in the common law system than to true legal interpretation.

Third, while in Hong Kong the power of legal interpretation is vested in the courts and in them alone, in China the NPCSC has decided to delegate part of its interpretation powers to other bodies. In this regard, the Resolution on Strengthening the Work of Legal Interpretation adopted by the NPCSC in June 1981 provides, inter alia, that the Supreme People's Court may interpret laws by deciding on questions of the concrete application of laws to judicial work.[31]

We now turn to the actual provisions of BL169. The article begins by declaring that the power of interpretation of the Basic Law is vested in the NPCSC. The statement, if taken alone, is a simple application of the Chinese constitutional principle that the NPCSC has the power of legal interpretation of the Basic Law, without any concessions for the special situation of the SAR. Indeed, when one proceeds to examine the remainder of the article, one finds nothing which limits the power of the NPCSC to interpret any provision of the Basic Law at any time and in any circumstance. The qualification at the end of the second paragraph that the exercise of the interpretation power by the NPCSC shall not affect judgments previously given by the SAR courts is only natural and logical, given the practical need to avoid the reopening of decided cases in any legal system.

---

29 Art 67(4) of the Chinese constitution (1982).
30 See, eg Albert H Y Chen, 'The Developing Legal System in China' (1983) 13 *Hong Kong Law Journal* 291, 307–309.
31 For the Chinese text of the resolution, see NPCSC Legal System Work Committee (ed), *Laws of the PRC 1979–1984* (Beijing: People's Press, 1985) 274–275.

The third paragraph of BL169 confers upon the SAR courts the power to interpret Basic Law provisions other than provisions 'concerning defence, foreign affairs and other affairs which are the responsibility of the CPG.' If the latter type of provision is involved, the SAR courts are bound to seek an interpretation of the relevant provision from the NPCSC. According to the 'Summary' prepared by the Secretariat of the Basic Law Consultative Committee,[32] this provision 'takes account of the current practice in the courts of Britain and the European Community.'[33]

From Hong Kong's point of view, the main drawback of BL169 is that even with regard to Basic Law provisions relating exclusively to the SAR's domestic affairs (and not to defence, foreign affairs and other affairs which are the responsibility of the CPG), the SAR courts do not have exclusive power of interpretation, but only have a power concurrent with that of the NPCSC, any previously given interpretation by the NPCSC being binding on the SAR courts. The possibility of abuse of its interpretation power by the NPCSC cannot be ignored. For example, if it exercises the power during the trial of a case before an SAR court for the purpose of securing a particular outcome in the case, then the SAR's judicial independence and autonomy will be seriously jeopardised, particularly if the case is concerned purely with a domestic matter of the SAR and not with matters such as defence, foreign affairs, or the central-SAR relationship. Although BL169 provides for consultation with the CBL before the NPCSC exercises its interpretation power, this is an inadequate safeguard because the CBL, however well structured, has only an advisory role.

In the light of the above, there is a strong need, if the worries of the people of Hong Kong are to be minimised, for the NPCSC to undertake not to exercise its interpretation power in respect of Basic Law provisions not relating to defence, foreign affairs, and

---

32 *The Draft Basic Law of the Hong Kong Special Administrative Region of the People's Republic of China (For Solicitation of Opinions) (with Introduction and Summary)* (Hong Kong: Secretariat of the Consultative Committee for the Basic Law, April 1988) 24, para 52.

33 Under art 177 of the EEC Treaty, the Court of Justice of the European Communities has jurisdiction, inter alia, to give rulings on the interpretation of the treaty and the validity and interpretation of acts (including regulations and directives) of Community organs. Where such a question is raised before a court of a member state, the court may refer it to the European Court 'if it considers that a decision on the question is necessary to enable it to give judgment.' But if the court is one 'against whose decisions there is no judicial remedy under national law,' the court *shall* bring the matter before the European Court. See generally de Smith (n 15 above), 115–116; P F Smith and S H Bailey, *The Modern English Legal System* (London: Sweet & Maxwell, 1984) 749–757.

other affairs which are the responsibility of the CPG (or, in other words, Basic Law provisions relating to the SAR's domestic affairs). The undertaking might be in the form of a resolution similar to the above-mentioned Resolution on the Strengthening of the Work of Legal Interpretation. The resolution can delegate to the SAR courts exclusive jurisdiction to interpret Basic Law provisions concerning the SAR's domestic affairs, while the power to classify whether a case involves such Basic Law provisions or provisions relating to defence, foreign affairs etc, as well as the power to interpret the latter provisions, remain completely vested in the NPCSC acting in consultation with the CBL. This, then, is probably the best compromise solution to the problem.

We now turn to BL170, which deals with the power and procedure of amendment of the Basic Law. The article vests the power of amendment in the NPCSC and regulates the right and procedure of submitting amendment proposals. Now the Basic Law is a law enacted by the NPC, and it is only logical that the NPC has full power to amend it.[34]

The last paragraph of BL170 states that no amendment to the Basic Law shall contravene 'the established basic policies of the PRC regarding Hong Kong.' Such basic policies are referred to in the preamble of the Basic Law, which also mentions that '[t]he basic policies of the PRC regarding Hong Kong have been elaborated by our government in the Sino-British Joint Declaration.' Hence any departure from such basic policies would in effect be a breach of the Joint Declaration. However, it should be noted that the JD is only binding on the PRC as a matter of international law. From the technical legal point of view, the NPC has full power to amend the Basic Law in a way which contravenes the JD and the 'established basic policies of the PRC regarding Hong Kong' as set out in the JD, and to delete the last paragraph of BL170 from the Basic Law. Unless the status of and guarantees regarding the SAR are entrenched in the PRC constitution itself, it is technically impossible to restrict the NPC's power to amend the Basic Law in whatever manner it sees fit. And even if the PRC constitution were amended to safeguard Hong Kong's position, the protection can still be eroded by future constitutional amendment.

Another point to note about BL170 is that the submission of

34 Article 62 of the PRC constitution expressly provides that the NPC has power to enact and amend basic statutes. See also art 31 under which the Basic Law of an SAR is to be enacted by the NPC. For general rules governing the right to propose bills before the NPC, see arts 9 and 10 of the Organic Law of the NPC 1982.

amendment proposals from the SAR is tightly regulated whereas there is no restriction on the right of the NPCSC and the State Council to propose amendments to the Basic Law. Under the draft article, the Hong Kong community may only submit a proposal for amendment of the Basic Law if it has been consented to by two-thirds of the members of the SAR legislature, two-thirds of the SAR deputies to the NPC, and the CE. Why should the procedure for merely proposing an amendment be made so difficult? After all, if the Central Government is against the proposal and argues against it before the NPC, it is highly unlikely that the NPC will adopt the amendment.

IV INSTITUTIONAL ARRANGEMENTS

The above section considers the central-SAR relationship under the BL by examining specific provisions in the draft. In this section, we shall focus on the institutions and actors involved in managing and operating that relationship. Seven elements will be briefly considered: (1) the NPC, (2) the NPCSC, (3) the CBL, (4) the State Council, (5) the Chief Executive, and (6) the SAR delegates to the NPC.

National People's Congress

The NPC, being the supreme organ of state power[35] and legislature of China, is responsible for the enactment and amendment of the Basic Law. As far as the practical operation of the SAR is concerned, it seems that it will not be in direct contact with the NPC. Like other regions of the PRC, the SAR will send deputies to the NPC in accordance with BL20.

As will be mentioned below, the SAR has a closer working relationship with the NPCSC and the State Council, both of which are subject to the authority of the NPC. The NPCSC is responsible to the NPC and reports to it on the work of the NPCSC;[36] the NPC has the power to 'alter or annul inappropriate decisions of the NPCSC.'[37] The State Council is also responsible to and reports on its work to the NPC.[38] Deputies to the NPC have the right to question the State Council on its performance.[39]

---

35 Art 57 of the PRC constitution.
36 Ibid art 69.
37 Ibid art 62 (11).
38 Ibid art 92.
39 Art 16 of the Organic Law of the NPC 1982.

Standing Committee of the NPC

Under the PRC constitution, the powers and functions of the NPC include the interpretation of laws[40] and the annulment of local regulations (made in the provinces and autonomous regions) which contravene the constitution or the law.[41] The Basic Law confirms the existence of these powers in relation to the SAR. As mentioned above, the NPCSC has powers to interpret the Basic Law (BL169) and to review SAR legislation as regards its conformity to the Basic Law (BL16). These powers are to be exercised in consultation with the CBL, which will be considered below. The NPCSC also has the right to propose amendments of the Basic Law (BL170). As regards the formation of the first SAR government, the NPCSC will appoint the members of the Preparatory Committee of the SAR (Basic Law, Annex III, paragraph 1).

Another responsibility of the NPCSC will be discharged at the time of the establishment of the SAR. It will then declare which part of the existing law cannot remain valid because it contravenes the Basic Law (BL172). The assignment of this power to the NPCSC is understandable if one accepts its power to interpret the whole of the Basic Law (BL169) and to review all post-1997 SAR legislation as regards its consistency with the Basic Law (BL16). From the viewpoint of the people of Hong Kong, however, it is important that the NPCSC should not draw up the list of laws to be invalidated on 1 July 1997 without extensive consultation with those familiar with the existing laws and legal system of Hong Kong.

Other powers to be exercised by the NPCSC in relation to Hong Kong include the following. It will decide on the number of seats to be given to and the election procedures for SAR deputies to the NPC (BL20). Any post-1997 modifications to the methods for selecting the CE and constituting the Legislative Council of the SAR as prescribed in Annexes I and II to the Basic Law have to be approved by the NPCSC (BL45, 67).

Committee for the Basic Law

Although the CBL is referred to in several articles of the Basic Law (BL16, 17, 169, 170), its status and composition are not provided for in the document itself. Some explanation of this is supplied by note 2 to the Basic Law, which records the content of 'the proposal on the establishment of the CBL of the HKSAR put

---

40 Art 67(4) of the PRC constitution.
41 Ibid art 67(8).

forward by the Sub-group on the Relationship between the Central Authorities and the HKSAR' of the BLDC. The BLDC has apparently decided that it is inappropriate for the drafting committee to include in its draft any provisions governing the constitution of the proposed CBL, because the terms of reference of the drafting committee oblige it to draft a law regulating the SAR only, and not any law dealing with the NPC system of which the proposed CBL will form a part.

The proposal on the CBL as contained in note 2 to the Basic Law is that the committee should be under the NPCSC consisting of both mainland members and Hong Kong members appointed by the NPCSC. The committee is to advise the NPCSC on the conformity of SAR legislation with the Basic Law (BL16), the applicability of national laws to the SAR (BL17),[42] and the interpretation (BL169) and amendment (BL170)[43] of the Basic Law. The significance of these four areas is that they all represent points of possible conflict of interests and of opinion between the Central Government and the SAR. The function of the CBL is therefore to resolve the conflict. However, the CBL is only advisory in nature and does not possess concrete decision-making power. The ultimate power to settle the dispute still lies with the central authority.

As discussed above, in federal systems the federal supreme court is the usual institution for conflict resolution between the central government and local governments and for interpretation and enforcement of the constitutional division of power between the federal authority and member states. The essential characteristics of the federal supreme court in this context are that it is a federal organ, and it is a judicial organ. The judicial function, at least according to traditional doctrines, is to be exercised in a neutral, impartial, objective, and rational manner. Hence a court which adheres to this judicial ideal would be the ideal guardian of the federal arrangement for division of power.

The question therefore arises as to whether the possible situations of central-SAR conflict to which the CBL proposal has been addressed can be better dealt with in a judicial forum. There are at least three possible variations of this approach. The relevant judicial authority can be a court of mainland Chinese judges, a court of Hong Kong judges, or a mixed court of both

42 There is probably a drafting defect here insofar as the proposal provides for advice by the CBL to the NPCSC, because under BL17 it is the State Council, and not the NPCSC, which determines whether national laws are to be applied to the SAR. In fact BL17 expressly provides for consultation between the State Council and the CBL.

43 BL170 is not clear as regards which body should consult the CBL in respect of proposed amendments to the Basic Law.

mainland and SAR members. The first alternative is hardly feasible because mainland Chinese judges have no or little experience of constitutional interpretation and judicial review of legislation, and do not have sufficient prestige even within mainland China and would not be trusted by the people of Hong Kong as arbiters of central-SAR conflicts. The non-viability of the second alternative, particularly from the point of view of the Central Government, has been discussed earlier in this chapter. The third option remains to be considered here.

The main difficulty with the idea of using a mixed tribunal of Chinese and Hong Kong judges to interpret the Basic Law, to enforce the division of power provided therein, and to settle central-SAR disputes in a manner accepted as authoritative and legitimate, is that the gulf between the mainland and Hong Kong judges is simply too wide and deep. Mainland judges have not yet achieved a status of complete independence from the state and Party apparatus; their techniques of constitutional and legal interpretation have not been sufficiently developed given the extremely short history of the rebuilding of the legal system in China.[44] These contrast sharply with the long and cherished common law traditions of judicial independence and sophisticated legal reasoning in judge-made law. Hence the probability of a mixed court arriving at a consensus on the proper judicial solution to problems of central-SAR conflict is minimal. Whether the decision goes in favour of the central authority or the SAR will probably depend entirely on the relative numbers of mainland and SAR judges sitting on the court. Where a 'court' is divided in this way, no meaningful judicial decision-making can take place. It is indeed doubtful whether such a body deserves the name of a 'court.'

If the above analysis is accepted as valid, then it is probably necessary to conclude that litigation followed by judicial decision-making is not the most appropriate method to resolve fundamental problems of central-SAR conflict. One has to turn to other methods of dispute settlement, which include negotiation and arbitration. While negotiation involves the contesting parties only, mediation means the interposition of a third-party mediator attempting to facilitate dialogue and achieve a reconciliation between the disputants. If the objective behind the proposal for the CBL is that it should perform such a mediating role, then the proposal is probably a step in the right direction.

---

44 See, eg Chen (n 30 above); Albert H Y Chen, 'Civil Liberties in China: Some Preliminary Observations' in Raymond Wacks (ed), *Civil Liberties in Hong Kong* (Hong Kong: Oxford University Press, 1988) ch 4.

State Council

Some articles in the Basic Law refer to the State Council,[45] and some refer to the CPG.[46] This is probably an inconsistency which should be removed when the draft is improved, because under the PRC constitution, the State Council is the CPG.[47] The reason why the term 'CPG' is used in parts of the Basic Law is probably that 'CPG,' and not 'State Council,' is the term used in the JD to describe the institution. For example, Annex I, section I, JD states that '[t]he HKSAR shall be directly under the authority of the Central People's Government of the PRC and shall enjoy a high degree of autonomy.' This principle is now stated in BL11, which uses the term 'CPG' rather than 'State Council.'

The main powers of the State Council in relation to the SAR are set out in chapter II of the Basic Law. It is responsible for defence and foreign affairs, and can authorise the SAR government to deal with relevant external affairs in accordance with the Basic Law (BL12, 13). It appoints the CE and principal executive officials of the SAR (BL14). It directs the SAR government to apply relevant national laws on defence, foreign affairs, national unity and territorial integrity (BL17). And it may issue certificates to the SAR CE on questions before the SAR courts concerning defence, foreign affairs or the executive acts of the Central Government (BL18).

Chief Executive

BL43 provides that '[t]he Chief Executive of the HKSAR is the head of the HKSAR and represents the Region.' It seems that the CE will represent the SAR in dealings both with the Central Government and with foreign countries.[48] The authorities to which the CE owes his or her duty are provided for in the second paragraph of BL43: he or she 'shall be accountable to the CPG and the HKSAR in accordance with the provisions of this Law.'

This principle of the dual accountability of the CE to the State Council and the SAR reveals the delicate nature of the position of this office. On the one hand, the CE is 'selected by election or through consultations held locally' (BL45) and is expected to advocate the interests of Hong Kong before the Central Government. On the other hand, he or she is appointed by the Central

45 BL17, 18, 19.
46 BL11, 12, 13, 14, 21, 22, 43, 45, 48, 72, ss 6 and 7 of ch V, and ch VII.
47 Art 85 of the PRC constitution.
48 Note in this regard BL48(9) which empowers the CE to deal with external affairs on behalf of the SAR.

Government (BL45) and is the visible symbol of the exercise of sovereignty by the national government in Hong Kong. This realisation of the presence of the central authority is not merely symbolic: the CE is bound 'to implement the directives issued by the CPG in respect of the relevant matters provided for in this Law' (BL48(8)).

SAR deputies to the NPC

The main function of the SAR-elected deputies to the NPC is to participate in the management of national affairs (BL20), which is the right and duty of the people of Hong Kong exercised and performed through their representatives. Presumably the deputies should also advocate the interests of Hong Kong before the NPC. It is interesting to note that these deputies are also given some role to play in the domestic politics of the SAR. For example, 5% of the seats in the Election Committee for the First Government of the SAR are assigned to these deputies and to members of the Chinese People's Political Consultative Conference. And as regards the amendment of the Basic Law, a proposal for amendment originating from the SAR must be consented to by, among others, two-thirds of the deputies from Hong Kong to the NPC (BL170).

V   OTHER ISSUES FOR CONSIDERATION

The way in which the Basic Law attempts to define and regulate the relationship between the central national authority and the SAR government has been discussed above. In this last section of this chapter, two major issues relevant to that relationship and yet omitted from consideration in the present Basic Law will be identified and explored.

The first issue concerns possible checks and balances on the State Council's exercise of its authority with respect to the SAR. BL48(8) requires the CE of the SAR to implement State Council directives in respect of 'the relevant matters provided for in this law.' What happens, however, if a directive of the State Council to the CE is ultra vires the Basic Law? This possibility is not covered by the Basic Law as it stands.

The position is even more worrying if one examines BL21 carefully. The first paragraph of this article provides, inter alia, that departments under the CPG 'shall not interfere in the affairs which the HKSAR administers on its own in accordance with this Law.' There is, however, no prohibition on the State Council itself interfering with matters within the SAR's autonomy. Is it intended that the SAR government will not have exclusive jurisdiction over the matters prescribed by the JD and the Basic Law to be within its autonomy after all? Real autonomy presupposes a true and effective division of power, which in turn requires a strict prohibition of acts infringing the scope of autonomy. It seems that the Basic Law is only concerned with preventing the SAR from exceeding the scope of its autonomy and not sufficiently concerned with restraining the State Council from trespassing on the SAR's autonomy. This imbalance needs to be rectified in any revision of the Basic Law.

It is submitted that the PRC constitution as it stands already supplies the basic principles for limiting unlawful behaviour by the State Council. In particular, article 67(6) and (7) of the constitution empowers the NPCSC to supervise the work of the State Council and to annul decisions or orders of the State Council which contravene the constitution or the laws. There is no reason why this idea cannot be assimilated into the Basic Law, given that the principles in the same article 67 of the constitution concerning interpretation of laws and review of local regulations contravening the laws have already been incorporated into the Basic Law with adaptations for the Hong Kong situation.

If this approach is accepted, then BL21 should be amended to extend the prohibition on unlawful interference with the SAR's domestic affairs to the State Council itself. At the same time, new provisions will have to be added enabling the SAR, when aggrieved by a State Council directive suspected to be ultra vires the Basic Law, to appeal to the NPCSC, which will resolve the matter on the basis of the recommendations of the CBL, in the same way as other points of central-SAR conflict are dealt with as discussed above.

The second major omission in the Basic Law relating to the central-SAR relationship is that the role of the Communist Party of China (CPC) in the SAR is not addressed. It is possible to defend or justify the omission by arguing that Party and state matters are separate, and the Basic Law is only intended to deal with the latter. On the other hand, even the PRC constitution itself has not omitted to state the principle of the leadership of the CPC in its preamble. The question may therefore be legitimately raised as to the extent to and the manner in which the principle, so fundamentally important in mainland China, is to be applied in the SAR.

This is a difficult question, and it is not for the author to advance any straightforward solution here. It suffices to point out that if CPC organs operating in the SAR control the SAR government behind the scenes, then the present debate and consultation on the Basic Law are wholly meaningless and futile. But in this regard, extreme pessimism does not seem to be justified: the affirmation of the principle that the CPC must operate within the framework of, and abide by, the state constitution and the law is, for example, an encouraging development in the PRC in recent years.[49] An express legal limitation in the Basic Law on the CPC's activities in the SAR is therefore one possible way to inspire confidence. Alternatively the PRC leaders might be able to think of other ways to assure the people of Hong Kong that the Basic Law, when enacted, will not just be a paper constitution but will be both the ideal and the reality of Hong Kong's future political life.

49 Chen (n 30 above) especially 301–302.

8 The Political System

JOSEPH Y S CHENG

INTRODUCTION

DURING the negotiations which led to the initialling of the Sino-British Joint Declaration on the Question of Hong Kong, the Chinese government indicated that the optimum solution to the question would be one which would re-establish Chinese sovereignty over the territory, with local Chinese residents being responsible for its administration.[1] In July 1984, the Hong Kong government published a Green Paper entitled *The Further Development of Representative Government in Hong Kong.*[2] The positions thus taken by both governments were a great boost to the morale of those who supported political reform and the democratisation of government in Hong Kong. Even ordinary citizens without much interest in political participation realised that, as colonial rule was to be terminated in 1997, and none of the parties concerned wanted the future Hong Kong Special Administrative Region to be directly administered by Beijing, the establishment of an SAR government with a high degree of autonomy, as subsequently stipulated in the Joint Declaration, would be a natural development.[3]

After the release of the Green Paper on representative government, however, the electoral system became a highly controversial issue as the electoral system discussed in the Green Paper finally extended to the core of the authority of the Hong Kong government — the Legislative and Executive Councils. At that time, many conservative business leaders openly opposed direct elections to the Legislative Council. On the other hand, the younger generation and the intelligentsia since then have been arguing that only an elected government can effectively promote

1 See *A Draft Agreement between the Government of the United Kingdom of Great Britain and Northern Ireland and the Government of the People's Republic of China on the Question of Hong Kong* (Hong Kong: Government Printer, 26 September 1984).
2 Hong Kong: Government Printer, July 1984.
3 For a good analysis of the traditional political apathy of the Hong Kong community, see Lau Siu-kai, *Society and Politics in Hong Kong* (Hong Kong: Chinese University Press, 1982).

the interests of the people and maintain Hong Kong's international status.

While the issues of direct elections and political parties remained controversial in Hong Kong, a consensus on certain basic principles certainly existed. In the first place, almost no one would oppose a gradualist approach. Political reforms differ from fiscal reforms in that the latter may substantially increase or decrease government revenue and expenditure and then reverse such increases or decreases in accordance with the needs of the times. Political reforms, however, under normal circumstances, can only proceed further and can hardly be reversed. There was also general agreement that the existing political institutions should be respected in the transitional period and that, as far as possible, they should serve as a basis for political reforms, with the aim of preserving their strong points.

Second, the political system of the SAR should be designed to achieve a high degree of stability. A presidential system, for example, gives the Chief Executive security of tenure and is therefore a relatively stable political system. An electoral system based on proportional representation, however, encourages a multi-party system; if this were combined with a parliamentary system, Hong Kong might well encounter the situation in Italy and some Western European countries where shifting coalitions of political parties result in frequent falls of government and frequent general elections. Hong Kong can ill afford such a scenario, and it might well lead to an early termination of whatever autonomy the territory might have been enjoying.

Third, the future SAR government should be an efficient one. Over-emphasis on separation of powers as well as checks and balances might lead to deadlock and confrontation between different parts of the government, resulting in political crisis and paralysis of government. A relatively independent Chief Executive with sufficient powers would help to guarantee the dedication and devotion of the heads of departments and other civil servants in his or her government and thereby maintain its high efficiency.

Finally, the SAR government must be subject to effective democratic supervision to prevent any abuse of power. 'Power corrupts, absolute power corrupts absolutely.' Effective democratic supervision guarantees liberty and the Rule of Law and also provides opportunities for political participation.

This consensus, however, has been considerably weakened because of the sharpening confrontation emerging in the community since late 1985 on the extent of democracy to be enjoyed by the ordinary people in the transitional period and after 1997. The conservative business community's position has been strengthened by Beijing's attempt to dampen the Hong Kong people's movement for democracy. Since late 1985, the British administration has also given up the initiative to shape political reforms in the transitional period.[4] To a large extent, the contradiction over the issue of autonomy and self-administration has become one between Beijing and the local democratic movement.

The political system has become probably the most controversial issue in the drafting of the Basic Law, partly because, while the Joint Declaration promises that Hong Kong's 'capitalist system and life-style shall remain unchanged for 50 years,' the colonial political system obviously has to be replaced; moreover, the Joint Declaration and its Annexes do not provide for a political system for the SAR.

Article 3(4) of the Joint Declaration states:

The Government of the Hong Kong Special Administrative Region will be composed of local inhabitants. The chief executive will be appointed by the Central People's Government on the basis of the results of elections or consultations to be held locally. Principal officials will be nominated by the chief executive of the Hong Kong Special Administrative Region for appointment by the Central People's Government.

The third paragraph of section I of Annex I further elaborates:

The legislature of the Hong Kong Special Administrative Region shall be constituted by elections. The executive authorities shall abide by the law and shall be accountable to the legislature.

As Beijing and London have never informed the Hong Kong community in a formal manner their interpretations of the above key paragraphs, controversies regarding the meaning of the executive authorities' accountability to the legislature, etc have often emerged.

Various concerned parties began to articulate their proposals on the political system of the future SAR since mid-1985, though general discussions started soon after the initialling of the Joint Declaration. Cha Chi-ming, a prominent conservative businessman and a member of the Basic Law Drafting Committee, presented a proposal entitled 'Basic Policies and Constitution for the Hong Kong Special Administrative Region' to the Chinese leaders during the first meeting of the BLDC, held in Beijing in July 1985.[5] It was said that Cha's proposal attracted much attention from the Chinese authorities and the Hong Kong government. On 10 December 1985, a signed article (under the

4 See Joseph Y S Cheng, 'Hong Kong: The Pressure to Converge' (1987) 63 *International Affairs* (London) 271–283.
5 For the Chinese version of Cha Chi-ming's proposal, see *Ming Pao*, 7–12 August 1985.

pseudonym Gu Xinghui) appeared in the newly published *The Mirror* (a pro-China Chinese-language monthly magazine) under the title 'Preliminary Discussions on the Future Basic Law Blueprint.' Although the Chinese authorities then claimed that they had no preconceptions about the political system of the SAR, it is obvious that they and the local business community approved of the proposals of Cha Chi-ming and *The Mirror*.

The above proposals were then followed by a few proposals from academics and one each from the 'democratic camp' and the 'conservative camp'. The Joint Committee for the Promotion of Democratic Political System, an umbrella group involving almost all political groups demanding democracy in Hong Kong, issued a declaration on 2 November 1986.[6] The Business and Professional Group of Members of the Basic Law Consultative Committee, consisting of more than 90 members of the committee, published its *A Proposal for the Future Structure of the Hong Kong SAR Government* in pamphlet form in September 1987, though the main points of the proposal had been reported by major newspapers in Hong Kong intermittently in 1986. This chapter does not intend to consider any of the above proposals in detail, although all the alternatives listed in the Basic Law released on 28 April 1988 had their origins from these proposals.[7]

CHIEF EXECUTIVE, EXECUTIVE AUTHORITIES, AND THE LEGISLATURE

Chief executive

BL44 of the Basic Law provides:

> The Chief Executive of the HKSAR shall be a Chinese national of no less than 40 years of age who is a permanent resident of the Region and has ordinarily resided in Hong Kong for a continuous period of 20 years.

It is common for constitutions to set a minimum age for the CE; the United States constitution stipulates that the President shall

---

6 A summary of the declaration appeared in all the major newspapers in Hong Kong on 3 November 1986.

7 The Basic Law was issued by the BLDC, while the Introduction and Summary were compiled by the BLCC. The whole set of documents, appearing in pamphlet form with separate Chinese and English versions, has been distributed freely since 29 April 1988 in Hong Kong. The Chinese version is the official version, while all quotations of the Basic Law in this chapter are from the English version.

be of no less than 35 years of age.[8] In the Hong Kong community, seniority commands respect and at any rate it is difficult to imagine how someone less than 40 years of age could become a credible candidate for the post of CE in this Chinese society. Nevertheless, it is equally legitimate to raise the need to set an upper age limit.

It is understandable that the CE should be a Chinese national, though the original permanent inhabitants of Hong Kong will be divided into two categories and those who are not Chinese nationals will have fewer political rights. In this connection, BL55 stipulates that members of the Executive Council 'shall be Chinese nationals who are permanent residents of the Region,' BL100 and 70 (alternative 1) require the same qualifications for a list of principal officials and the President of the Legislative Council respectively, while such qualifications do not apply to members of the Legislative Council as well as judges and other members of the judiciary of the SAR. Judges and other members of the SAR judiciary may even be recruited from other common law jurisdictions, including judges sitting on the Court of Final Appeal (BL91 and 81). It is difficult to defend that, because of the temporary lack of available talents, the Basic Law allows judges from other common law jurisdictions to sit on the Court of Final Appeal, while for reasons of sovereignty, it stipulates that the Director of Audit, Commissioner of Immigration, and Inspector General of Customs and Excise must be Chinese nationals (BL100).

To allay the fears of the local community, BL44 also requires that the first CE of the SAR should at least have ordinarily resided in Hong Kong since 1977; this is only of symbolic value as there are certainly members of the Communist Party of China (CPC) working in Hong Kong since before that date. In order to better preserve the capitalist system in Hong Kong, it may be more logical to provide that the CE should not be a member of the CPC. BL47 appears to be redundant, as a declaration of assets by the CE to the Chief Justice of the Court of Final Appeal on a confidential basis serves a very limited purpose.

According to BL46, the term of office of the CE shall be five years; and he may serve for no more than two terms. This is a reasonable arrangement, as the CE should not stay in power for more than ten years. Since the term of office of members of the Legislative Council shall be four years (BL68), the arrangement

---

8 Article II, section 1.5 of the constitution of the United States; see Ralph Mitchell, *CQ's Guide to the US Constitution* (Washington, DC: Congressional Quarterly Inc, 1986) 62.

provides better continuity and stability of government. In the unlikely event that the CE shall be directly elected, there may be a problem of too many elections, resulting in too frequent mobilisation of the mass electorate.

BL45 reaffirms what is stipulated in the Joint Declaration:

> The Chief Executive of the HKSAR shall be selected by election or through consultations held locally and be appointed by the Central People's Government.

It had been hoped that this appointment would be a mere formality to demonstrate China's sovereignty over Hong Kong; however, Chinese officials responsible for Hong Kong affairs indicated that the appointment would be a 'substantial' one, implying a veto power in the hands of the CPG. If the latter refuses to appoint the CE elected in the manner as outlined by alternative 2 or Annex 1 of the Basic Law, then there will be a constitutional crisis with a serious adverse impact on the stability and prosperity of the territory. It will obviously be politically prudent for the Chinese authorities to indicate their preferences and objections before the selection process so as to influence the outcome and thus to avoid the actual use of their veto power. It appears that the community is willing to concede that the CE has to be someone acceptable to Beijing.

To be in line with the above method of selection, the CE 'shall be accountable to the Central People's Government and the HKSAR in accordance with the provisions of this Law' (BL43). Nowhere in the entire section on the CE is it mentioned that the CE has to be accountable or responsible to the Legislative Council. On the other hand, BL64 of the following section on the executive authorities stipulates:

> The executive authorities of the HKSAR must abide by the law and shall be accountable to the Legislative Council of the HKSAR. . . .

It appears therefore that the CE does not have to be accountable to the Legislative Council, while only the executive authorities (treated in a separate section of chapter IV Political Structure of the Basic Law) have to be accountable to the Legislative Council. This certainly is not in accord with the general understanding of the Hong Kong community concerning the promise in the Joint Declaration that 'the executive authorities shall abide by the law and shall be accountable to the legislature.' On the other hand, BL59 states that the government of the SAR is the executive authority of the Region, and BL60 states that the CE of the SAR is the head of the government of the Region. This may be interpreted to mean that the CE is part of the executive authorities and therefore has to be accountable to the Legislative Council. (See p 193 below.)

Obviously the ambiguity has to be removed. In fact, a member of the BLDC proposed that BL60 should be rewritten as follows:

> Members of the executive authorities shall include: (1) the Chief Executive; (2) principal officials nominated by the Chief Executive and appointed by the Central People's Government (officials corresponding to the Secretary level); (3) the Executive Council, including the Chief Executive and members of principal officials appointed by him.[9]

In this connection, a member of the BLDC (the same member?) also suggested revising BL43 to read as follows:

> The Chief Executive of the HKSAR is the head of the Region and the head of the executive organs of the Region, representing the Region and leading its executive organs, and shall be accountable to the Central People's Government, the HKSAR, and the legislature of the Region in accordance with the provisions of this Law.[10]

BL43 also raises the following question: the CE's accountability to the CPG can be well defined because the CPG is a concrete entity and controls his appointment; on the other hand, the CE's accountability to the SAR is largely symbolic and has not been defined by the Basic Law. BL48(8) further states that the CE has 'to implement the directives issued by the Central People's Government in respect of the relevant matters provided for in this Law.' The PRC constitution promulgated in 1982 clearly stipulates that the State Council is 'the highest organ of state administration' and it has the power 'to exercise unified leadership over the work of local organs of state administration at different levels throughout the country, and to lay down the detailed division of functions and powers between the Central Government and the organs of state administration of provinces, autonomous regions and municipalities directly under the Central Government.'[11]

It is not sufficiently clear in what way and to what extent the SAR differs from the provinces, autonomous regions, and municipalities in its accountability to the Central Government. Is the SAR government also one of the 'local organs of state

9 'A Collection of Opinions and Suggestions of Some Members in Regard to the Articles Drafted by Their Respective Special Subject Sub-groups' (henceforth referred to as 'Collection of Opinions and Suggestions') included in the Basic Law pamphlet, p 99; the page number refers to the page in the English version of the pamphlet.
10 Ibid 96.
11 Articles 85 and 89.4, *The Constitution of the People's Republic of China* (adopted on 4 December 1982 by the Fifth National People's Congress of the People's Republic of China at its Fifth Session) (Beijing: Foreign Languages Press, 1983) (henceforth referred to as *The Constitution*), 63 and 66.

administration' as defined by the PRC constitution? Moreover, the State Council is one of the three parties which have been empowered by the Basic Law to propose amendments to the Basic Law. With the consent of the National People's Congress, it can seek to expand its power vis-à-vis the SAR government (BL170). Article 1 of Annex 1 of the Joint Declaration is equally unclear. On the one hand it states that the 'HKSAR shall be directly under the authority of the Central People's Government' and on the other stipulates that 'the executive authorities shall abide by the law and shall be accountable to the legislature.'

BL48 defines the powers and functions of the CE. The SAR political system as outlined in the Basic Law conforms to the consensus described above. The CE has powers and functions similar to the United States President, though the former probably has even larger powers vis-à-vis the legislature. According to BL48 to 52, bills passed by the Legislative Council have to be signed by the CE before being promulgated as laws (BL48.3). If the CE considers that a bill passed by the Legislative Council is not compatible with the overall interests of the SAR, he may return it to the Legislative Council within three months for reconsideration. If the Legislative Council passes the original bill again by no less than a two-thirds majority, the CE must sign and promulgate it within one month (BL49). The CE, however, has one further option which is not available to the United States President: he may still refuse to sign it and dissolve the Legislative Council instead. He may also dissolve the Legislative Council when the latter refuses to pass the budget or other important bills and consensus cannot be reached after consultations. Before dissolving the Legislative Council, the CE should ask for opinions from the Executive Council, and he may dissolve the Legislative Council only once in each term of office (BL50). This power to dissolve the Legislative Council is balanced by the risks that the CE has to take into consideration: he shall have to resign when the new Legislative Council has again passed with a two-thirds majority the original bill in dispute which the CE has twice refused to sign, leading to the dissolution of the previous Legislative Council; or when the new Legislative Council still refuses to pass the budget or any other important bill which the previous Legislative Council has refused to approve (BL52).

In order to ensure the smooth functioning of the government when disagreement arises between the CE and the Legislative Council, BL51 also provides that if the Legislative Council refuses to pass the budget bill or when it is impossible to approve any appropriation of public funds because the Legislative Council has already been dissolved, the CE may, during the interim period prior to the formation of a new Legislative Council, approve temporary short-term appropriations in accordance with the level of expenditure of the previous fiscal year.

The strength of the CE and the weakness of the Legislative Council are further demonstrated by the CE's power to approve the introduction of motions regarding revenue or expenditure to the Legislative Council (BL48.10) and to decide, in the light of security and public interest, whether government officials or other personnel in charge of government affairs should testify or give evidence before the Legislative Council (BL48.11). If the CE can, without having to give reasons, reject any motion presented to the Legislative Council regarding revenue and expenditure, then basically the Legislative Council can only respond to the CE's proposals regarding revenue and expenditure. It is not sufficiently clear whether the Legislative Council can reject certain items of the budget, though it does not appear likely. If the Legislative Council can only accept or reject the budget as a whole and the refusal to pass the budget will lead to its dissolution, the Legislative Council's power over government revenue and expenditure will be very limited indeed. Under such circumstances, the Legislative Council may to a large extent have to rely on the pressure of public opinion to persuade the CE and the executive authorities to accept the views of the Council in the course of consultation between the two branches of government. This is the actual situation today.

The CE's power to exempt government officials or other personnel responsible for government affairs from testifying or giving evidence before the Legislative Council will severely hamper the latter's function as a watch-dog of the CE and the executive authorities. Considerations of security and public interest are not sufficient reasons for preventing the Legislative Council from calling government officials or other personnel in charge of government affairs to testify or give evidence. Certainly the testimony or the giving of evidence can take place in closed sessions. In the United States, the Chairman of the Joint Chiefs of Staff and the Director of the Central Intelligence Agency also testify and give evidence before the Congress. The provision in the Basic Law assumes that the CE has a greater concern for security and public interest than members of the Legislative Council, yet such an assumption is obviously subject to dispute.

On the other hand, the CE's power of appointing and dismissing the principal officials of the SAR government is quite limited. He may nominate them and report such nominations to the CPG for appointment and may propose to the CPG the removal of the principal officials (BL48.5). The Basic Law does not specify the criteria according to which the CPG will approve the CE's nominations and his proposals for dismissing the principal officials. If the CPG refuses to approve the CE's proposal to remove some of the principal officials, it will cause substantial difficulties within the SAR government. The lack of well-defined power of dismissal of the principal officials will also affect the CE's status as head of government.

A better arrangement would be to give the Legislative Council the power to endorse the CE's nomination of principal officials, and refusal of endorsement should be limited by the Basic Law to the following two conditions: (1) when the portfolio of a nominated principal official involves an obvious conflict of interests; for example, if the principal official nominated to head the transport portfolio comes from a family having a substantial stake in an important corporation in the public transport sector; and (2) when the qualifications and credentials of a nominated principal official fail to meet the requirements of the post. This would enhance the Legislative Council's power vis-à-vis the CE and act as a healthy means of checks and balances. The CE, however, should have full authority to dismiss the principal officials. It can only be hoped that the CPG's power to approve the CE's nominations and proposals of dismissals of the principal officials will only be a formality to demonstrate China's sovereignty over Hong Kong, as any rejection of the CE's nominations and especially the proposals of dismissals of the principal officials will compromise the SAR government's autonomy. The employment of advisers at or above the director level by the CE should not require the approval of the CPG (BL48.5); and it is inconsistent that the Basic Law does not require the approval of the CPG for the removal of such advisers.

According to BL55, members of the Executive Council, an organ for assisting the CE in policy-making (BL54), may be principal officials of the executive authorities, members of the Legislative Council, and public figures (BL55). That members of the Legislative Council may concurrently serve as members of the Executive Council is undesirable as it violates the principle of separation of powers and the provision in the Joint Declaration that 'the executive authorities shall . . . be accountable to the legislature.'

If the purpose of the above arrangement is to improve co-ordination between the legislative and executive branches of the government, as indicated by some members of the BLDC, then the objective may be better fulfilled by the establishment of the following formal and informal arrangements: (1) scheduled sessions between the Executive Council and the committee chairmen of the Legislative Council; (2) executive sessions as well as informal sessions of individual committees in the Legislative Council inviting the principal officials (and their subordinates) concerned to attend; (3) advisory bodies established under the executive authorities (BL65) involving both the senior members of the Legislative Council interested in the policy area and the principal officials responsible for the same policy area; (4) all kinds of informal communication between the two branches of the government.

According to BL56, the Executive Council appears to have a high status and a means of checking the impressive powers of the CE. BL56 is a superficial and largely meaningless replica of the existing colonial system. In the present British administration, appointments to the Executive Council are to be made by the Crown, that is, the Secretary of State for Foreign and Commonwealth Affairs; and the Commander of the British Forces, the Chief Secretary, the Financial Secretary, and the Attorney General are ex officio members of the Executive Council. The appointments of these senior government officials also have to be approved by the Secretary of State according to the Civil Service Regulations. In this way, the need for the Governor to consult the Executive Council on all important matters of policy constitutes a means of checks and balances, which is especially significant in view of the almost dictatorial powers of the Governor. In the case of the CE of the SAR, he has full authority to appoint and dismiss members of the Executive Council, and it is difficult to see how the need to consult the Executive Council will similarly constitute a means of checks and balances. It should be noted, however, that an earlier draft of the Basic Law stipulated that members of the Executive Council should be nominated by the CE and appointed by the CPG and that if the CE did not adopt a majority opinion of the Executive Council, he should register his specific reasons and report them to the CPG for the record.[12]

Executive authorities

The ambiguity concerning whether the CE is part of the executive authorities and whether or not he has to be accountable to the Legislative Council has already been discussed. BL64, however, clearly states:

12 Articles 9 and 10 of Section 1 of Chapter 4 'The Political Structure of the HKSAR' in the draft articles presented by the Sub-group on the Political Structure of the SAR to the BLDC meeting in August 1987; for the text of these draft articles, see *Ta Kung Pao*, 25 August 1987.

The executive authorities of the HKSAR shall abide by the law and shall be accountable to the Legislative Council of the HKSAR in the following respects: They shall implement laws passed by the legislature and already in force; they shall present regular reports on their work to the Legislative Council; they shall answer questions raised by members of the Legislative Council; and they shall obtain approval from the Legislative Council for taxation and public expenditure.

The accountability of the executive authorities to the Legislative Council is therefore quite narrowly defined. Implementation of laws passed and presentation of regular reports are by no means effective measures of enforcing accountability on the part of the executive authorities, and the powers of the CE to approve the introduction of motions regarding revenue or expenditure to the Legislative Council (BL48.10) and to decide, in the light of security and public interest, whether government officials or other personnel in charge of government affairs should testify or give evidence before the Legislative Council (BL48.11) will also severely circumscribe the remaining two measures of accountability on the part of the executive authorities to the Legislative Council.

It is significant to note that some members of the BLDC objected to this narrow definition of accountability and attempted to broaden it by suggesting an amendment of BL64 to read thus:

The executive authorities of the HKSAR must abide by the law and shall be accountable to the legislature of the Region. They shall: (1) implement laws passed by the legislature and already in force; (2) present regular reports on their work to the legislature; (3) be subject to supervision by the legislature; (4) answer questions raised by members of the legislature, and be subject to or assist in investigations by the legislature on special issues; and (5) obtain approval from the legislature for taxation and public expenditure, and be subject to supervision by the legislature in respect of public expenditure.[13]

BL62 defines the powers and functions of the government of the SAR which are largely uncontroversial. However, as the powers and functions of the CE are separately defined by BL48, it again implies that he is not part of the government of the SAR which 'is the executive authorities of the Region' (BL59).

To allay further the fears of the local community and in line with BL44, BL61 requires that:

The principal officials of the HKSAR shall be Chinese nationals who are permanent residents and have ordinarily resided in Hong Kong for a continuous period of 15 years.

13 'Collection of Opinions and Suggestions' 99.

Note 4 of the Basic Law indicates that members of the BLDC held that, in general, principal officials should be selected from among public servants. However, they can also be selected from among prominent members of society other than public servants. Principal officials of the latter type would be remunerated as public servants working on contract. They would leave the service on expiry of their terms of office. This actually follows the present practice. Note 4 also reveals that transfers of principal officials and increase of officials to the Secretary level must be reported to the CPG for approval.

The legislature

BL67 provides that the Legislative Council of the SAR shall be constituted by a combination of direct and indirect elections and BL68 stipulates that the term of office of members of the Legislative Council shall be four years.

According to BL71, the President of the Legislative Council has extensive powers and functions; he shall:

(1) preside over meetings;
(2) decide and control the agenda;
(3) decide on the time and duration of meetings;
(4) call special meetings during the recess; and
(5) exercise other powers and functions as prescribed in the rules of procedure of the Legislative Council.

In view of such powers of the President of the Legislative Council, and in view of the CE's power to dissolve the Legislative Council (BL50) and the Legislative Council's power regarding impeachment of the CE (BL72.9), it is highly inappropriate for the CE to serve concurrently as President of the Legislative Council (alternative 2 of BL70). This not only violates the principles of separation of powers and checks and balances which were agreed upon by the BLDC in its early stage of deliberations, but it should also be noted that even in the Westminster model, the British Prime Minister does not serve concurrently as Speaker of the House of Commons. It is therefore much more appropriate for the President of the Legislative Council to be elected from among the members of the Legislative Council (alternative 1 of BL70). In this case, like the CE, he 'shall be a Chinese national of no less than 40 years of age, who is a permanent resident of the Region and has ordinarily resided in Hong Kong for a continuous period of 20 years' (alternative 1 of BL70).

BL72 defines the powers and functions of the Legislative Council which, as far as the article is concerned, includes the normal powers and functions of a legislature. However, the powers and functions of the Legislative Council of the SAR are considerably limited by the extensive powers of the CE and the narrow definition of the accountability of the executive authorities (which most probably do not include the CE) to the Legislative Council as discussed above. BL73 further reinforces such limitations on the powers of the Legislative Council. Regarding bills relating to revenue and expenditure, bills relating to government policies, and bills relating to the structure and operation of the government, members of the Legislative Council may only introduce them with the prior written consent of the CE (alternative 1 of BL73). Alternative 2 of the same clause, however, appears to be more lenient and states:

> Bills which do not relate to public expenditure or public policies may be introduced individually or jointly by members of the council.

The impotence of the Legislative Council to control government revenue and expenditure has been analysed above; and there will be a danger that 'government policies' or 'public policies' may be so broadly defined as to render members of the Legislative Council almost powerless to introduce bills. The author therefore supports the suggestion of a member of the BLDC that bills relating to public expenditure or public policies should be jointly proposed by no less than one-tenth of the members of the legislature, but that the prior written consent of the CE should not be required.[14]

BL72.9 empowers the Legislative Council to pass a motion for the impeachment of the CE, which is a very important characteristic of a system of separation of powers. The impeachment procedure is appropriate, and it can only be hoped that the CPG's decision to remove the impeached CE is just a matter of formality demonstrating China's sovereignty over Hong Kong. It is difficult to imagine how an impeached and therefore totally discredited CE could be allowed to retain his office through the support of the CPG without severely damaging political stability in Hong Kong. Under such circumstances, the last clause of BL72.9 'and report it to the Central People's Government for decision' should be amended to read 'and report it to the Central People's Government for the removal of the Chief Executive.'

The section on the legislature remains silent on its power to impeach members of the executive authorities and the Executive Council as well as the power of a certain number of members of

14 Ibid 101.

the Legislative Council to call special meetings during the recess (this power seems to lie solely in the hands of the President of the Legislative Council according to BL71.) It is therefore hoped that amendments will be made to provide such powers to the Legislative Council and its members. It is reasonable that the same power and procedure of the Legislative Council to impeach the CE should be extended to include at least all principal officials of the executive authorities.

Further, a member of the BLDC suggested that a provision for the establishment of standing committees and ad hoc committees should be added to BL72 which defines the powers and functions of the Legislative Council, though another member held that such a provision should be covered by the standing orders of the legislature.[15] Experiences of legislatures in various countries have well demonstrated that a system of standing committees and ad hoc committees allows members of a legislature to specialise and cultivate their expertise vis-à-vis the executive branch of the government and the civil servants and thereby enables them to play a more effective role in policy-making as well as supervision of the executive branch. After all, article 70 of the PRC constitution promulgated in 1982 provides for the establishment of standing committees by the NPC; and the Legislative Council in Hong Kong today also shows such a trend of development.[16]

In addition, a member of the BLDC proposed that BL72 should also include the following clause: The legislature and its subordinate committees shall have the power to summon the person concerned to appear before them to testify and give evidence.[17] This power is in fact implied and restricted by BL48.11 which grants the CE the power to 'decide, in the light of security and public interest, whether government officials or other personnel in charge of government affairs should testify or give evidence before the Legislative Council.' As the power is already implied, it may as well be clearly stated in BL72. It should be noted that the committee system and the power to summon witnesses have contributed much to the effective role assumed by the American Congress in a system of separation of powers.

BL76 and 77 grant members of the Legislative Council immunity from legal action in respect of their speeches made at meetings of the Legislative Council and protection from arrest when attending or on their way to a meeting of the Legislative

15 Ibid.
16 Art 70 of *The Constitution*, 56.
17 'Collection of Opinions and Suggestions' 101.

Council. Such protection certainly facilitates members of the Legislative Council to speak freely in voicing their criticisms of the CE and the executive authorities. The circumstances listed in BL78 which will disqualify members of the Legislative Council from office also appear fair.

Note 6 of the Basic Law, however, raises a serious question. It states that whether or not members of the legislature should be required to resign after being appointed principal officials in the executive authorities remains to be studied. As the executive authorities shall be accountable to the legislature according to the Joint Declaration and BL64, it is only natural that members of the legislature have to resign after being appointed principal officials in the executive authorities. Moreover, the Legislative Council has the power to propose impeachment of the CE (and, one hopes, all principal officials of the executive authorities and members of the Executive Council as well). Further, it has already been suggested that a number of formal and informal arrangements may be established to improve co-ordination between the legislative and executive branches of the government without violating the principles of separation of powers and checks and balances.

It is not intended to discuss the judicial organs in this chapter; suffice it to point out here that independence of the judiciary from the other branches of the SAR government appears to be well safeguarded. The main threat, however, comes from the power of the Standing Committee of the National People's Congress to interpret the Basic Law (BL169) and that of the NPC to amend, while the power to propose an amendment to the Basic Law shall be vested in the NPCSC, the State Council, and the SAR (BL170). Moreover, BL17 states that certain PRC laws will be applied in the SAR. The above aspects are of considerable concern to the legal profession in the territory.

DISTRICT ORGANISATIONS AND PUBLIC SERVANTS

District organisations

The section on district organisations is brief and reaffirms the present situation of the British administration in Hong Kong where there is only one tier of government despite the talk of a three-tier structure of government. BL96 states that district organisations which are not local organs of political power may be established in the SAR, thus guaranteeing that power will remain concentrated in the hands of the SAR government. District organisations, however, may be responsible for providing services in such fields as culture, recreation, and environmental sanitation. Note 8 of the Basic Law also indicates that members of the BLDC held that if the present three-tier structure were retained, district boards should still be district consultative bodies.

The author concurs with such views; in fact an ideal arrangement may be to combine the existing Urban Council, Regional Council, and the 19 district boards into about five to six larger district boards which will basically be consultative bodies at the district level with responsibility for the provision of services listed in BL96. BL97 which provides that the powers and functions of the district organisations and their composition shall be prescribed by law reflects a flexible attitude towards the future evolution of district organisations. This is certainly wise.

Public servants

The section on public servants is similarly uncontroversial. BL98 stipulates that public servants must be permanent residents of the SAR which is the normal practice in almost all countries; while BL100 allows the flexibility that the SAR government may also employ British and other foreign nationals as advisers to government departments and, when there is need, may recruit qualified candidates from outside the SAR to professional and technical posts in government departments.

In order to attract public servants serving the establishment of the SAR to remain in employment, BL99 promises that they may retain their seniority with pay, allowances, benefits, and conditions of service no less favourable than before. It is rather unusual for this type of promise to be written into a constitution, but it may well be necessary. Likewise, BL101 which guarantees public servants of the present British administration their promised retirement benefits, and BL102 which promises the retention of the existing system of recruitment, employment, etc for public servants, are aimed at achieving the same purpose. The BLDC obviously goes to considerable lengths to maintain the loyalty and morale of the civil servants of the British administration and induce them to stay on and serve the SAR government.

BL100 reaffirms the almost identical provisions in the Joint Declaration. The requirement of Chinese nationality for the list of posts contained in BL100 has been discussed in the previous section. This requirement is probably related to the British government's attempt to maintain a certain role in the SAR government. In late 1983 and early 1984, when the British government finally agreed to return Hong Kong's sovereignty and administration to China in 1997, it tried to retain a number of 'sensitive' positions in the future SAR government for the British, for example, the posts of Attorney General, Commissioner of Police, and so on. The Chinese government firmly rejected such demands as they were regarded as an infringement of Chinese sovereignty over Hong Kong. Section IV of Annex I of the Joint Declaration already rules out British and other foreign nationals from serving as 'heads of major government departments (corresponding to branches or departments at Secretary level) including the police department, and as deputy heads of some of those departments' in the SAR government.

METHOD FOR SELECTING CE OF THE SAR, METHOD FOR CONSTITUTING LEGISLATIVE COUNCIL OF THE SAR, AND METHOD FOR FORMATION OF FIRST GOVERNMENT AND FIRST LEGISLATIVE COUNCIL OF THE SAR

The method for selecting the CE and the method for constituting the Legislative Council of the SAR are probably the most controversial issues in the drafting of the Basic Law. In 1987, there was already an intense debate on the introduction of direct elections to the Legislative Council in 1988. The issue at stake is the extent of democracy in the SAR. As the CE wields significant powers in the SAR political system, the method for selecting the CE naturally becomes the bone of contention between the advocates for democracy and the conservative business community supported by Beijing.

Though there are five alternatives listed in Annex 1 of the Basic Law which deals with the selection of the CE, the real contest is between alternative 1 and alternative 2. The latter was presented by the advocates for democracy in the declaration issued by the Joint Committee for the Promotion of Democratic Political System on 2 November 1986. According to this proposal, the CE shall be nominated by no less than one-tenth of the members of the legislature and directly elected by a territory-wide general election with universal franchise. Direct election by universal franchise is obviously the most democratic method and more in accord with the spirit of the modified presidential system of government analysed above which bestows on the CE a large degree of independence relatively free from any major checks and balances, except the threat of impeachment. Direct election of the CE, however, involves substantial mobilisation and might bring about serious divisions and even confrontation within the community. If there were too many candidates, then there would be confusion. To guarantee the legitimacy of the CE, he would have to receive an absolute majority of the votes cast. It is therefore likely that two rounds of elections would be required, following the French system of presidential election: that is, if no candidate receives an absolute majority of votes cast in the first round, then the two candidates securing the most votes in the first round enter the second round.

If the CE is selected in this way, then his or her appointment by the CPG (BL45) can only be a matter of formality demonstrating China's sovereignty over Hong Kong. If the CPG refused to appoint the person elected as CE by universal franchise, there would certainly be a constitutional crisis with a serious adverse impact on the stability and prosperity of the SAR.

One may reasonably speculate that both Beijing and the local conservative business community would like to have a considerable measure of control over the choice of the CE of the SAR government, so as to make sure that the selected candidate would be acceptable from their point of view. The conservative business community also wants to avoid the possibility of having a directly elected CE who is unacceptable to Beijing. Based on such considerations, the Business and Professional Group of Members of the BLCC offered a proposal which has become alternative 1 in Annex 1 of the Basic Law.

The gist of this alternative is that the CE shall be elected by an electoral college. Members of the electoral college shall include: members of the legislature, representatives of district organisations, representatives of corporate bodies and non-corporate permanent organisations, and representatives of various functional constituencies (including industry, commerce, finance, professions, education, labour, religious communities, social services, and the public servants), totalling about 600 in number. Communities and organisations with seats in the electoral college may elect their representatives by a democratic procedure in accordance with their own rules. Each elected representative shall vote in an individual capacity. Then the electoral college shall elect a nominating committee of 20 members from its own members. The nominating committee shall nominate three candidates for the office of the CE. Members of the nominating committee cannot run for the office of, nor vote in the election of, the CE. Finally, the electoral college shall vote on the nominations by the nominating committee. A candidate must win over half of the votes in order to be elected; if necessary, a second round of voting shall be conducted for the two leading candidates.

Advocates for democracy criticise this proposal as an attempt to ensure that the conservative business community will control a majority in the electoral college, given its composition. Moreover, such an electoral method does not involve ordinary people and offers no chance for their participation.

Alternative 3 presented by former Supreme Court judge Simon Li is basically a repetition of alternative 2; it is less specific on the procedure of selecting the CE, but it has a more detailed plan on the composition of the electoral college which again shall have no more than 600 members. It is generally assumed that the conservative business community shall be able to control an absolute majority of such an electoral college.

As alternative 3 provides that any person with the qualifications prescribed by BL44 and nominated by no less than 50 permanent residents of the SAR can become a candidate for the CE, there may well be a great number of candidates, which would create a minor procedural problem for the electoral college.

Alternative 4 is an even more conservative proposal presented by Cha Chi-ming, suggesting that the CE shall be selected by an advisory group through consultation. The advisory group shall be composed of 50–100 advisers who shall be selected by the Executive Council, presumably on the basis of open nominations. Members of the advisory group will be appointed by the CE after approval by the CPG. Each advisory group must be formed six months before the expiry of the term of office of the incumbent CE. However, if both the advisory group and the CPG agree that the incumbent CE should serve another term, there is no need to form a new advisory group.

Cha Chi-ming proposes that this selection method should apply to the second or third CE. Then the subsequent CEs shall be elected by an electoral college composed of former members of the Legislative Council and the Executive Council, former CEs, and former principal officials appointed by the CPG. The advisory group shall nominate three candidates for the office of the CE and, after the approval of the CPG, the CE shall be voted on by the electoral college. It is significant to note that Cha's proposal is the only one that stipulates that the CPG should approve the list of candidates before election by the electoral college.

The final alternative was proposed by Louis Cha, the Hong Kong co-convenor of the Sub-group on Political Structure of the BLDC. This was supposed to be an attempt to forge a consensus and, to some extent, also incorporated a proposal of the pro-Beijing education workers in Hong Kong who could not find a BLDC member to present their proposal. According to this alternative, the CE shall be elected by all the voters of Hong Kong on a one-person-one-vote basis. The three candidates, however, shall be nominated by the 'Nominating Committee for the

Election of the Chief Executive of the HKSAR' through consultation or by ballot after consultation.

Louis Cha's proposal supports the direct election of the CE on a one-person-one-vote basis, and allows the advocates for democracy to secure a slightly larger slice of the membership of the Nominating Committee than that of the electoral college in alternative 3. The proposal, however, satisfies the conservative business community by apparently offering it the control of the nomination process with an absolute majority in the Nominating Committee. The composition of the Nominating Committee also recognises the political status of deputies to the NPC and of members of the Chinese People's Political Consultative Conference.

Louis Cha's proposal leaves the Nominating Committee to formulate a procedure for consultation or balloting regarding the nomination of candidates for the office of CE. This procedure may well be crucial to achieving a compromise. If each member of the Nominating Committee can support only one candidate, and the three candidates who receive the most members' support shall be formally nominated to be elected subsequently by all the voters of Hong Kong on a one-person-one-vote basis, then there is a good chance for the pro-democracy lobby to accept the alternative. The lobby can count on securing about a third of the seats in the Nominating Committee and get its leader nominated as one of the three candidates who may then be elected on a universal franchise basis.

It is not expected that Beijing and the conservative business community will accept such a procedure, as they will then fail to make sure that the elected CE will be acceptable to them. If members of the Nominating Committee can indicate support for three candidates, then the conservative business community with its absolute majority in the Nominating Committee will control the nomination process; and if the procedure for consultation or balloting regarding the nomination of candidates for the office of CE is left to the decision of the Nominating Committee, it is likely that such a procedure will be adopted and will not be acceptable to the pro-democracy lobby.

Those who are familiar with the united front tactics of the Chinese authorities may note that the proposals of the pro-democracy lobby and Cha Chi-ming respectively are now at the two ends of the political spectrum, while Louis Cha's proposal is presented as a compromise formula. Four out of the five alternatives contain an electoral college, with Cha Chi-ming's advisory group being the least democratic and Louis Cha's Nominating Committee most liberal. So even the adoption of Louis Cha's proposal may be presented as a considerable concession on the part of Beijing and the conservative business community to the local pro-democracy lobby, though such a proposal yields nothing substantial.

As a vague promise to the pro-democracy lobby and while supporting the argument of the conservatives that the development of democracy takes a long time, BL45 of the Basic Law states:

> The method for selecting the Chief Executive as prescribed in Annex I may be modified in the light of actual situation in the HKSAR and in accordance with the principle of gradual and orderly progress. Such modifications shall require the endorsement of a two-thirds majority of the members of the Legislative Council of the HKSAR and the consent of the Chief Executive, and shall be submitted to the Standing Committee of the National People's Congress for approval.

BL67 offers the same provision concerning the future method for constituting the Legislative Council of the SAR.

Annex II, which deals with the method for constituting the Legislative Council of the SAR, presents four alternatives. As BL67 already states that the Legislative Council shall be constituted by a combination of direct and indirect elections, all four alternatives accept that at least 25% of the seats shall be directly elected by a universal franchise and that at least 25% shall be elected by functional bodies. As the powers of the Legislative Council are considerably less than those of the CE, the differences among the four alternatives on the method for constituting the Legislative Council of the SAR are less significant.

Alternative 2 comes from the Joint Committee for the Promotion of Democratic Political System based on its declaration issued on 2 November 1986, and was presented by Szeto Wah to the BLDC. It suggests that no less than 50% of the members shall be directly elected in a general election based on universal franchise, no more than 25% shall be elected by the functional bodies, and no more than 25% shall be elected by district organisations, that is, district boards, the Urban Council and the Regional Council, or other similar organisations.

Martin Lee, however, proposes that all the members of the legislature of the SAR should be elected by districts through direct election on a one-person-one-vote basis. To counterbalance Lee's proposal, Simon Li, supported by Xu Chongde from Beijing, suggests that all the members of the legislature of the SAR should be elected by the functional bodies. These two proposals are only presented as Note 3 and Note 2 of Annex II respectively.

Alternative 1, on the other hand, comes from the Business and Professional Group of Members of the BLCC which was presented by Raymond Wu to the BLDC. According to this proposal, the Legislative Council shall be composed of 80 persons, with 50% elected by functional bodies, 25% directly elected by districts, and 25% elected by the same electoral college proposed by the group for the election of the CE.

The group further suggests that the term of office of the members of the legislature shall be four years, and half the members shall be elected every two years. The functional bodies shall elect half of their members to the legislature every two years. The direct election in the districts and the election by the electoral college shall be held alternately every two years, while district direct elections and election of the CE shall take place in the same year. Such arrangements are well worth considering.

Regarding district direct elections, the group suggests that Hong Kong shall be divided into ten constituencies, with two seats for each constituency, and the two candidates with the highest and second highest number of votes shall be elected. The group has not specified whether each voter can vote for just one candidate or two candidates in the two-seat constituencies; this specification may have significant impact on the election outcomes. If voters can vote for only one candidate, then it will favour the conservative business community, assuming that most district direct elections will be contests between candidates supported by the conservative business community and those endorsed by the pro-democracy lobby and that the former's supporters are in a minority. By securing slightly more than one-third of the votes in a constituency, the former can win one half of the seats.

Alternative 3 is the most conservative among the four and was presented by Cha Chi-ming. He suggests that the legislature of the SAR shall have 60 members, with 30% of the members elected by the same advisory group he proposed for the selection of the second or third CE and later for the nomination of the three candidates for the office of CE, 40% of the members shall be elected by functional bodies, and 30% shall be elected directly by the districts.

Both alternative 1 and alternative 3 maintain that the proposed methods for electing members of the legislature are 'package' deals, that is to say, direct district election is conditional upon the acceptance of the other two types of election. One unique characteristic of Cha Chi-ming's proposal is that his alternative stipulates that at least one-third of those members elected by the advisory group among non-advisers shall be principal officials, and the rest shall be members of the Executive Council and other public figures. Cha Chi-ming believes that members of the legislature must include members of the Executive Council and principal officials so as to strengthen the links between the executive and the legislature, and his proposal concerning the method for constituting the Legislative Council of the SAR attempts to ensure this. The author has earlier suggested ways to strengthen the links between the executive and the legislature without violating the principle of separation of powers by electing members of the Executive Council and principal officials to the Legislative Council, and he also strongly believes that the principle of separation of powers must be strictly observed.

Alternative 4 is again presented by Louis Cha as a compromise formula. According to his alternative, the composition of the legislature of the SAR shall be as follows: 30% of the members from business circles, 25% from the professions, 20% from grassroots organisations, and 25% through district general elections.

As in Annex 1, the proposals of the pro-democracy lobby and Cha Chi-ming respectively are again at the two ends of the political spectrum. Louis Cha's alternative, similar to alternatives 1 and 3, allows the conservatives to gain a majority in the Legislative Council; but it offers more to the advocates for democracy than alternatives 1 and 3 do.

The four alternatives are as yet brief outlines; and for obvious reasons, they have not gone into details regarding the electoral system and the distribution of seats within the broad categories of functional bodies, district organisations (grassroots organisations), business circles, etc. While such distribution can be troublesome, the detailed arrangement of the electoral system may well be more controversial and may even lead to confrontation; a significant example has been discussed above. As the existing ten district board constituencies of the electoral college will be entirely replaced by direct elections to the Legislative Council in 1991,[18] it will be interesting to observe how this will affect the proposals in the Basic Law concerning the indirect election to the Legislative Council from district (grassroots) organisations. The Basic Law should also include a provision for the establishment of an independent and neutral Electoral Commission to be responsible for the holding of elections so as to relieve principal officials — who will be political appointees in the SAR — from the job.

Note 4 of Annex II indicates that a member of the BLDC raised the controversial issue of the nationality of members of the Legislative Council, and it was suggested that studies must be

18 See *White Paper – The Development of Representative Government: The Way Forward* (Hong Kong: Government Printer, February 1988).

made of the right to vote and to stand for election of Hong Kong permanent residents who have moved to a foreign country (but might not have acquired foreign nationality). It appears that the BLDC wants to play down the issue, as it has already been pointed out that at least seven (out of 23) BLDC members from Hong Kong hold foreign passports.[19] While it is certainly legitimate to argue against the right of SAR permanent residents holding foreign passports to stand for election to the Legislative Council, the fact that by 1997 a significant portion of community leaders may hold foreign passports poses a serious problem. Further, there are also people who concurrently hold passports from countries such as the Dominican Republic, Argentina, etc; people who have gained the right of permanent residence in a foreign country though not foreign nationality; and people whose spouses hold foreign passports or have secured the right of permanent residence in a foreign country: all these cases are very difficult to check. It is therefore less controversial if the BLDC itself is made a precedent for the Legislative Council.

Annex III, which deals with the method for the formation of the first government and the first Legislative Council of the SAR, reflects China's position which was first revealed by Lu Ping, Deputy Secretary-General of the BLDC, in October 1987 when the committee's Sub-group on Political Structure met in Guangzhou.[20] It is significant that Annex III does not include the alternatives proposed by individual members of the BLDC, but only registers them in 'A Collection of Opinions and Suggestions of Some Members in Regard to the Articles Drafted by Their Respective Special Subject Sub-groups' attached to the Basic Law.

Annex III indicates that, in 1996, the NPC shall establish a Preparatory Committee of the SAR composed of mainland members and of Hong Kong members who shall constitute no less than 50% to be appointed by the Standing Committee of the National People's Congress. This Preparatory Committee shall in turn establish the 'Election Committee for the First Government of the HKSAR.' The Election Committee shall be composed entirely of permanent residents of Hong Kong with 25% being professionals, 25% from labour and grassroots and religious organisations, 20% being political figures of former times, and 5% from among the Hong Kong deputies to the NPC and members of the National Committee of the Chinese People's Political Consultative Conference. The Election Committee shall

19 See Emily Lau, 'Breach of Promise?' *Far Eastern Economic Review*, Vol 140, No 19 (12 May 1988) 36; pp 94-95 above.
20 *South China Morning Post*, 7 and 9 October 1987.

recommend the candidate for the first CE through local consultation or through local election after consultation, and report the recommended CE to the CPG for appointment. The term of office of the first CE shall be the normal term. The Election Committee will also elect the first legislature of the SAR whose term of office shall be two years.

Critics have expressed fear that Beijing will then control the formation of the first government and the first Legislative Council; they are not convinced by Beijing's arguments that for the sovereignty reason, elections cannot be held in Hong Kong while the British authorities are still responsible for the administration of the territory and that for the same reason, the 'through train' idea, that is, the existing Legislative Council in Hong Kong will automatically become the first (or provisional) legislature of the SAR on 1 July 1997, cannot be accepted.[21] It is significant that both the Joint Committee for the Promotion of Democratic Political System and the Business and Professional Group of Members of the BLCC supported the 'through train' idea now rejected by Beijing. The Chinese authorities' concession is that all members of the former Hong Kong Legislative Council can be candidates for membership in the first (or provisional) legislature of the Region.

Besides the arrangements proposed by Beijing, members of the Sub-group on Political Structure from Hong Kong put forward five other alternatives. Cha Chi-ming's alternative substitutes an advisory group of no less than 50 persons for the Election Committee to select the CE and elect members of the legislature nominated by the CE in conjunction with the Executive Council. The term of office of all the members of the first government shall not exceed three years.[22]

The second alternative advanced by Liu Yiu-chu also agrees that the first CE shall be selected through local consultation held by a consultation committee elected from and by the members of a 'Preparatory Committee for the Implementation of the Basic Law' to be appointed by the NPC. A provisional legislature shall be elected by an electoral college about which no details have been provided. The first legislature shall then be elected and formed within 12 months after the establishment of the first government of the SAR.[23]

A third alternative was presented by the Business and Professional Group of members of the BLCC which again supports

21 Ibid.
22 'Collection of Opinions and Suggestions' 105.
23 Ibid 105–107.

the formation of an electoral college by a 'Preparatory Committee for the First Government of the HKSAR' to be appointed by the NPCSC. The electoral college shall be responsible for drawing up the procedures for the selection of the first CE (through consultation, or by election following nomination through consultation) and the election of the first legislature.[24]

The alternative presented by Martin Lee on behalf of the pro-democracy lobby suggested that the NPCSC shall establish a 'Preparatory Committee for the First Government of the HKSAR' in 1996 whose members shall all be Chinese nationals selected from among the permanent residents of Hong Kong. The first CE shall be elected by a general and direct election held by the Preparatory Committee in accordance with the Basic Law, meaning that the method of selecting the first CE should not differ from that of his or her successors. The alternative proposes that persons who are members of the Hong Kong Legislative Council in June 1997 shall automatically become members of the first legislature of the SAR.[25]

The final alternative presented by Maria Tam is simply a suggestion to postpone the decision on the arrangements.[26]

It appears that the Chinese authorities have already made up their minds and the above alternatives may not attract too much attention of the local community and, as a result, will have very limited chance of being adopted. Martin Lee's alternative is based on two principles: the method of selecting the first CE should not differ from that of his successors and the application of the 'through train' idea concerning the first legislature. The other three alternatives all contain an electoral college in various forms which will control the selection or at least the nomination of candidates for the office of CE. Such electoral colleges will also have a large measure of control over the election of the first legislature. Cha Chi-ming's alternative is even less democratic than the one presented in Annex III, while the second and third alternatives are yet too vaguely defined to merit detailed scrutiny.

CONCLUSION

The political system outlined in chapter IV of the Basic Law presents an 'executive dominant' system in which the CE will have powers similar to those of the present British Governor.

---

24 Ibid 107–108.
25 Ibid 108–109.
26 Ibid 109–110.

The Legislative Council constituted by a combination of direct and indirect elections will have only limited powers. As analysed above, it has very limited initiative on the revenue and expenditure of the government; and if it rejects the budget introduced by the CE and the executive authorities, it will be dissolved. The Legislative Council has no control over the appointments of the CE or the removal of the principal officials; further, its watchdog role is circumscribed by the CE's power not to allow government officials to testify or give evidence before the Legislative Council.

As the CE has to be accountable to the CPG but not to the Legislative Council of the SAR, and the appointment as well as removal of the CE and principal officials have to be approved by the CPG, this certainly affects the autonomy of the SAR. According to article 101 of the 1982 constitution of the PRC, local people's congresses, at their respective levels, 'elect, and have the power to recall, governors and deputy governors, or mayors and deputy mayors, or heads and deputy heads of countries, districts, townships and towns.'[27] Article 104 further provides that 'the standing committee or a local people's congress at and above the county level ... decides on the appointment and removal of functionaries of state organs within the limits of its authority as prescribed by law. . . .'[28] According to article 9 of the The Organic Law of the Local People's Congresses and the Local People's Governments of the PRC revised by the Fifth Session of the Fifth National People's Congress in 1982, the local people's congresses have the power to remove members of the local people's governments at their respective levels.[29] Article 28.8 further grants to the Standing Committee of a local people's congress at and above the county level the power to decide on the appointment and removal of the secretary-general, agency hands, bureau director, etc of its corresponding local people's government. Such appointments and dismissals have to be reported to the local people's government at a higher level for the record.[30] Similar provisions exist for the organs of self-government of

27 *The Constitution* 74.
28 Ibid 76.
29 'The Organic Law of the Local People's Congresses and the Local People's Governments of the PRC' was adopted by the Second Session of the Fifth National People's Congress in 1979. It was revised according to the 'Resolution on Certain Revisions of "The Organic Law of the Local People's Congresses and the Local People's Governments of the PRC" ' adopted by the Fifth Session of the Fifth National People's Congress in 1982. For the text of the revised law, see *Renmin Ribao* (Beijing), 16 December 1982.
30 Ibid.

national autonomous areas. It does not appear logical that the CPG should have more control over the appointment and dismissal of the CE and principal officials of the SAR than their counterparts in other local people's governments within the PRC, while the CE and principal officials of the SAR are less accountable to the Legislative Council of the SAR than their counterparts in other local people's governments within the PRC to their corresponding local people's congresses.

More significantly, it appears that the Chinese authorities want to have a certain measure of control over the formation of the first government and the first Legislative Council of the SAR. Articles of the Basic Law, like any constitution, can only provide the bare skeleton of the political system which also involves numerous precedents, conventions, practices, and regulations to be established through actual implementation of the Basic Law. The first two or three years after 1997 will therefore be crucial. If, in the first two years, both the CE and members of the Legislative Council are selected and elected respectively by the same Election Committee, it will be difficult for a system of checks and balances to function properly and will therefore adversely affect the evolution of the political system of the SAR.

The author's analysis of BL56 may provide a hint. There is obviously an attempt to retain the political structure of the existing colonial government as both Beijing and the conservative business community take it as part of the foundation for Hong Kong's economic success and political stability. A statement by the former Chairman of the Hong Kong Stock Exchange, Ronald Li, at an international investment conference, perhaps best reflects the conservative business community's attitude. Li declared:

> Hong Kong is a colony. It is a dictatorship, although a benevolent one. It is and has been a British colony, and it's going to be a Chinese colony, and as such it will prosper. We do not need free elections here.[31]

The colonial government in Hong Kong is certainly a benevolent one; there is ample liberty in the territory and the Rule of Law is observed. This colonial government, however, has to be accountable ultimately to a democratic government willing to defend freedom and the Rule of Law; and this is the guarantee of its benevolence.

A survey conducted in 1985 by Kuan Hsin-chi and Lau Siu-kai of the Chinese University of Hong Kong revealed that 61.7% of the respondents believed in the ability of the Hong Kong people to run Hong Kong well, while 16.9% thought otherwise and

31 *South China Morning Post*, 17 June 1987.

21.4% had no opinion. On the other hand, however, only 22.3% of the respondents believed that China would truly let Hong Kong people rule Hong Kong, as against 43.9% who proclaimed no confidence in the Chinese promise and 33.8% who had not made up their mind. In addition, 62.3% of the respondents agreed or strongly agreed with the general statement that the political fate of Hong Kong people was beyond their control.[32]

It appears that political expectations and confidence have been in decline since 1985.[33] Survey results released in mid-May 1988 indicated that 56.7% of the respondents who had picked up copies of the Basic Law had not read the document, while 35% had read a small part of it. Among those who knew of the Basic Law, only 6.9% said they would comment on various articles of the draft, while 34.7% indicated that they had not yet decided and 58% were not prepared to give their views. Of those who were prepared to give their views, they did not seem to be aware of the channels offered by the BLCC while ironically 30.8% of them chose to rely on the district boards and the District Offices of the Hong Kong government.[34] To some extent, neither Beijing nor the BLCC has convinced the community that it is eager to listen to the views of Hong Kong people.[35] Meanwhile, a survey conducted in early May 1988 reflected that 24% of the respondents wanted to emigrate, and the percentage went up to 45.5% among those who had tertiary education and above.[36] A return to traditional political apathy and making preparations to emigrate (among those who have the means of doing so) are natural responses.

To arrest these trends, the Chinese authorities must refrain from significant interference in the territory's political development. Their attempts to reserve in their own hands the final say in all important matters have unfortunately created such an impression, and the Basic Law has only reinforced such views. They must also demonstrate once again their willingness to listen and respond to the community's demands. Few people in Hong Kong will take part in open demonstrations to fight for democracy, but many well-educated citizens are aware that measures of

32 See Kuan Hsin-chi and Lau Siu-kai, 'The Civic Self in a Changing Polity: The Case of Hong Kong,' paper to be published by *The Asian Journal of Public Administration*.
33 See Joseph Y S Cheng, 'Hong Kong: The Decline of Political Expectations and Confidence,' to be published by *The Australian Journal of Chinese Affairs*.
34 *Ming Pao*, 16 May 1988 and *South China Morning Post*, 16 May 1988.
35 See Andy Ho, 'Confused DB members to put their case to drafters,' ibid, 17 May 1988 and 'Some basic mistakes,' ibid, 18 May 1988.
36 *Ming Pao*, 16 May 1988.

checks and balances are essential for the future political system. Given that the powerful CE will have to be acceptable to Beijing, freely contested elections to the legislature based on universal suffrage remain the most effective means of political participation and deterrence of the government's abuse of power. They are a necessary guarantee of the freedom of expression as well as the foundation for the survival and development of the existing political groups. Ordinary people must be given legitimate channels to articulate their interests too; after all, the business community has successfully secured BL105 which guarantees no major increase in government expenditure and the business community's tax burden. In the absence of the above provisions, the present prosperity may only be perceived by those with the required assets and qualifications as the final opportunity to make more money before emigration.

9 The Legal System and Constitutional Issues

PETER WESLEY-SMITH

THE term 'legal system' has no precise meaning,[1] and the topics it frequently embraces tend to converge with political or constitutional matters. Its focus is plainly law, but it is usually concerned also with the institutions and personnel who make, administer, and enforce legal rules and principles and with the procedures by which they do so.[2] Aspects of the legal system as thus conceived are dealt with in other chapters of this book; the present chapter discusses issues not considered in detail elsewhere, though some overlap is inevitable.

Under the Joint Declaration on the Question of Hong Kong Hong Kong's social and economic systems are to remain unchanged (JD3(4)) and the judicial system shall be maintained (section III, Annex I), but no mention is made of the legal system as such. In some respects the content of the legal system is of course to be substantially altered by the Basic Law; the general principle, however, appears by implication to be that matters not expressly referred to will continue along with the laws which define them. Accordingly, 'one country, two systems' (a slogan raised to constitutional respectability by its incorporation into the preamble) permits the maintenance of a legal system which may radically differ from the legal system in mainland China.

THE LEGAL SOURCES OF LAW

There are two principal categories of law covered by the Basic Law: laws previously in force in Hong Kong or made after 1997 by the Special Administrative Region, and laws which emanate from the PRC. The former comprises common law, equity,

---

1 See Lawrence M Friedman, *The Legal System: A Social Science Perspective* (New York: Russell Sage Foundation, 1975) ch 1.
2 A superficial guide to the local system is provided by Peter Wesley-Smith, *An Introduction to the Hong Kong Legal System* (Hong Kong: Oxford University Press, 1987).

ordinances, subsidiary legislation, and customary law (BL8), supplemented by SAR-enacted laws (BL17).

Laws emanating from the PRC include the Basic Law itself (BL17) and laws enacted by the NPC or its Standing Committee, applied in accordance with BL17. Other PRC laws will, it seems, be in force so far as military forces sent by the Central People's Government are concerned (BL13). Will mainland government officials, and permanent residents of the PRC, be subject to the general law of China while visiting Hong Kong? The Basic Law is silent on this question. Neither is it stated whether Hong Kong citizens visiting the mainland will be amenable to the jurisdiction of Chinese courts, applying Chinese law, in respect of acts done in Hong Kong. This is a somewhat startling omission. Although the Criminal Law of the PRC 1980 applies to all who commit crimes within the PRC,[3] and the SAR will be part of the PRC (BL1), it may be that the Basic Law provides an exception regarding crimes committed within the SAR. However, Hong Kong people deserve specific assurances on this point.

An important issue not addressed in the Basic Law is whether the Chinese constitution will apply in the SAR. One of the Basic Law Consultative Committee's special groups decided in February 1987 that the constitution is *valid* in Hong Kong but not necessarily *applicable* (a somewhat obscure distinction); some provisions of the constitution are clearly *not* applicable to the SAR, such as articles 1 and 5 proclaiming the socialist system or article 24 regarding education and sports; other provisions, such as articles on the national flag and emblem and articles 31 and 62(13), clearly *are* applicable. 'As to exactly which articles are applicable or otherwise, further discussion is required.'[4] The Basic Law Drafting Committee may be expecting that, under the third paragraph of BL17, the State Council, after taking the advice of the Committee for the Basic Law, will direct which articles of the Chinese constitution are to take effect. This is quite unsatisfactory: we need such information before the Basic Law is perfected and promulgated.

With respect to laws previously in force, several issues arise. First, does 'previously' mean prior to the Joint Declaration, prior to adoption of the Basic Law, or prior to 1 July 1997? Article 3(3) of the Joint Declaration states that the laws *currently* in force will remain basically unchanged. The ordinary meaning of BL8

---

3 See W S Clarke, 'Double Jeopardy, Overlapping Jurisdiction and the Attorney General of Hong Kong' (1986) 16 *Hong Kong Law Journal* 90, 91.
4 Final Report on the Relationship Between the Basic Law and the Constitution: CCBL-SG/RCS-OO-FR02-870213(E).

suggests that all laws in force in Hong Kong at midnight on 30
June 1997 shall be maintained. Two exceptions must be noted.
The list of sources in BL8 does not include laws emanating from
the United Kingdom; thus prerogative legislation, such as the
Letters Patent and Royal Instructions, and any unrepealed Acts
of Parliament previously applicable to Hong Kong will fall away
as the SAR comes into being. The other exception is previous
laws which contravene the Basic Law. But who is to decide which
laws contravene the Basic Law? This is considered below.

Second, by what mechanism are laws previously in force
maintained? By BL172, maintenance of the previous laws is
apparently not automatic with the dawning of 1 July 1997, for
such laws 'shall be adopted' at the time of the establishment of
the SAR. (This may, however, simply be a translation weakness,
as the problem is apparently not evident in the Chinese version.)
Under Annex III the government and legislature are to be
inaugurated on 1 July 1997. Laws previously in force expire with
the demise of British sovereignty in accordance with the Hong
Kong Act 1985; this is so because they are in force in British
Hong Kong by virtue of the Queen's prerogative, an incident of
her sovereign authority. (Ordinances and subsidiary legislation
take effect through the legislative competence of the Governor,
as advised by the Legislative Council, under the Letters Patent.
Once the Letters Patent lapse the legislature is deprived of power
and its laws disappear unless retained by some other technique.
And the colonial legislature cannot legislate for territories other
than British Hong Kong, such as the SAR. Common law and
equity are part of current Hong Kong law because, and only
because, they are imported into Hong Kong by the Application of
English Law Ordinance. Chinese law and custom exist through
the New Territories Ordinance or general principles of imperial
constitutional law. None of these sources can survive the expiry
of British jurisdiction over Hong Kong.) Thus there will be a
period — from midnight on 30 June 1997 to the moment when
the first SAR legislature adopts them — during which the
previous laws are not in force, leaving a vacuum in Hong Kong
law. It is not clear that the second paragraph of BL172 contradicts this conclusion. The new legislature could of course adopt
the previous laws with retrospective effect, but retrospective laws
are objectionable in principle and this would seem a poor way for
the SAR authorities to commence their work.

Third, laws previously in force shall not be 'adopted' if the
Standing Committee of the NPC declares them to be in contravention of the Basic Law (BL172). One question is: when is the
Standing Committee to make such a declaration? If it is to do so
some time after establishment of the SAR, the legislature will

have to delay adoption of the laws, thus exacerbating problems associated with the hiatus in Hong Kong law. Another question is whether judicial review is to apply in respect of laws previously in force. BL8 provides for the maintenance of previous laws other than those contravening the Basic Law. Standing alone, this would imply that the courts may strike down prior legislation or decisional law as ultra vires, but BL172 seems to suggest that only the Standing Committee may decide which laws are in conflict with the Basic Law; as the more specific provision, BL172 would prevail over BL8. The reference in BL172 to annulment or revision of laws 'later discovered to be in contravention of this Law' implies that only legislative means are available for dealing with offending prior laws. At the same time, as discussed below, there are several clauses which seem to assume that SAR judges may determine whether the Basic Law over-rides ordinary law, including laws previously in force. In the face of BL172 it remains entirely ambiguous whether judicial review of laws from the British period is to apply.

Fourth, what is meant by 'the common law'? It is presently defined as the common law of England and in the practice of the Hong Kong courts it appears to mean decisional law other than equity.[5] The retention of English law is not inconsistent with Chinese sovereignty (English law remains, for example, part of the law of Singapore and Malaysia), but the spirit of the Basic Law, or at least the emphasis given to sovereignty by Chinese leaders and publicists, suggests that the law of England should no longer be in force in Hong Kong in any form. (By the same token, appeal to the Judicial Committee of the Privy Council is not inconsistent with non-British sovereignty — witness, again, Singapore and Malaysia — yet that body is to have no jurisdiction in the SAR.) This is reinforced by BL83, which authorises the SAR courts to refer to precedents in other common law jurisdictions. The present Hong Kong government has not yet indicated whether the Application of English Law Ordinance will be amended prior to 1997. If the common law remains as the common law of England it will presumably persist as such into the SAR period, unless declared to be in contravention of the Basic Law. But if it is not qualified by any reference to England the SAR judges will have an enhanced ability to adapt it and mould it in accordance with the circumstances of the territory. 'Equity' is not currently defined as English equity: the assumption has probably been that it could be nothing else. In the SAR the judges could identify it not by its source (the law developed in

5 See Peter Wesley-Smith, 'The Reception of English Law in Hong Kong' (1988) 18 *Hong Kong Law Journal* 183.

the Court of Chancery) but by its content, which may mean the same thing but avoids reference to the law of the former imperial power; that is, equity could be regarded as decisional law, revealed in the judgments of courts in any common law jurisdiction, which supplements and ameliorates the common law.

At present, identification of the common law in many instances depends at least in theory on its interaction with Acts of Parliament. This is because until 1966 Hong Kong received 'the law of England' as it existed on 5 April 1843; repeal of that formula in 1966 did not mean that only 'pure' common law, unaffected by any pre-1843 English legislation which abolished common law rules, was thence in force in Hong Kong, and thus to determine the 'modern' common law it is necessary to consider the 'inferential' application of much old statute law from England.[6] This will presumably continue to be the case after 1997, at least if the existing Application of English Law Ordinance remains largely unaltered in content, and therefore 'the laws previously in force in Hong Kong' will retain the English connection. It is difficult to see how this could be avoided or to imagine that it should offend sentiments of Chinese nationalism and sovereignty.

Fifth, customary law has become part of Hong Kong law by two separate devices. The first is legislative provision, represented solely by section 13 of the New Territories Ordinance in relation to land in the New Territories; the maintenance of the New Territories Ordinance in this respect gives rise to no technical problems. Nevertheless Chinese law and custom, predicated upon the usages of a peasant society, might in some respects fall foul of the guarantee of equality of all Hong Kong residents in BL24. A specific privilege is granted to persons descended through the male line from indigenous villagers of 1898 (BL128). In other respects the customary bias in favour of males, for example, might be regarded by the courts as discrimination on the ground of sex.

The second means by which custom enters colonial law is through the non-reception of English law: that is, pre-British law and custom survive in a ceded colony unless replaced, and when English legislation or decisional law is rejected as causing injustice or oppression there has been no replacement of the prior law. After 1997 there will be no reception of English law (including the rule regarding retention of pre-cessional law and custom), which is the precondition for customary law to survive.

6 See Peter Wesley-Smith, 'The Effect of Pre-1843 Acts of Parliament in Hong Kong' (1984) 14 *Hong Kong Law Journal* 142.

Thus there can be no 'new' discovery by the courts that some customary rule is applicable in the SAR. That does not present a practical problem, as no such judicial decision is imaginable in any event.

Virtually all Chinese law and custom which the courts had previously recognised was abrogated by local statute in 1971. However, the position of inhabitants who had acquired some kind of customary status (as, say, a concubine or an adopted son) prior to the appointed day (7 October 1971) remains unaffected. Customary law therefore continues to be of importance in Hong Kong, though it declines as those who enjoy its benefits or suffer its burdens die off. It is possibly arguable that customary law, being retained only because English law was inapplicable, cannot exist after the abolition of English law, since the general reception of English law had provided the rationale for its retention in the first place. This contention would be defeated if it is held that BL8 maintains Hong Kong law as at 30 June 1997 and preserves such Chinese custom as had by then been acknowledged. Determination of SAR law would in that event be dependent upon a consideration of the applicability of English law in the colonial period.

THE LEGISLATURE

The most obvious issue concerning the legislature is the method of forming the Legislative Council. This is discussed in Chapter 8. The first question raised here is: what *is* the legislature of the SAR under the Basic Law?

In the present constitution, the legislature of Hong Kong — the body which makes laws for the peace, order, and good government of the colony — is not LegCo but the Governor, by and with LegCo's advice and consent (LP7(1)). LegCo can pass a bill but the bill does not become law until the Governor assents to it (the resulting ordinance not usually coming into operation until publication in the *Gazette*). This was confirmed in the *Rediffusion* case,[7] which also illustrated a practical consequence of the distinction. Letters Patent and Royal Instructions in 1985 conferred legislative power on the Council alone, but this appears to have been in error. By RI23 LegCo may make standing orders, and in this case the Council is a true, separate legislature in its own right; on all other matters the Council

7 *Rediffusion (HK) Ltd v AG* [1970] AC 1136, 1153 ('the legislature of Hong Kong consists of the Governor and the Legislative Council. The latter alone is not the legislature, it is the deliberative part of it').

merely advises the Governor and consents to the passing of bills. The Governor is not required to assent to bills presented to him.

BL66, in contrast, announces that LegCo is the legislature of the SAR. The intention appears to be the creation of a presidential rather than a parliamentary system; that is, the Chief Executive, even if President of LegCo under alternative 2 of BL70, will not be a member of the Council. The CE's functions nevertheless include the signing of bills passed by the Council and the promulgation (presumably meaning publication) of laws (BL48). Without the CE's signature, no bill can become law (BL75). The CE is not obliged to sign (BL49); he may if necessary dissolve LegCo (BL50), and although LegCo may force his resignation (BL52) a bill may remain unsigned.

BL72, therefore, in stipulating that LegCo shall have the power to 'enact, repeal or amend laws,' is out of harmony with other provisions. LegCo will *not* be the legislature of the SAR in the usual sense. It may, *on its own*, establish its own rules of procedure (BL74), but only to that extent is it an independent legislature. The United States Congress may over-ride a presidential veto and in such circumstances is a genuine legislative body; the SAR's LegCo will, however, be a deliberative assembly with no authority 'on its own' to make laws.

The second issue to be considered here is the legislative competence of the SAR legislature. There is no equivalent of RI26, requiring bills in certain categories to be reserved for the royal assent. LP8, however, permitting the Queen to disallow ordinances, is in effect adopted (though in a limited form) in BL16: a law shall immediately cease to have force on being returned for reconsideration or revoked by the Standing Committee of the NPC. The Hong Kong legislature, as now (RI28), must report all enactments to the sovereign authorities (in the SAR, to the Standing Committee: BL16). Reporting is for the record only and 'shall not affect the entry into force of such laws.' Therefore the reporting requirement does not restrict the legislature of the SAR in its competence to make law, although its ability to preserve its enactments in force is overshadowed by the Standing Committee's 'disallowance' power.

The NPC authorises the SAR to enjoy legislative power (BL2); the SAR 'is vested with legislative power' (BL16). The phrase now used refers to power 'to make laws for the peace, order, and good government of the colony' (LP7(1)) and this has been held to be a plenary power within limits, with the operation and force of sovereign legislation.[8] Thus the Hong Kong legislature may

8 See Peter Wesley-Smith, *Constitutional and Administrative Law in Hong Kong* (Hong Kong: China and Hong Kong Law Studies Ltd, 1987–88) Vol II, 262.

freely delegate its legislative authority, provided it does not entirely divest itself of its law-making capacity, and may enact laws contrary to fundamental moral principles or international law. Whether the SAR legislature will enjoy the same power is uncertain, but there is no reason in principle why it should not. However, it will not be free to disregard limits imposed by its own constitution.

The only express limitation on legislative competence in the Basic Law is contained in BL10:

> No law enacted by the legislature of the Hong Kong Special Administrative Region shall contravene this law.

From Hong Kong's point of view, the Basic Law will be an absolutely rigid constitution. Only the NPC may amend it, and the SAR legislature may only consent to an amendment proposal (by a two-thirds majority) which is also consented to by two-thirds of Hong Kong's deputies to the NPC and by the CE (BL170). An ordinance which contravenes the Basic Law may be revoked by the Standing Committee or returned for reconsideration (BL16). Whether it may be deprived of force — declared ultra vires — by the courts of the SAR is considered below; to anticipate, it seems essential that the courts should have the power to review legislation for breach of constitutional norms and thus to invalidate ab initio any law which contravenes the Basic Law. Laws which, for example, restrict the rights and freedoms of Hong Kong residents beyond the necessity for maintaining national security, public order, public morals, etc (BL39) will be vulnerable to judicial review.

The present Hong Kong legislature may not make laws which are repugnant to Acts of Parliament extending to the territory by their own terms. Similarly, it may be argued, PRC laws applied in the SAR under BL17 will be superior to Hong Kong ordinances, for two reasons. First, such PRC laws, enacted by the NPC or its Standing Committee, will be 'outside the limits of the high degree of autonomy' of the SAR. Second, the NPC, at least, enacts 'basic statutes' (article 62 of the Chinese constitution), such as the Basic Law itself, and ordinances must be inferior to the Basic Law and by implication to all other basic statutes including those concerning defence, foreign affairs, and the expression of national unity and territorial integrity. The extent of legislative power in the SAR must be determined by reference to the whole of the Basic Law, with its description of Hong Kong as a *local* administrative region enjoying a mere high degree of (not total) autonomy (BL11), and its stipulation that the CPG is responsible for foreign affairs (BL12) and defence (BL13) of the SAR. This does not necessarily mean that the legislature may not enjoy *concurrent* legislative power over foreign affairs and defence, but where PRC laws in these areas apply to the SAR, local laws in conflict with them must give way. The repugnancy doctrine is an inevitable consequence of the 'one country' portion of 'one country, two systems.' But whereas BL18, for example, is explicit on the SAR courts' lack of jurisdiction over cases relating to defence and foreign affairs, clauses concerning legislative jurisdiction rely on implication and thus contain an element of uncertainty.

SAR legislation which is in conflict with articles of the Chinese constitution applied to Hong Kong must also fail. Unless we know precisely which constitutional provisions are in force after 1997 the legislature must be over-cautious and lawyers unable to advise their clients with confidence.

It is assumed that such constitutional common law as remains relevant to the SAR and is not inconsistent with the Basic Law will continue in force. Thus if the courts retain their authority to review legislation, the legislature will remain subject to the threat of judicial interference for failure to comply with procedural requirements in the making of law; for example the courts might be asked to declare that it would be unlawful for the CE to sign a bill which had not received the votes of more than half of LegCo's members present (see BL74).[9]

The only limitation which 'peace, order, and good government' imposes on the present Hong Kong legislature is said to relate to extraterritoriality: Hong Kong may not make laws having *any* extraterritorial operation, according to the strict doctrine, or, as is now the orthodox view, which possesses no genuine nexus with the territory. BL12, however, states that the CPG authorises the SAR to deal with relevant external affairs on its own. Thus it can be inferred that laws having effect beyond the SAR's boundaries, provided they are 'relevant' to the SAR, will be within the legislature's competence.

Should the CE be President of LegCo? BL70 is undecided. The BLCC's special group on political structure noted that, as Speaker, the CE might serve as a bridge between the legislative and executive authorities, thus improving communication, co-ordination, and efficiency while enhancing the CE's prestige. On the other hand the proposal was not in accordance with the spirit of the separation of powers; it would greatly increase the CE's workload, and if the CE were not elected it would violate the provision in the Joint Declaration that the legislature shall be

9 See the *Rediffusion* case (n 7 above).

constituted by elections.[10] It might be observed that the CE's prestige is unlikely to need enhancement and that the separation of powers, in the sense of a strict division between executive and legislative branches of government, is not now exhibited by the British or Hong Kong constitutions and is not a sine qua non of liberty. The CE could preside without being a member of the Council, and the presidential system, as noted above, seems to be assumed in other parts of the Basic Law. The Green Paper of July 1984 proposed that the Governor be replaced as President of LegCo prior to 1997 by a presiding officer elected by unofficial members of the Council from among themselves. The White Paper of November 1984 stated that the general view adopted by the public was in favour of making no significant change during the following few years. The issue was raised again in the Green Paper of May 1987, where the suggestion was recorded that the dual role of the Governor as head of the executive and impartial Speaker might lead to a conflict of interest. But 'the way forward,' said the subsequent White Paper, was to stand still in relation to the presidency of LegCo in the near future.

There are obvious conflicts of interest between the CE and LegCo under the Basic Law. LegCo is to debate the CE's work reports, deal with complaints, and, in the event of a serious breach of law or dereliction of duty by the CE, pass a motion for his impeachment (BL72). The greater threat to the principle of 'Hong Kong people ruling themselves' comes from the CE rather than from abuse of its authority by the elected LegCo, and for this reason the first alternative in BL70 is manifestly preferable to the second.

THE JUDICIARY

If the judiciary is 'the least dangerous branch,' it is also crucial to the operation of any constitutional system and a vital mechanism for the protection of citizens from arbitrary government. Restrictions on the jurisdiction of the courts need to be approached with great circumspection.

In present-day Hong Kong there is very little which is beyond the purview of the courts. With limited exceptions, events occurring outside the territory cannot give rise to criminal proceedings. Some matters, such as declarations of war, recognition of a foreign government, and delimitations of territorial boundaries, are classified as Acts of State and in respect of them

10 Final Report on the Relationship Between the Legislature and the Executive Authorities (passed by the Executive Committee on 8 August 1987): CCBL–SG/POS–WGO3–FRO1–870730(E).

the courts defer to the executive branch. Certain individuals possess sovereign or diplomatic immunity. Judges in the common law tradition are otherwise hostile to all suggestions that they lack jurisdiction over disputes raising questions of law. Legislative attempts to oust their jurisdiction regarding executive behaviour have largely been futile, and prerogative acts are in principle as reviewable in the courtroom as acts done under statutory authority. Without the judges' pervasive role as guardians of the law and the public interest, the Rule of Law as a fundamental precept of the constitution could hardly be said to exist.

In this context the third and fourth paragraphs of BL18 are positively alarming. The SAR courts are to have no jurisdiction over cases relating to defence, foreign affairs, and the executive acts of the CPG. Whether a case so relates, it seems, is to be conclusively determined by the NPCSC or the State Council. (On the question of the meaning of BL18, however, see below.)

The first point to note is that the CE's statement is unchallengeable whether the case is directly or remotely connected with defence or foreign affairs or completely unconnected. Experience gives no reason for confidence in the honest exercise of such a discretion even by executive governments subject to parliamentary control. And it makes no sense to create a limitation and permit the body thereby limited to determine the ambit of the limitation; this is a familiar assumption in Hong Kong's administrative law. Second, under BL17, PRC laws concerning defence and foreign affairs shall be applied locally; they will be part of the law of the SAR. The legality of acts done in the realm of defence and foreign affairs could therefore be measured against formal, binding, statutory standards. To deny the courts their customary role in determining whether executive action is in accordance with pre-existing law is a negation of judicial power. BL18 does not propose a narrow exception but a hole wide enough, as the saying goes, to permit the egress of a coach-and-four. Third, the phrase 'the executive acts of the Central People's Government' imposes no limit; it could refer to anything from the arrest of a dissident to expropriation of property without compensation and beyond. There are certain matters which the courts would certainly regard as not 'justiciable,' primarily matters of state involving wide questions of policy; the appointment of the CE is a clear example. If BL18 is designed to avoid interference by the courts in matters such as these it is strictly unnecessary. If nevertheless inclusion of the prohibition in the Basic Law is desired as a kind of insurance against intrusive judges, the clause requires a much narrower and more precise formulation.

It must be emphasised that BL18 represents a startling

departure from the common law.[11] Damage done to private property in the exercise of admitted prerogative powers, such as in the defence of the realm, must be adequately compensated for, and the courts may determine whether the prerogative is properly invoked. Under the Act of State doctrine there may be executive acts ('inter-governmental Acts of State') which represent the supreme authority of the state and are therefore uncontrollable by the state's judicial organs. But these acts involve 'catastrophic change' such as war or annexation of territory; they do not concern themselves with domestic matters subject to a regime of law. When the government claims sovereign authority to interfere directly with the legal rights of individuals the courts demur unless the individuals are foreigners and the offending acts occurred beyond the boundaries of the state; jurisdiction over acts performed in Hong Kong would only be lost if the individuals were enemy aliens. The Crown may lodge a binding certificate as to certain matters, but the type of situations in which the 'certificate Act of State' doctrine is applicable is strictly limited; only such questions as whether a state of war exists, whether a person's claim to sovereign immunity is justified, or whether a foreign government is recognised by the Crown may be conclusively determined in this way. BL18 is not so confined. It permits the CPG to interfere directly in SAR affairs on any matter without being subject to judicial review, provided the Standing Committee or the State Council issues a certificate to the CE.

In the December 1987 draft, BL18 was part of BL81 though with a crucial difference in meaning:

> The courts shall have power to adjudicate all cases in the HKSAR other than those relating to defence, foreign affairs, and the executive acts of the Central Committee [sic!], *over which the courts do not have jurisdiction under the legal system previously in force in Hong Kong* (italics supplied).

The last phrase evinces an intention to maintain the common law Act of State doctrine; BL18 does not.[12] It is not the Hong Kong

11 See Wesley-Smith (n 8 above) ch 8.
12 The August 1987 draft (cl 5 of s 4 of ch 4) did not include this provision but a note referred to a clause, endorsed in principle by the sub-groups on the relationship between the Central Government and the SAR and on political structure, which began: 'Except for cases relating to defence and foreign affairs and the executive acts of the Central Government over which the HKSAR courts, *in accordance with the previous legal system in Hong Kong*, do not have jurisdiction, the courts of the HKSAR shall enjoy the power of adjudication for all other cases in the HKSAR' (italics supplied). For the views of the BLCC's special group on law (4 November 1987): see CCBL–SG/LES–RPO1(E)–871030.

way to allow the executive authorities carte blanche to do as they will without redress in the courts; it may be the PRC way, but to provide for it in the SAR is not faithful adherence to the 'two systems' portion of 'one country, two systems.'

It is pointed out in Chapter 1 of this book that judicial review of both administrative and legislative action is an integral part of Hong Kong's present constitution. As we have just seen, under BL18 judicial review of certain executive acts is denied, while judicial review of laws previously in force is rendered doubtful by BL172 (p 175 above). But the argument in favour of measuring SAR enactments against the standard of the Basic Law is a strong one. The courts are to exercise judicial power (BL79), and it is the very essence of judicial power to decide between conflicting laws; the judicial system previously in practice in Hong Kong, which incorporates judicial review of legislation, shall be maintained (BL80); the Court of Final Appeal is to have the power of final adjudication (BL81), which would be impossible without the power of judicial review; and the courts may interpret the Basic Law in the process of adjudication (BL169), without being required to defer to the Standing Committee unless the case involves the interpretation of BL provisions concerning affairs which are the responsibility of the CPG. Further, many English-speaking courts have deemed judicial review of legislation 'an indispensible, implied characteristic of a written constitution';[13] it is a necessary consequence of the Rule of Law;[14] and without it the promise in the Joint Declaration of protection for rights and freedoms would be impossible to respect. In principle, all the legal sources of Hong Kong law ought to be subject to review by the courts, the Basic Law being regarded as fundamental law superior to common law, equity, ordinances, subsidiary legislation, and Chinese law and custom.

This extends also to PRC laws applied under BL17: if laws enacted by the NPC or its Standing Committee are in force yet do not relate to defence or foreign affairs or national unity or territorial integrity, or if in any event they contravene the Basic Law, the courts in the SAR ought to have the power to disregard them. Otherwise BL17, like BL18, could be used to subvert all the guarantees laid down in the Joint Declaration and the SAR constitution. Whether the CPG would approve is a quite separate

13 Felix Frankfurter, 'John Marshall and the Judicial Function' (1955) 69 *Harvard Law Review* 217.
14 Stanford H Kadish, 'Judicial Review in the High Court and the United States Supreme Court' (1959) 2 *Melbourne University Law Review* 4, 6.

matter. There can be no doctrine of 'implied repeal' of the Basic Law by ordinary NPC legislation (that is, legislation not complying with BL170). Nevertheless, challenge to the vires of PRC law on the basis that it does not in fact relate to defence or foreign affairs, etc would involve an interpretation of the meaning of defence, foreign affairs, etc in the Basic Law, thus requiring submission to the Standing Committee in accordance with BL169.

The SAR courts should in addition be regarded as empowered to declare void any improper amendments to the Basic Law itself. BL170 restricts NPC amendments to those which have been studied by the Basic Law Committee and which do not 'contravene the established basic policies of the People's Republic of China regarding Hong Kong.' The PRC's basic policies regarding Hong Kong have been set out in the Joint Declaration (referred to in the preamble), a solemn international treaty registered with the United Nations. Thus no amendment which contradicts the Joint Declaration can be valid. Since amendment is the responsibility of the NPC, not the CPG (the State Council, according to article 85 of the Chinese constitution of 1982), BL169 does not oblige the SAR courts to seek an interpretation from the Standing Committee before making their final judgment. (A further intriguing question is whether the courts would review the Standing Committee's exercise of its 'disallowance' power in BL16.)

The question of interpretation is dealt with in other chapters of this book. It is an obvious necessity that SAR courts be empowered to interpret the Basic Law:

> A law which is to be applied by a court, but is not to be interpreted by a court, is a solecism simply unknown to our conceptions of legality and the legal process.[15]

BL169 does not deny this. The courts must of course interpret BL169 itself and determine whether a case 'involves an interpretation of the provisions of this Law concerning defence, foreign affairs and other affairs which are the responsibility of the Central People's Government'; they must also construe Standing Committee interpretations and decide how they apply to the cases before them. There are manifest difficulties, not least delay, in the operation of the obligation to seek the Standing Committee's views.

---

15 Charles L Black, Jr, *The People and the Court: Judicial Review in a Democracy* (New York: Macmillan, 1960) 15.

Other matters affecting the judiciary are not so controversial:

Appointment of judges

The present Judicial Service Commission is strictly advisory; in practice the Governor delegates the selection of judicial officers (ranging from an adjudicator in the Small Claims Tribunal to a Justice of Appeal) to the Chief Justice, who chairs the Judicial Service Commission and is further advised by an informal (and possibly unconstitutional) judicial appointments committee. BL87 refers only to the appointment, by the CE on the recommendation of an independent commission, of district judges and above; BL90 maintains the previous system of appointment for magistrates and presiding officers. It seems that in the SAR the CE *must* accept the commission's recommendations on the appointment of judges, whereas for other judicial officers the arrangements will depend on the pre-1997 position. There is an opportunity here to amend the much-criticised Judicial Service Commission Ordinance[16] and, in the process, to remove the Governor's discretion regarding *all* judicial appointments. The so-called Judiciary Bill, not yet published but which is supposed to reorganise the whole judicial service so as to remove all connections with the public service, should be proceeded with well before 1997 (compare note 7 to the Basic Law).

Removal of judges

The procedures in BL88 are similar to those presently existing (though without, of course, the participation of the Judicial Committee of the Privy Council) and they follow the provisions of the Joint Declaration. BL89, by requiring the endorsement of LegCo for removal of judges of the Court of Final Appeal, is an interesting adoption of a US-style check-and-balance.

Judicial independence

SAR courts shall 'exercise judicial power independently and free from any interference' (BL84). Judicial officers 'shall be chosen by reference to their judicial and professional qualities' (BL91), not by their political reliability; their immunity is maintained (BL84); those serving before 1997 will retain the perquisites of

---

16 By, for example, removing the Attorney General from its membership and prohibiting the Chief Justice from by-passing members by consulting just two other members (as s 3(3) now permits).

office on terms 'no less favourable than before' (BL92); retirement benefits may not be diminished (BL93). New appointees to the judicial service are not guaranteed equal pay with their pre-1997 brethren and, as now, there is no provision that salaries shall not be subject to annual vote in the legislature.

Court structure

The Court of Final Appeal is of course a new body, replacing the Judicial Committee of the Privy Council. (Incidentally, vesting the SAR with 'independent judicial power, including that of final adjudication' (JD3(3)), does not necessarily entail abolition of appeals to the Judicial Committee, since the Committee could be considered a court *of the SAR*. But BL81 reposes the power of final adjudication in the Court of Final Appeal in the Region.) The Judicial Committee hears only a handful of appeals from Hong Kong each year and it may be wondered how the Court of Final Appeal will be organised and whether the judges who compose it will sit on the High Court as well.[17] The 'High Court' is not, as now, the lower tier of the Supreme Court but includes both the Court of Appeal and the clumsily-named 'Court of the First Instance' (BL80). Will the Court of the First Instance possess the appellate jurisdiction of the present High Court? (Note that the BLCC translation adopts more familiar terms — those currently in use — for the names of the courts.) BL80, by maintaining 'The judicial system previously in practice in Hong Kong,' might be held to prohibit the creation of new special courts and tribunals, which would be unfortunate.

Chief Justice

BL72 and 89 refer to 'the Chief Justice of the High Court,' BL47 and 88 to 'the Chief Justice of the Court of Final Appeal.' Are there to be two Chief Justices or, as is presumably intended, one Chief Justice who heads the judiciary and is able to sit on either superior court? (Again, the BLCC translation distinguishes between the 'chief judge' of the Court of Final Appeal and the 'chief judge' of the Supreme Court.) A report passed by the Executive Committee of the BLCC on 12 June 1987 stated:

> The Chief Justice should be the Chief Judge of the Court of Final Appeal and in keeping with the [criterion] that the judges of the Court

17 The report referred to in n 18 below says that judges of the Court of Final Appeal should not sit in the Court of Appeal; a fortiori, presumably, they should not sit in the High Court (Court of the First Instance) either.

of Final Appeal should not be members of the Court of Appeal or high court judges, the Chief Justice should only sit in the Court of Final Appeal.[18]

Precedent

The Hong Kong courts now regard themselves as bound by all decisions of the Privy Council and all decisions of the House of Lords on matters of English law.[19] If the common law and equity applying in the SAR are not considered English law but part of a separate system of Hong Kong law (see above) there can be no question of post-1997 decisions of courts outside the SAR court structure being binding. Whether pre-1997 Privy Council and House of Lords decisions should retain their present status may depend, in theory, on whether the new Court of Final Appeal regards itself as having the same freedom as the Privy Council and House of Lords to overturn its own decisions.[20] But Hong Kong courts have never been much concerned with the theory of precedent, and it seems likely that in the SAR the political reality of the change in sovereignty and the creation of a new legal order will force an attitude of genuine independence. The judges 'may refer to precedents in other common law jurisdictions' (BL83); they might well continue to be in sympathy with 'prevailing sentiments of a homogeneity of culture and tradition throughout the British Empire, reinforced by the mystique of a univocal common law as "a brooding omnipresence in the sky"';[21] doubtless they will recognise the utility of preserving a high degree of consistency with precedents elsewhere, particularly England. Ultimately, however, the decisional law of the SAR will be determined by SAR judges. The only threat to their autonomy is represented by Standing Committee interpretations of the Basic Law under BL169.

18 Final Report on Some Aspects of Final Adjudication and the Judicial System of the SAR, and the Role of an Independent Prosecuting Authority (passed by the Executive Committee on 12 June 1987), prepared by the special groups on law and the political structure of the SAR: CCBL–SG/LES/POS–FR01–870603(E).
19 See Peter Wesley-Smith, 'The Effect of *de Lasala* in Hong Kong' (1986) 28 *Malaya Law Review* 50; 'Recent Decisions on Precedent in Hong Kong' (1986) 16 *Hong Kong Law Journal* 268.
20 See A R Blackshield, *The Abolition of Privy Council Appeals: Judicial Responsibility and 'The Law for Australia'* (Adelaide: Adelaide Law Review Association, 1978) 53–59.
21 Ibid 47.

Judicial power

The courts of the SAR are to exercise the judicial power of the Region (BL79). This may mean that only *courts* may exercise judicial power and that courts may exercise *only* judicial power. If so, BL79 might well become, like its counterpart in the Australian constitution, a fertile source of constitutional litigation.

DEPARTMENT OF JUSTICE

The government is to be composed of departments, bureaux, divisions, and commissions (BL60 and note 3 to BL48(5)). The three main departments are the Department of Administration (presumably equivalent to the branches and departments, etc under the Chief Secretary), the Department of Finance (incorporating the branches and departments, etc under the Financial Secretary), and the Department of Justice. The heads are, respectively, the Administrative Secretary, the Financial Secretary, and the Secretary of Justice. What are the functions of the Department of Justice?

Such a body, abolished in 1959, was re-established in China 20 years later with the following tasks:

> To exercise unified control over the various organs under the Court; manage and train judicial cadres; set up and manage higher academic institutes on political and legal affairs; institute a system of notary lawyers; popularize the legal system; compile laws and decrees; establish contacts with other ministries and do other judicial and administrative work so as to insure the enforcement of all stipulations and state laws.[22]

In addition, the Department of Justice is responsible for training lawyers and procurators, supervising lawyers' work, and controlling lawyers' qualification and disqualification.[23] But few of these functions can be intended for the Department of Justice in the SAR. The judicial system previously practised, which leaves judicial administration to the Chief Justice and the registrars, is to be maintained except for changes consequent upon establishment of the Court of Final Appeal (BL80); educational institutions of all kinds, including those training lawyers, may retain

22 'Late Report: Fifth NPC Standing Committee Closes,' FBIS 13 September 1979, L18–L19, quoted by Stanley B Lubman, 'Emerging Functions of Formal Legal Institutions in China's Modernization' (1982) 3 *China Law Reporter* 195, 220.
23 Albert H Y Chen, 'The Developing Legal System in China' (1983) 13 *Hong Kong Law Journal* 291, 312.

their autonomy (BL144) and the educational system previously practised shall continue (BL142); notaries already exist; Hong Kong residents shall have the right of choice of lawyers to protect their rights and interests (BL34); and the methods of assessing and accrediting professional qualifications previously practised in Hong Kong may be maintained (BL150). This leaves popularisation of the legal system, compilation of laws, and ensuring the enforcement of laws (not prosecutions, which in China are the responsibility of the procuracy). The reference in BL63 to 'the prosecuting authority' suggests that prosecutions are not to belong to the Secretary of Justice.

The office of Attorney General is not mentioned in the Basic Law, and presumably the Department of Justice is to take its place. The Attorney General is now the 'compiler' of the statute book, and in various ways (as a senior member of ExCo, Chairman of the Chief Secretary's Legal Affairs Policy Group, Chairman of the Law Reform Commission, etc) he is involved with ensuring respect for the law. He has not been known to play an active role in popularising the legal system. One of his main functions, of course, is the initiation of criminal proceedings.

A report by the BLCC's special groups on law and the political structure of the SAR, issued in June 1987,[24] stated:

> A Minister of Justice potentially combines not only the roles of the Attorney General who may or may not be another official under his jurisdiction but also has responsibilities for immigration, security, the administration of the courts, prisons, perhaps the police and other matters which are related.

One proposal was that:

> Since the future Attorney General may be a political appointee, an independent prosecuting authority should be set up and that the head of such authority would be statutory, totally independent of the Attorney General and free from any interference.

It is not clear from the report that this proposal was endorsed by all members, but the report did recommend a provision which

---

24 See the report cited in n 18 above. For references to the question of instituting a Ministry of Justice in England: see John Ll J Edwards, *The Attorney General, Politics and the Public Interest* (London: Sweet & Maxwell, 1984) 193n. See also Jack I H Jacob, *The Fabric of English Civil Justice* (London: Stevens & Sons, 1987) 255–257. 'It is unfortunate that the name Minister of Justice has a sinister sound to many English ears, despite the fact that such a minister is commonly found in the most respectable countries': R M Jackson, *The Machinery of Justice in England* (Cambridge: University Press, 6th ed 1972) 547.

appears as BL63. Further, it was suggested that the role and accountability of the Attorney General be delineated by the SAR legislature. The report concluded:

> The question of the desirability of having a Minister of Justice was discussed but it was considered that in the context of Hong Kong, the combining together of the various tasks which are at present divided amongst various secretariats would not entail any benefits. Furthermore, if the Minister of Justice were to assume a wider function, the [power] at present exercised by the Attorney General either becomes fused with or confused with the power of the Minister of Justice. Concern was expressed that the Minister of Justice may exercise too wide a jurisdiction. It was considered undesirable that the holder of one office should simultaneously exercise functions relating to the judiciary, law and security. If there were to be a Minister of Justice and an Attorney General, it was clear that there would have to be a clear delineation of the roles, in particular the role of the Attorney General. The Attorney General's functions should therefore not be augmented into that of a Minister of Justice.

Since note 3 to the Basic Law refers separately to the Police Division and the Immigration Service Division, the Secretary of Justice cannot be intended to take over these functions. It seems likely that the Department of Justice will not be involved with judicial administration, legal education, or the supervision of lawyers; the Secretary will perform all the present functions of the Attorney General except for the institution of criminal proceedings, and his duties will not be augmented by new areas of responsibility. To call him a Secretary of Justice is somewhat misleading.

OTHER MATTERS

A few other points relating to the legal system may be briefly discussed.

Language

The only reference in the Basic Law to language is BL9:

> In addition to the Chinese language, the English language may also be used by the executive authorities, legislature and judicial organs of the Hong Kong Special Administrative Region.

This is in line with a provision in Annex I to the Joint Declaration. Does it mean the predominance of Chinese or equal status for Chinese and English? What are its ramifications for the literary sources of law, including the Basic Law itself?

The BLCC's special group on law favoured the ultimate development of a bilingual legal system in Hong Kong.[25] The difficulties in achieving this goal are immense, but the present Hong Kong government has committed itself to the project. All legislation is to be drafted in both languages, and both versions are to be equally authentic.[26] There is no intention to translate any portion of the common law into Chinese, and the higher courts will probably continue to use oral English. The BLCC report noted the convenience of maintaining the use of English in the higher courts, because of the language in which the legal training of most members of the legal profession has been conducted, the difficulty of translating common law legal concepts into Chinese, and the fact that English is the language of international trade, finance, and technology. The special group concluded that 'a functional approach should be adopted in tackling the language problem of the legal field brought about by the establishment of the SAR. Objective elements such as the availability of Chinese-proficient judges, lawyers and interpreters, etc, should be taken into consideration.'

BL9, which implies bilingualism, makes no provision for the gradual development of a fully bilingual system for the law. Few persons involved in the Hong Kong legal system now believe that both languages can be in equal use by 1 July 1997; in practice, therefore, BL9 is likely to be in some respects a dead letter for many years after the SAR is founded. A more attractive formulation would allow the SAR legislature to determine how bilingualism is to be achieved and over what period.

It has already been announced that the Basic Law is not to be available in English in a form equally authentic with the Chinese version.[27] But if the courts may interpret the Basic Law (BL169), and judges from other common law jurisdictions — who cannot be expected to be familiar with Chinese — may sit on the Court of Final Appeal (BL81), and many judges and lawyers in the SAR

25 Final Report on Language of the Law (passed by the Executive Committee on 8 August 1987): CCBL-SG/LES–WG01–FR02–870612(E). See also Albert H Y Chen, '1997: The Language of the Law' (1985) 15 *Hong Kong Law Journal* 19 and, for a sceptical view, Henry Litton, 'A Question of Interpretation,' *Far Eastern Economic Review* 7 April 1988, p 82.

26 See the Interpretation and General Clauses (Amendment) Ordinance 1987 and the Official Languages (Amendment) Ordinance 1987. These statutes will continue through 1997 unless regarded as inconsistent with the Basic Law (see BL172).

27 See Emily Lau, 'A Language Problem,' *Far Eastern Economic Review* 18 February 1988, p 34.

period will be illiterate in Chinese, the lack of an authentic translation of the post-1997 constitution will be a serious impediment to genuine judicial power.

Access to law

BL34 preserves the right of access to lawyers and the courts and the right to challenge in the courts 'the actions of the executive organs or their personnel' (in the BLCC translation, 'the actions of the executive or members of the executive ... '). Do 'the executive organs' include the CE? Chapter IV on political structure seems to distinguish between the CE (section 1) and 'the executive authorities' (section 2); BL64 (which is in section 2) follows Annex I to the Joint Declaration in specifying that the executive authorities shall abide by the law, but no clause in section 1 similarly obliges the CE (being 'dedicated to his/her duties' (BL47) has a somewhat different meaning). In ordinary constitutional parlance a CE is an executive organ or authority, and the CE is head of the SAR government (BL60) which constitutes the executive authorities (BL59). It can therefore be assumed that the CE, like lesser personnel charged with executive power, must abide by the law (and be accountable to LegCo under BL64) and is not subject solely to investigation by committee for a 'serious breach of law' (BL72(9)). But the juxtaposition of clauses leaves regrettable room for doubt. It should not be even faintly arguable that the CE in the SAR is in a more favoured position than the colonial Governor by virtue of immunity from judicial process.

Jury system

'The principle of trial by jury previously practised in Hong Kong shall be maintained' (BL85). Some provision for maintenance of the jury system is certainly desirable, but it would be unfortunate if BL85 were to prohibit improvements or extensions of jury trial.

Localisation

Only permanent residents who are Chinese nationals may be CE (BL44), members of the Executive Council (BL55), principal officials (BL61), President of the LegCo (BL70, first alternative), or holders of certain posts (BL100), and a period of ordinary residence is required in some instances (20 years for the CE and President of LegCo, 15 years for principal officials). Thus 'localisation' in the executive and legislative spheres is constitutionally ordained. But no such provisions apply to the judiciary.

Redress of grievances

The CE's functions include the handling of petitions and complaints (BL48(13)), while the LegCo may 'receive and deal with complaints' (BL72(8)). This is presumably not intended to preempt the powers of the proposed ombudsman, whose office is not mentioned. A BLCC special group concluded that, after 1997:

> An ombudsman's office should be set up as an independent statutory body to deal with complaints. The ombudsman should be nominated by the chief executive, approved by the legislature and appointed by the Central People's Government.[28]

The special group also recommended that the Independent Commission Against Corruption should remain independent and be accountable only to the CE. The Basic Law says that a 'Commission Against Corruption shall be established' (BL57) and refers to the Commissioner Against Corruption in BL100 but ignores the ombudsman. This should not be taken to imply that the ombudsman's office is undesirable or constitutionally forbidden.

Committee for the Basic Law

This is referred to in note 2 but will presumably earn its own separate clause in the next draft. Its role in advising the NPC and the Standing Committee is obviously of first importance; without knowing its composition or how its members are to be chosen one cannot assess its desirability,[29] and failure to incorporate such details into the draft considerably diminishes the ability of

28 Although 'Another view has also been expressed that the Commissioner for Administration/Ombudsman should be appointed by the chief executive after approval by the legislature': Final Report on Security, Law and Order, ICAC, and Other Avenues of Complaint (passed by the Executive Committee on 12 June 1987): CCBL–SG/POS–WG05–FR01–870610(E).

29 See the Final Report on the Basic Law Committee (by the special group on law; passed by the Executive Committee on 5 December 1987): CCBL–SG/LES–RP04–871201(E) and Opinions on 'HKSAR Basic Law Committee' by the special group on the relationship between the Central Government and the SAR (passed by the Executive Committee on 5 December 1987): CCBL–SG/RCS–RS03–871111(E).

Hong Kong people to comment on the proposed constitutional system.[30] Some such body is a common feature of autonomous regions elsewhere.[31]

CONCLUSION

It is perhaps too much to expect elegant or uplifting language in the Basic Law, but we can legitimately demand of the drafters that the SAR constitution be clear, readily comprehensible, consistent, coherent, and capable of being obeyed. At another level, we can insist that there be no significant deviation from the Joint Declaration, that there be a genuine high degree of autonomy for the SAR, and that 'one country, two systems' be thoroughly respected. Finally, the public response to the discussion draft is entitled to careful consideration in good faith before the BLDC completes its work. This chapter reveals some grave deficiencies of both drafting technique and substance. The whole exercise of soliciting opinions will be a sham if the next draft of the Basic Law is not greatly improved.

30 See the Final Report on the Basic Law Committee (by the special group on law; passed by the Executive Committee on 5 December 1987): CCBL–SG/LES–RP04–871201(E) ('It would not be fair to the Hong Kong public to keep them in the dark about the precise terms of reference, criteria for membership (as distinguished from actual membership), etc of the BLC while expecting them to discuss and accept the provisions of the draft Basic Law which refers to the BLC'). The division of the CBL into two committees (political and legal) proposed by the special group on law is thoroughly deserving of endorsement.

31 See Hurst Hannum and Richard B Lillich, 'The Concept of Autonomy in International Law' in Yoram Dinstein (ed), *Models of Autonomy* (New Brunswick and London: Transaction Books, 1981) 215.

10 Protection of Civil Liberties

JOHANNES CHAN

CONCEPTUAL BACKGROUND

The following is an edited version of a dialogue which allegedly took place in a meeting between members of the Basic Law Drafting Committee and members of the Basic Law Consultative Committee:

A: The Basic Law is like the son of the PRC constitution. How can the Basic Law, as a piece of local legislation, exclude the provisions of her mother constitution without becoming a bastard child?

B: Oh, no! This is never the intention. The mother constitution is like the sun, right up in the middle of the sky. It shines on every part of the land, and brings warmth and peace to the people. But in a small corner of the land, could there not be a coloured sunshade, so that the sunshine filtered through is not red in colour?

C: The people of that corner are too fragile, and even the filtered sunshine is too strong for them. Could we not have an opaque sunshade, just for that little corner?

This dialogue reflects the basic problems of the idea of 'one country, two systems.' Politically it is the first attempt in the world to make socialism and capitalism cohabit under one single regime. Constitutionally it represents an unwilling marriage between a highly sophisticated westernised legal system and an embryonic socialist legal structure. Economically it brings together a highly competitive capitalist system and an inferior but ambitious and rapidly changing economy. Legally it attempts to build up a sandwiched structure: at the bottom of this structure is the common law protection of human rights, upon which is superimposed a politically powerful socialist regime. Yet this socialist framework itself is engulfed by an international order of human rights. Can such a system work? How are these different ideologies and orientations reflected in the Basic Law? How can they be reconciled with one another, particularly in the context of human rights? What difficulties, both conceptual and practical, have been encountered in the drafting process? How are they resolved, if at all?

The basic problem is how much emphasis should be put on 'one country' and how much on 'two systems.' The nationalists insist that sovereignty must be manifest in designing the system of the SAR, whereas the pragmatists stress that political confidence and economic viability should be the primary concern. Neither could be entirely right, or entirely wrong. As there are to be two systems, the two systems must be insulated from one another and must be able to function independently, efficiently, and smoothly. Yet as one single country, there should be doors and windows which allow free flow between the two systems. These are probably all uncontroversial. The controversy is: how many windows should be open? And can the doors be locked?

DRAFTING PROCESS

From April 1985 to April 1988 seven plenary sessions of the BLDC were held. The timetable of the drafting process was agreed at the first plenary session. The 'structure' of the Basic Law was adopted at the second plenary session, and at the same time, five sub-groups were set up to work on the detailed provisions of five specified topics. Each member of the committee was allowed to join not more than two sub-groups. The two most controversial topics — the central-local relationship and the political system of the SAR — attracted all of the most outspoken Hong Kong members, most of the senior PRC members, and almost all the lawyers from both sides. The restriction on the number of sub-groups one could join resulted in a poorly staffed (in terms of common law legal expertise) sub-group on the fundamental rights and duties of Hong Kong residents. The sub-group was jointly chaired by Simon Li, a retired judge of the Court of Appeal of Hong Kong, and Wang Shuwen, Director, Institute of Legal Research, Chinese Academy of Social Science. The rest of the Hong Kong members included Tam Yiu-chung, a Legislative Councillor who represents the pro-China labour unions, Lau Wong-fat, another Legislative Councillor who represents the interests of the indigenous inhabitants of the New Territories, Peter K K Kwong, Bishop of the Hong Kong and Macau diocese of the Anglican Church, and a Buddhist monk, Kwok Kwong, President of the Hong Kong Buddhist Association. The other two mainland members of this sub-group are Chen Xen, Secretary to the Central United Front Office, and Lin Hengyuan, Chairman of the legal group of the National Political Consultative Committee. Lin was a practising lawyer before 1949, and took part in drafting the 1978 constitution of the People's Republic of China. One should not overlook the fact that the sub-group was staffed by three members, one from the New China News Agency and the background of the other two being unknown.[1] Apparently, it is these supporting staff who actually prepared the various drafts. The sub-group's lack of common law expertise resulted in a draft which bears close resemblance to the PRC constitution. The background of the members may also explain the presence of some of the provisions in chapter III of the Basic Law.

Drafting a bill of rights for Hong Kong is a highly technical task. It requires familiarity with the common law system and, in particular, with the operation of the existing legal system in Hong Kong. Yet the only member in the sub-group who is familiar with the Hong Kong legal system is Simon Li. Being one of the two convenors of the sub-group, understandably he exerted a dominant influence on the proceedings. However, some of his views were not shared by the legal profession in Hong Kong. It was therefore unfortunate that the proceedings of the sub-group were almost closed to the legal profession, at least at the early stage of the drafting process.

The first draft by the sub-group was produced in November 1986.[2] The draft which the sub-group produced five months later was almost identical to the first. It was only in the third draft, produced in August 1987, that some significant changes were made. This might partly be the result of the lobbying efforts of the legal profession in Hong Kong. A few influential essays by lawyers and academics found their way into the proceedings of the sub-group as working papers, and some of the recommendations contained in these essays were adopted, or appeared as minority views in the explanatory memorandum of the subsequent drafts of December 1987 and April 1988.[3] Nevertheless,

1 See *Ming Pao* 22 April 1986. The two other members were staff provided by the mainland.

2 The reports containing the various drafts may be found in the 'Collection of Documents' of the 3rd, 4th, 5th, 6th and 7th plenary sessions of the BLDC, compiled by the BLDC Secretariat after each respective plenary session.

3 See Report on the Discussion on the 'Principles and Specific Questions regarding the Fundamental Rights and Freedoms of Hong Kong Inhabitants' BLCC (4 November 1987). Also see J Chan, 'Comments on the Third Report of the Sub-group on Fundamental Rights and Obligations of Hong Kong Residents' (1987) 181 *Wide Angle* 74 (in Chinese); J Chan, 'Comments on the Discussion Paper on Fundamental Rights of Residents in the Basic Law' in A Chen and J Chan, *Human Rights and the Rule of Law—The Challenges of Hong Kong's Transition* (Hong Kong: Wide Angle Press, 1987) 94–103 (in Chinese); J Chan, 'Basic Law and the Rights and Freedoms of Hong Kong Residents' ibid 76–84; and A Chen, 'International Human Rights Covenants and Hong Kong' ibid 85–93. The last four papers were included by the BLDC Secretariat as reference materials for the BLDC.

despite strong criticism by the legal profession of some provisions, chapter III of the Basic Law of April 1988 is on the whole
fairly similar to the first draft produced by the sub-group in
November 1986.

ANALYSIS OF THE BASIC RIGHTS

Chapter III, entitled 'the fundamental rights and duties of
residents,' runs from BL23 to BL42. BL23 defines the meaning of
'Hong Kong SAR residents.' Various fundamental rights are set
out in BL24 to BL41. BL42 sets out the obligation to abide by the
laws of the SAR. On top of these one has to add the right of property ownership (BL6), the principle of jury trial (BL85), rights
enjoyed by litigants in civil and criminal proceedings (BL86),
political rights of participation in state affairs (BL20), rights
concerning land (BL126–128), and various social, economic, and
cultural rights in chapter VI. In this chapter the history and
content of the major provisions will be analysed. Social,
economic, and cultural rights will be the subject of Chapter 11.

Obligation clause (BL42)

It seems odd to examine the obligation clause first when the
purpose of this section is to examine fundamental rights! Perhaps
the presence of an obligation clause itself is odd enough. To a
Western lawyer duties are just another way of looking at rights.
Once there is a right there is a correlative duty on other persons
not to violate the right. Certain basic rights are inherent in the
nature of human beings. They transcend national legislation,
which has to comply with this higher order of human rights. Thus
it does not make much sense to talk about duties independently
of rights. However, in some socialist theories, there are no such
things as inherent rights of mankind. Rights and duties form
different components of a collective society and are ultimately
determined by the relations of production. Rights come from the
constitution and the law. To enjoy certain rights one has to
discharge certain obligations. This ideological difference is
reflected in the drafting process of the Basic Law. For example,
the title of chapter III is nearly identical to the corresponding
chapter in the PRC constitution. Since the title refers to duties,
BL42 is insisted upon by the mainland members. To a common
law lawyer this clause seems to be stating the obvious, and
acceptance of this clause does not by itself impose any real
obligation. Yet its absence would not be acceptable to the
mainland members. Indeed, in the drafting process it has been

queried whether there should be more provisions on obligations in order to redress the balance between rights and duties. Among those mentioned are duties to take care of and respect the national flag, national emblem, and national song, and to respect national leaders (see the 'Collection of Opinions of Drafting Members on the Preamble, General Principles, and the Provisions of Chapters Two, Three, Seven and Nine,' compiled by the Secretariat of the BLDC in May 1987). These suggestions did not, however, receive adequate support in the BLDC.

BL42 applies to both Hong Kong residents and other persons in Hong Kong. This is again obvious: any person within the jurisdiction should abide by the laws of the SAR. However, it seems that the phrase 'other persons' does not include legal persons and members of the garrison. All rights and freedoms contained in chapter III are hinged on the concept of Hong Kong residents. Accordingly, when the phrase 'other persons' is used as opposed to Hong Kong residents, it should probably be confined to natural persons. This is unfortunate as there is no reason why a legal person should not receive constitutional protection of its freedom of expression or right to judicial remedies. It would be sad if a company deprived of its right to property ownership were also deprived of its right to seek judicial remedies. Whether members of the garrison would be caught by this provision has been discussed, but the conclusion is not clear (see the explanatory note to article 19 of the Progress Report of 13 April 1987 in 'Collection of Documents for the Fourth Plenary Session of the Drafting Committee,' Secretariat of the BLDC, 1987). However, exclusion of the members of the garrison is not significant, as they are clearly under the same duty by virtue of BL13. In addition, members of the garrison shall abide by nationwide laws irrespective of whether these laws apply to the SAR or not. Two questions arise from BL13: first, what should be the position if there is a conflict between nationwide law and the law of the SAR? This may, for instance, arise in a case of succession when a member of the garrison dies in Hong Kong. Second, if a member of the garrison commits a crime in Hong Kong, should he be subject to the jurisdiction of the Hong Kong court or to some court martial? Space limitation does not allow discussion of either question here.

Equality before the law (BL24)

It may be interesting to compare BL24 with article 26 of the International Covenant on Civil and Political Rights and article 5 of Annex 1 of the Sino-Portuguese Joint Declaration:

Article 24

All Hong Kong residents shall be equal before the law, regardless of their nationality, race, ethnic origin, language, sex, occupation, religious belief, political views, educational level and property status.

Article 26

All persons are equal before the law and are entitled without any discrimination to the equal protection of the law. In this respect, the law shall prohibit any discrimination and guarantee to all persons equal and effective protection against discrimination on any ground such as race, colour, sex, language, religion, political or other opinion, national or social origin, property birth or other status.

Article 5

The inhabitants and other persons in the Macau Special Administrative Region are equal before the law and shall be free from discrimination, irrespective of nationality, descent, sex, race, language, religion, political or ideological belief, educational level, financial status or social condition.

This comparison reveals two deficiencies in BL24. First, it does not include the right to non-discrimination. Second, it does not prohibit unequal treatment on the basis of social condition (or social origin), birth, or ideological belief.

While the phrase 'equality before the law' has found its way into many international and national instruments, its elusive character has made it less popular in many modern bills of rights. Canada adopted this phrase in her Bill of Rights 1960; yet it was amended to 'every individual is equal before and under the law and has the right to equal protection and equal benefit of the law without discrimination . . .' in the Canadian Charter of Rights and Freedoms 1982.[4] New Zealand, in her proposed Bill of Rights 1985, dropped the phrase altogether and preferred to state simply the right to freedom from discrimination.[5] The Canadian experience is worth noting. The plain meaning of the phrase is that every person, be he a king, a nobleman, the devil, or an idiot, will be subject to the Rule of Law. No one is above the law, and no one will be spared the full rigour of the law. Yet it is equally clear that it is impossible, and indeed unfair, to apply the same law to all persons. It would be absurd to say that a male worker should be entitled to maternity leave, or a juvenile offender should be subject to the same treatment as an adult offender. In other words, equality before the law does not prohibit class legislation. What it requires is that the law should be applied

4 For a detailed account: see Hogg, *Constitutional Law of Canada* (Toronto: Carswell, 2nd ed 1985) 787–802.
5 *A Bill of Rights for New Zealand* (New Zealand Home Office, 1985) 85–87.

equally to every person within the class. This is accepted by the Canadian Supreme Court[6] where 'equality before the law' was defined as 'equality of treatment in the enforcement and application of the law.' However, such a requirement would not be infringed even if the law levies a birth tax on every new-born male child. This is a fairly narrow, and unfortunate, interpretation. In order to prohibit discrimination based on unreasonable classification, many modern bills of rights include the right to freedom from discrimination. It is thus suggested that BL24 be amended as follows:

> Hong Kong residents shall be equal before the law, and shall be entitled to the equal protection of the law without discrimination on grounds of nationality, race, ethnic or social origin, language, sex, occupation, religious or ethical belief, political views, education level, birth, property or marital status.

The author has included four additional grounds for non-discrimination. Social origin does not appear in the present formulation. This term is included in the International Covenant as well as the Sino-Portuguese Joint Declaration. It would outlaw the famous 'five black categories' prevailing in the Cultural Revolution. Inclusion of 'birth' would mean that any distinction on the basis of illegitimacy would be unlawful, whereas 'marital status' would render a law imposing different tax rates on the basis of marriage discriminatory. The last addition of ethical belief needs some explanation. In the first and second drafts the phrase *zong jiao xin yang*, which could mean 'religion and belief' or simply 'religious belief,' was used. Some people expressed concern that this ambiguous wording would allow discrimination on the basis of political beliefs. In the third draft of August 1987, the phrase was amended to become *zong jiao, xin yang*, that is, 'religion and belief.' This did not lessen the worries. So it was further amended in the fourth draft to *zong jiao, xin yang, zheng jian*, which is the present version. Yet this seems to divide beliefs into either religious or political beliefs. People may raise conscientious objections to a lot of issues which can be classified as neither religious nor political. Thus the author would propose the inclusion of 'ethical belief.'

It is not clear whether BL24 applies only to government action or is intended to regulate private relationships among ordinary citizens as well. Under the existing legal system in Hong Kong, it is still doubtful whether an action of discrimination exists under common law.[7] BL24 provides a constitutional basis for such an

---

6 *AG of Canada v Lavell* (1974) 5 SCR 1349.
7 See *Bladauria v Board of Applied Arts and Technology* (1980) 105 DLR (3d) 707.

action, at least in the public sector. Extension of BL24 to private actions may have a profound impact on a lot of purely economic or contractual relationships. The potential use of BL24 depends very much on the imagination of the judiciary. As time passes, it may well prove to be the most powerful provision in chapter III.

Right to vote and to stand for election (BL25)

The limitation under BL25 of the right to vote and to stand for election to those who have reached 21 years of age has been under some criticism. This is unnecessarily rigid, and would make it extremely difficult to change the age requirement when circumstances warrant it in the future. In fact, the first draft of chapter III was released at more or less the same time as the Law Reform Commission's report on the age of majority. The Law Reform Commission, after two years' study, recommended the lowering of the age of majority from 21 to 18. Although the voting age was expressly left out from their terms of reference, the Commission expressed the view that there was no reason why it should not be brought into line with the general lowering of the age of majority. The recommendations of the Law Reform Commission (on matters within their terms of reference) were warmly received and will soon be implemented by the Hong Kong government.

Despite such background and strong criticism from many sectors, the age of election was still specified in the Basic Law. Even more disappointing is that the BLDC never explained the rationale for retention of the provision. In the fourth report (December 1987) the sub-group stated, in the explanatory note, that 'after research and consultation the age of 21 for election is considered appropriate.' This could hardly be considered a satisfactory explanation.[8]

The Basic Law has to be in force until 2047. Public perceptions of what should be the proper age of election could change with social circumstances. It would certainly be more flexible if the

8 In an informal discussion with some of the members of the sub-group, the author asked what research had been carried out and who had been consulted. The answer was that 'research and consultation' referred to the meetings with various sectors of people in Hong Kong by a delegation of mainland BLDC members led by Lu Ping in early January 1986. The delegation stayed in Hong Kong for several weeks only. The people they met were not selected on any rational or scientific basis. The topics of discussion ranged widely, and any conclusion reached would necessarily be superficial and unrepresentative. It would be disappointing if this was what 'consultation' and 'research' meant.

age of election could be left to the future legislature. It is suggested that BL25 be rewritten as follows:

> Permanent residents of the Hong Kong SAR shall have the right to vote and the right to stand for election as prescribed by law.

Another problem arises from BL20, which provides for election of deputies of the SAR to the National People's Congress. Presumably the age requirement in BL25 would apply to BL20. Yet it has been suggested that the Organic Law of the National People's Congress and the relevant Electoral Law should apply to the SAR. Under article 3 of the Electoral Law of the National People's Congress and People's Congresses at All Levels, the age when one exercises one's right to vote is 18. This raises an important question of possible conflict between a nationwide law applicable to the SAR and the Basic Law, on which no answer is provided by the Basic Law. Equally silent is the question of conflict between nationwide laws and local laws. On this particular aspect, probably the more specific provision of the Electoral Law would prevail over the more general provision of BL25. If this were so it might create the awkward situation of BL25 prevailing over the corresponding provision in the PRC constitution (see below) but yet itself being subject to a national law (ie the Electoral Law) on exactly the same subject matter!

A further problem with BL20 is that only those Hong Kong residents who are Chinese nationals are entitled to participate in state affairs. While it may not be an unreasonable requirement, it depends on how widely the words 'state affairs' would be construed. Incidentally, although it is not expressly spelt out, the right to stand for election in BL25 is subject to other provisions in the Basic Law which lay down other limitations, on age, nationality, or otherwise, in relation to various principal positions of the SAR government (see BL43, 61 and 100). The restriction of so many top positions in the government and the civil service to Chinese nationals among permanent SAR residents may well frustrate and lower the morale of many civil servants who have applied for or obtained foreign passports. Many of them may wish to stay in Hong Kong for as long as possible. Yet there may be no point in working up the civil service ladder when one can already see the limits of one's future career.

Freedom of expression, assembly, and association (BL26)

BL26 is one of the most important provisions in chapter III: it covers three major freedoms: freedom of expression, freedom of association, and freedom of assembly. Given the importance of this provision, it is surprising that BL26 attracted only a little attention. This is partly because attention was diverted to the limitation of 'in accordance with law' in the earlier drafts, a subject which will be discussed more fully below. As far as the substantive provision is concerned, the criticism raised is typical of the conflict between the demands of 'brevity' and 'clarity.' On freedom of speech, it has been pointed out that it is unclear whether it includes the right to receive information of all kinds regardless of frontier. Under section 2 of the Official Secrets Act 1911, the right to official information is almost non-existent. This British Act, which applies to Hong Kong by Order in Council, would not survive the change of sovereignty. At the same time, BL22 would require the SAR government to enact, inter alia, laws against espionage and spying. In order to ensure that section 2 of the Official Secrets Act is not reproduced, it has been suggested that the right to information should be entrenched in the Basic Law.

Another suggestion which has been put forward is to entrench the right to form and join political parties and organisations. This proposal has to be understood in the context of the debate about direct election of the legislature and the Chief Executive in Hong Kong. One of the arguments against direct election is that it would result in the emergence of political parties. In order to please and win the support of the masses, these political parties would inevitably advocate more welfare policies, which may not be in the best interests of the Hong Kong economy. This is known as the 'free lunch' argument. Besides, once political parties are allowed in Hong Kong, the most powerful political party would no doubt be the Communist Party across the border. The democrats, on the other hand, argue that the existence of political parties is not a bad thing. The consistent party line, better use of resources, and the maintenance of internal discipline are among the advantages mentioned. Pressure groups have emerged in Hong Kong since the 1980s. Most them are politically oriented and take a prominent and active part in elections at district levels. They may worry about their existence after 1997 and would, understandably, like to see the right to form political parties and organisations entrenched.

A liberal interpretation of freedom of speech and freedom of association may well render the above suggestions redundant. While the right to official information, because of its special nature, would probably be worth writing into the Basic Law, it is difficult to see how freedom of association would not include the freedom to form or join a political party or organisation. Besides, it may not be easy to determine whether a particular association is a political organisation or not. While the author tends to think this suggestion unnecessary, there is at least no harm, given the

political context of Hong Kong, to insert this right into BL26 in
order to ease the worry.

It may be interesting to note that freedom of the press, freedom
of demonstration, and freedom to strike, which are in BL26, are
not included in the corresponding provision in the PRC constitution. Indeed, freedom to strike, which existed in the 1978
constitution, was deliberately taken out in the 1982 constitution.
Would freedom to strike in the Basic Law be ultra vires the PRC
constitution? This raises a wider and more complicated question
of the relationship between the PRC constitution and the Basic
Law. It is not only politically but also theoretically impossible to
exclude the constitution in the Basic Law. The problem is indeed
inherent in the concept of 'one country, two systems.' The Basic
Law cannot deny the authority or status of national organs such
as the NPC, or the national flag, or Beijing as the capital of the
country, which are all laid down in the constitution. Indeed, to
exclude the PRC constitution in the Basic Law would itself be
unconstitutional! On the other hand, it is certainly the intention
of Beijing to preserve the existing capitalist system and life-style
in Hong Kong. Attempts have been made during the drafting
process to spell out which constitutional provisions could and
should apply; these attempts soon proved futile, and it was
accepted that such an abstract classification was impossible and
unrealistic. This insoluble problem was eventually dealt with in a
subtle way in BL17, which, despite much criticism of its
linguistic ambiguity, may be regarded as first-class drafting.
Without referring to the constitution, it seems to imply that only
those constitutional provisions which 'give expression to
national unity and territorial integrity and which, in accordance
with the provisions of the [Basic Law], are outside the limits of
the high degree of autonomy of the Hong Kong SAR' will apply
to the SAR. It is therefore submitted that whenever a provision
exists in both the Basic Law and the PRC constitution, it is the
Basic Law which prevails, insofar as the SAR is concerned. In
other words, the whole of chapter III of the Basic Law will
exclude all the corresponding provisions on fundamental rights
and duties in the PRC constitution. Thus when BL34 of the PRC
constitution provides that 18 should be the voting age, and BL24
of the Basic Law specifies 21 as the voting age, it is necessarily
implied that BL24 is the over-riding provision!

Freedom of the person (BL27 and 28)

BL27 protects Hong Kong residents from being unlawfully
arrested, detained, imprisoned, or searched. BL28 goes on to
prohibit unlawful search and intrusion into a resident's home or

other premises. With respect, these two articles seem to be stating the obvious. If the arrest, detention, or search is unlawful, there is already a remedy under the existing law. Yet if the arrest, detention, or search is lawful but oppressive, these two clauses provide no additional protection. Suppose a person is waiting for his friend in the street. A police officer, with no reasonable grounds whatsoever, forms an intuitive suspicion of him and searches him bodily. Nothing is found and he is released. Can he bring an action against the police officer or the government for violation of BL27? Under section 54 of the Police Force Ordinance, a police officer can stop and search any person about whom he or she has an intuitive suspicion. We may think this is draconian and despotic, but it is, nevertheless, lawful!

Most powers of arrest, detention, and search are granted by legislation. In Hong Kong there are over 70 provisions in different ordinances which give powers of arrest to police and other public officers. Indeed, the law is so vague and incomprehensible that no one really knows exactly what the law is.[9] The existence of BL27 does not improve the situation. Obviously what has to be guarded against is arbitrary rather than unlawful deprivation of liberty. 'Arbitrary' is a concept universally adopted in many international and national instruments. Article 9 of the International Covenant on Civil and Political Rights protects persons against arbitrary arrest and detention. The suggestion to replace 'arbitrary' by 'unlawful' has, however, been expressly rejected in the drafting process. In tracing the drafting history of the relevant provision in the International Covenant, which lasted almost two decades, Hassan concluded that it was clear that the word 'arbitrary' was accepted by the international community to mean both 'illegal' and 'unjust.'[10] The author would submit that the word 'arbitrary' connotes the absence of legal authority, compliance with legal procedure, and an objective standard for assessment, in addition to the exclusion of improper or extraneous considerations and an element of irrationality, unfairness, and unreasonableness. A lawful power may still be arbitrary if the power is oppressive or unreasonably vague. It is therefore recommended that the word 'lawful' be replaced by 'arbitrary' in BL27 and 28. The author would also add that the rejection of the word 'arbitrary' by the BLDC was

---

9 Johannes Chan, 'Police Power of Arrest and Seizure' in *Law Lectures for Practitioners 1988* (Hong Kong: Hong Kong Law Journal, forthcoming).
10 P Hassan, 'The International Covenant on Civil and Political Rights: Background and Perspective on Article 9(1)' (1973) 3 (No 2) *Denver Journal of International Law and Policy* 153.

probably due to the elusive meaning conveyed by its Chinese translation (*ren yi*).[11] However, linguistic problems should never be an excuse for a complete denial of substantive justice.

'In accordance with law' and the limitation clause (BL39)

This takes us to the concept that rights and freedoms are only protected 'in accordance with law.' It was argued that no freedom is absolute and there must be legitimate restrictions of rights and freedoms. From this basic proposition, it was inferred that no one should be allowed to transgress the law in the name of exercising his rights and freedoms. Thus the phrase 'in accordance with law' appeared in many provisions on fundamental rights in the first draft produced by the sub-group. In particular, BL15 of the first preliminary draft provided that 'the rights and freedoms of Hong Kong residents shall not be limited save in accordance with law.' This concept of 'in accordance with law' is dangerous, as it would mean that fundamental rights and freedoms would be left at the mercy of the legislature, with no restriction on the enactment of draconian laws at all. Now one of the major functions of a bill of rights is to restrain the legislature from arbitrarily taking away fundamental rights, and this function would be completely defeated by the formula of 'in accordance with law.' Strong criticisms were voiced and it was suggested that this phrase should be deleted. The drafters were, however, unhappy about its deletion. Eventually, in November 1987, a proposal by this author was accepted as a 'trade off' for replacing BL15 and the phrase 'in accordance with law' in most of the provisions.[12] This proposal appears as the present BL39. It recognises the worry about unlimited freedom, and tries to strike a balance between protection of human rights and legitimate restriction on reasonable grounds. The clause itself is modelled closely on typical limitations clauses in international human rights instruments in order to bring in international jurispru-

11 See the *Report on the Exchange Session between the Special Group on Fundamental Rights and Duties of Hong Kong Inhabitants and Members of the Corresponding Sub-group of the Drafting Committee,* (BLCC, 4 November 1987).

12 See Appendix 1, *Report on the Discussion on the 'Principles and Specific Questions regarding the Fundamental Rights and Freedoms of Hong Kong Inhabitants'* (BLCC, 4 November 1987). The full submission can be found in J Chan, 'Comments on the Third Report of the Sub-group on Fundamental Rights and Obligations of Hong Kong Residents' (1987) 181 *Wide Angle* 74. The author made a slight amendment in the published version: see n 15 below.

dence to assist interpretation. If any restriction could not be justified under this article, such restriction would be unconstitutional and judicial remedies would be available.

Under BL39, any restriction must be shown to be 'necessary' and necessity should be decided by the court. Necessity, as interpreted by current international jurisprudence, means the existence of a pressing social need and the requirement of proportionality in relation to any measures adopted (vis-à-vis the legitimate needs).[13] However, what is necessary in a socialist state may be different from that which is necessary in a capitalist city, and what is necessary in a totalitarian country would be different from that in a liberal democratic society. Thus in many international human rights instruments, it is required that the restriction be 'necessary in a democratic society.' This is not a mere political statement, as there are plenty of jurisprudential analyses and court decisions on the meaning of this phrase. Briefly speaking, the essence of a democratic society is plurality, tolerance, and broadmindedness.[14] Free political debate has been held to be at the core of a democratic society. Certainly it is the intention that the SAR is to remain a free and democratic society, and any restriction should be examined in this context. In such circumstances, it is submitted that this intention should be clearly spelt out.[15] This will bring the Basic Law into conformity with numerous leading international human rights instruments and allow reference to be made to many common law countries with a similar phrase in their constitutional bills of rights. More specifically, it is suggested that the last sentence of BL39 should be amended to read:

> ... but such restrictions shall not go beyond the necessity for the maintenance of national security, public order, public safety, public health, public morals and for the safeguarding of the rights and freedoms of other persons in a free and democratic society.

Despite amendment to the earlier draft of BL39, the phrase 'in accordance with law' is still retained in BL5, 23, and 41. BL5 was

---

13 *Sunday Times v UK* (1979) 2 EHRR 245; *Handyside v UK* (1978) 1 EHRR 737; *Dudgeon v UK* (1981) 4 EHRR 149.

14 Ibid. See also *Lingens v Austria* (1986) 8 EHRR 407; *Re Compulsory Membership of Journalists Association* (1986) 8 EHRR 165.

15 The phrase 'in a democratic society' was not included in the author's submission to the BLDC because it was considered that a proposal without this contentious phrase might be more politically acceptable at that time, and would stand a better chance of being accepted. This phrase appeared in the version which was published subsequently: see n 3 above and J Chan, 'Comments on the Discussion Paper on Fundamental Rights of Residents in the Basic Law' in A Chen and J Chan, *Human Rights and the Rule of Law – The Challenges of Hong Kong's Transition* (n 3 above) 94–103 (in Chinese).

drafted by a different sub-group of the BLDC. It is submitted that BL39 is sufficient to mitigate the worry about unlimited freedom. The formula 'in accordance with law' may well put the legislature above the Basic Law. The author would suggest that the redundant phrase 'in accordance with law' in BL5 and 23 be deleted.

BL41 is a little more complicated and requires slightly different treatment. At present, the restriction on legislative encroachment of rights and freedoms in BL39 only applies to Hong Kong residents. It does not apply to rights and freedoms of persons other than Hong Kong residents, who can only enjoy their rights and freedoms in accordance with law. So the rights and freedoms of transient tourists, expatriate businessmen, or newly arrived foreign clergy would all be at the mercy of the legislature. It is difficult to see why a foreigner's freedom of expression or right to judicial remedies should be subject to more stringent controls than those of a Hong Kong resident. The present drafting is unfair to foreigners and would be detrimental to the status of Hong Kong as an international city.

It is accepted that foreigners may not enjoy the right to free entry to the SAR, the right to election, and the right to social welfare. Special rules may have to apply to them. However, the present formulation goes far beyond these rights and covers every fundamental right. An alternative formulation of BL40 is therefore suggested:

> Persons in the Hong Kong SAR other than Hong Kong residents shall, insofar as applicable, enjoy the same rights and freedoms co-extensive with those of Hong Kong residents as prescribed in this chapter.

Freedom and privacy of communication (BL29)

This provision extends the common law, which has not yet recognised privacy as an actionable right.[16] It requires the SAR government to enact law to protect privacy of communication. The scope of this article depends on the meaning of 'communication.' It is clear from the drafting process that communication includes not only 'written correspondence' (*tong xin*), a phrase which has been rejected, but also any kind of oral or electronic communication.[17] Privacy is a complicated area of the law. It

16 *Malone v Metropolitan Police Commissioner* [1979] Ch 344.
17 In the second report of the sub-group it was said that correspondence (*tong xin*) was a better word as 'communication' (*tong xin*) included telephone and telex, which were subject to licencing requirements. Thus the word 'correspondence' was preferred. This reasoning was severely criticised by the author in a written submission to the sub-group: see J Chan, 'Comments on the Discussion Paper on the Fundamental Rights of Residents in the Basic Law' (n 3 above) 97.

may be desirable, for the purpose of smooth transition, to have a law enacted on this subject before 1997.

BL29 is also interesting in another aspect: it even prevails over BL39! Under BL29, a department or individual may infringe residents' freedom and privacy of communication only if (and on no other ground) such infringement is for the purpose of meeting the needs of public security or of investigation into criminal offences. This is more restrictive than the general limitations in BL39. It is welcome and the only thing the author would suggest is to add the requirements of 'arbitrariness' and 'necessity' in the second sentence of BL30, which would then read:

> No department or individual may, on any ground, arbitrarily infringe upon the residents' freedom and privacy of communication except in cases where such infringement is necessary in a democratic society to meet the needs of public security or of investigation into criminal offences and is in accordance with legal procedures.

Freedom of movement (BL30)

BL30 guarantees (1) freedom of movement within the SAR; (2) freedom of emigration to other countries and regions; (3) subject to the holding of a valid travel document, the freedom to travel and the freedom of entry and exit; and (4) unless restricted by law and subject to the holding of a valid travel document, freedom to leave the SAR without special authorisation. There is some overlapping among the various headings.

Under international law, the freedom to return to one's own country is a fundamental human right, for otherwise that person would be rendered stateless. The right to return to one's own country should not depend on the possession of any travel document. Yet the present formulation denies the right of Hong Kong residents to return to the SAR without a valid travel document. Under BL23 Hong Kong permanent residents have the right of abode in the Hong Kong SAR. The right of abode should by itself carry the right to return to the SAR without being subject to further restrictions. Thus it is submitted that the right of entry should not be subject to the requirement of a valid travel document.

How about the right to travel and the right to exit? The requirement of a valid travel document could be a serious impediment even to these freedoms. The right of abode does not necessarily include the right to a travel document. In the first preliminary draft of the sub-group, it was provided in the equivalent article that 'the government of the Hong Kong SAR shall, in accordance with law, issue travel documents to the [Hong Kong] residents to guarantee they can realise the above freedom.' This clearly means that Hong Kong residents have a right to obtain travel documents. However, this sentence was deleted in the second preliminary draft on the ground that such a right was already guaranteed by the present BL162.[18] With respect, this seems to have overlooked the difference in wording between the two clauses. Under BL162 the SAR government is empowered to, but is under no obligation compare, issue passports and travel documents to Hong Kong residents. In other words, BL162 is just an enabling provision. This is further reinforced by the positioning of BL162: it is placed under chapter VII, entitled 'external affairs.' The whole of chapter VII deals with the powers the SAR will enjoy in relation to external affairs, which, but for this chapter, would be under the jurisdiction of the Central Government. Besides, under common law, the issue of passports and travel documents is a prerogative power which may not be subject to judicial review.[19] If the government refuses to issue a passport, there is no legal remedy. Moreover, it is usually clearly stated in a passport that it remains the property of the government, which can revoke the passport at any time. It is unclear how far these prerogative powers are to be preserved or adopted after 1997. Yet what is clear is that nowhere in the Basic Law is there provided a right to a travel document. In many countries the right to a travel document is an inherent right of a citizen. It is suggested that such a right should be included in either BL23 or BL30.

Freedom of religion (BL31)

No provision in chapter III has generated so much discussion as the provision on freedom of religion. This is partly attributable to the active involvement of the representatives of the religious sector in both the BLDC and BLCC, and partly due to the fear about the restrictive religious policies practised across the border. One may recall that Peter Kwong and Kwok Kwong are both members of the sub-group on fundamental rights and obligations of Hong Kong residents. Both of them are also members of the sub-group on education, science, and culture, which was responsible for drafting chapter VI of the Basic Law. Their influence can probably be seen in the fact that one-third of the provisions in chapter VI concern religion or religious bodies to some extent. There are six other clergymen on the BLCC.

18 Explanatory note to clause 8 of the second preliminary draft (April 1987).
19 This is probably the case notwithstanding *Council of Civil Service Unions v Minister of State for the Civil Service* [1985] AC 374: see W S Clarke, 'Freedom of Movement' in R Wacks (ed), *Civil Liberties in Hong Kong* (Hong Kong: Oxford University Press, 1988) 338. Compare, however, *R v Foreign Secretary, ex p Everett* [1987] *The Times* 10 December.

Among them is Father Louis Ha, a firm supporter of the democrats, and probably the most prominent figure. Besides, many church leaders have experienced persecution during the Cultural Revolution and are anxious to protect religious freedom after 1997.[20] Apart from the active involvment of clergymen, two provocative articles by Xin Weisi brought the discussion on religious freedom to an unprecedented climax.

There are two main types of relevant provision in the Basic Law: one on protection of religious freedom and another on protection of religious organisations.[21] BL31 protects freedom of conscience, which has a wider scope than just religious belief. It then sets out the freedom of religious belief and the freedom to preach and to carry out and participate in religious activities in public. BL148 further provides that the government of the SAR shall not restrict religious activities which do not contravene the laws of the SAR. The major argument about BL31 again concerns 'brevity' versus 'clarity.' A proposal along the lines of article 18(1) of the International Covenant on Civil and Political Rights was made and now retained as a minority view.[22] While article 18(1) is certainly more elegantly drafted, the author tends to think that the difference is not really significant.

Experience elsewhere suggests that most litigation on religious freedom arises in the private sector with economic implications. In the United States, the First Amendment has been used to deny state aid to religious schools. This is unlikely to be a problem in Hong Kong, as BL148 clearly states that religious organisations shall enjoy the right to receive financial assistance and to run seminaries and other schools according to their previous practice. A more worrying area is the practice of compulsory morning prayers or attendance at services in some religious schools. Teaching courses on religion in schools would be protected under BL144. Yet some schools make it compulsory for their students to take papers on religious knowledge in the School Certificate Examination. Such practices may well infringe the freedom of religious belief.

It has also been suggested that a third paragraph be added to BL31:

> No person shall be subject to discrimination or impairment of his or her civil rights on grounds of religious belief.

---

20 It was said that many believers were called upon to prepare themselves for defending their religion in case of possible religious persecution in future; others were advised to memorise Bible texts in case they were banned: Iris Y L Tsang, 'Religious Freedom and the Basic Law' (1987) 38 *Tripod* 51.
21 See BL 148, 149, 156, and 157.
22 *The Draft Basic Law*, p 96.

This proposal was included as part of the author's earlier proposal of a non-discrimination clause in connection with equality before the law. Yet it seems that the proposal was supported only half-heartedly by the religious sectors. Realising that many religious organisations may impose the requirement of a particular religious belief for employment, they were somewhat hesitant in putting forward such a proposal, which may cut both ways. Indeed, it is known that some schools run by religious organisations would only employ teachers with the same religious belief. Such a practice would certainly not survive a non-discrimination clause, provided the clause applies to relationships among private individuals.

Another controversial topic is the relationship between church and state. The debate was provoked by an article by Xin Weisi in a leading Chinese newspaper.[23] Some observers believed that Xin Weisi was a *nom de plume* of the New China News Agency, and his view reflected the official thinking of the Central Government. Together with his second article two months later,[24] he has generated at least 16 articles in response.

In brief, Xin advocated that the church should stand aloof in relation to politics. He expressed concern about politicisation among certain Catholics and some Protestant denominations. According to him, the proper role of religion was in spiritual and ethical matters, whereas politics concerned power struggles in the materialistic world. Thus direct involvement of the church as a body in politics was beyond the boundary of religious activities, and clergy propagating their own political ideas in religious gatherings were abusing their position. Religious involvement in politics would lead to a conflict between the state and religion, and would ultimately lead to greater restrictions on religious freedom. Hence he called for the principle of separation of church and state to be written into the Basic Law.

At the same time, Xin also advocated strict adherence to the principles of non-subordination, non-interference, and mutual respect between the religious organisations of the SAR and their counterparts on the mainland. If religious organisations in Hong Kong were to request the mainland not to interfere with policies in the SAR, then the former should not themselves interfere with the religious policies of the mainland by criticising or preaching,

23 Xin Weisi, 'The Basic Law and Religious Freedom' *Ming Pao* 5 December 1986.
24 Xin Weisi, 'Further Discussion on the Basic Law and Religious Freedom' *Ming Pao* 3-4 February 1987. For a summary of the debate: see Peter Barry, 'A Discussion on "Separation of Church and State" in Hong Kong after 1997' (1987) 38 *Tripod* 63.

in the name of religious freedom. In other words, religious freedom is a concession which would not be allowed to blossom beyond the four corners of this small territory.

Responses to Xin's articles came from churches, believers, academics, journalists, and even some atheists. Most of them attacked the semantic ambiguity of the meaning of 'church' and 'politics' in Xin's article. Others criticised Xin's view of the church as outdated and Marxist. Human rights and social injustice were the proper concerns of the church, it was argued, and at least for the Roman Catholic Church, this role has received the blessing of the Second Vatican Council.[25] Others were worried that this might be the prologue to future controls on religious activities. When the debate became more and more heated, some of the responses tended to be rather emotional.

It is not clear whether it is because of the strong reaction of the religious community that the principle of separation of church and state was not included in the Basic Law. However, BL148 provides that the government of the SAR shall not restrict religious activities which do not contravene the laws of the Region. It begs the question of what are religious activities and whether political participation would fall outside the meaning of religious activities. It would be unfortunate if the principle of separation of church and state were sneaked into the Basic Law in such a subtle way. Yet as Barry pointed out, this topic is being hotly discussed in both church and secular circles in many places around the world. Apart from the political implications in the Hong Kong context, the question should probably call for more reflection and rational discussion. The principles of non-subordination, non-interference, and mutual respect, however, found their way into BL156. This phrase is taken from the Joint Declaration. It has been interpreted by some to mean that religious organisations are not allowed to preach across the border, nor to set up any branches or affiliated organisations on the mainland.[26] This is unnecessary, as any religious organisation which wants to preach on the mainland will be subject to the law on the mainland. On the other hand, it would be difficult to prevent mainland religious organisation from coming to the SAR to preach, as to do so would infringe the strongly defended freedom of religion here. An even more worrying feature of this phrase is that, according to Xin, any criticism of the religious

25 *Church in the Modern World*, 7 December 1965, para 76, quoted in Peter Barry, ibid.
26 'No preaching in the mainland after 1997 by the local church' *Ming Pao* 22 May 1988.

policies of the Central Government by the local church as a body would infringe this principle. To what extent this would affect freedom of expression in the SAR remains to be seen.

Right to social welfare (BL35)

This provision is a clear result of political compromise. Unlike civil and political rights, the right to social welfare is not a right enforceable in a common law court. In October 1987 the Hong Kong government decided not to establish a central provident fund. If this happened after 1997, could the government be sued under BL35? The issue would simply not be justiciable. Or suppose the government, faced with a serious deficit budget, proposed to cut down public assistance. Persons who had been receiving such assistance might petition the court and allege violation of BL35. Let us assume that the court is prepared to entertain the application and hold that there is a violation. What could the government do when there is simply not enough money? It would probably have to cut down other expenses in order to meet the court order. In so doing other public works such as transportation and road construction projects would have to be delayed. It would cause unnecessary strain and inflexibility on a tight budget, and would likely be unbeneficial to society at large. Insistence on huge expenditure on welfare items in times of depression might even lead to the collapse of a government, a situation not unheard of around the world. In most countries welfare rights and social policies are included in a chapter called directive principles, which are guidelines to the executive government and enforced only in the political forum. It is therefore suggested that BL35 should be removed to chapter VI, a chapter on executive policies, which should be expressly stated to be not cognisable in a court.

Rights of the indigenous inhabitants of the New Territories (BL40)

The rights of the indigenous inhabitants of the 'New Territories' can be grouped under six major categories:

(1) exchange of land (the letter 'A' and letter 'B' systems) or compensation upon resumption;
(2) the right of male descendants to build a small house under the 'Small House Policy';
(3) funeral and burial conventions;
(4) rate exemption policy for rural houses;
(5) symbolic rental of village lots; and

(6) the official status of the Heung Yee Kuk as a consultative body.[27]

The system of exchange of land, the rate exemption policy, and the symbolic rental of village lots were developed in the 1970s under the special political circumstances which existed at that time. It is doubtful whether they deserve mention in a constitutional document when, first, they relate to features of the New Territories which are dying out, and second, they represent privileges which, in a way, are rather unfair to the majority of Hong Kong residents. After all, they involve purely economic and property rights which are well secured under BL6 and 128 of the Basic Law. The same could probably be said about funeral and burial conventions and the 'Small House Policy.' There have been disputes in the past when construction of public utilities required the removal of tombs or caused destruction of 'feng shui.' Yet most of the disputes were settled eventually by monetary compensation. As far as the 'Small House Policy' is concerned, the entitlement is based on the existence of male descendants and there is doubt as to whether it should be preserved. The status of the Heung Yee Kuk raises the wider question of the political structure of SAR, which is considered in a different chapter. On the whole, there is no convincing reason why the rights of indigenous inhabitants of the New Territories should be singled out and specially protected by the Basic Law. But again, political considerations have prevailed.

Right to property ownership (BL6)

BL6 on the right to private property has an interesting history. Right from the very beginning chapter III has been criticised for its omission of any provision on protection of private property.[28] The reply was that such a provision existed as BL6 in chapter I, which provided better protection because it was intended that the provisions in chapter I were not subject to amendment. Nevertheless, the problem of chapter I, or indeed the whole of the Basic Law, is that it is unclear as to which provisions are intended to be legally enforceable and which are not. That the SAR is an inalienable part of the People's Republic of China or that the socialist system and policies shall not be practised in the SAR for 50 years are clearly provisions unenforceable in the local

27 Liu, 'Problems of the Lawful Rights of the Indigenous Inhabitants of the New Territories' (1986) 165 *Wide Angle* 65.
28 See J Chan, 'Comments on the Discussion Paper on Fundamental Rights of Residents in the Basic Law' (n 3 above).

court. Indeed, most provisions in chapter I seem to be incapable of enforcement in court. Given the nature of chapter I, doubts have been raised as to the enforceability of BL6. A right to property ownership is the cornerstone of a capitalist system. It would be awkward if such an important right were not included in the chapter on fundamental rights! This argument did not impress the drafters until a very late stage. A new sub-group was set up at the sixth plenary session, charged with the duty of putting together all the provisions submitted by the various sub-groups and making improvements in style. In their working report presented to the seventh plenary session, BL6 was replaced by a short article that 'the right to property ownership shall be protected by the Hong Kong SAR government.' The original BL6 was re-enacted in chapter III as a new BL26. This was a preferable approach which, unfortunately, was not adopted by the seventh plenary session. BL6 remains where it is.

The elegant drafting of BL6 probably accounts for the lack of criticism of it. The first sentence sets out the right to property ownership. Property should probably be construed in the widest sense, which would include tangible and intangible property as well as real and leasehold property. The second sentence provides for adequate compensation for lawful acquisition, which should be calculated in accordance with the real value of the property concerned. There is much litigation in the past on land compensation where constitutional issues were raised.[29] Because of the meaning of 'real value of the property concerned' in BL6, the article is likely to be fertile soil for litigation in the future.

International covenants (BL38)

Specific reference to the two International Covenants in the Joint Declaration aroused a fervent hope that Hong Kong will, for the first time, have a constitutional code of human rights commensurate with international standards. At the same time, critics had not been slow to point out that the two covenants, as international treaties, were not enforceable in the domestic courts.[30] They have to be implemented by the local legislature. There is almost unanimous support by writers in Hong Kong for the entrenchment of at least the International Covenant on Civil and

29 *Winfat Enterprises Ltd v AG* [1987] HKLR 34; *Home Restaurant Ltd v AG* (1986) HCt, MP No 2135 of 1986.
30 See J Chan, 'Basic Law and the International Covenant' in A Chen and J Chan (n 3 above) and references in J Chan, 'A Bill of Rights for Hong Kong?' in R Wacks (ed), *Civil Liberties in Hong Kong* (n 19 above) at n 5 thereof.

Political Rights by giving it legal effect through the Basic Law. It was a great disappointment when the drafters failed to live up to this expectation.

The earlier draft of BL39 was almost a replica of the relevant provision of the Joint Declaration, which shows no intention to entrench the International Covenants at all. It was only under pressure from the legal profession that some cosmetic modifications were made. The present BL39 requires the SAR to implement through legislation the provisions of the International Covenants as applied to Hong Kong. To the credit of the drafters, this is more positive than its predecessor. Nevertheless, unless and until such legislation is perfected, the International Covenants are not fully enforceable in our local courts. Even when such laws are in force, being ordinary laws made by the local legislature they are not entrenched and are themselves subject to repeal. It seems that the BLDC never intended to entrench the International Covenant in the Basic Law. What was envisaged was that the provisions of the International Covenants have been or will be transformed into local law. Thus the provision on the inherent right to life is regarded to have been implemented by the law on the offence of murder. The drafters defended their stand by pointing out that this is the existing system.

With respect, this is a disappointingly short-sighted and unimaginative approach. The drafters were charged with a task which was unprecedented. The object of chapter III is to ensure effective protection of human rights after the change of sovereignty (or its exercise). The relevant consideration for the drafters should be whether entrenchment would afford better protection of human rights. They should not be tied down by the existing system. Retention of the present system in this regard means that implementation of the International Covenants would depend very much on the initiative and perceptions of the executive; such implementation would necessarily be in an ad hoc, reactive, and piecemeal fashion. The British experience in protecting civil rights by way of such piecemeal, ad hoc legislation has resulted in the UK's distinguished record under the European Convention of Human Rights: for many years it has been the country receiving the largest number of complaints of violations of the European Convention and with the largest number of judgments entered against it!

It is regrettable that the drafters did not see fit to exploit the wisdom and meticulous drafting of the International Covenants, the drafting of which took almost two decades. In terms of clarity, comprehensiveness, and detail, the provisions on substantive rights in chapter III compare poorly with the International Covenant on Civil and Political Rights. There is no reference to the right to life,[31] the right not to be subjected to torture or to cruel, inhuman, or degrading treatment or punishment, the right not to be subjected to medical or scientific experimentation without free consent, the right not to be held in servitude, the right to privacy, or the right to non-discrimination in the enjoyment of fundamental rights and freedoms. The extensive procedural safeguards for a person who has been lawfully arrested are reduced to minimum brevity in BL86. There are no restrictions on derogation of fundamental rights in times of emergency. It is not clear whether freedom of speech under BL26 includes the right to seek and receive information and ideas of all kinds. Nor is it clear, ironically, whether freedom of religious belief includes freedom to preach in private!

This is not to undermine the hard work of the drafters in the last two years. The easiest way to remedy these defects is to give legal effect to the International Covenants. Despite repeated calls from lawyers and academics, the drafters still refused to entrench the International Covenants, this time by referring to drafting difficulties. With respect, there are at least three different formulae which have been proposed, and technicality is no excuse at all. Because of the different nature of the rights involved, the two covenants should receive slightly different treatment. It is submitted that BL38 be replaced by the following article:

> The provisions of the International Covenant on Civil and Political Rights as applied to Hong Kong shall be enforceable in the courts of the Hong Kong Special Administrative Region and shall, to the extent of inconsistency, prevail over any law of the Hong Kong Special Administrative Region.
>
> The provisions of the International Covenant on Economic, Social and Cultural Rights as applied to Hong Kong shall be implemented, and if appropriate, through legislation, by the Hong Kong Special Administrative Region.

Alongside the pressure to entrench the International Covenants in the Basic Law, there is growing pressure to have a bill of rights enacted in the transitional period. It may simply repeat the relevant provisions in the two International Covenants. This idea was first advocated in 1985, although it did not arouse any response at that time.[32] Nonetheless, the pressure of international human rights law was gradually felt in Hong Kong. In

---

31 The right to life was considered and rejected by the sub-group on the ground that it might prohibit the death penalty, a subject on which there is no public consensus.

32 J Chan, 'Basic Law and the Bill of Rights' (n 30 above) 72–74.

1984 the local Court of Appeal held that the Universal Declaration of Human Rights formed no part of the domestic law and could not be enforced as such (*Re Wong Chun-Sing and Ng Fook-yiu* [1984] HKLR 71). In 1987 the High Court, and a dissenting judge in the Court of Appeal, expressly referred to the guarantee of freedom of expression in the International Covenant of Civil and Political Rights in discharging an injunction against the publication of the book *Spycatcher* by a local newspaper (*Attorney General of the United Kingdom v South China Morning Post* (1987) CA, Civ App No 114 of 1987, (1987) HCt, HCA No 4644 of 1987). And in the recent Film Censorship Ordinance 1988 (No 25 of 1988), article 19 of the International Covenant on Civil and Political Rights on freedom of expression was expressly referred to. In the last days of office of the former Attorney General Michael Thomas, a working party was set up to look into the question of a bill of rights. The working party was chaired by the Attorney General himself, and consisted of top officials, from the British side of the Sino-British Joint Liaison Group and the Legal Department, distinguished private lawyers, and legal academics. Although all members sat in a private capacity, it could probably be considered as the first 'official' attempt towards the enactment of a bill of rights in the transitional period. Within three months the working party has even produced a draft human rights bill. Yet it was also at this point that the working party was dissolved upon the expiry of office of Mr Thomas as Attorney General.

Due process of law and the right to judicial remedies (BL34 and 86)

In the common law system, the court is always regarded as the ultimate guardian of human rights. The right of access to the courts and procedural guarantees of fairness are endowed with great importance in the protection of human rights, as evidenced by the invariably lengthy details of these rights in numerous international human rights conventions and national constitutions. BL34 guarantees the right of access to the court and the right to judicial remedies. However, nowhere in chapter III is there any mention of procedural guarantees of fairness. These should include, at the very least, the right to a fair and open trial by a competent, independent, and impartial tribunal established by law, the right to a fair and open trial without delay, the right to have the case tried in one's presence, the right to address and persuade the tribunal before determination of the case, and, in criminal cases, the celebrated presumption of innocence. These omissions were defended on the ground that these rights are

Protection of civil liberties

already guaranteed by the laws of Hong Kong.[33] With respect, this argument shows complete ignorance of the function of a constitution. Many rights in chapter III are already guaranteed by our laws. If this argument were right, we might as well scrap the whole of the chapter! One of the functions of a constitution is to spell out explicitly those rights which are agreed by society at large as the most important rights and to recognise their status in a constitutional framework. Existing laws can be changed at any time. A constitution should lay down restrictions on the legislature from arbitrary abrogation of these rights by the enactment of laws.

It has also been argued that procedural fairness is already safeguarded by BL86 which provides that 'in criminal or civil proceedings in the Hong Kong Special Administrative Region, the principles previously applied in Hong Kong and the rights previously enjoyed by the parties to the proceedings shall be maintained.' BL86 is deficient in a number of respects. First, our civil and criminal procedures keep on changing according to the needs of society. So what are 'the principles'? And when we refer to the 'principles previously applied in Hong Kong,' what time frame are we talking about? Is it 1997, when the Basic Law comes into force? Or 1990, when the Basic Law is promulgated? BL86 lacks the precision which characterises a common law system. Second, BL86 does not mean a lot to a layman. If the principles of a fair and public trial and the presumption of innocence are so important in our system of administration of justice, there is no reason why they should not be expressly spelt out. Recent arrests in Singapore only reinforce our belief in the importance of the right to a fair trial without delay.

It is submitted that the following clause be added to the present BL34:

In the determination of their civil rights and obligations, or of any criminal charge against them, all Hong Kong residents are entitled to a fair and public hearing within a reasonable time by an independent, competent, and impartial tribunal established by law. Everyone charged with a criminal offence shall be presumed innocent until proved guilty according to law.

BL34 provides that Hong Kong residents shall have the right to challenge in the courts the actions of the executive organs or their personnel. Presumably this would include judicial review of the decisions of the Chief Executive, either because of the general principle of equality before the law so that the CE should receive no preferential treatment in the absence of express privilege or

33 *Report on the Exchange Session* (n 9 above) para 1.5.2.

immunity, or because of BL60 which stipulated that the CE is the head of the SAR, so that he must fall within the meaning of 'personnel' in BL34.

In an explanatory note to this provision in the fourth Report (December 1987) it was said that whether this provision enabled an action to be brought against central state organs or their personnel would have to be further considered. This is an alarming proviso if central organs or their personnel are immune from local judicial procedure. Yet this would probably be the case as the court has no jurisdiction over any executive act of the Central People's Government under BL18.

While it has not been clearly spelt out in the Basic Law, it is submitted that the court has power to review the constitutionality of any legislation. Under BL169 the local court may interpret some of the provisions of the Basic Law in adjudicating cases before them. BL10 further provides that 'no law enacted by the legislature of the Hong Kong SAR shall contravene this Law.' Thus the local court could strike down any law which purports to limit the basic rights and freedoms set out in the Basic Law and which could not be justified under BL39, although the consequences of such a judicial declaration on the impugning laws are not entirely clear. Besides, the supremacy clause in BL10 does not cover national law which applies to Hong Kong by virtue of BL17. Would these laws be subject to judicial review by the local court?

A WINDOW: TREASON

Treason is a very sensitive area. Although everyone knew that this question had to be tackled somehow at some stage of the drafting process, no one seemed willing to be the first to raise it. It was not until Spring 1987 that this vexed question was finally raised in the context of the application of nationwide laws to the SAR. The experience of the political trials of dissidents in the name of treason or like offences across the border is too fresh in the minds of many Hong Kong inhabitants. Thus when the suggestion of applying PRC laws on treason to the SAR was made, the idea immediately received strenuous opposition. For the first time in the drafting process, the Hong Kong members of the BLDC presented a united front. It was clear that the existing laws of Hong Kong on treason could not survive the change of sovereignty. It was also clear that Beijing would not be happy with a lacuna. The discussion almost came to a deadlock until a suggestion was made that the existing laws of Hong Kong on treason be examined. A paper on treason was then submitted to the BLDC. Eventually a compromise was reached: the SAR was to draft its own law on treason in a manner that was familiar to a common law lawyer, and the Central Government would not interfere in this sensitive area by the application of national law. Thus BL22 was drafted in such a way that the SAR government was under a duty to enact law to prohibit any act designed to undermine national unity or subvert the CPG. It was intended that this clause should be exhaustive, notwithstanding anything in BL17. While the approach is certainly a salutary one, the present drafting does not seem to have achieved such intention.

Under BL17, apart from foreign affairs and defence, the Central Government can apply to the SAR any laws which give expression to national unity and territorial integrity and which, in accordance with the provisions of the Basic Law, are outside the limits of the high degree of autonomy of the SAR. It is clear that the law of treason must fall under either 'defence' or 'laws which give expression to national unity and which are outside the high degree of autonomy of the Hong Kong SAR.' There is therefore nothing to prevent the Central Government from introducing its law on counter-revolutionary crimes to the SAR so as to make it exist alongside the SAR laws on treason. Besides, the courts of the SAR might have no jurisdiction to try any case on treason, which must fall within the scope of defence. So how and where would a defendant charged with these offences be tried? Would he be entitled to lawyers of his own choice under BL34 and the rights 'previously enjoyed in any criminal proceedings' under BL86?

Another source of anxiety comes from the phrase 'to undermine national unity and to subvert the Central People's Government,' which bears close resemblance to the provisions on counter-revolutionary crimes under the PRC Criminal Code. What types of law are contemplated? Would it suffice to change all references to Her Majesty, the Queen, or like words in the present Crimes Ordinance to the CPG? Or are some other new laws contemplated? What would be the consequence if the laws enacted by the SAR government do not satisfy Beijing?

While it is conceded that some laws on treason in the SAR are necessary, could it not be left to the future legislature and be dealt with in the same way as all other crimes? Is it necessary to spell it out in the Basic Law? From a pragmatic point of view, the only purpose BL22 serves is to frighten off people from Hong Kong. Confidence is not likely to be boosted by a provision like this. On the other hand, with the existing BL17, complete removal of BL22 may result in an even worse position: the Central Government alone will determine what law on treason should apply to the SAR.

If the intention of the drafters in enacting BL22 is to ensure that no nationwide law on treason or like offences should apply to the SAR, this should be expressly spelt out. This may be done by inserting a phrase 'other than those laws which are covered by BL22' immediately after the words 'the limits of the high degree of autonomy of the Hong Kong Special Administrative Region' in the third paragraph of BL17. Besides, an additional paragraph should be inserted at the end of BL22:

> Notwithstanding anything in the Basic Law, the courts of the Hong Kong SAR shall have exclusive jurisdiction over trials of any offence arising from this article.

Since we are dealing with offences under Hong Kong law, it is only right that the defendant should be tried by Hong Kong courts.

DOOR WITHOUT LOCK: INTERPRETATION . . .

Consider this hypothetical case. The SAR government, pursuant to the Crown Lands Resumption Ordinance, resumes certain parcels of land for the purpose of public development. Compensation is awarded according to the formula laid down in the Ordinance. The residents are unhappy with the amount of compensation. Negotiation with the government does not result in anything fruitful. So they bring an action against the government for breach of BL6, claiming that the amount of compensation does not reflect the real value of the property concerned. Thus the only issue to be tried by the court is whether the formula laid down in the Crown Lands Resumption Ordinance complies with BL6.

If the claims of the residents are successful, it may cost the SAR government a fortune. Before the case is set down for trial, the SAR government invites the Standing Committee of the National People's Congress (1) in pursuance of BL169, to interpret the meaning of compensation in BL6; and (2) in pursuance of BL172, to determine whether the relevant provision in the Crown Lands Resumption Ordinance is in contravention of BL6 of the Basic Law. The NPCSC decides both questions in favour of the SAR government. Under BL169, this interpretation is binding on the local courts, and would affect all those cases insofar as judgments have not been rendered. Thus the claim of the residents is bound to be defeated well before they have a chance to argue it in court. The proceedings in the NPCSC are closed-door proceedings. The residents do not have a right to address the Standing Committee, which acts on the advice of the Committee for the Basic Law, a strange animal whose functions, powers, and composition are yet unknown at this stage. The residents may not even be given the reasons for the decision by the NPCSC. Nor would there be any channel for appeal. Where are the minimum safeguards for procedural fairness envisaged in BL86?

The author has deliberately chosen a politically neutral case. There are a lot of cases which may be potentially embarrassing to the government or would cost the government a fortune. This is inevitable as long as there is an independent judiciary. Yet the provision on final interpretation puts the SAR government, when faced with a legal suit, in a 'heads I win, tails you lose' situation. The result may be that the judiciary cannot decide against the government's wishes, or if they do so, they will be 'corrected.' How could any investor have confidence in such a system?

Besides, experience elsewhere suggests that once there is a bill of rights, there will be a lot of constitutional litigation. All criminal cases could easily be turned into cases involving constitutional dispute, and a competent lawyer would have no difficulty in framing a constitutional issue in almost any case. There are all sorts of reasons why lawyers or litigants would like to resort to the NPCSC for rulings. Sooner or later the NPCSC would be flooded with all these cases, most of which would probably be purely economic in nature rather than politically sensitive. It would be practically impossible for the NPCSC to handle this volume of work. It would delay and lengthen a lot of legal proceedings. The provision that the interpretation of the NPCSC would not affect those cases where judgments have been rendered would not be of much consolation, as it can easily be side-stepped by taking preliminary points or invoking interlocutory proceedings. It would also be a mockery to the system of administration of justice if the most essential part of the litigation is decided behind closed doors by a body which is not familiar with the common law system.

The best solution lies in granting to the Hong Kong courts the final interpretation power on matters which fall within the limits of the autonomy of the SAR. The integrity and credibility of the legal system could not be maintained without such a final power of interpretation. Counter-arguments based on the existing system of appeals to the Judicial Committee of the Privy Council are misleading, because:

(1) the Judicial Committee of the Privy Council is a court staffed by the best judges, and not politicians, in England;
(2) it is a trial in open court, and litigants have the right to make representations before the court renders its judgment (ie advice to the Queen);

(3) all internationally recognised procedural safeguards are observed in appeals to the Privy Council;

(4) both the Hong Kong and the British legal systems belong to the common law system; and

(5) in hearing an appeal from Hong Kong, the Privy Council applies Hong Kong law and is itself bound by Hong Kong law.

None of these features is applicable to the proceedings of the NPCSC or the CBL.

A less satisfactory, but still possible, solution is to include in BL169 detailed provisions on how the power of interpretation is to be exercised by the NPCSC if it is to retain final interpretation power. The author would suggest the following principles of interpretation for consideration:

(1) apart from foreign affairs and defence, the NPCSC shall not exercise its power of interpretation of any part of the Basic Law unless there is a request from the Court of Final Appeal of the SAR;

(2) no question of interpretation shall be referred to the NPCSC unless such a question is necessary for the determination of any issue in the case before the Court of Final Appeal; however, such referral per se shall not be a ground for staying any proceedings before the court; no appeal shall lie against a decision of the Court of Final Appeal not to refer the case to the NPCSC;

(3) in referring any question, apart from those involving foreign affairs and defence, to the NPCSC for interpretation, the Court of Final Appeal shall state its own interpretation on the question;

(4) the NPCSC shall interpret the Basic Law as referred to it by the Court of Final Appeal in accordance with the principles of interpretation applicable to the common law system in the SAR and in the light of the JD and preamble to the Basic Law;

(5) any interpretation by the NPCSC shall be supported by reasons, and if appropriate, by relevant legal authorities;

(6) any interpretation by the NPCSC shall not affect any existing proceedings in the SAR, irrespective of whether judgments have been rendered or not;

(7) no interpretation by the NPCSC shall be binding on the local court until such interpretation is published in the SAR; the Court of Final Appeal of the SAR shall publish any such interpretation as soon as practicable.

These principles are designed on the basis that the legal system of the SAR should be self-contained and functioning efficiently.

The integrity and credibility of the legal system cannot be maintained if there are many loopholes. It is submitted that these principles of interpretation should be included in BL169 and the phrase 'and other affairs which are the responsibility of the Central People's Government' in the third paragraph of the clause should be deleted.

Executive acts of the Central People's Government

BL26 guarantees freedom of expression. Suppose a writer in the mainland has written a book on 'Humanism in a Socialist Society,' which is prohibited from publication on the mainland. A Hong Kong publisher manages to obtain the copyright from the author, and decides to publish the book on a serial basis in a leading Chinese newspaper in the SAR. The New China News Agency warns the publisher concerned not to publish the book. Shortly thereafter, all the books are seized by the SAR government. The publisher seeks a declaration from the local court that he has the constitutional right to publish the book under BL26 and that the books have been unlawfully seized.

The government argues that the court has no jurisdiction in this case, as it concerns the 'executive acts of the Central People's Government' under BL18. The CE of the SAR, upon receipt of a certificate from the State Council, issues a certificate to that effect. This certificate is binding on the court, which has no alternative but to dismiss the case of the publisher, no matter how reluctant the court may be. It is absurd to empower the executive to oust the jurisdiction of the court when it is the very act of the same executive that is being challenged. The argument that this could equally happen under the common law concept of 'Act of State' is misleading. The anomalous concept of 'executive acts of the Central People's Government' goes beyond the common law concept of 'Act of State,' which is already preserved in the second paragraph of BL18. Besides, the most crucial difference is that the meaning of 'Act of State' is determined by the court. When the government pleads the defence of Act of State, it is the court, and not the executive, which determines whether the case falls within the meaning of the phrase. Whether the executive or the judiciary should make the decision may not make a lot of difference on the mainland when there is no separation of powers. But once we accept a system with separation of powers, the court should be the master of its own house. The ambivalent concept of 'executive acts of the Central People's Government' provides another potential avenue for violation of fundamental rights without remedies. It is suggested that this concept of 'executive acts of the Central People's Government' be removed altogether.

CONCLUSION

Chapter III has an ambitious objective. It has to preserve the existing rights and freedoms under the common law and, in particular, the residual principle that everything that is not forbidden is lawful. In some areas it even extends the common law. Being the supreme law in the SAR, it entrenches fundamental rights and freedoms and imposes restrictions on the powers of both the executive and the legislature. At the same time, it attempts to bring home international standards of protection of human rights. Perhaps the task is too onerous for any draftsmen. In building up such a complicated structure, the draftsmen have forgotten that any sheltered place needs a roof!

Human rights cannot be protected without the back-up of an autonomous and self-contained legal system. Yet the legal system portrayed by the Basic Law is a crippled system, with its hands tightly tied under the concept of 'sovereignty.' Under the common law system, the court is the ultimate place where one can take shelter from the storm of oppression. But who is going to hide himself at a ruined castle, with a wide-open gate and full of broken windows? Many of the criticisms on the ambiguous drafting of the relevant provisions in the Basic Law have already been raised. However, in addressing these issues, one must not lose sight of a more fundamental question: what is meant by 'one country, two systems'? The concept would entail, at the very least, that each of the systems would be able to function independently, efficiently, and smoothly.

Throughout the drafting process we have heard a lot about sovereignty. We have heard arguments that a sovereign country must be able to interpret all the laws of a local district. We have heard that the laws of a local district cannot exclude the power of a national organ. These are all very nice arguments if we are talking about one sovereign state. At the same time, in order to have two different systems working efficiently and smoothly within one single sovereign regime, one has to recognise that there are many intrinsic theoretical problems which are probably insoluble. The solution, it is submitted, is to put aside sovereignty for a while and give a little more thought to practicality. The sole reason why the problem of Hong Kong could be resolved in the Sino-British negotiations was because pragmatism prevailed. Under this consideration of pragmatism the Peoples' Republic of China was prepared to accept the consequences of the unequal treaties. Under this consideration the novel idea of 'one country, two systems' was conceived. Under this consideration socialism could be shelved and not applied to this small territory. Also under this consideration the four cardinal principles in the PRC constitution could be suspended in relation to Hong Kong. And now, if pragmatism is not the primary concern in designing the structure of the SAR, and if sovereignty is blindly insisted upon, 'one country, two systems' would soon become 'one country, two crippled systems.' Without final interpretation power and exclusive jurisdiction, at least in the area of protection of human rights, the legal system would at best be a lame duck system. Without a self-sustained legal system, no matter how perfectly chapter III is drafted, protection of human rights is nothing but an illusion.

11 Economic, Social, and Cultural Aspects

NIHAL JAYAWICKRAMA

NATURE OF CONSTITUTIONS

JOHN Marshall, Chief Justice of the United States and one of the draftsmen of the American constitution, thought that a constitution 'to contain an accurate detail of all the subdivisions of which its great powers will admit, and of all the means by which they may be carried into execution, would partake of the prolixity of a legal code, and could scarcely be embraced by the human mind. It would probably never be understood by the public.' In his view, therefore, its nature 'requires that only its great outlines should be marked, its important objects designated, and the minor ingredients which comprise those objects be deduced from the nature of the objects themselves.'[1] Writing 140 years later, K C Wheare reaffirmed the principle that the ideal constitution should be as short as possible, and should contain 'the very minimum, and that minimum to be rules of law.'[2]

The constitution of a country, therefore, is primarily a law. It is a law which states, in clear and concise form, the essential features of the state. These include the composition and powers of the principal institutions of government, and their relationship with each other and to the inhabitants of the country. The constitution is the supreme law of the country, not only in the sense that it is superior to all other laws, but also because it is the basis upon which the sovereign people have agreed to be governed. Most constitutions in the Commonwealth and many others that have been democratically adopted possess these characteristics. For example, the 1946 constitution of Ceylon, which was drafted by a constitutional commission and accepted by the State Council on the eve of independence, and which served that country well for a quarter of a century, consisted of 92 sections, organised under nine chapters, dealing successively with preliminary matters, including interpretation; the

1 *McCulloch v Maryland*, 4 Wheaton 316, 4 L Ed 579 (1819).
2 K C Wheare, *Modern Constitutions* (Oxford: Oxford University Press, 1966) 34.

Governor-General; the legislature; delimitation of electoral districts; the executive; the judicature; the public service; finance; and transitional provisions, repeals, and savings.[3] The 1963 constitution of Malaysia, being that of a federal state, contains, in addition, provisions which seek to regulate relations between the federation and the states.[4] Since the early 1960s, a chapter on fundamental rights and freedoms has become an indispensable feature of a national constitution.[5]

In socialist states, however, a constitution is not only a legal document, but also an important political manifesto.[6] A socialist society is regarded as a natural, logical stage on the road to communism. To reach that ultimate ideological goal of communism, the state must proceed upon a well regulated path. That path is delineated, in accordance with Marxist-Leninist theory, by the Communist Party; and the march is led by the legislature, the supreme organ of state power. The constitution confirms the achievements of the past, and proclaims the tasks and goals that lie ahead. For example, the 1977 constitution of the Union of Soviet Socialist Republics, recognising that the USSR is now a 'developed socialist society,' states in its preamble that:

> The supreme goal of the Soviet state is the building of a classless communist society in which there will be public, communist self-government. The main aims of the people's socialist state are: to lay the material and technical foundation of communism, to perfect socialist social relations and transform them into communist relations, to mould the citizen of communist society, to raise the people's living and cultural standards, to safeguard the country's security, and to further the consolidation of peace and development of international co-operation.

Accordingly, it proceeds in its substantive provisions to affirm and proclaim the 'principles' and 'aims' of the socialist state.[7] Similarly, the 1982 constitution of the People's Republic of China 'affirms the achievements of the struggles of the Chinese people of all nationalities' and notes that the basic task of the

---

3 The Ceylon (Constitution) Order in Council 1946.
4 See part VI of that constitution.
5 For a recent example, see the Belize Independence Order 1981, chapter II.
6 'The Party regarded the Constitution as an affirmation of the gains of the revolution and, at the same time, as a proclamation of the basic tasks and goals of the building of socialism . . . .' (Leonid Brezhnev, in his address to the May 1977 Plenum of the Communist Party Central Committee, quoted in Edward McWhinney, *Constitution-making: Principles, Process, Practice* (Toronto: University of Toronto Press, 1981) 51.)
7 These are contained in five chapters entitled: the political system; the economic system; social development and culture; foreign policy; defence of the motherland (32 articles).

nation in the years ahead 'is to concentrate its effort on socialist modernisation.' It then defines this basic task in the form of general principles, and calls upon the people, state organs, armed forces, political parties, public organisations, and all enterprises and undertakings to accept the constitution 'as the basic norm of conduct' and 'ensure its implementation.'[8]

Influenced perhaps by the strong moral content implicit in the programmatic declarations found in socialist constitutions, constitution-makers in liberal democracies have now begun to include a package of attractive, abstract, but unenforceable propositions of political, economic, and social objectives. The 1937 constitution of Ireland contained ten 'directive principles of social policy' which were 'intended for the general guidance of the Oireachtas'; these principles 'shall not be cognisable by any court.'[9] The 1949 constitution of India included a more comprehensive and updated statement of 'directive principles of state policy' which 'shall not be enforceable by any court' but which 'are nevertheless fundamental in the governance of the country.'[10] The 1972 constitution of Sri Lanka enunciated 'principles of state policy' which, while neither conferring legal rights nor being enforceable, could be invoked by the state to validate a bill that sought to restrict the exercise or operation of a fundamental right or freedom.[11] These principles, typical of

8 Preamble to the constitution. See also chapter 1: general principles.
9 Art 45.
10 Art 37. 'The purpose of the Directive Principles is to fix certain social and economic goals for immediate attainment by bringing about a non-violent social revolution. Through such a social revolution the Constitution seeks to fulfil the basic needs of the common man and to change the structure of our society. It aims at making the Indian masses free in the positive sense. Without faithfully implementing the Directive Principles, it is not possible to achieve the Welfare State contemplated by the Constitution . . . .' (per Hegde and Mukerjee JJ in *Kesavananda v State of Kerala* [1973] supp SCR 1, 343).
11 Chapter V. In 1973, the Constitutional Court of Sri Lanka held that the Associated Newspapers of Ceylon Ltd (Special Provisions) Bill which, inter alia, sought to alter the status of a private company by vesting 75% of the total number of shares of the company in the Public Trustee on behalf of the government and reducing the total existing shareholdings of shareholders to a maximum of 25% with a maximum limit of 2% per individual shareholder, had the effect of depriving the members of the company of their right to freedom of speech and of association. However, the constitution was not infringed since these restrictions on the exercise and operations of fundamental rights were being imposed in the interests primarily of the principles of state policy; in particular: (a) the development of collective forms of property; (b) the raising of the moral and cultural standards of the people; (c) the elimination of economic and social privilege, disparity, and exploitation and the ensuring of equality of opportunity to all citizens. (*Re Associated Newspapers of Ceylon Ltd (Special Provisions) Bill* (1973) 1 Decisions of the Constitutional Court of Sri Lanka 35.)

those which found their way into the short-lived constitutions of Bangladesh (1972), Ghana (1979), and Nigeria (1979), and the somewhat more durable ones of Papua New Guinea (1975), Malta (1975), and Guyana (1980), included such objectives as that 'the state shall endeavour to eliminate economic and social privilege, disparity and exploitation, and ensure equality of opportunity to all citizens,' and 'the state shall endeavour to ensure social security and welfare.' An Indian judge has described these directive principles as constituting, together with the fundamental rights and freedoms, 'the true conscience of the constitution.'[12] However, having regard to their virtually non-existent practical value, their continued presence in contemporary constitutions is probably due to a need on the part of constitution-makers to appease their own conscience after having invested legislatures with absolute and uncontrolled law-making power.

Hong Kong has been administered during the past 147 years as a British colony. Its constitutional evolution has followed the basic pattern applied in other British territories overseas, but at an incredibly slower pace. With its non-representative legislature and a nominated executive still accountable to the British government, Hong Kong is today at the stage of constitutional development that Ceylon was at in 1910. The written constitution of Hong Kong consists of two brief documents, the Letters Patent passed under the Great Seal of the United Kingdom, and the Royal Instructions passed under the Royal Sign Manual and Signet. The former create the office of Governor, prescribe his powers, duties, and functions, and deal with the constitution of the Executive and Legislative Councils and the tenure of office of judges and other public officers. The latter deal with the composition of the two councils, the nature of proceedings therein, and the Governor's powers in relation thereto. Perhaps more important than the written documents is the unwritten constitution of Hong Kong: the conventions that have developed by which the British government rarely exercises the full extent of its absolute powers, but permits Hong Kong to govern itself with a high degree of autonomy, through consultation and consensus, albeit at rarefied, elitist levels.

This style of government, unique in the volatile Southeast Asian environment in which Hong Kong is geographically situated, has no doubt contributed immensely to the territory's economic success. By consistently following a policy of 'positive non-intervention,' the Hong Kong government has left the way

12 Chandrachud J in *Kesavananda v State of Kerala* (n 10 above).

open for pragmatic, uninhibited decision-making, determined almost solely by the interplay of market forces. The government has confined itself to providing the infrastructure necessary for economic development, such as water supply, health facilities, public housing, education, a communication network, and a reliable legal and administrative framework. This policy of minimum regulation has led to the creation of a free, open society which, in turn, has given rise to significant public confidence in the territory.

Had the Joint Declaration on the Question of Hong Kong not intervened, Hong Kong's constitutional evolution this century, as it moved slowly but inexorably to its logical end, would probably have resulted in a more representative legislature with its own elected chairman and, to meet the demands of the international community, a constitutional bill of rights. But the agreement entered into between the United Kingdom and the People's Republic of China on the future of Hong Kong, involving as it does the transfer of sovereignty, has necessitated the preparation of an entirely new constitutional instrument. A transfer of sovereignty is today as anachronistic a concept as any extension of the lease of the New Territories would have been. The problems raised by such a transfer are compounded by the reality that the new sovereign is not a liberal democracy sympathetic to the laissez-faire aspirations of Hong Kong, but one committed to an alien, incompatible ideology, aggressively on the march towards communism. In this context, the constitution assumes a significance which previously it has not had for Hong Kong. It becomes the pivot upon which the continued freedom and prosperity of the territory rests.

THE JOINT DECLARATION

A draftsman of a constitution could not have asked for instructions in more specific or clearer terms than are contained in the Joint Declaration. At the same time, the basic policies of the PRC regarding Hong Kong as stated in the Joint Declaration and their elaboration in Annex I contemplate a relationship between two territories which is unique in constitutional history. If a sovereign state committed to the achievement of communism under the 'guidance of Marxism-Leninism and Mao Zedong Thought'[13] were to permit a newly acquired special administrative region to continue to adopt its 'previous capitalist system and life-style' (section I, Annex I, JD), that region would need to be

13 Preamble to the 1982 constitution of the People's Republic of China.

insulated by law from the over-arching influence of its mother country more effectively than any federating state has yet been from its federation. Indeed, if two vibrant and powerful, but mutually antagonistic, economic and social systems were to co-exist peacefully and progress within the territorial borders of a single state, then the tangible link between them can only be their common sovereignty. The Joint Declaration has been made upon that premise, and it is the draftsman's duty to bear in mind that dichotomy when he seeks to give legal effect to the proposition contained in the treaty that:

> the Hong Kong Special Administrative Region will enjoy a high degree of autonomy, except in foreign and defence affairs which are the responsibilities of the Central People's Government (JD3(2)).

The Joint Declaration states that 'the current social and economic systems in Hong Kong will remain unchanged, and so will the life-style' (JD3(5)). Annex I elaborates this further:

> ... the socialist system and socialist policies shall not be practised in the Hong Kong Special Administrative Region and ... Hong Kong's previous capitalist system and life-style shall remain unchanged for 50 years (section I).

These statements are capable of two interpretations. They can mean that Hong Kong's capitalist system and life-style will remain frozen for 50 years. Alternatively, they can mean that Hong Kong may continue to adopt its current social and economic systems for the next 50 years, without interference, notwithstanding the transfer of sovereignty. One is mandatory, the other is merely permissive. A decision on which interpretation was intended by the two signatory governments must precede any attempt at drafting the Basic Law.

If what was intended was that Hong Kong's capitalist system and life-style shall remain frozen for 50 years, the SAR's 'high degree of autonomy' would necessarily be circumscribed within the framework of that system. The Basic Law would then prescribe mandatory guidelines for the SAR's legislature and executive, and these would be policed by the PRC. Laws which transgress these guidelines would be struck down by the Standing Committee of the National People's Congress. Hong Kong would be subjected to a rigid totalitarian system dictated by an ideological commitment similar to that in socialist countries marching towards communism, except that in the case of the SAR the onward march would be in the opposite direction. This interpretation would be consistent with a desire on the part of the PRC to have at its disposal, as it has had for the past 40 years, a capitalist enclave or entrepôt through which it can reach out to the financial centres and free markets of the world.

This interpretation, however, ignores at least three important considerations.

First, such enforced rigidity is incompatible with an elected legislature.[14] A free election presupposes competing political forces, each seeking to attract the support of more voters than the others. Such support may be secured, for example, by the offer of an attractive package of welfare benefits to the lower income groups in the electorate. But the implementation of that promise may involve increased public spending (and consequently, a variation of tax policy) or may be construed as a socialist measure: both contrary to the idea of the frozen capitalist framework. It is the history of regimented societies that once a people's aspirations have been raised, it is not possible to avoid fulfilling them except through the use of military force, as was witnessed in Hungary, Czechoslovakia, and Poland in recent years. The use of the military is generally a destabilising factor in the economy.

Second, while the march towards communism is usually characterised by strict regimentation, so as not to deviate from orthodox theory and principles, the same is not true of the development of capitalism. Socialism implies regulation, since the resources necessary for increased public spending can best be ensured by strict state control over the commanding heights of the economy. Capitalism, on the other hand, is the product of a free economy, and the buoyancy of a free economy depends entirely upon the free play of a variety of market forces. It is unlikely, for instance, that the flow of capital into the SAR can be secured by legislation, for no consumer can be forced to part with his money against his will, or that potential investors can be dragooned into the region by the fiat of a state whose constitution requires it to engage in 'combating capitalist ideas.'[15]

Third, every economic or social system is subject to the vicissitudes of external forces such as the collapse of linked currencies or share markets, natural forces such as epidemics or earthquakes, and human forces such as rising aspirations and dissatisfaction with the status quo. Any one or more of these often unforeseen events or occurrences may require modification of the system, either temporarily or for protracted periods, or even a radical restructuring. In such circumstances, the heat generated will hardly be conducive to the continuation of a frozen state.

14 See section I, Annex I: 'The legislature of the Hong Kong Special Administrative Region shall be constituted by elections.'
15 Art 24 of the 1982 PRC constitution.

The other possible interpretation is that the SAR *may* continue to adopt its current social and economic systems after the transfer of sovereignty. This appears to be a more reasonable interpretation since it respects the wishes of the inhabitants of Hong Kong and accords to them the same flexibility of decision-making that they have hitherto enjoyed; and it has, no doubt, contributed significantly to the creation of the free, open financial and commercial centre that Hong Kong is today. Moreover, it is consistent with the concept of 'one country, two systems.'[16] This interpretation, however, would require the drafter not only to identify with a high degree of specificity the matters in respect of which the PRC may exercise authority over the SAR, but also to prohibit mainland state organs from interfering in any manner in respect of all other matters.

This result may be achieved by resorting to standard drafting techniques:

(1) In federal constitutions, powers are distributed between the government of the whole country and the governments of the constituent parts. For example, the 1950 constitution of India contains a Union legislative list over which the Parliament of India has exclusive authority; a State legislative list over which state legislatures have exclusive authority; and a concurrent legislative list over which both Parliament and the state legislatures have authority, with parliamentary legislation prevailing in the event of repugnancy. Parliament has exclusive authority over any residual matters.[17] The executive power of the Union extends generally to matters with respect to which Parliament has legislative authority.[18] Any dispute between the government of India and a state is resolved by the Supreme Court of India which also has final appellate jurisdiction to determine 'a substantive question of law as to the interpretation of the constitution.'[19] This is the usual federal model, although variations are not uncommon. For example, under the 1900 constitution of Australia, only the powers of the federal Parliament are enumerated;[20] state legislatures enjoy residual power.[21]

The relationship between the PRC and the SAR will not be that of a federal state and one of its constituent units, not merely because the PRC is not a federation, but also because the SAR

16 This principle is referred to in the preamble to the Basic Law.
17 Arts 245–248 of the Indian constitution.
18 Art 73.
19 Arts 131, 132.
20 Ss 51, 52 of the Australian constitution.
21 S 107.

will be financially independent of the CPG in every respect. However, there is much in the technique of the distribution of powers in federal constitutions that can usefully be absorbed into the Basic Law. There are also lessons that can be learnt from the innumerable disputes that have arisen on whether a particular matter falls within the subjects enumerated in one list or in the other, or even in the third concurrent list — lessons which point unwaveringly in the direction of a single unambiguous list of subjects.

Accordingly, the Basic Law ought to specify that the PRC will have legislative and executive authority only in respect of the defence of the SAR and the conduct of its foreign affairs (subject to the exceptions referred to in section XI of Annex I to the Joint Declaration), and that in respect of all other matters, the SAR will have and enjoy autonomous legislative, executive, and judicial power. These other matters will, no doubt, include the economy, education, science, culture, sports, religion, labour, and social services.

(2) A statement of justiciable rights and freedoms, binding on all the institutions of government, is another technique that is available to the draftsman. In the event of an infringement, the aggrieved party would be entitled to a remedy through the judicial process. For instance, in respect of education, the Basic Law should include in such a statement the following provisions:
(a) Parents and, where applicable, legal guardians, shall have the right to choose for their children schools, other than those established by public authorities, which conform to such minimum standards as may be laid down or approved by the government of the SAR, and to ensure the religious and moral education of their children in conformity with their own convictions.
(b) Individuals and bodies, including religious organisations, shall have the right to establish and direct educational institutions, subject always to the observance of the principles set forth in paragraph (a) above and to the requirement that the education given in such institutions shall conform to such minimum standards as may be laid down by the government.
(3) A statement of 'directive principles of state policy' is a technique being commonly resorted to now, ostensibly for the purpose of giving a high moral content to a constitution. However lofty the sentiments expressed therein may be, they are likely to be ignored or even deliberately disregarded if, as is often the case, such a statement is either preceded, or followed, by a provision in the following terms:

The provisions of this chapter do not confer or impose legal rights or obligations, and are not enforceable in any court or tribunal. No question of inconsistency shall be raised in any court or tribunal.[22]

It is not, therefore, suggested that the Basic Law should contain anything in the nature of such a statement. However, the concept of 'directive principles of state policy' may be usefully adopted for the purpose of limiting the authority of the organs of state power in the PRC in relation to the SAR if it is clearly stated that such principles shall operate as rules of law.

The Joint Declaration states that the basic policies of the PRC regarding Hong Kong, as set out in article 3 and as elaborated in Annex I, will be stipulated in the Basic Law. Some of these policies relate to the institutions of government, their structure and composition, and these should, no doubt, be incorporated in those sections of the Basic Law that deal with the exercise of legislative, executive, and judicial power in the SAR. Some others relate to the rights and freedoms of the inhabitants, and they ought properly to find expression in a bill of rights included in the Basic Law. The remaining declarations of policy are principally those which seek to guarantee that the PRC will not interfere with the current social and economic systems in Hong Kong.

It would seem appropriate for these declarations of policy regarding non-interference with the social and economic systems chosen to be followed in the SAR to be included in the Basic Law as a statement of directive principles of state policy, laid down by the National People's Congress and binding on all organs of state power in the PRC. Such a statement should probably include the following provisions in lesser or greater detail:

(1) The SAR may use its financial resources exclusively for its own purposes. The CPG shall neither levy taxes on, nor recover any payments from, the SAR.

(2) The SAR may formulate and implement its own monetary and financial policies, issue its own convertible currency, and continue markets for foreign exchange, gold, securities, and futures.

(3) The SAR may formulate and implement its own economic and trade policies, and may maintain and develop economic and trade relations with other states and regions. It may establish official and semi-official economic and trade missions in foreign countries.

22   1978 constitution of the Democratic Socialist Republic of Sri Lanka, s 29. See 1937 constitution of Ireland, art 45 and the 1975 constitution of Malta, art 22, for similar provisions.

(4) The SAR may retain the status of a free port and continue a free trade policy, including the free movement of goods and capital.

(5) The SAR shall be a separate customs territory. It may participate in relevant international organisations and trade agreements (including preferential trade arrangements). It may exclusively enjoy export quotas, tariff preferences, and other similar arrangements obtained by it. It may issue its own certificates of origin for products manufactured locally, in accordance with prevailing rules of origin.

(6) The SAR may grant access to its ports to all ships other than foreign warships (access for which requires the permission of the CPG). The SAR may maintain its own systems of shipping management and shipping regulation. It may maintain a shipping register and issue related certificates in the name of 'Hong Kong, China.'

(7) (a) The SAR may maintain its own system of civil aviation management and its own aircraft register.

   (b) The CPG shall act in consultation with the SAR government in making arrangements for air services between the SAR and other parts of the PRC by airlines incorporated and having their principal place of business in the SAR and by other airlines of the PRC.

   (c) The CPG shall take account of the special conditions and economic interests of the SAR in concluding air service agreements for air services between other parts of the PRC and other states and regions with stops at the SAR, and air services between the SAR and other parts and regions with stops at other parts of the PRC. Representatives of the SAR government may participate as members of delegations of the government of the PRC in air service consultations with foreign governments concerning arrangements for such services.

   (d) In respect of all scheduled air services to, from, or through the SAR which do not operate to, from, or through the mainland of China, the SAR government may, acting under specific authorisation from the CPG,

      (i)   renew or amend existing agreements or arrangements;

      (ii) negotiate and conclude new agreements providing routes for airlines incorporated and having their principal place of business in the SAR, and providing rights for overflights and technical stops;

      (iii) negotiate and conclude provisional arrangements where no air service agreement with a foreign state or region is in force;

and the SAR government may,

    (iv) negotiate and conclude with other authorities all arrangements concerning the implementation of such air service agreements and provisional arrangements;

    (v) issue licences to airlines incorporated and having their principal place of business in the SAR;

    (vi) designate such airlines under such air service agreements and provisional arrangements; and

    (vii) issue permits to foreign airlines.

(8) The SAR government may issue its own travel documents for entry into and exit from the SAR, and apply immigration controls on entry, stay in, and departure from the SAR by persons from foreign states and regions.

(9) The SAR government may formulate and implement its own policies in the fields of culture, education, science, and technology, including policies regarding the educational system and its administration, the language of instruction, the allocation of funds, the examination system, the system of academic awards, and the recognition of educational and technological qualifications.

DRAFTING TECHNIQUES

The drafter of the Basic Law has preferred to ossify the existing social and economic systems of Hong Kong, rather than offer the SAR the freedom to develop itself according to its own genius. The essential characteristic of the document is strict regimentation. It is structured on the lines of socialist constitutions. Indeed, in the tradition of Marxist-Leninist ideology, its preamble affirms the fulfilment of 'the long cherished common aspiration of the entire Chinese people for the recovery of Hong Kong,' while the main body of the draft proceeds to 'prescribe the system to be practised in the Hong Kong SAR.' It is the very antithesis of that informal, often illusory, framework within which successive colonial administrations have endorsed the manifestation of an economic miracle.

Some of the provisions of chapters V and VI seek, quite unabashedly, to freeze the existing systems. For example, 'The Hong Kong dollar, as the legal tender in the Hong Kong SAR, shall continue to circulate and remain freely convertible' (BL114).

When one recalls that the principle agreed upon in the Joint Declaration was that 'The Hong Kong dollar, as the local legal tender, shall continue to circulate and remain freely convertible' (section VII, Annex I), one wonders whether the drafter perhaps thought that his task was merely to reproduce the contents of the treaty in the form of numbered sentences. The commitment made by the PRC government in the Joint Declaration was surely that the SAR will have the right to issue its own convertible currency without having to conform to the national monetary system. If so, the drafter ought to have expressed the rule of law in that form, thereby placing the SAR in control of its monetary system without imposing on it a duty, as it has done by this clause, which will require policing by the PRC.

BL130 ('The Hong Kong SAR shall maintain Hongkong's previous systems of shipping management and shipping regulation') and BL135 ('The Hong Kong SAR shall continue the previous system of civil aviation management in Hong Kong'), by imposing constitutional injunctions, which stultify development in these related areas of shipping and aviation management, must necessarily have the effect of eventually transforming these two vibrant lifelines of Hong Kong's economy into fossilised relics of a past era.

BL152 states that:

The Hong Kong SAR shall maintain the policy previously practised in Hong Kong in respect of subventions for organisations in fields such as education, medicine, culture, arts, recreation, sports, social welfare and social work. Staff previously serving in subventioned organisations in Hong Kong may remain in their employment in accordance with the previous system.

If this constitutional provision is intended to be taken seriously, it would at first retard, and eventually halt, the development of numerous subvented programmes such as the School Medical Service Scheme and primary and secondary education in the SAR, by prohibiting the government from responding to the changes that must inevitably occur, phase by phase, during a 50-year span. It would also inhibit any extension of government assistance to new attempts of private initiative thrown up by socio-economic pressures. Equally catastrophic for subvented organisations would be the claims likely to be made by staff serving on 30 June 1997 that they have acquired, by virtue of BL152, a right to serve in perpetuity notwithstanding retirement age or physical or mental infirmity.

The impracticability of attempting to 'freeze' an existing system is particularly evident in relation to education. The Joint Declaration states that:

The Hong Kong SAR shall maintain the educational system practised in Hong Kong. The Hong Kong SAR shall on its own decide policies in the fields of culture, education, science and technology, including policies regarding the educational system and its administration, the language of instruction, the allocation of funds, the examination system, the system of academic awards and the recognition of educational and technological qualifications (section X, Annex I).

The Basic Law gives expression to that policy declaration in the following terms:

Article 142
The Hong Kong SAR shall maintain the educational system previously practised in Hong Kong.

Article 143
The government of the Hong Kong SAR shall, on its own, formulate policies on education, including policies regarding the educational system and its administration, the language of instruction, the allocation of funds, the examination system, the system of academic awards and the recognition of educational qualifications.

BL142 will, therefore, require the SAR to 'maintain the system previously practised in Hong Kong.' Accordingly, the power of the SAR government to formulate policies regarding the educational system under the next clause will necessarily have to be exercised within the framework of the 'system previously practised in Hong Kong.' No other interpretation is possible if legal effect is to be given to both these clauses. Not only will this interpretation frustrate any attempt to refashion the SAR educational system to meet the needs and demands of the twenty-first century, it will also enable a future law on educational change to be challenged in court on the ground of repugnancy to the Basic Law. Such problems could, of course, have been avoided if the Basic Law had merely provided, as the Joint Declaration must surely have intended, that the SAR may formulate and implement its own policies in the field of education.

Apart from seeking to freeze the existing systems, the draftsman has also fallen into the error of attempting to prescribe directives of policy for the SAR government: a task that was not contemplated in the Joint Declaration. That has probably been done in the wholly mistaken belief that capitalism can survive only if, like the march towards communism, its progress is chartered on an irrevocable, pre-determined plan, or in the naive hope that the emergence of social and political forces can be stemmed by rigid constitutional injunctions.

Some of these 'directives' are relatively harmless and inconsequential. For example, it is unlikely that in the absence of BL109 ('The Government of the Hong Kong SAR shall create conditions and take measures for the maintenance of the status of the Hong Kong SAR as an international financial centre') the SAR government would have embarked on a self-destructive rampage through the region's financial and monetary institutions. Equally, it would be fanciful to imagine that the motivating force for any initiatives in the field of public health would be BL145, which states that:

> The Government of the Hong Kong SAR shall promote the development of medical and health services . . . .

Other 'directives' or programmatic declarations are potentially debilitating or are capable of seriously disrupting the hitherto stable economic and social structure of Hong Kong. At least four such 'directives' can be immediately identified:

Article 105
The government of the Hong Kong SAR shall follow the principle of measuring expenditure by revenues in drawing up its budget.

The government of the Hong Kong SAR shall, over a number of fiscal years taken as a whole, maintain a basic balance between total budgetary revenues and expenditure.

In principle, the rate of increase of the budgetary revenues and the expenditure of the Hong Kong SAR shall not exceed that of the gross domestic product over a number of fiscal years taken as a whole.

Article 107
The Hong Kong SAR shall continue to practise a low tax policy.

Article 111
No exchange control policies shall be applied in the Hong Kong SAR.

Article 115
The issue of Hong Kong currency shall be backed up by a reserve fund of no less than 100 per cent freely convertible currency.

The proposed legal requirement that the growth rates of budgetary revenue and expenditure shall not exceed the growth rate of the gross domestic product is believed to have been included at the insistence of some Hong Kong members of the Basic Law Drafting Committee, fearful of demands for excessive welfare after the transfer of sovereignty.[23] A previous proposal that 'public expenditure of the Hong Kong SAR should not exceed 20 per cent of the gross domestic product' had been modified to reach the present version.[24] It is foolhardy to believe that social and economic forces can be held in check by constitutional restraints of this type. Moreover, as one commentator has already noted, the constitutional rules as to the drawing up of the budget contained in BL105 will leave the future SAR government with few alternatives in financial policy formulation:

---

23 Tang Shu-hung, 'Basic Law – Its Economic Stipulations' (1988) 166 *Welfare Digest* (Hong Kong Council of Social Welfare) 4.
24 Ibid.

the SAR Government will be unable to introduce a surplus budget to cool down demand under an overheated economy or a deficit budget to boost investment during an economic recession.[25]

The relative size of the public sector ought to be determined, from time to time, by the relevant authorities in the SAR government in accordance with the fiscal and economic needs of the time. To stipulate by law that it shall not exceed the gross domestic product is to make economic management justiciable in court. Judges of the SAR will be called upon to decide not whether the Financial Secretary has acted in the best interests of the Region, but whether he has conformed to the predetermined principles prescribed in the Basic Law, regardless of the devastating effect the application of such principles may have, in the special circumstances of the time, on the social and economic life of the community.

The other injunctions of the Basic Law contained in BL107, 111 and 115 will require the SAR government to continue to practise a low tax policy, apply no exchange control, and ensure that the issue of Hong Kong currency is always backed up by a reserve fund of no less than 100% freely convertible foreign currency. These are, no doubt, aspects of current economic policy in the territory. They are probably principles of good financing too. However, their transformation into mandatory rules of law may raise a multitude of unprecedented legal problems: What is a 'low' tax policy? Will the lowering of the salary tax with a corresponding increase in the profits tax infringe the Basic Law? Does the word 'continue' have the effect of freezing the tax structure as on 30 June 1997? Will a supplementary finance bill be subjected to judicial review on the ground that it alters the basic balance between revenue and expenditure? Is the enforced artificial value of the Hong Kong dollar secured by keeping it pegged to the US dollar a subtle form of exchange control? Will resort to the floating exchange rate system (which may disrupt the reserve fund) be unconstitutional? It would surely imperil the economic health of the SAR if sound financial management is to be overshadowed by issues such as these being raised and argued in the region's courtrooms by lawyers and judges.

If it is considered necessary that, in order to assuage fears that may exist in any quarter, certain stipulations relating to the economy ought to be included in the Basic Law, the preamble appears to be the proper place for their inclusion. They will then

25 Tsang Shu-ki, 'Too much detail on economy may create problems' *South China Morning Post* 29 April 1988.

not be enforceable rules of law, but guidelines for the governance of the SAR. They will be the underlying premise upon which the NPC has, by a basic law, created the Special Administrative Region of Hong Kong.

CONCLUSION

In its review of economic policy in 1987, the Hong Kong government states that:

> Economic policy in Hong Kong is to a large extent dictated, and constrained, by the special circumstances of the Hong Kong economy. Owing to its small and open nature, the economy is vulnerable to external factors, and government actions designed to offset unfavourable external influences are of limited effectiveness. Further, the government is of the view that, except where social considerations are regarded as over-riding, the allocation of resources in the economy will normally be most efficient if market forces are relied on and if government intervention in the private sector is kept to a minimum. This basically free-enterprise, market-disciplined system has contributed to Hong Kong's economic success.[26]

Whether, and for how long, Hong Kong can continue to enjoy that economic success after it has become a minuscule part of an enormous socialist (or perhaps communist by then) state, will depend on the degree of autonomy it continues to enjoy. No constitutional prescriptions can serve as a substitute for such autonomy. What Hong Kong will require as it readjusts itself to a new sovereign is continued freedom of action and flexibility of movement. In the context of a conflict of ideologies, that freedom and flexibility can only be guaranteed by the Basic Law. It would be a tragic mistake for the BLDC to assume, as it appears to have done, that by packaging the territory in cellophane, inserting it into a time capsule, and releasing it wishfully into what is believed to be a frozen historical vacuum, Hong Kong's 'previous capitalist system and life-style' will remain unchanged for 50 years.

26 *Hong Kong 1988* (Hong Kong: Government Printer, 1988) 59.

12 Foreign, External, and Defence Affairs

RODA MUSHKAT

HONG Kong has long functioned as a de facto city-state, enjoying extensive autonomy in the conduct of its internal and external affairs. The People's Republic of China has signalled its intention, both formally and informally, to allow the Hong Kong Special Administrative Region considerable freedom of action in the domestic arena after 1997. A reasonably high degree of autonomy has also been promised in the external sphere, although the commitments made in this respect imply a greater measure of central guidance.

While the management of external affairs raises sensitive issues of sovereignty, wide discretionary powers in this domain are viewed as an essential component of the strategy designed to maintain Hong Kong's status as a key actor in the international economic system. It is necessary, therefore, to try to establish to what extent the SAR will be able to control its relations with external parties.

The starting point for such analysis should be the Sino-British Joint Declaration on the Question of Hong Kong which provides for the 'one country, two systems' model of autonomy and confers validity upon the SAR legal order. In other words, the standard of interpretation and evaluation of the envisaged division of responsibilities between the Central Government of the PRC and the Region is the international law which governs the Joint Declaration. Stipulations in the Basic Law ought thus to be examined with a view to ascertaining their convergence with the Sino-British agreement and conformity to generally accepted international legal norms pertaining to autonomous schemes.

The specific issues explored in the present chapter are definitional concerns stemming from the conceptual approach adopted by the drafters of the Basic Law, application problems which may have impact upon the relationship between the 'central' authorities and the Hong Kong 'periphery,' and the policy implications of the assumption of responsibility by China for the conduct of SAR foreign and defence affairs. The ultimate objective of the exercise is to determine whether Hong Kong will be able to enjoy the 'high degree of autonomy' which its residents rightfully expect.

THE SINO-BRITISH AGREEMENT ON THE QUESTION OF
HONG KONG

Further to the broad identification of the sovereign power as
located with the CPG (JD3(2)), the Sino-British accord provides
that the SAR 'will enjoy a high degree of autonomy, *except in
foreign and defence affairs which are the responsibilities of the
Central People's Government.*' At the same time, under section
XI of Annex I the Region 'may on its own, using the name "Hong
Kong, China," maintain and develop relations and conclude and
implement agreements with states, regions and relevant international organisations in the appropriate fields, including the
economic, trade, financial and monetary, shipping, communications, touristic, cultural and sporting fields.'[1] In its role as an
autonomous entity, the SAR may also 'participate in international organisations and conferences not limited to states.' In
addition, '[r]epresentatives of the Hong Kong Special Administrative Region Government may participate, as members of the
delegations of the Government of the People's Republic of
China, in international organisations or conferences in appropriate fields limited to states and affecting the Hong Kong Special
Administrative Region, or may attend in such other capacity as
may be permitted by the Central People's Government and the
organisation or conference concerned, and may express their
views in the name of "Hong Kong, China".' Indeed, the CPG
undertakes 'to ensure that the Hong Kong Special Administrative Region shall continue to retain its status in an appropriate
capacity in those international organisations in which the
People's Republic of China is a member and in which Hong
Kong participates in one capacity or another.' The PRC's
undertaking also extends to facilitating where necessary the
'continued participation of the Hong Kong Special Administrative Region in an appropriate capacity in those international
organisations in which Hong Kong is a participant in one
capacity or another, but of which the People's Republic of China
is not a member.'

Consistent with the emphasis upon the development by the
territory of external ties, the Sino-British agreement stipulates
the establishment, with the approval of the CPG, of consular and
other official or semi-official missions in the SAR (section XI,
Annex I) as well as official and semi-official SAR economic and
trade missions in foreign countries (section VI, Annex I). The
SAR's 'external' status is further enhanced by the authority

---

1 A special provision concerning participation in international trade agreements
  is contained in s VI. Wide powers are also granted for the 'specific functions
  and responsibilities of the Hong Kong Special Administrative Region Government in the field of shipping' (s VIII) and civil aviation (s IX).

granted to it by the PRC to issue passports and travel documents as well as to conclude agreements for the mutual abolition of visa requirements (section XIV, Annex I). Finally, to demonstrate the SAR's sincere desire to accept obligations as an active member of the international community, appropriate arrangements are projected for the application in the Region of relevant international agreements (section XI, Annex I).

With respect to defence, while such affairs are to be managed (and funded) by the CPG, the maintenance of public order in the SAR should be the responsibility of the SAR government and the military forces sent by the CPG to be stationed in the Region for the purpose of defence 'shall not interfere in the internal affairs of the Hong Kong Special Administrative Region' (section XII, Annex I).

THE BASIC LAW

The Basic Law, which has been widely expected to inject greater substance into the notion of the 'high degree of autonomy' pledged under the Joint Declaration and to define in a more unequivocal fashion the areas of responsibilities of the CPG and the SAR government, has in effect generally reproduced the agreement, including some of its vague provisions.

Certain modifications and additions pertaining to the areas of foreign relations and defence have nonetheless been incorporated. Thus, added to other undefined key terms such as 'foreign affairs' and 'relevant external affairs' are laws enacted by the National People's Congress or its Standing Committee which 'give expression to national unity and territorial integrity' and which are 'outside the limits of the high degree of autonomy of the Hong Kong Special Administrative Region.' Under BL17 such laws will apply in the Region by way of promulgation or legislation under the directives of the State Council whenever there is the need to apply them. A new class of cases — namely, cases relating to the 'executive acts' of the CPG, which like cases relating to foreign affairs and defence are to be removed from the jurisdiction of the SAR's courts — has also become part of the Basic Law (BL18) in clear deviation from the JD. Further restraints have likewise been imposed upon the local judiciary in connection with all three categories of cases: '[C]ourts of the Hong Kong Special Administrative Region shall seek the advice of the Chief Executive whenever questions concerning defence, foreign affairs or the executive acts of the Central People's Government arise in any legal proceedings.'

The provisions pertaining to 'external affairs' are largely a duplication of their counterparts in the JD. Covered are the

SAR's participation (in various forms) in international agreements and organisations (BL158–161) as well as other 'externally oriented' activities such as the authorisation given by the CPG to the government of the SAR to issue passports and the control granted to the SAR over entry into, stay in, and departure by persons from foreign states and other regions (BL162). Also included are articles governing the establishment of official and unofficial missions representing the SAR (BL164) and those carrying representative functions in the Region (BL165).

The Basic Law reiterates the CPG's responsibility for the defence of the SAR and its undertaking to refrain from interference through the military forces stationed in the territory. A new provision was thought to be necessary, however, to allow the SAR, 'in times of need, [to] request the Central People's Government for assistance from the garrison in the maintenance of public order and disaster relief' (BL13).

DEFINITIONAL CONCERNS

Some conceptually challenging questions have emerged under the Joint Declaration and have not been resolved in the Basic Law. One crucial issue concerns the scope of 'foreign affairs' and 'defence.' The problem stems from the fact that neither term is formally defined and that the distinctions employed, such as between foreign and external affairs or defence and public order, tend to obscure rather than elucidate their meaning.

Foreign affairs

Commentators have pointed out, for instance, the difficulty, indeed futility, of attempting to separate external economic affairs from foreign affairs, given that in the 'real world,' 'all power struggles are essentially economic in nature . . . , economic blockade has been a widely used political weapon for half a century . . . , infiltration is a common international practice . . . [and] the economic and strategic power of multinational corporations often exceeds those of small states.'[2]

Others have queried the nature of the relationship between foreign affairs for which the PRC is responsible and the 'relevant external affairs' with which the SAR is authorised to deal on its own (BL12), or more specifically whether the latter is a 'sub-set'

2 Liu Yiu-chu, 'The Scope of "Foreign and Defence Affairs",' an unpublished paper written for discussion by the Future of Hong Kong Law Study Group, 29 May 1985.

of the former.[3] At least one provision which is included in the chapter on 'external affairs' reflects a measure of involvement in what is generally considered as 'foreign affairs' through participation by representatives of the SAR 'as members of delegations of the Government of the People's Republic of China in negotiations at the diplomatic level directly affecting the Hong Kong Special Administrative Region conducted by the Central People's Government' (BL 158). It is nonetheless unclear that the 'relevant external affairs' referred to in the chapter on the relationship between the central authorities and the SAR (chapter II) correspond to the 'external affairs' which form the subject matter of chapter VII.

Little guidance may be derived from international legal practice, since no uniformity can be established among the various autonomy arrangements. Hannum and Lillich, who surveyed 22 non-sovereign entities, observe that notwithstanding the 'almost-universality' of the reservation to the central or sovereign government of general authority to conduct foreign relations on behalf of the autonomous entity, there are considerable 'nuances' of these powers (eg formal or informal consultations on matters of foreign policy between the local and national governments).[4]

It is also arguable that analogies with entities such as the Turkish Federate State of Cyprus, the Emirates of the UAE, or even Greenland and the Netherland Antilles, are inappropriate in view of Hong Kong's level of development and sophistication and its active participation in the international system.

Indeed, it is Liu Yiu-chu's contention that 'foreign affairs' in the PRC/SAR context should be restrictively interpreted to mean 'that part of SAR's role in international interaction [ie, not to be equated with China's foreign affairs in general] which . . . international law from time to time reserves exclusively to sovereign states,'[5] or what political scientists sometimes refer to as 'high' foreign policy.[6] Covered presumably are declarations of recog-

---

3 See Law Society Working Party on the Draft Basic Law, *Comments on the Draft Basic Law* (December 1987 version) (hereafter *Law Society Comments*).

4 See Hurst Hannum and Richard B Lillich, 'The Concept of Autonomy in International Law' in Yoram Dinstein (ed), *Models of Autonomy* (New Brunswick and London: Transaction Books, 1981) 233.

5 Liu Yiu-chu (n 2 above) 5.

6 See, eg R E Jones, *Changing Structure of British Foreign Policy* (London: Longman, 1974) 9–10. In contrast, 'low' foreign policy (eg agreements on international credits, monetary reforms, agreements of transnational industrial and scientific projects, etc), while absorbing governments fully, 'does not occupy the high international stage where issues of peace and war and rise and fall of nations are the traditional dramatic themes.' And although statehood is

nition of foreign states, of war and peace or of belligerency and neutrality, claims relating to territorial sovereignty, military or defence alliances, and membership in organisations whose primary purpose is the maintenance of international peace and security. Such a definition of 'foreign affairs' would serve to reaffirm PRC's sovereign position with respect to the SAR ('one country') and highlight, at the same time, the distinct nature of the SAR ('two systems') with its own 'foreign affairs' orientations, core interests, values, and objectives.[7] It might also narrow the areas thought to be 'grey.' Thus, for example, the responsibility for conducting extradition relations — while evidently containing a 'foreign affairs' element, but not inevitably a matter of high statecraft[8] — may legitimately be regarded as within the SAR's 'external' powers alongside the authority to 'maintain and develop relations and conclude and implement agreements with states, regions and relevant international organisations in the appropriate fields, including the economic, trade, financial and monetary, shipping, communications, tourism, cultural and sports fields' (BL159; JD3(10) and section XI, Annex I) as well as the control over 'entry into, stay in and departure from the Hong Kong Special Administrative Region by persons from foreign states and other regions' (BL162; JD, section XI, Annex I).[9]

not irrelevant to these concerns, it 'commands something less than a monopoly of influence over them.' As noted by Wallace, low policy typically would be decided upon below the cabinet level of government, often by officials dealing directly with the relevant foreign organisations in a semi-autonomous way. See W Wallace, *Foreign Policy and the Political Process* (London: Macmillan, 1971) 50–52.

7 For a discussion of these concepts see K J Holsti, *International Politics. A Framework for Analysis* (Eaglewood Cliffs, NJ: Prentice Hall, 4th ed 1983).

8 Mann observes the change in British law and policy with respect to extradition from a conception of 'great prerogative power supposed to be an incident of sovereignty' (*Brown v Lizars* (1905) 2 CLR 837, 852 per Griffiths CJ) to a position where, as in issues of immigration and control of aliens, 'very little [is] left of the prerogative': F A Mann, *Foreign Affairs in English Courts* (Oxford: Clarendon Press, 1986).

9 In fact, it may be argued with some conviction that extradition matters fall most appropriately within the criminal justice system to be regulated as part of the domestic legal system. See Janice Brabyn, 'Extradition and the Hong Kong SAR' (1988) 20 *Case Western Reserve Journal of International Law* (forthcoming). Alternatively, Brabyn contends that classification of extradition as 'foreign affairs' does not necessarily preclude the granting of responsibility for the 'judicial aspects of extradition' to the SAR. Another proposal examined by Brabyn seeks to avoid the issue of classification altogether through the devolving of a specific power on the SAR to conclude extradition agreements while 'reserving a power of veto to be exercised by the CPG within a fixed period after the signing of the treaty.'

More problematic perhaps is the categorisation of 'asylum' matters. Evidently, requests for 'political/diplomatic' or permanent asylum are within the sovereign discretion of states. Yet, the issue of 'temporary territorial refuge' may arguably be handled by whichever entity is in effective control of the territory and whose immediate interests are most directly affected. It is the latter which incurs the respective international obligations and hence should logically be responsible for the relevant decision-making. An autonomous SAR government would be in a position to pursue an independent refugee policy.

Finally, a restrictive approach to 'foreign affairs' would be in line with prevailing notions of sovereignty. Recent studies confirm that the key attribute of sovereignty is not necessarily active participation in international life but rather the state's 'constitutional independence' (in the sense that its constitution is not part of a larger constitutional arrangement).[10] Indeed, states may choose to opt out of international life (like Burma for much of the 1960s and early 1970s) or they may find it difficult to play an international role because of refusal of other states to have dealings with them (eg South Africa), yet their sovereignty or constitutional independence is not thereby affected. By the same token, it is evident that international participation, including membership in international organisations, is not limited to sovereign states.[11] In fact, non-sovereign entities may act, for certain purposes, as 'international persons.' Only sovereign states, however, are *full* international persons, by virtue of their constitutional independence, whereas the international activity of non-sovereign entities is based on a specific grant or permission of the sovereign superior.[12]

Needless to say, constitutional independence does not mean a completely free internal or external hand[13] but neither the amount of a state's 'legal freedom' (ie control over the extent of one's legal obligations) nor its acceptance of jurisdictional limits

10 See A James, *Sovereign Statehood. The Basis of International Society* (London: Allen & Unwin, 1986).

11 Hong Kong is an obvious case in point. Other examples include the states of the West German Federation which have the right, with the consent of the Federation, to make treaties on matters within their jurisdiction and the cantons of Switzerland which may do likewise on specified matters. The constituent republics of the Soviet Union are non-sovereign members of the UN.

12 James (n 10 above) 26–27.

13 For a discussion of international legal and political restraints upon states' behaviour see ibid 52–57, 228–240, 245–253; see also I Detter de Lupis, *International Law and the Independent States* (Aldershot, Hants: Gower, 2nd ed 1987).

(including submission to some form of third-party adjudication) detracts from its sovereignty or its eligibility to participate in a full and regular manner in international relations.[14]

By retaining control over matters of 'high' foreign policy only, the PRC's sovereignty is by no means derogated from,[15] since regardless of who exercises the relevant authority, the source of governmental authority would lie with the Central Government and any restrictions are accepted on a consensual basis.

Defence

Under BL13, '[t]he Central People's Government is responsible for the defence of the Hong Kong Special Administrative Region.' Again, questions arise as to the scope and extent of such responsibility. Ordinarily, 'defence' of a territory may cover both external and internal security affairs or generally the 'maintenance of the integrity and security' of a territory.[16] Under the Joint Declaration (JD3(11), section XII, Annex I) and BL15, however, matters of 'public order' fall within the ambit of the SAR as part of its general management of internal affairs. Furthermore, the non-intervention of PRC's military forces in the 'local' affairs of the Region is expressly guaranteed (BL13; JD section XII, Annex I).

Internal security duties, including the control of civilian disturbances,[17] are thus to be removed from the domain of the 'defence exception.' In addition, certain matters (such as the prevention of infiltration by illegal migrants), hitherto possibly classified as 'external defence,' are to be vested with the SAR government (BL15). Other 'external defence' functions currently

---

14 As stated by Judge D Anzilotti, '[t]he restrictions upon a State's liberty, whether arising out of ordinary international law or contractual engagements, do not as such in the least affect its independence. As long as these restrictions do not place the State under the legal authority of another State, the former remains an independent State however extensive and burdensome these obligations may be': Independent Opinion, *Customs Regime Between Austria and Germany* PCIJ (1931) Series B, No 41, p 58.

15 In fact the PRC's sovereignty would not have been affected had it agreed to have *all* relevant foreign relations and defence affairs conducted by the SAR. See illustrations in James Crawford, *The Creation of States in International Law* (Oxford: Clarendon Press, 1979).

16 See statement of the official tasks of British troops in Hong Kong, cited in Norman Miners, *The Government and Politics of Hong Kong* (Hong Kong: Oxford University Press, 4th ed 1986) 19.

17 See, however, the statement by Deng Xiaoping that the troops stationed locally 'will go into action ... when turmoil and big riots occur': speech reproduced under the title 'Current Policies and Prospects for Hong Kong,' *Beijing Review* 4–10 January 1988, pp 14, 17.

within the parameters (theoretically at least) of the British forces in Hong Kong (ie those connected with protection against invasion from the mainland and containment of limited incursion by the PLA or local militia) would cease to be of relevance after 1997.

It may therefore be concluded that the scope of 'defence' in the context of the PRC/SAR relationship is confined to the protection of the Region from foreign aggression, and intervention locally under the pretext of 'defence' could rarely be justified. Thus, for example, intervention based upon 'fears that the local police force might not be able to handle its new responsibilities of controlling civilian disturbances' or would succumb to opportunities of corruption arising out of its new duties of controlling illegal immigration[18] would clearly be ultra vires. In a similar vein, 'laws which relate to defence' are to be interpreted 'purposively,' namely, only laws which have as their 'direct and immediate object'[19] the military defence of the SAR should be applied in the Region (by virtue of BL17, para 3).

Executive acts of the CPG

While not touching directly upon the issues of foreign and defence affairs, the reference to this new (ie not alluded to in the JD) 'exclusionary domain' of the Central Government in a provision relating to foreign affairs and defence may warrant attention in the present analysis. Indeed, it is submitted (subject to observations made later concerning the acceptability of any special measure of exclusion of such acts from the scope of the local courts' jurisdiction) that a reasonable interpretation of 'executive acts of the CPG' would take account of the *noscitur a sociis* rule ('a thing is known by its associates') and delimit this dangerously broad category to acts which constitute the exercise of exclusively sovereign powers (not shared with ordinary citizens) and involving relationships with a foreign state/entity.[20] Such an interpretation would seem to accord with the intention of the drafters who, motivated by a strong desire to 'fade out the

18 Expressed by a Chinese official in the Joint Liaison Group as reported in S Leung, 'Working Towards a Strategic Withdrawal' *South China Morning Post* 21 November 1987, p 15.

19 Test laid down in *Australia Communist Party v The Commonwealth*, extracted in L Zines and G J Lindell, *Sawer's Australian Constitutional Cases* (Sydney: Law Book Co, 4th ed 1982) 505.

20 See H W R Wade, 'Procedure and Prerogative in Public Law' (1985) 101 *Law Quarterly Review* 180, 192–193.

colonial colour,' sought to avoid the use of terms such as 'prerogative acts' or 'Acts of State' while retaining a similar notion.[21]

National unity and territorial integrity

The definitional ambiguities which are a feature of the BL are exacerbated by the vague concept of 'national unity and territorial integrity,' representing a body of PRC laws which, like those concerning foreign affairs and defence, is applicable in the SAR (BL17).

As a 'preambular' term, 'national unity and territorial integrity' may be presumed to reinforce the status of the SAR as 'an inalienable part of the People's Republic of China' (BL1). In an introductory context the phrase may also serve to emphasise the 'unitary' nature of the PRC and the intent to avoid formation of a federation.[22] Additionally, it may imply the notion of 'mutual solidarity between the various parts of the realm.'[23]

Yet, it is not clear how the scope of any relevant legislation could extend beyond what is already covered by laws relating to foreign and defence affairs. Arguably, any internal action which may be considered an infringement of national unity and territorial integrity would be *within* 'the limits of the high degree of autonomy of the Hong Kong Special Administrative Region' as a matter of public order.

As it stands, this undefined category of laws is unacceptable, giving rise to local fears of unchecked interference by the Central Government in SAR affairs.[24]

21 This is reflected in examples of such acts cited by one drafter which include the appointment of the SAR's Chief Executive and other principal government officials, deployment of troops, dissolution of the local legislature, and amnesty. See report by Yau Shing-mu, 'After a Year Drafters Solve a Sticky Legal Problem,' *Hong Kong Standard* 3 August 1987, p 1.

22 Note the statements made in the *People's Daily* following the signing of the Joint Declaration: 'First of all, to safeguard China's sovereignty, unity, and territorial integrity is a basic principle we should adhere to in establishing special administrative regions. Our country should be a unified country. There is only one China in the world, and that is the People's Republic of China. It exercises sovereignty over its special administrative regions. Ours is a socialist country with a unitary system. It is not a federal country. . . . The special administrative regions are local administrative regions under the unified central leadership. They are not member states. . . .': 'Renmin Ribao on Special Administrative Regions' *FBIS, China*, 2 October 1984, p K19.

23 See I Foighel, 'A Framework for Local Autonomy: The Greenland Case' in *Models of Autonomy* (n 4 above) 37.

24 See Frank Ching, 'Draft is a Minefield of Legal Ambiguities' *South China Morning Post* 13 May 1988.

APPLICATION ISSUES

Another set of questions emerge in connection with the application or legal/judicial aspects of the basic division of responsibilities concerning foreign affairs and defence. It is a moot point, for example, to what extent the PRC's foreign policy (as distinct from its legislative manifestations) would constitute the foundation of legal rules or contribute to the formation of public policy in the SAR and hence be of relevance in the decision-making process of local courts.

Foreign affairs and defence laws

Evidently, *laws* which relate to foreign affairs and defence will apply in the SAR 'by way of promulgation[25] or legislation on the directives of the State Council whenever there is the need to apply any such law in the Region' (BL17).

International agreements

Similarly, international agreements to which the PRC is a party may be extended to the SAR upon a decision of the CPG 'in accordance with the circumstances and needs of the Region and after seeking the views of the government of the Region' (BL161). No stipulation is included, however, regarding the domestic application of such treaties or, in other words, whether the treaties form part of the SAR's law and thus are enforceable by the local courts.[26] Arguably, in the light of BL17, unless the treaties are part of the 'laws previously in force in Hong Kong' or 'enacted by the legislature of the Hong Kong Special Administrative Region' or incorporated in 'laws enacted by the National People's Congress or its Standing Committee which relate to defence and foreign affairs' or 'give expression to national unity and territorial integrity' they would not form part of the laws of the SAR.

25 As pointed out by commentators, clarification of this mode of enactment is required since no such procedure exists under the present legal system. See *Law Society Comments* (n 3 above 5).

26 It is not clear whether any changes are envisaged from the current practice (following English law) of requiring generally 'enabling legislation' to give internal effect to treaties, while allowing some instances of 'application' of 'unincorporated treaties' (eg as aid to construction). See R Higgins, 'United Kingdom' in F G Jacobs and S Roberts (eds), *The Effect of Treaties in Domestic Law* (London: Sweet & Maxwell, 1987) 123–139. It may be noted that the Chinese position on this issue (and in general on the question of the relationship between international law and domestic law) is rather ambiguous. See the brief inquiry in R Mushkat, 'The Transition from British to Chinese Rule in Hong Kong: A Discussion of Salient International Legal Issues' (1986) 14 *Denver Journal of International Law and Policy* 171, 193.

Foreign policy

Of greater concern perhaps is the judicial effect of foreign policy or attitudes of the political organs as such. It is submitted that there is merit in the view expressed by Mann[27] that only where the executive intervenes to protect alleged interests of foreign relations would the courts be justified in invoking public policy to support or deny private rights. It is equally to be expected in the light of international legal practice[28] that in matters that affect the sovereignty of the PRC (eg attempts by a foreign state to exercise jurisdiction in respect of acts performed outside the jurisdiction of that country), prejudice its security, or imperil its diplomatic relations, SAR judges would act upon the CPG's expression of its view.

Cases relating to foreign affairs and defence

On the other hand, under the Basic Law the jurisdiction of the local courts would seem to be totally ousted in 'cases relating to defence and foreign affairs, which are the responsibility of the Central People's Government, and cases relating to the executive acts of the Central People's Government' (BL18) (see pp 251–257 above). By rendering all such cases non-justiciable per se, a severe restriction is imposed upon the SAR courts which is inconsistent with both the judicial power postulated in the Joint Declaration and constitutional doctrines hitherto affecting the decision-making process by local judges.

Under the present system, recently 'rationalised and modernised'[29] following the House of Lords decision in *Council of Civil Service Unions v Minister for the Civil Service*,[30] acts of the executive affecting private rights would be subject to review if they are 'amenable to the judicial process,'[31] notwithstanding the 'elevated' source of power. Thus while 'judges are unlikely to consider themselves competent to review prerogative decisions such as a declaration of war, commutation of a death sentence or negotiation of a treaty'[32] they would not refrain from reviewing,

27 Mann (n 8 above) 9–10.
28 For illustrations of relevant British judicial practice: see *Re Westinghouse Uranium Contract* [1978] AC 547, 616 (per Lord Wilberforce), 631 (per Viscount Dilhorne), 650 (per Lord Fraser) and *R v Lewes Justices, ex parte Home Secretary* [1973] AC 338, 412.
29 See Peter Wesley-Smith, *Constitutional and Administrative Law in Hong Kong* (Hong Kong: China and Hong Kong Law Studies Ltd, 1987–88) Vol I, 125.
30 [1985] 1 AC 374.
31 Ibid 398.
32 Wesley-Smith (n 29 above) 126.

for example, proceedings relating to compulsory retirement of an immigration officer by the Governor.[33]

Nor are all matters concerning foreign affairs and defence beyond the scope of judicial power, particularly when incorporated in statutory instruments. It should also be emphasised that while the conduct of foreign affairs may not attract judicial review, courts are not prevented from adjudicating upon other aspects of the cases before them. Thus where certain questions arise in the course of proceedings concerning facts, circumstances, or events which are 'peculiarly within the cognisance of the Executive'[34] (eg extent of territory, existence of a state of war, belligerency, or neutrality, determination of status which entitles one to immunity from process, or recognition of a state or government) British/Hong Kong judges would be expected (by virtue of the principle that the courts should in such matters 'speak with the same voice as the Executive')[35] to seek the executive's statement or certification.[36] Once granted, such a statement or certificate would be binding and conclusive. Yet, the legal effects of the certified 'facts of state' (as well as the interpretation of the certificate itself) is a matter that falls solely within the province of the judiciary.[37]

Indeed, to preserve the basic policy of judicial independence[38] — laid down in the Joint Declaration (JD3(3), section III, Annex I) — SAR judges must not permit the expression of executive policy to usurp entirely the judicial function[39] and

33 See *Re Fong Hin-wah* [1985] HKLR 332.
34 Mann (n 8 above) 23.
35 *Re Westinghouse Uranium Contract* [1978] AC 547, 617.
36 It is conceivable that BL draftsmen envisaged this type of judiciary/executive exchange when providing in the latter part of para 3 of BL18 that the '[c]ourts of the Hong Kong Special Administrative Region shall seek the advice of the Chief Executive whenever questions concerning defence, foreign affairs or the executive acts of the Central People's Government arise in any legal proceedings.' Other interpretations are nonetheless possible. It has been suggested, for example, that this provision is merely an elaboration on the procedure involved in applying the first part of the paragraph, namely, that whenever any party or the court believes that the case might be one involving defence, foreign affairs, or the executive acts of the CPG, the court must refer the matter to the CE who will determine whether the case relates to those matters. If it does, then the court will not hear the case at all. See *Law Society Comments* (n 3 above) 10–11.
37 Mann (n 8 above) 52.
38 It should be emphasised that according to Lillich and Hannum 'a free and independent judiciary forms part of the governmental structure of all the politically autonomous entities surveyed' (n 4 above) 228.
39 For a similar sentiment: see US District Court Northern District California, *Bank of China v Wells Fargo Bank & Union Trust Co* 104 F Supp 59 (1952) at 63. The court held that after the State Department had determined which of

must guard against the 'trap' of 'what may begin by guidance as to the principles to be applied and end in cases being decided irrespective of any principle in accordance with the view of the Executive as to what is politically expedient.'[40]

While acknowledging the 'independent judicial power of the Hong Kong Special Administrative Region' and the jurisdiction of SAR courts 'over all cases in the Region' subject (only) to restrictions imposed under the Hong Kong legal system (BL18), the Basic Law proceeds to impose new and unacceptable restraints. Such incongruence with legitimate expectations appears to stem largely from confusion concerning such notions as 'acts of state,' 'facts of state,' and 'non-justiciability.' This pitfall could perhaps have been avoided by adopting the proposal made by a member of the Basic Law Drafting Committee[41] which omits any reference to 'executive acts of the Central People's Government' while retaining the notion of current (limited) restriction pertaining to the request for executive advice 'in accordance with the principles and legal precedents of the common law when questions concerning foreign affairs and defence arise in any legal proceeding.'

Clearly, independent judges in an autonomous regime may be trusted not to 'embarrass or interfere with the Executive'[42] or hurt the national interest, by applying the general principle of 'judicial restraint and abstention' which is 'inherent in the very nature of the judicial process.'[43]

As a final note it may be pointed out that the Act of State doctrine as a bar to judicial investigation of the validity of acts of foreign governments is not a rule of general international law.[44] In fact, as observed by Mann, there is 'no trace' of such a doctrine outside Anglo-American law and there is on the other hand 'much authority of the greatest weight for its rejection in Europe.'[45]

the two governments of China was entitled to act on behalf of that state, the court might still evaluate the legal significance of the acts of both governments.

40 Mann (n 8 above) quoting Lord Cross of Chelsea in *The Philippine Admiral* [1977] AC 373, 399.
41 See 'Collection of Opinions and Suggestions by Some Members in regard to the Articles Drafted by their Respective Subject Sub-groups' annexed to the Basic Law booklet, pp 91, 94.
42 The rationale underlying the 'Act of State' doctrine: see the leading American decision in *Baker v Carr* 369 US 186 (1962).
43 *Buttes Gas v Hammer* [1982] AC 888, 932 (per Lord Wilberforce).
44 See J G Starke, *Introduction to International Law* (London: Butterworths, 9th ed 1984) 105.
45 Mann (n 8 above) 175–176.

PRC military forces

The discharge of the CPG's defence responsibilities over the SAR raises some 'practical' issues concerning the role, status, and composition of the military forces sent by the CPG to be stationed in the Region (BL13).

First, in view of the few external security challenges likely to be faced by the SAR (at least of a degree requiring full-scale military involvement) and the fact that internal security functions are to be handled by the SAR police (with clear assurances of non-interference of the PRC), one may query the role and necessity of a Chinese garrison in the territory. The stipulation in the Basic Law for a discretionary power to be granted to the SAR to request, in times of need, the CPG's assistance 'in the maintenance of public order and disaster relief' (BL13) seems to indicate that a 'back-up' role is envisaged for the forces.[46] Evidently, notwithstanding the limited scope of activities by the military, the PRC would 'not entertain any suggestion that it should not send soldiers here because it is considered an essential symbol of transfer of sovereignty.'[47] The very presence of a Chinese contingent might also be viewed as a deterrent both internally and externally.

Second, ambiguity also surrounds the status of the Chinese military forces to be stationed in the SAR, especially in the light of the provision that '[a]part from abiding by nation-wide laws, members of the garrison shall also abide by the laws of the Hong Kong Special Administrative Region' (BL13). In addition to 'disturbing the normal operation of conflict of laws rules (eg regarding capacity to marry),'[48] such a provision erects a hybrid entity of no clear designation or status.

While the PRC may wish to enhance the notion of territorial sovereignty, it must also pay heed to the autonomous structure of the SAR with respect to which the Chinese force may be most appropriately designated as a 'visiting force.' As such, it would also be subject to established principles of international law (although a specific agreement regulating the terms and conditions governing the stationing of the forces in the SAR is evidently more desirable) which emphasise the functional approach to jurisdic-

---

46 According to one observer, such a role is reserved for the specially trained units of the People's Armed Police (PAP). See H Dikkenberg, 'New Arm of the Law in 1997' *Sunday Morning Post* 23 August 1987.

47 D Wong, 'China May Put 5000 Troops Here Britain is Told Possible PLA Total' *Hong Kong Standard* 19 December 1987. Note, however, the CPG's pledge not to station its troops in Taiwan under the nine-point unification proposal: 'Deng Xiaoping on China's Reunification' *Beijing Review* 8 August 1983, p 5.

48 *Law Society Comments* (n 3 above) 3.

tion issues. In other words, local jurisdiction need not extend to matters of internal administration of the force or related to the performance of its duties or generally where the integrity and efficiency of the force may be impaired.[49]

Finally, an issue of particular concern to Hong Kong people[50] is whether they will be liable to conscription into the Chinese armed forces. The application in the SAR of laws enacted by the National People's Congress or its Standing Committee which relate to defence (BL17), coupled with the fact that '[u]nder the Nationality Law of the People's Republic of China all Hong Kong Chinese compatriots ... are Chinese nationals,'[51] renders such a development a likely prospect.

External affairs

The application of the Basic Law provisions pertaining to external affairs is to a large extent inextricably bound up with the questions identified earlier in the discussion concerning the scope of the SAR responsibility for external affairs. Specifically, the reference to the SAR's authority 'on its own, using the name "Hong Kong, China" [to] *maintain and develop relations and conclude and implement agreements* with states, regions and relevant international organizations in the appropriate field ... ' (BL159) (in contrast with the phrase 'shall, on its own, *formulate policies*' incorporated with respect to the SAR's responsibilities in the fields of education (BL143), science and technology (BL146), culture (BL147), sports (BL151), and labour laws and policies (BL155)) may give rise to issues such as whether the SAR may decide which agreements to conclude, which organisations and conferences are affecting the SAR, or which are the appropriate fields; whether the PRC would entertain a request initiated by the SAR for inclusion in China's delegations to various international organisations or conferences; and whether the PRC retains a right to veto relations and agreements contemplated by the SAR (in the appropriate fields).

The extent of 'participation' by the SAR in international organisations and conferences also requires further clarification. While provision is made (BL160) for an 'expression of views' by the representatives of the SAR when participating in international organisations or conferences under the name 'Hong Kong, China,' the Basic Law fails to guarantee the Region's

---

49 This approach is currently applied under the United Kingdom Forces (Jurisdiction of Colonial Courts) Order 1965 and 1967.

50 See *Hong Kong: Arrangements for Testing the Acceptability in Hong Kong of the Draft Agreement on the Future of the Territory* (Cmnd 9407, 1984).

51 Chinese Memorandum of 1984 attached to the Joint Declaration.

'right' to vote independently, including the right to cast a vote contrary to that of China.[52] Nor does the Basic Law stipulate the SAR's 'right' to speak independently and contrary to China when there is a conflict of interests between the two in international forums it attends as a member of the delegation of the PRC.[53]

Other issues relating to 'participation' in international forums, and which are not addressed in the Basic Law, are claims/liabilities arising from violation of international agreements and sanctions. As aptly suggested by members of the Basic Law Consultative Committee's Special Group on External Affairs, relevant clauses should be incorporated in the Basic Law to ensure that when the SAR suffers damage in connection with its participation in an international organisation· or agreement under the name of 'Hong Kong, China' it should be able to submit claims in a separate capacity[54] (whereas if the damage to SAR interests occurred in the course of participation as part of the PRC contingent, China's responsibility to bring claims on behalf of the SAR should be confirmed).[55] Similarly, the SAR's ability to form its own policy with respect to sanctions against other participating members too should be acknowledged in the Basic Law.[56]

Also of significance regarding the SAR's autonomous conduct of external affairs is the question of extension to the territory of international agreements to which the PRC is or becomes a party (BL161) without distinction as to subject matter. Again, a proposal made by the Special Group on External Affairs — that 'China should relinquish the power of making agreements for the HKSAR in fields such as economy, trade, finance and monetary, shipping, communications, culture, sports, etc'[57] — may be fully endorsed.

Finally, since the autonomous status of the SAR depends largely upon its acceptance as such by the international community, the PRC's willingness to promote it as a separate entity must be properly reflected in the Basic Law. A few areas where a firmer undertaking on the part of the PRC may be desirable have been identified in the Final Report of the Special Group on External Affairs. These include participation in agreements which are limited to states and where China has no intention of

52 See Special Group on External Affairs, 'Final Report on Arrangement for and Form of Participation in International Organisations/Agreements' (passed by the Executive Committee on 14 March 1987), 4.6.2.
53 Ibid 4.6.1.
54 Ibid 4.9.1.
55 Ibid.
56 Ibid 4.9.2.
57 Ibid 4.8.2.

participating;[58] participation in agreements under the auspices of international organisations which impose restrictions upon non-sovereign territories signing conventions;[59] and continuation or resumption of participation by the SAR in agreements/organisations from which China has withdrawn.[60]

POLICY IMPLICATIONS

The allocation of responsibilities between the PRC and the SAR in the policy domain encompassing foreign, external, and defence affairs will inevitably affect all facets of societal management in the territory after 1997. The external dimension of the policy steering system can be neither compartmentalised nor neatly separated from the domestic dimension and any initiatives undertaken in support of foreign, external, and defence objectives are likely to have system-wide repercussions.[61]

One aspect of the policy environment which will probably undergo change is the general perception of Hong Kong as a politically neutral entity engaged almost exclusively in the pursuit of a narrow set of conventional economic goals. As an integral part of the Chinese body politic, and as a component of the PRC foreign affairs apparatus, it may not be able to maintain close relations, commercial and otherwise, with countries which have no diplomatic ties with China and may lose its status as an effective intermediary between the PRC and such countries.[62] This may not only prove costly in terms of business opportunities lost but may have the serious consequence of undermining Hong Kong's image as an autonomous entity.

In the extreme case of China imposing sanctions upon another country, Hong Kong will have to take similar action, thus incurring the risk of being seen as an active player in the game of international power politics. This will be inconsistent with the aim of promoting itself as a territorial unit motivated primarily by the desire to live by the principles of free trade.[63]

58 Ibid 4.2.3.
59 Ibid.
60 Ibid 4.7.
61 For an illuminating discussion of linkages between domestic and external policies: see J N Rosenau (ed), *Linkage Politics* (The Free Press, 1969).
62 See Y C Jao, 'Hong Kong's Economic Prospects After the Sino-British Agreement: A Preliminary Assessment' in Hungdah Chiu et al (eds), *The Future of Hong Kong: Toward 1997 and Beyond* (New York, Westport, London: Quorum Books, 1987) 84, 86. See also Y C Jao, 'Hong Kong's Future as a Free Market' (1986) 22 *Issues and Studies* 111, 139.
63 See *Hong Kong 1988* (Hong Kong: Government Information Services, 1988) 74: 'Hong Kong believes in free trade. The aims of Hong Kong's external commercial relations policy are thus to safeguard its rights and to discharge its obligations in the pursuit of free trade.'

At the regional level, Southeast Asian countries may reassess their position vis-à-vis PRC-dominated Hong Kong. These countries have traditionally considered the British colony as part of the non-Communist bloc. Malaysia and Singapore also share with Hong Kong common values rooted in British norms of government. They may feel, therefore, the need to assume greater distance between themselves and the SAR (eg no longer channel their communications through the territory or even impose restrictions upon travel to and from the territory).[64] Bilateral relations with Taiwan may prove even more problematic in the event of the latter opting to sever direct ties with the SAR.[65] Trade flows between Taiwan and the territory, and other forms of exchange, are of considerable benefit to Hong Kong, both economically and psychologically, and a Taiwanese disengagement would doubtless constitute a severe financial and political blow.

Perhaps less threatening, but nonetheless costly, will be the loss of membership in the Commonwealth and the privileges which are associated with it. The unavailability of British support, which occasionally has greater impact than Chinese diplomatic manoeuvres, will also render the SAR more vulnerable, for without it problems requiring international co-operation (eg repatriation of refugees)[66] may be more difficult to manage.

Another potentially negative factor is policy instability within China and its implications for the SAR. Specifically, factional disputes in Beijing over foreign policy may spill over into other

64 See Frank Ching, *Hong Kong and China: For Better or For Worse* (New York: China Council of the Asia Society and the Foreign Policy Association, 1985) 73.

65 Given Taiwan's continued rejection of unification and its strong commitment to the maintenance of the status quo, it might consider it strategically prudent to 'unlink' itself from Hong Kong and China. For an analysis of the Taiwanese position see Hungdah Chiu, 'Prospects for the Unification of China' in Chiu (ed), *Symposium on Hong Kong: 1997* (Maryland: School of Law, University of Maryland, Occasional Papers/Reprint Series in Contemporary Asia Studies, 1985) 81–94. See, however, D F Simon, 'Taiwan's Political Economy and the Evolving Links between the PRC, Hong Kong, and Taiwan' (1986) 6 *AEI Foreign Policy and Defence Review* 42, 50 for the view that, while the 'chances for Taiwan's incorporation into the Hong Kong-PRC economic sphere will be strongly resisted,' current economic ties will be maintained.

66 Especially in view of China's hard-line policy vis-à-vis Vietnam. See R G Sutter, 'Peking's Relations with Vietnam and Korea: Implications for Future Change in Peking's Foreign Policy' (1987) 23 *Issues and Studies* 92.

policy domains in the PRC[67] — a development from which the territory, in the absence of a British buffer, may not be immune. The effects need not be indirect. Under the pretext of responding to a 'foreign affairs' policy crisis China could interfere in the internal affairs of the SAR in violation of the letter and spirit of the Joint Declaration. The vagueness of the relevant terms in the Basic Law will facilitate direct interference, possibly in a form which cannot be reconciled with notions of genuine autonomy.[68]

CONCLUSION

The preceding analysis has revealed conceptual and practical flaws in the BL provisions relating to foreign and defence affairs. The ambiguity permeating these provisions suggests that interpretation by power-holders, rather than pre-determined legal constraints, will be the key factor shaping the dynamics of the relationship between the Central Government and the SAR in that particular domain.

The problem is compounded by the absence of a dispute settlement mechanism which might inspire the confidence of all affected parties. Additional barriers to Hong Kong's autonomous functioning may be erected by control-minded central officials wedded to the notion of 'indivisible sovereignty.'[69] Autonomy for the SAR, contrary to China's potential claims, is not merely a domestic issue. It is hoped that the final draft of the Basic Law will be more in tune with international legal norms pertaining to autonomous entities.

67 See K Lieberthal, 'Domestic Politics and Foreign Policy' in H Harding (ed), *China's Foreign Relations in the 80s* (New Haven: Yale University Press, 1984) 43–70. For a significant example: see discussion of the serious effects of a backlash against the 'open door' policy in M Yahuda, *Towards the End of Isolationism: China's Foreign Policy After Mao* (London: The Macmillan Press, 1983) 239.

68 For an indication of such eventuality: see Deng Xiaoping's speech on the 'Current Policies and Prospects for Hong Kong' (n 17 above) 17: 'Suppose after 1997 someone in Hong Kong denounces the Chinese Communist Party and curses China: we will allow them to do so, but if they turn abuse into action and try to turn Hong Kong into a base of opposition to the mainland in the name of "democracy" how should it be dealt with? We will definitely interfere.'

69 See Ch'in Fu, 'Restoring Hong Kong is Perfectly Valid in International Law' (1983) 4 *Journal of International Studies* 3, 3–8.

Part III

General Commentaries

13 In Search of Pragmatic Solutions

DENIS CHANG

GENERAL APPROACH

THE concept of 'one country, two systems' was born of a pragmatism that has caught the world somewhat by surprise. 'It does not matter whether the cat is black or white so long as it catches mice,' said Deng Xiaoping. Hong Kong heaved an audible sigh of relief, hoping that it was meant to be part of the cat and not one of the mice and believing that pragmatism, and not just ideology, had been assimilated into the real politics of China and had become the very instrument of China's salvation.

The primary purpose of this short commentary is not to ask whether the hope is well founded or whether the faith has been misplaced, but to offer a few reflections on how best to go about solving some of the seemingly intractable problems which have arisen in the implementation of the concept of 'one country, two systems' and which in my view the first draft of the Basic Law has yet to resolve with any real measure of success.

In the first place, I believe that to achieve the much-needed breakthrough all those who are concerned in the making of this most uncommon law must strive to rise above partial perspectives and go beyond the mind-set of one country, one system. Both courage and imagination are needed in designing a new political order which will give to the Chinese unitary state 'some of the characteristics of a composite state.'[1] Over-emphasis on the unitary nature of the Chinese state and the imperative of 'realising sovereignty' can easily obscure other essential characteristics of the new political structure. On the other hand, indifference or insensitivity to the national goals of reunification and modernisation can also undermine the rationale of the enterprise.

Second, whilst it is absolutely essential to ask whether the Basic Law complies with the Sino-British Joint Declaration on the Question of Hong Kong, the proper test, as I see it, is not bare compliance but full and generous implementation. I think that China is unlikely to win the confidence of Hong Kong people

1 Yan Jiaqi, Hongqi No 6 (16 March 1985) 18–19.

without being magnanimous. 'Give more, not less' should be the governing motto. This is particularly so in autonomy-related areas of the Basic Law. A high degree of autonomy can never be credibly achieved unless there is included in the equation a 'generosity factor.' As explained below, there must be a willingness on the part of China to translate rules of self-restraint into constitutional rules of action and ways of acting. In my view, China can afford to be generous.

Third, the broad basic specification of the Joint Declaration in relation to division of powers between the Central People's Government and the Hong Kong Special Administrative Region is as follows:

> Except for foreign affairs and defence which are the responsibilities of the CPG, the Hong Kong SAR shall be vested with executive, legislative and independent judicial power, including that of final adjudication (section 1, Annex I, JD).

A pre-requisite of achieving a high degree of autonomy for the SAR is, therefore, real *division of powers* and not mere *division of functions* between Central Government and SAR organs. In other words, the relevant SAR organs must in *all* three spheres be given *exclusive* jurisdiction within their scope of autonomy. This means that, in general, Central Government organs must not have concurrent jurisdiction within the SAR's autonomy.

It is precisely in areas where the two systems overlap or where power relations between Central Government and SAR organs are involved that the search for pragmatic solutions is hardest because it is here that doctrinal principles, more often than not, are invoked. No one should be so naive as to suppose that the pragmatism of the modern Chinese leadership is free from ideology, despite the increasing tendency in recent years to see things in terms of technology and despite the common aspiration of so many people in Hong Kong and China to ensure, as far as humanly possible, that the Basic Law will stand up to world scrutiny at least as a piece of legal technology. Pragmatism, however, does not imply a disregard for principle. What it does signify is a continuing willingness to search for practical ways and means of balancing or resolving competing or conflicting principles, to find workable and credible solutions. The 'credibility factor' should thus form one of the design principles of the new political order.

RULES OF SELF-RESTRAINT

The above approach, in my view, should help us to find concrete solutions to quite a few critical problems which have vexed the minds of the BLDC members.

Three such problems concern the jurisdiction of the SAR courts (BL18), the interpretation of the Basic Law (BL169), and the power of nullification of SAR laws by the Standing Committee of the National People's Congress (BL16).

The NPCSC is the organ of legislative interpretation and legal supervision under the PRC constitution. Its powers of interpretation and legal supervision, under the constitution, extend to laws, 'basic' or otherwise. A problem, therefore, arises as to how, short of amending the PRC constitution, the powers of the Standing Committee can be restricted or modified in relation to the SAR.

The current draft of the Basic Law seeks to address the problem only in a very limited fashion. It lays down the broad procedural rule that the Standing Committee shall, before giving an interpretation of the Basic Law, or before declaring any law of the SAR as being not in conformity with the Basic Law or legal procedures, first consult its Committee for the Basic Law (which is envisaged to comprise members drawn from both mainland China and Hong Kong). Neither the interpretation of the Standing Committee nor the nullification of laws will have retroactive effect under BL169 and 16 respectively. Beyond these rules, however, the Basic Law as it stands in no way inhibits the jurisdiction of the Standing Committee. Consequently, there is nothing to stop the Standing Committee from exercising jurisdiction in relation to matters purely internal to the SAR. On the other hand, the jurisdiction of the Hong Kong courts is curtailed under BL18 and 169 which exclude from the courts' purview not only matters relating to defence and foreign affairs but also 'executive acts of the CPG' (whatever that means).

I for one think that the only fully satisfactory long-term solution is for the Chinese authorities to cause the PRC constitution to be amended so as to remove all possible argument on some of the issues mooted in this commentary and in particular to stipulate that the Standing Committee's powers in relation to the SAR will be restricted to matters relating to defence and foreign affairs (as distinguished from external affairs and from purely domestic affairs of the SAR). Such an amendment is the only legally secure way of removing the logical difficulty of trying by means of provisions in a law which is subordinate to the constitution to restrict powers given to a central organ by the constitution itself.

I would not be too surprised, however, to find that more than logic would be required to persuade China to take such a course within the time-frame set for the drafting of the Basic Law and at this stage of China's own constitutional development. Pending amendment to the PRC constitution, a 'lateral' approach would be necessary to modulate the powers given by the constitution to the Standing Committee. Such an approach would continue to emphasise the absolute necessity in principle of devolving a generous measure of power to the region (so that, for example, the SAR courts would be given no less jurisdiction than what the Hong Kong courts currently enjoy), but it would also seek to lay down a number of practical rules of self-restraint governing the exercise of such power as would be retained by the central authorities.

The first rule of self-restraint is that the Standing Committee will refrain from exercising any powers of interpretation of the Basic Law in matters which pertain purely to the internal affairs of the SAR. The second rule is that in respect of matters outside the scope of the high degree of autonomy (defence and foreign affairs as distinguished from those external affairs which are delegated to the SAR) the Standing Committee will refrain from exercising its powers of interpretation except when its jurisdiction has been invoked by specified organs or through specified channels and after reference to an organ of mediation such as the Committee for the Basic Law. The third rule is that disputes or difficulties over classification of issues will be referred to the Committee for the Basic Law whose advice will by convention be accepted by the Standing Committee.

A separate set of rules in relation to the Standing Committee's power of disallowance of SAR laws can be constitutionalised. Because the Joint Declaration merely stipulates that SAR laws should be reported to the Standing Committee for the record (no mention being made of any power of disallowance), the simplest rule is that the Standing Committee will refrain from exercising any disallowance powers it may have under the Chinese constitution. It should in any event not exercise any power of disallowance of any law that pertains purely to the internal affairs of the SAR. As for laws which are alleged to trespass on matters reserved to the central authorities a procedure can be devised whereby reference of the issue can be made by the Standing Committee in the first instance to the Court of Final Appeal of the SAR. The Standing Committee should, pending the determination of the reference, refrain from exercising its power of review of the constitutionality or legality of the law in question. This is in addition to the fundamental principle, already incorporated in the Basic Law, that no decision by the Standing Committee shall have retrospective effect.

What, it might be asked, would be the status of these or similar rules of self-restraint if constitutionalised? The answer would depend on the manner in which they were constitutionalised: as substantive rules of devolution of power, as procedural rules of exercise of power, or simply as constitutional conventions.

Constitutional conventions are of course of pivotal importance in common law jurisdictions and serve to modulate the
plenitude of prerogative power theoretically vested in the sovereign and to regulate relationships between and within Central
Government and regional organs. Without these conventions —
which are not rules of law but are habitually upheld as a matter of
practice — the Commonwealth of Nations would not have been
possible and the Westminster-style constitutions would not have
developed in the way that they have done. Seeking to reconcile
the supremacy of Parliament with the principle of equality of
status between 'autonomous communities' within the Commonwealth by making a distinction between *status* and *function*, the
Balfour Declaration of 1926, for example, created a framework
for the British Commonwealth based on conventional relationships. The Statute of Westminster put the relationship on a more
secure basis by formalising, *as a constitutional convention*, the
rule of self-restraint that no law thereafter made by the British
Parliament would extend to any of the Dominions as part of the
law of that Dominion otherwise than at the request and with the
consent of that Dominion. By this method, the exercise of power
was in practice regulated without infringing the supremacy of
Parliament.

Many post-colonial territories have incorporated in their
constitutions the UK conventions usually with modifications
and sometimes simply by reference.[2] The Singapore constitution
of 1958 applied the constitutional conventions partly by reference and partly by spelling them out. What is important to bear
in mind is that unless it is made clear that these conventional
rules are not justiciable in the courts, conventions incorporated
in a written constitution become rules of law enforceable in the
courts. There is, however, nothing to prevent such rules from
being expressly preserved simply as constitutional conventions
or characterised as directive principles which are fundamental
but are non-justiciable.

The Basic Law of course is not a constitution based on
the Westminster model. It is a Chinese law which is also
the foundational law of the SAR and thus a vehicle whereby the
common law system is to be preserved basically unchanged.
While there is no ready-made set of conventions governing the
relationship between Central Government and regional organs
which can be taken over wholesale, there is nothing to prevent
the Basic Law from creating constitutional rules of different
kinds, designating some of them as conventional rules, thus
inducing artificially the birth and accelerating the growth of

2 See, eg the constitution of Ceylon, s 4(2).

constitutional conventions. This does not mean that we should not, as far as possible, seek to regulate the power relationships between and within central and regional organs by clear and justiciable rules of law, substantive and procedural. Furthermore, whatever method is adopted there should still be effective devolution of power to enable the SAR to exercise full legislative, executive, and independent judicial power including that of final adjudication, subject only to the principle that defence and foreign affairs are the responsibilities of the CPG. Conventional rules of self-restraint can never be a substitute for effective devolution of power but will be of help in the regulation of the exercise of such power as has been retained.

DIFFERENTIATION AND MEDIATION

I described the proposed Committee for the Basic Law as 'an organ of mediation' because that would appear to be the role envisaged for it in the Basic Law. Consisting of both mainland and Hong Kong members the Committee would, according to the current .draft, advise the Standing Committee on such questions as interpretation and amendment of the Basic Law, the constitutional validity and legal-procedural regularity of SAR laws, and any proposed application of nationwide laws. Whatever the final shape of the relevant provisions, some organ of mediation would seem desirable to help resolve difficulties which would inevitably arise in the theory and practice of 'one country, two systems.' If such an organ were to perform a role remotely similar to that envisaged in the current draft, its political and legal functions should be clearly separated on the operational level (without denying the ultimate relationship between politics and law on another level). A committee of jurists drawn from both systems should be set up within the organ to deal with legal issues.

Mediation between the systems implies that the systems will remain differentiated though each will form part of one country. This differentiation will be destroyed if the SAR does not have a corpus of law which is operationally 'hived off' from the mainland system. Operational integrity does not mean that there is no meeting-point between the two systems. It means that the SAR system should be virtually self-contained for all practical purposes. For example, it should in practice be unnecessary, when interpreting provisions in the Basic Law pertaining purely to the internal affairs of the SAR, to look beyond the four corners of the Basic Law to the PRC constitution, other mainland laws, or Central Government directives. I call this 'the four-corner principle,' which is really a product of the pragmatic approach required to make the concept of 'one country, two systems' work. What is needed, at this early stage of the development of the concept, is a functional jurisprudence that pays attention not only to the 'pure' structural principles of the Basic Law or its juristics, politics, and economics, but also and no less importantly to what I would call its 'pragmatics.'

An illustration of what I mean by a functional approach or the pragmatics of the Basic Law relates to the manner in which the need to have an authentic English version of the Basic Law can be met. Quite apart from the international status of Hong Kong and the importance of English as the language of international trade and commerce, English is the mother tongue of the common law. Furthermore, Hong Kong has begun to enact laws in English and Chinese, both versions being equally authentic. There should, therefore, be an authentic English version of the Basic Law if the operational integrity of the SAR system is to be protected. Indeed there is a need for an English version which enjoys functional equality with the Chinese version. However, the Basic Law is a law enacted by the NPC in Beijing. To expect the NPC to enact an authentic version in English is already regarded by some people as quite unrealistic, let alone a version which is equally authentic with the Chinese. What then is the solution? A possible and, in my view, pragmatic solution is for Beijing to cause to be produced an English translation which the NPC then authorises the SAR legislature to adopt for use in the SAR as an authentic version. This will preserve the flexibility Beijing may want as regards the manner in which it will oversee the production of the English translation without necessarily having to go through any legislative procedures in Beijing to give legal status to the translation, delegating the latter task to the SAR. An authentic version, unlike a mere translation, may be used in the courts without the need for further proof as to its accuracy. If authorised by the NPC or its Standing Committee (and under BL19 'the Hong Kong SAR may enjoy other powers granted to it by the NPC, the Standing Committee of the NPC or the State Council') the SAR will even be able to pass legislation to the effect that the version shall enjoy equal status in the courts of the SAR with the Chinese version. To facilitate the production of an authentic version, an appropriate advisory organ consisting of mainland and Hong Kong members should be set up in the form of a Basic Law Language Committee, beginning work as soon as possible and certainly long before the final draft is produced. A positive response from China to such a suggestion will vastly increase people's confidence in the entire enterprise of 'one country, two systems.'

Another example of a functional approach concerns the way in which the SAR's relationship with the PRC constitution has to be worked out. One can see the logical difficulty of trying in the Basic Law to exclude provisions in the very constitution under which it is promulgated. If China does not amend the constitution, it will be necessary to develop a functional jurisprudence which will simply presuppose (as an irrebuttable principle of law that goes to the jurisdiction of the organ of interpretation and to the Basic Law's own legitimacy) that *the PRC constitution itself,* on its true construction in accordance with the tenets of socialism with Chinese characteristics, already permits the exclusion, for a specified time and from a defined part of China's territory, of the socialist system and socialist practices. This pragmatic approach takes cognisance of the fact that the SAR is the product of the exercise of power by the NPC and the State Council under article 31 of the constitution. The exercise of power carries with it the exclusion of everything else which is inconsistent with the realisation of the SAR model specified by the NPC. This means the consequential exclusion of the mainland corpus of law. It also means that in relation to the SAR, implementing the PRC constitution means in practical terms no more and no less than implementing the Basic Law, the PRC constitution 'applying' only to the extent necessary to give coherence and legal validity to the Basic Law in the spirit of 'one country, two systems.'

The principle of operational integrity will, however, sadly be undermined if BL16, 18, or 169 mentioned above or BL17 is enacted in its present form. I can quite understand why there should be machinery to enable the Central Government to implement laws relating to foreign affairs and defence but the formula 'other laws which give expression to national unity and territorial integrity' is terribly ambiguous and much too wide. The mainland draftsmen have made it clear that their intention is only to let in 'a few laws' such as those relating to the establishment of the national capital, the national flag and anthem, boundaries, the limits of territorial waters, and the Nationality Law. If that be the case a more acceptable solution is to enumerate these items either by listing out the specific laws or in the manner similar to what I have just done, using terms which are sufficiently specific and yet allow for future laws of the same kind to be included.

Two basic flaws should be pointed out in BL21, a clause which is clearly intended to enshrine the principle of non-interference so essential to the SAR's autonomy and the integrity of its systems. The clause provides that 'Departments *under* the Central People's Government . . . shall not interfere in the affairs which the Hong Kong SAR administers on its own in accordance with this Law.' The CPG is defined in the PRC constitution as the State Council. Surely the CPG itself should not interfere in affairs within the SAR's autonomy since autonomy is conferred on the SAR under BL2 not by the CPG but by the NPC. That is the first flaw in BL21. The second may be found in paragraph four of the clause which provides that people from other parts of China must apply for approval for entry into the SAR without saying that the approval must include that of the SAR government.

The principle of non-interference will become an acid test of the credibility of the new political order. A paradox of 'one country, two systems' is that the objective of national unity is best achieved by keeping the two systems operationally separate. This is not the same as saying 'good walls make good neighbours' because nobody would be so foolish as to think that Hong Kong could just build a wall, close the gate, and keep the keys on the Hong Kong side of the border. There would always be a master key on the other side. In fact the Basic Law is not a wall. It is the foundation of a unique structure that at once seeks to link as well as separate features from two vastly different systems. Therein lies the challenge as well as cause for anxiety.

THE CREDIBILITY FACTOR

Speaking less figuratively, the credibility of the Basic Law will be tested particularly in two areas of perennial concern to Hong Kong people, namely, the protection of our rights and freedoms and the degree of autonomy the SAR will in reality enjoy.

As regards civil liberties many people have a natural and healthy scepticism of paper promises and parchment guarantees. Every freedom has its limits and a corresponding duty can be found for every right. It is, however, precisely because it is so easy to destroy freedom and vitiate rights by reformulating and qualifying them that a bill of rights is unlikely to be credible if it departs from the language and content of relevant international conventions.

Chapter 3 of the Basic Law which deals with civil liberties contains a number of grave deficiencies, only three of which need be mentioned here. There is, first, the failure to give effect *in the Basic Law itself* to the provisions of the International Covenant on Civil and Political Rights and the International Covenant on Economic, Social and Cultural Rights as applied to Hong Kong, the implementation of these covenants being indeterminately left under BL38 to the future SAR legislature. Second, such rights as *are* spelt out come closer in language to the PRC constitution than the international covenants, hence creating discrepancies.

Third, many important rights and freedoms are merely stated to be 'protected by law' and thus liable to be curtailed by almost any old law passed by the barest majority in the future SAR legislature, a point which should be brought into sharp focus when reflecting on the relationship which exists between democracy and freedom.

A pragmatic, and in my view credible, solution is for the Basic Law simply to incorporate by reference the applicable international covenants and give them over-riding effect (insofar as they are not merely directive principles) without affecting additional rights as are given or preserved by the Basic Law. In this way many of the deficiencies can be remedied and common law freedoms can be translated into constitutionally-protected rights.

As regards the realisation of a high degree of autonomy, the credibility of the Basic Law will be tested not only by reference to the power which is devolved on SAR organs but also by the freedom of Hong Kong people to choose their own people to run the SAR. Thus it would make good practical sense for China to give the local inhabitants a real say in selecting their Chief Executive and members of the legislature, in relation to the formation of either the first government or subsequent governments. In my view a good political structure is more likely to be achieved by a system of government which is broadly and democratically based than by one which is not. Furthermore, a system of checks and balances should be devised on the principle that power should be distributed among sound and credible institutions without creating a paralysis of power in the centre of government. I believe these are important points which should be borne in mind when evaluating the various power structures created or preserved by the Basic Law and the different options under BL45, 67, and 171 (and set out in the Annexes).

There was a time when many people believed that China would be happy to go along with the idea of developing a representative government in Hong Kong at a pace which would ensure that a fully-elected legislature would be in place by 1 July 1997 and that China would readily accept that something similar to a 'through train' method of formation of the first government would be less likely to de-stabilise Hong Kong than a dismantling exercise. The 'through train' theory is now completely derailed and very little if anything can be salvaged from the wreckage if the method stipulated under BL171 and Annex III is adopted, a method which the Hong Kong people will be quick to see as amounting to nothing more than a disguised appointment system because, under the clause, the 'Election Committee' will be

formed by a Beijing-appointed Preparatory Committee of mainland and Hong Kong members.

If there is anything which the people here fervently believe,
and which needs no demonstration, it is China's ever-present
ability to 'realise sovereignty' over Hong Kong. Being pragmatic,
the people here will judge China by its actions during the
transitional period and particularly by the manner in which it
seeks to exercise control and by the behaviour of Communist
Party cadres. Most of the immediate action after the promulgation of the Basic Law will revolve around the formation of the
first government and of the Committee for the Basic Law. A
pragmatic approach will not ignore the fact that irrespective of
how 'democratic' future governments in the SAR are supposed to
be under the Basic Law, most people are likely to remain
unconvinced that this is how things will work out if the first
government is seen to be nothing more than a creature of Beijing.
People will see China's vision of 'one country, two systems'
faithfully mirrored in the first government and legislature of
Hong Kong. I sincerely hope that the vision that finally emerges
will be a more positive and encouraging one than that mirrored
in the first draft of the Basic Law.

14 Strong Government in the SAR

HENRY LITTON

INTRODUCTION

THE Basic Law is a patchwork quilt of many hues. Its draftsmen in Beijing, and the members of the Basic Law Drafting Committee, have laboured long and hard (the first session of the Drafting Committee was held three years ago, on 1 July 1985). As the introduction to the draft makes clear, extensive consultations with many different groups of people have taken place during the drafting process. Perhaps because so many hands have been involved in its making, the result is a cloth composed of many overlapping segments; the colours clash and the pieces do not fit. The Basic Law is intended to be Hong Kong's security blanket, protecting the Hong Kong Special Administrative Region from violent change, safeguarding its capitalist system and life-style for 50 years after 1997. In its present form, the Basic Law is likely to have the opposite effect. It risks smothering the SAR by the weight of its inconsistencies.

DRAFTING CONSTRAINTS

This chapter will focus upon those chapters dealing with the nuts and bolts of the new system established under the Basic Law. These are principally: chapter V dealing with the economy and chapter VI dealing with education, science, culture, sports, religion, labour, and social services. Herein lies the functional core of the SAR, and if the systems here do not work, the rest of the fabric will be mere show, however brilliantly conceived they may be.

Before these two chapters are examined in depth, the fundamental aims of the Basic Law, and the corresponding drafting restraints, have to be recognised. The main points are these:

(1) In Annex I to the Joint Declaration on the Question of Hong Kong, the government of the PRC undertook to enact and promulgate a Basic Law, stipulating that after the establishment of the SAR (under article 31 of the constitution of the PRC) the 'socialist system and socialist policies' of the PRC shall not be practised in the SAR and that 'Hong Kong's

previous capitalist system and life-style shall remain un-changed for 50 years.' This undertaking effectively rules out the formula of a brief statement of basic principles for the SAR (the sort of constitution which, according to Napoleon, was the ideal model: short and vague. Or like article VII of the present Letters Patent: 'The Governor, by and with the advice and consent of the Legislative Council, may make laws for the *peace, order, and good government* of the Colony').

(2) The Joint Declaration fulfilled 'the long cherished common aspiration of the entire Chinese people for the recovery of Hong Kong' (see the preamble to the draft). According to article 62 of the constitution of the PRC, the Basic Law of the SAR will be a basic statute of the state, enacted by the highest legislative body of the state, the National People's Congress. Accordingly, the principles of national unity and territorial integrity are ones which cannot be compromised.

(3) And yet, to give effect to the principle of 'one country, two systems,' a high degree of autonomy must be guaranteed for the SAR in the Basic Law.

These somewhat conflicting principles clearly make the task of the BLDC a most difficult one. Making every allowance for these constraints, there are nevertheless inherent contradictions and inconsistencies in the draft which must be ironed out before the Basic Law is promulgated by the NPC in 1990.

CHAPTER V: THE ECONOMY

Many of the articles under this chapter are aimed at giving practical effect to BL2: 'The National People's Congress author-ises the Hong Kong SAR to exercise a high degree of autonomy in accordance with the provisions of this Law,' and are accordingly necessary for the fulfilment of the main aim. For example, BL104 clearly intends to say that the *government* of the SAR shall use its revenues exclusively for the purposes of the SAR; as such, it is perfectly all right. BL104 provides both a protection and a restraint. It protects the government of the SAR from demands for financial assistance from the Central Government, provincial governments, and other mainland authorities. It is also a restraint. It prevents the government from spending money for extraneous purposes. Thus, if BL104 had been in force in 1982, the Hong Kong government would not have been able to donate $21m to the Falklands Fund at the time of the Falklands War, and a vote by the Finance Committee for such a purpose would have been ultra vires. Few people would, perhaps, have quar-relled with such a result.

BL106 is to the same effect. Although the opening sentence of BL 106 is a little curious ('The HKSAR shall practise an independent taxation system') the intention of the clause, read as a whole, is clear: the government of the SAR shall have autonomy in levying taxes, free of interference by the Central Government.

BL115 deals with the system for issuing currency and specifically enables the government of the SAR to authorise designated banks to issue Hong Kong currency: a clause which is particularly important since it has always been the practice of the Hong Kong government to take instructions from the Foreign and Commonwealth Office in relation to the issue of currency.

BL119 entrenches the SAR as a 'separate customs territory' and enables the SAR, using the name 'Hong Kong, China,' to participate in trade arrangements such as the General Agreement on Tariffs and Trade and arrangements regarding international trade in textiles. And BL120 specifies that export quotas, etc which are obtained by the SAR shall be 'enjoyed exclusively by the Region.'

The clauses referred to above all have one objective in common: to give practical effect to the high degree of autonomy promised in the Joint Declaration; and since the technique of a broad and general statement of principles for the Basic Law is not possible, these detailed provisions, to fortify Hong Kong's economic autonomy, are plainly necessary.

What is regrettable is that, mixed up with the clauses referred to above (clauses which entrench Hong Kong's autonomy and freedom from mainland interference), are clauses with wholly different objectives. They set out the *policies* to be pursued by the government; policies to be pursued for *50 years* irrespective of the prevailing circumstances; and they tie the hands of the government in such a way as to hamper its ability to govern. In some cases, the provisions for entrenching Hong Kong's autonomy (and thereby *strengthening* the government's powers to withstand outside interference) and those which tie the government's hands (and thereby *weakening* it) are contained in the same clause. For example BL115, which vests the authority to issue Hong Kong currency in the government of the SAR, goes on to say:

> The issue of Hong Kong currency shall be backed up by a reserve fund of no less than 100 per cent freely convertible foreign currency.

This would preclude the government from backing up the currency by the holding of gold or other precious metals.

Another example of a clause emasculating the government is BL111 which (in part) states:

Markets for foreign exchange, gold, securities and futures shall continue.

This plainly will preclude the future government from passing laws suppressing the operation of markets in foreign exchange and futures contracts, however desirable in the public interest such suppression might be.

There are many clauses under chapter V, putting restraints upon the government of the SAR, which are equally curious. BL112 and 117, which to some extent overlap, are examples of such clauses.

BL112 states:

The government of the HKSAR shall safeguard the free flow of all capital within, into and out of the Region.

BL117 (second paragraph) states:

The government of the HKSAR shall safeguard the free movement of goods, intangible assets and capital.

The duty of safeguarding the *free flow* (BL112) or *free movement* (BL117) of capital suggests that there is a corresponding right which the courts would recognise and protect. If this be correct, then an enactment of the local legislature such as the new section 21L of the Supreme Court Ordinance would appear to be ultra vires the Basic Law. Section 21L in effect empowers the High Court to restrain anyone from removing assets out of the jurisdiction. (This gives statutory force to a practice of the courts, in existence for over a decade, of making what are called *Mareva* injunctions. The object of such an injunction is to protect the plaintiff in legal proceedings from obtaining an empty judgment, and such relief is given where there are good grounds for believing that the defendant is liable to the plaintiff on a monetary claim and is likely to remove his assets from Hong Kong unless restrained.) A provision of law such as section 21L of the Supreme Court Ordinance, on the face of it, offends the principle of free flow and free movement of capital as enshrined in BL112 and BL117: a provision which a defendant after 1 July 1997 would surely invoke in resisting a *Mareva* injunction.

There are other provisions in chapter V which, if promulgated, would create problems for the government later on. For example BL123 appears to display a heavy bias in favour of industry and technology; the same bias is seen in BL146 which requires the government to formulate policies on science and technology. Nowhere in the Basic Law, over the whole of the 172 articles, is there any reference to the need for protecting the natural environment or combating the deleterious effect of industry upon the living environment. Thus, it could be argued that the effect of BL123, together with the absence of any counterbalancing provisions elsewhere in the Basic Law, have the effect of making *all* environmental protection statutes ultra vires, such as the present Air Pollution Control Ordinance and the Water Pollution Control Ordinance.

CHAPTER VI: EDUCATION, SOCIAL SERVICES, ETC

This chapter seeks to constitutionalise part of the professional and social scene in Hong Kong and to freeze it on canvas. Some of the clauses are quite extraordinary, for example: BL145 which requires the government of the SAR to 'promote the development of Western and Chinese traditional medicine. . . .' Why, one might ask, confine the focus to two sets of medical concepts when, for all one knows, others more valid and more beneficial might emerge in the course of the next 50 years? Consider also BL155, which requires the SAR (meaning, presumably, the *government* of the SAR) to formulate labour laws and policies 'in the light of economic development, social needs and the specific circumstances of labour-management consultations.' Why confine the consideration of economic development and social needs to the formulation of *labour* laws? Surely factors such as Hong Kong's economic development and social needs are relevant to the formulation of most laws? Or is the focus in BL155 on 'labour-management consultations'? And what would happen to statutes passed by the local legislature, or subsidiary legislation passed by (say) the Commissioner for Labour, *without* sufficient (or any) consultation?

There are many similar examples of odd concepts being constitutionalised in the Basic Law.

What is particularly objectionable in chapter VI is this: the Basic Law seeks to create entrenched pockets of power among interest groups and to make them immune from control by the government of the SAR. An extreme example of this is in BL150 which (in the third paragraph) requires the government of the SAR to maintain the professional organisations recognised prior to the establishment of the Region; the paragraph then goes on to say:

> . . . and these organisations may, *on their own*, assess and accredit professional qualifications.

This gives a degree of autonomy to professional bodies which has never been enjoyed by such bodies. It is highly questionable whether it is in the public interest that there should be such autonomy given to self-interested groups. At present, the professional qualifications of persons such as lawyers, doctors, and accountants are regulated by statute; the governing bodies of these professions do *not* decide 'on their own' the qualification to practise. It cannot be in the public interest that total autonomy be given to these professions, whose governing bodies are elected from year to year. Their policies as regards professional qualifications could change from year to year. If BL150 is intended to safeguard the existing professional organisations from encroachment by untrained and unqualified people, then the way the clause is worded at present, it could have the opposite effect. For if the *government* of the SAR is rendered powerless by the Basic Law from passing laws generally in the public interest to regulate the professions, then all it takes is one *coup d'état* in any one of these professional bodies for the rules of professional qualification to change. Assume, for example, that the Council of the Law Society should, in 1998, declare that solicitors over the age of 50 should compulsorily retire and be disqualified from practice: is the government of the SAR powerless to interfere? The rules made by the professions concerning the conduct and etiquette of members may safeguard the honour of the professions and uphold their high standards today; what is there to prevent the governing bodies from changing the rules tomorrow, if BL150 were in place?

BL154 gives to voluntary organisations providing social services the *right*, on their own, to decide their *forms* of service according to law. This clause puts the status of voluntary agencies at an extraordinarily high level and will create pockets of power over which the SAR government will have no control. Are *all* voluntary welfare agencies equally well motivated? Has there not been the odd abuse in the past by some of these bodies and will it not occur again? What if their powers were used, not in the general public interest, but to advance the selfish interests of those in charge of such groups?

CONCLUSION

To ensure that the people of the SAR will enjoy a high degree of autonomy, and that their present life-style be preserved, it is essential that the *government* of the SAR be strong. There is nothing that could stand between the pressure exerted by the yearnings and aspirations of one billion mainland people, many with their noses pressed against the door of the SAR, and the people of the SAR, except a strong and honest SAR government. To strip the government of its powers of effective functioning is to ensure that the Region will lose its identity. Its distinctive life-style will be submerged by the weight of numbers, as surely as night follows day.

15 Chinese Nationality in the Basic Law

FRANK CHING

THE official draft of the Basic Law contains a number of references to 'Chinese nationals.' For example, it divides permanent residents of the future Special Administrative Region into 'Chinese nationals' born in Hong Kong, 'Chinese nationals' who have resided in Hong Kong for at least seven years, 'persons of Chinese nationality' born outside Hong Kong whose parents belong to the first two categories, and certain 'persons of non-Chinese nationality' (BL23).

In addition, the draft says that the Chief Executive 'shall be a Chinese national' aged 40 or above (BL44). Also, the 'principal officials' of the SAR 'shall be Chinese nationals who are permanent residents' (BL61).

In the section on the legislature, the draft says that the President of the Legislative Council 'shall be a Chinese national' (BL70, alternative 1), though it does not make the same requirement of any other member of the legislature.

However, nowhere in the Basic Law is there any explanation as to the criteria for determining the nationality of residents of Hong Kong. For that, presumably, we will have to turn to China's nationality law.

BL17 of the Basic Law says that certain laws enacted by the National People's Congress or its Standing Committee 'which give expression to national unity and territorial integrity' shall apply in Hong Kong as needed. Presumably, China's nationality law will be such a law. And it is the nationality law that will be used to determine whether a person is or is not a Chinese national.

The only Chinese statement relating specifically to the nationality of people in Hong Kong is the Chinese memorandum accompanying the Joint Declaration on the Question of Hong Kong. In it, the Chinese government said:

Under the Nationality Law of the People's Republic of China, all Hong Kong Chinese compatriots, whether they are holders of the British Dependent Territories Citizens' Passport or not, are Chinese nationals.

Taking account of the historical background of Hong Kong and its realities, the competent authorities of the Government of the People's

288

Republic of China will, with effect from 1 July 1997, permit Chinese nationals in Hong Kong who were previously called British Dependent Territories Citizens to use travel documents issued by the Government of the United Kingdom for the purpose of travelling to other states and regions.

The above Chinese nationals will not be entitled to British consular protection in the Hong Kong Special Administrative Region and other parts of the People's Republic of China on account of their holding the above-mentioned British travel documents.

The memorandum shows that China does not recognise possession of the British Dependent Territories Citizens' (BDTC) passport — and presumably its successor, the British National (Overseas), or BN(O), passport — as an indication of nationality. In fact, the memorandum carefully uses the term 'travel documents' rather than 'passports,' a word with connotations of nationality, when referring to the British-issued documents.

The Chinese position is that BDTC and BN(O) passport holders are merely using British-issued travel documents but such people do not necessarily possess British nationality.

The statement 'all Hong Kong Chinese compatriots, whether they are holders of the "British Dependent Territories Citizens' Passport" or not, are Chinese nationals' sounds sweeping and conclusive. It has been interpreted to mean that in China's eyes all ethnic Chinese are by definition Chinese nationals.

This is very far from the truth. For one thing, China's population is far from being homogeneous, with the government recognising that some 55 different ethnic groups — including Tibetans, Koreans, Uigurs, Kazakhs, Uzbeks (who are Caucasians), and Mongols — make up the Chinese nation.

The term 'ethnic Chinese' normally refers to the dominant ethnic group in China, the Han people. The rich diversity of China's many peoples is officially acknowledged both in the Chinese constitution and in the Chinese currency, where banknotes are inscribed with the main minority languages.

China's ethnic pluralism was reflected in the earliest flag of the Republic of China, which consisted of stripes of five colours to represent the country's five main ethnic groups.

Moreover, China's nationality law, promulgated in 1980, sets forth the circumstances in which Chinese nationals can lose their nationality, and the circumstances in which non-Chinese nationals can acquire such nationality. Hence, no person can be labelled a 'Chinese national' or a 'non-Chinese national' merely because of ethnic origins.

And while the words 'all Hong Kong Chinese compatriots . . . are Chinese nationals' sound sweeping, the statement is in fact no more than a tautology. 'Compatriot' is not a legal term; its everyday meaning is 'a fellow countryman.' Hence all that the Chinese memorandum says in effect is 'All Hong Kong Chinese nationals . . . are Chinese nationals.'

China's position on BDTC passport holders is, in fact, ambiguous. This is reflected in the setting up of the Sino-British Joint Liaison Group in the aftermath of the signing of the Joint Declaration. The British side included a senior Hong Kong official, Eric Ho, as part of its delegation. China took exception to this because Mr Ho was the holder of a BDTC passport (as well as of a New Zealand passport). In order to secure the acceptance of Mr Ho, the British government had to convert his passport into an authentic United Kingdom passport. Armed with his new passport, Mr Ho was recognised by the Chinese side as a member of the British delegation. However, when Mr Ho was replaced by another Hong Kong official, Donald Liao, the Chinese side did not insist that he, too, be given an authentic United Kingdom passport in order to take his place in the British delegation.

These two events show that, whatever China's nationality law says, the Chinese government's position may change with changing circumstances. In fact, whether the Chinese government should have recognised Mr Ho's United Kingdom passport is an interesting question. After all, from China's viewpoint, Hong Kong is Chinese territory. Can China recognise the right of a foreign government to confer arbitrarily foreign citizenship on a Chinese national residing in Chinese territory? From the standpoint of sovereignty and national dignity, it is difficult to see how China can allow any foreign government the right to turn Chinese nationals in China overnight into foreign nationals merely by giving them a foreign passport.

Similarly, the popular notion that the Chinese government will take the fact of possession of a BDTC or BN(O) passport to be proof of Chinese nationality is facile. The implication is that China is willing to accept a document issued by another government as an indication of Chinese nationality. However, no sovereign nation, certainly not China, can allow another sovereign nation — in this case Britain — to confer or withhold Chinese nationality through the issuance of special passports.

The confusion in the minds of Chinese officials regarding Chinese nationality was also evident in the formation of the Basic Law Drafting Committee and the Basic Law Consultative Committee. When an official of the State Council's Hong Kong and Macau Affairs Office, Lu Ping, visited Hong Kong in early 1986, a member of the Hong Kong Legislative Council, Helmut Sohmen, proposed that foreign constitutional experts be invited to help draft the Basic Law. Mr Lu brushed this suggestion aside, remarking that China does not need foreigners to help draft the Basic Law.

However, many of the leading members of the BLDC and the BLCC turned out to be ethnic Chinese holding foreign passports — not BDTC passports but authentic United Kingdom passports. Either China had not realised that legally they were foreigners or China had not considered their nationality to be important. But Chinese officials were clearly embarrassed when key members of the BLDC were disclosed as foreign nationals. Nonetheless, they continue to serve the BLDC.

Presumably, ethnic Chinese such as those referred to above who are holders of foreign passports will be barred from the posts of Chief Executive, principal officials, and President of the Legislative Council. However, China's nationality law does provide for the resumption of Chinese nationality by 'aliens who were once of Chinese nationality' who apply for restoration of Chinese nationality 'provided that they have legitimate reasons.' Foreign nationality before 1997, therefore, need not bar an individual from high office after 1997, provided that person is willing to give up his or her foreign nationality.

The crux in determining the nationality of Hong Kong people is the definition of the word 'abroad' as it appears in China's nationality law. Article 9 states:

> Any Chinese national who has settled abroad and who has been naturalized there or has acquired foreign nationality of his own free will automatically lose Chinese nationality.

The question is, does residence in Hong Kong constitute living 'abroad'? The Chinese memorandum would suggest not, since it does not recognise holders of BDTC passports as British nationals. However, people who have acquired United Kingdom passports after having fulfilled the five-year residency requirement — 'settled abroad' in the words of the nationality law — are recognised as British nationals.

However, in this area, too, China's behaviour is ambiguous. Chinese public security and customs authorities clearly consider travel to Hong Kong as going 'abroad.' Posters seen on the streets of Guangzhou put up by public security authorities warn against 'leaving the country illegally.' Flights from China to Hong Kong constitute international flights, and long-distance telephone calls to Hong Kong constitute international calls.

Moreover, the border at Shenzhen/Lowu is clearly regarded as an international border. And foreign diplomats in Hong Kong, all of them accredited to the British government, are routinely fêted by Chinese officials in Hong Kong as members of the diplomatic corps. Such consistent behaviour over a long period of time would appear to constitute recognition of British jurisdiction in Hong Kong, regardless of pronouncements from time to time that Hong Kong is and always has been Chinese territory.

All available evidence indicates that China has been eager to resolve disputes with other countries on nationality issues. Before China's nationality law was promulgated in 1980, it had reached agreement with a number of countries in Asia to resolve the problems of people with disputed or dual nationality. In almost all cases, such as the accords with Indonesia, Malaysia, the Philippines, and Thailand, China permitted the individuals concerned to decide for themselves what nationality they preferred to have.

The agreement with Burma in 1960 to resolve border disputes was especially interesting, since it involved the exchange of certain pieces of territory and their inhabitants. According to the agreement, the inhabitants in an area to be transferred by one side to the other should, after the transfer, be regarded as citizens of the other side to which the area now belongs. However, the principle of voluntarism was observed. Anyone wishing to retain his or her original nationality could state so within a year after the coming into effect of the treaty and move into the territory of the original side within two years.

China's refusal to recognise holders of Hong Kong British passports as British nationals appears to be dictated primarily by political considerations. Holders of such passports — plus those eligible to apply for these documents — constitute about half the population of the territory. As one official of the Xinhua News Agency, speaking privately, put it, 'How can we accept that half the population of Hong Kong are foreigners, subject to British control?'

Both of the English-language newspapers in Hong Kong have carried many letters to the editor written by people who fear that Chinese nationality will be imposed on them through the connivance of the British and Chinese governments. To prevent this from happening, tens of thousands of people are leaving Hong Kong every year, either to settle abroad permanently or to obtain an 'insurance policy' in the form of a foreign passport. Such a course of action would, of course, not be necessary if Britain had not taken away from its Hong Kong nationals the right of abode in the United Kingdom.

In a real sense, it is Britain that deprived its Hong Kong subjects of British nationality by changing the law and taking away from them the right of abode in the United Kingdom. Given this fact, it is difficult to see how China could have acted differently. If China had recognised holders of BDTC and BN (O) passports as foreign nationals, the following questions would immediately arise: What country are they nationals of? If they commit crimes in Hong Kong, can they be deported to Britain? Since Britain would not accept responsibility for these people, it was almost inevitable that China had to assume responsibility, and to do so by acknowledging them to be its own nationals and not foreigners.

To signify its non-recognition of BDTC passports, Chinese officials routinely refuse to stamp visas on these documents when presented by Hong Kong Chinese. Even in this area, however, there are exceptions. In one case, for example, an international news agency sent a journalist from Hong Kong to be based in Beijing as a foreign correspondent. That person held both a BDTC passport and a re-entry permit, which is the document normally used by 'Hong Kong compatriots' when travelling to China. The Chinese Foreign Ministry requested that the journalist use only his BDTC passport when entering or leaving China. One reason for this action could have been to limit his freedom to travel in the same way that other foreign correspondents were restricted. Compatriots from Hong Kong normally have almost unlimited access to all parts of the country.

In a more recent case, a holder of a BDTC passport approached the Chinese Visa Office in Hong Kong and applied for a visa. He was told to use a re-entry permit. However, when he protested that he was not a Chinese national, he was asked to swear a statutory declaration to that effect. Once that was done, the Visa Office agreed to stamp his BDTC passport.

The above may indicate that, even in the case of Hong Kong, China has not abandoned the principle of voluntarism. However, for holders of BDTC and BN(O) passports with no right of abode in Britain or any other country, that does not present them with any additional option, save that of being stateless.

16 Autonomy

ALBERT C Y HO

THE chapter is divided into two parts: the first part is an analytical study of the constitutional origin and nature of the Basic Law, with some comments on certain constitutional issues arising from such analysis; the second part is a critical evaulation of certain important provisions on the basis of one of the objectives the Basic Law seeks to achieve, namely, to confer a high degree of autonomy on the SAR.

CONSTITUTIONAL ORIGIN OF THE BASIC LAW

The authority of the Basic Law stems from article 31 of the constitution of the People's Republic of China. Article 31 empowers the National People's Congress to enact law to prescribe the systems to be instituted in special administrative regions set up by the state. There is, however, no express provision in this article empowering the NPC to disregard the directive or prohibitive principles appearing in other parts of the constitution. If one adopts a strict literal approach in construing article 31 within the four corners of the constitution (without reference to other political but non-legal documents or proclamations), the most probable and natural conclusion is that the power under article 31 shall be exercised within the confines of and subject to the constraints imposed by other parts of the constitution, which is understood to be applicable to the state as a whole.

On the other hand, it has been suggested that in construing article 31, one may adopt a more flexible, liberal, and purposive approach and refer to other documents such as relevant official reports, government statements and proclamations concerning the use of article 31. If such an approach (which is quite often accepted as a proper approach in construing constitutional documents, though not necessarily ordinary legislation) is adopted, the natural and probable conclusion is that article 31 vests in the NPC a special legislative authority, enabling it to create a constitutional framework for SARs and to legitimise the preservation of capitalist economic and social systems therein. The enabling power of article 31 allows it to over-ride other provisions in the constitution such as articles 1, 6, 10, etc which prescribe and direct that socialist policies and ideology must be strictly adhered to. Hence there is no question of a contravention of the constitution, and the Basic Law should not be declared ultra vires article 31 and liable to be annulled by the NPC in the future.

The most satisfactory solution, for the purpose of removing any doubt and demonstrating the long-term (at least 50 years) commitment of the Chinese government to the implementation of 'one country, two systems,' in relation to Hong Kong is to amend or re-write article 31, or even replace article 31 with a new article in the constitution, containing as many paragraphs as may be required, clearly defining the constitutional status of the SAR under the Chinese constitution, and expressly permitting the SAR to maintain a capitalistic economic and social system within its territories.

Distinguishing features of the Basic Law

Like ordinary state statutes, the Basic Law is to be enacted and promulgated by the NPC. There is no requirement that the Basic Law has to be passed by a special majority of NPC delegates. However, unlike an ordinary state statute, the Basic Law has a special constitutional origin as discussed above. It also has several other salient features which make it different and distinct from ordinary state statutes.

As the Basic Law is to be enacted under a constitutional provision and serves as the constitutional foundation for the SAR, it will or should exclude the application of many provisions of the Chinese constitution to the SAR. Apart from articles 1, 6, and 10, which uphold the principles of Marxist-socialist policies, many other provisions which serve to bring the regional governments of the provinces and municipalities directly under the unitary and centralised control of the Central Government should also be excluded from application to Hong Kong. Further, as the SAR will have its own bill of rights entrenched in the Basic Law, the whole of chapter 2 (on the fundamental rights and duties of citizens) of the Chinese constitution, which is framed in the context of a socialist system, should also be inapplicable to the SAR. The constitutional problem that remains to be solved is the ascertainment of those provisions which remain applicable to the SAR, after the enactment of the Basic Law.

The Basic Law, once enacted and promulgated, cannot be amended like an ordinary statute. There are two forms of entrenchment under the Basic Law. One is a substantive entrenchment appearing in the fourth paragraph of BL170, which provides that 'no amendment to this Law shall contravene the basic policies of the PRC regarding Hong Kong.' Therefore, the NPC will have to irrevocably abandon, renounce, or pledge to restrain its power to amend in this respect. The second form of entrenchment is a procedural one, namely, a special procedure is prescribed for effecting amendment. The special procedure is also entrenched in BL170, which requires all amendments to be properly proposed by the Standing Committee of the NPC, the State Council or the SAR. The manner of exercising this proposal power by the SAR is also specifically prescribed in the same article. Further, all lawful proposals to amend shall be preceded by prior consultation with the Committee for the Basic Law. Although both forms of entrenchment have been subject to strong criticism in that the meaning of 'the basic policies' has not been clearly spelt out in the substantive entrenchment provision, and that the procedural entrenchment provision does not confer sufficient freedom on the SAR to propose on its own motion, the entrenchment provisions of the Basic Law still make it clearly distinct and distinguishable from ordinary state statutes.

Interpretation of the Basic Law

As in the case of any ordinary state statute of the PRC, the power to interpret the Basic Law is vested in the NPCSC under BL169, which follows the spirit of article 62 of the Chinese constitution. Some drafters of the Basic Law maintain that the retention of this power is essential for the exercise of sovereignty over the SAR. However, this does not rule out the possibility of concurrent power of interpretation being exercised by the SAR judiciary. On mainland China, the Supreme People's Court does exercise full power to interpret all statutes for the purpose of adjudication.

Unlike an ordinary state statute, the Basic Law will form the legal foundation of all laws applicable in the SAR, and will itself be part of Hong Kong law (BL17). Within the legal system of the SAR, the courts exercise judicial power of interpretation of the law and the power of final adjudication. These are clearly provided in the Joint Declaration on the Question of Hong Kong. Further, the local judiciary is expected and empowered to act independently, not only vis-à-vis the SAR executive and legislature, but also vis-à-vis the Central Government. In this respect, the SAR judiciary is very different from its counterpart on the mainland, as the Chinese constitution in article 128 prescribes that the 'Supreme People's Court is responsible to the NPC and its Standing Committee. Local people's courts at different levels are responsible to the organs of state power which created them.'

In order to reconcile the principles of judicial independence and of SAR courts exercising the power of final adjudication with the principle that the NPCSC should enjoy some power to interpret the Basic Law so as to give effect to Chinese sovereignty, it is suggested that the NPCSC should confine and constrain its power of interpretation to certain parts of the Basic Law in the following specified and circumscribed situations:

(1) The NPCSC should only interpret those provisions of the Basic Law concerning the relationship between the central and SAR governments for the sole purpose of ensuring that the SAR, whether by its executive or legislative acts, will not transgress the limits of its jurisdiction and unlawfully usurp the powers of the Central Government. Vice versa, the legislative and executive acts of the CPG should also be subject to similar review by the NPCSC.

(2) Such interpretation by the NPCSC should *only* be made at the request of either the SAR or Central Government or both, and *not* by any individual or private or public organisation. The subject matter concerning which the interpretation by the NPCSC is made should be confined to legislative and executive acts of the two governments only and not extend to the acts of any other parties or individuals.

(3) It is of paramount importance that the NPCSC should refrain from interpreting any Basic Law provisions relating exclusively to matters within the high degree of autonomy enjoyed by the SAR. Moreover, the NPCSC should not use its power of interpretation as a means of interfering with the exercise of the power of final adjudication by the SAR courts or of influencing the outcome of adjudication in any pending or anticipated litigation.

(4) The procedures to be followed before the NPCSC exercises its power of interpretation should be clearly laid down. In particular, the composition, functions and procedures of the Committee for the Basic Law should be fully spelt out. It is imperative that the SAR government's representatives should be given an opportunity to be heard fully and fairly, and that all interpretations, when issued, should be accompanied by written reasons.

(5) The SAR judiciary should be vested with full power to interpret each and every part of the Basic Law, so as to enable it to carry out its judicial function smoothly and without disruption.

The retention by the NPCSC of the power to interpret those provisions of the Basic Law concerning the relationship between the central and SAR governments will suffice for the purpose of enabling the NPCSC to maintain the constitutional and political link between the two governments and hence to realise Chinese sovereignty over the SAR. All other powers of interpretation are capable of being delegated and should be delegated without reservation. It is therefore submitted that BL169 should be substantially re-drafted. The practical necessity of sustaining 'one country, two systems' and 'the high degree of autonomy' of the SAR warrants the demand for such delegation and division of power concerning the interpretation of the Basic Law.

Like the state statutes establishing national autonomous areas within China, the Basic Law will function to establish an SAR entrusted with a wide range of powers for its self-governance. But quite unlike the former statutes, the Basic Law should, in an unprecedented manner and to an unprecedented extent, impose limitations on the power of the supreme legislative and executive organs of the state, namely the NPC, its Standing Committee, and the Central Government, in relation to the governing of the SAR. It is only by limiting and restraining the power of these organs that the Basic Law may be able to sustain the integrity of a political, social, and economic system which is different and distinct from the system existing on the mainland. The Basic Law, if properly drafted and implemented, can serve as a bulwark safeguarding the autonomy and integrity of the political, social, and economic systems of the SAR.

Authority of the Basic Law

The Basic Law is a legal document having the force of law within the SAR. It enjoys a higher status than ordinary laws, as it functions to legitimise the status of laws previously in force in Hong Kong, and to empower the SAR legislature to make new laws, and to amend or repeal the existing law. It is provided in various articles of the Basic Law, namely articles 8, 10, and 172, that the laws previously in force and those enacted by the SAR legislature shall not contravene the Basic Law, otherwise they are liable to be annulled or revoked. The above provisions create several problems.

First, by which authority and through what procedures can a law of the SAR be annulled? Should it be by way of constitutional judicial review before the SAR courts, or by way of non-judicial review or preview by the NPCSC, or by both channels concurrently? This question is related to that of the interpretation of the Basic Law discussed above.

Second, are all the provisions of the Basic Law capable of being interpreted judicially, or, in other words, are they all intended to be justiciable and enforceable as legal rules binding on the legislature, the executive, and all private individuals and legal entities? For many articles in chapters I, II, IV, VII, and IX, the answer is obviously in the affirmative. How about the others? Most if not all of the articles in chapter V (on economy) and chapter VI (on education, science, culture, sports, religion, labour, and social services) are no more than directive principles and policies, which are extremely flexible in meaning and construction. To give a rigid and restricted meaning to these provisions for the purpose of enforcing their observance as legal rules will lead to disastrous consequences, as all the discretion in the formulation of social and economic policies by the executive and legislature will then be usurped by the judiciary. On the other hand, to attribute a liberal and flexible meaning to these policies will make them no more than declarations of good faith and intention, which cannot be applied and enforced in a court of law.

It is worth mentioning here that although chapter III (on fundamental rights and duties of citizens) contains general declaratory principles, it is capable of being and should be fully justiciable. BL39 has set out an objective test for balancing various public interests and fundamental private rights, and the power to strike a balance, it is submitted, should be expressly and exclusively entrusted to the SAR courts. There are ample judicial precedents laid down by reputable courts of many foreign countries which have justiciable bills of rights, and also by the European Court of Human Rights. The SAR judiciary should certainly refer to these foreign decisions for assistance and guidance.

Third, for those provisions of the Basic Law which are intended to be and are capable of being justiciable, what are the effects and consequences of their being applied to annul or revoke an ordinary law or legislation? BL16 stipulates that the annulment of any legislation by the NPCSC has no retroactive effect. How about those laws which are declared to be in contravention of the Basic Law by a court of law exercising its power of constitutional judicial review, or by the NPCSC exercising its power of interpretation under BL169? It is absolutely necessary that the status of those laws which are annulled because they contravene the Basic Law be clearly stated; in particular, an answer has to be provided as regards whether these contravening laws are null and void ab initio, or are only voidable and terminated as from the time of their being declared void.

Objectives of the Basic Law

The Basic Law is to be enacted pursuant to the obligations under the Joint Declaration. In giving a fair, liberal, and purposive construction to the letter and spirit of the Joint

Declaration in the light of various official explanations and commitments made to the public by the Chinese government at or about the time of its promulgation, the Basic Law is commonly expected and understood to achieve the following objectives:

First, to provide for the resumption of Chinese sovereignty over Hong Kong in 1997 and, upon such resumption, the establishment of a special administrative region pursuant to article 31 of the Chinese constitution.

Second, to confer a high degree of autonomy on the SAR government save and except in relation to defence and foreign affairs, and to delineate the power relationship between the Central Government and the SAR government.

Third, to set out the constitutional structure of the SAR government, including a fully elected legislature, a responsible executive, and an independent judiciary vested with the power of final adjudication.

Fourth, to restrain the SAR government from encroaching on fundamental human rights, by laying down a bill of rights, and to declare certain directive principles of social, economic, and cultural policies.

Fifth, to provide for a smooth transition from the rule of the British colonial government to the first SAR government with a view to preserving continuity.

To achieve the stated objectives, the Basic Law should be drafted within the confines of and in accordance with the letter and spirit of the Joint Declaration. Further, the drafters of the Basic Law should take into full account not only the consensus and understanding of the two signatory countries to the Joint Declaration, but also the common understanding and expectation of the people of Hong Kong, who gave their approval and endorsement to the Joint Declaration when it was promulgated and ratified.

As the Joint Declaration is a public document, having the legal status of an international bilateral treaty and registered with the United Nations, its provisions must be construed according to rules which are most commonly adopted or universally recognised, and its wording should bear its plain, natural, and ordinary meaning which is that commonly understood and accepted by the people of Hong Kong, who are to be most intimately affected by it.

It is suggested that the drafting of the Basic Law should follow the same principles. Further, the Basic Law should, as far as possible, be self-contained and self-explanatory. In other words, any party who has not participated in the drafting process should be able to comprehend its meaning fully, accurately, and precisely, without having to refer to other documents or authorities for guidance or direction.

Concepts of 'exercise of sovereignty' and 'the high degree of autonomy'

Implementation of the historic experiment of 'one country, two systems' requires mastery of the political art of balancing two seemingly conflicting concepts of 'sovereignty' and 'autonomy' by the creation of a constitutional model which can successfully synthesise these two concepts. It is suggested that this 'synthetic model' be created on the basis of the following principles:

(1) The Central Government should devolve or delegate as much power as possible to the SAR government, save and except those powers which are recognised in international law to be exercisable only by a sovereign state, such as defence and those foreign affairs relating to diplomacy, and those powers which are clearly necessary for the purpose of preserving the constitutional relationship between the Central Government and the SAR, such as the power to interpret certain provisions of the Basic Law and to amend it.

(2) The reservation of minimal but sufficient powers to realise the exercise of sovereignty should be a basic and important policy underlining the drafting of the Basic Law. It will demonstrate, on the one hand, the capacity of the Central Government to tolerate the preservation of capitalism and its integral structures within the SAR, which will inevitably remain under the predominant political influence of China no matter what political system the SAR is going to adopt. On the other hand, it will allow the maximum degree of devolution of power to the SAR government, thus enabling it to enjoy the highest scope of autonomy that is consistent with the realisation of Chinese sovereignty over the SAR.

(3) Further, there should be a clear delineation and division of power between the Central Government and the SAR government. This is normally worked out in other constitutions by drawing up either a list of powers to be reserved for the Central Government, or a list of those to be fully delegated to the autonomous government; the residual powers will then belong to the government which does not enjoy the powers set out in the list. In some countries, such as Canada and India, the constitution provides for two separate lists of powers respectively for the central and provincial governments. Sometimes there is a third

list of concurrent powers exercisable by both governments jointly or severally.

(4) The idea of a clear separation of powers is related to two other concepts inherent in a high degree of autonomy: first, the power to be delegated to the SAR government must be exclusively exercisable by it; in other words, there should be an area of exclusive jurisdiction for the SAR government; second, the Central Government should be restrained by the Basic Law from intermeddling in or interfering with the exercise of any power within the exclusive jurisdiction of the SAR government.

(5) If there is an area of concurrent jurisdiction of both governments, it may cover two major areas:

(a) affairs related to the constitutional relationship of the central and SAR governments, such as the interpretation and amendment of the Basic Law, the selection of the Chief Executive (which includes the final appointment, whether ceremonial or substantive, by the Central Government);

(b) affairs that affect or regulate the bilateral but non-political relationship between the mainland and the SAR, such as the control of movement and immigration of people, reciprocal enforcement of judgments and other forms of juridical assistance, control of movement of traffic between the two places.

(6) In order to maintain and sustain the integrity of the political, social, and economic systems of the SAR, it is a prerequisite that the SAR government and, in particular, its CE and legislators, should derive their support and mandate to rule primarily from the people of the SAR through a democratic process. Only a democratic order based on universal suffrage and an internal system of balance of powers will ensure the government's accountability to the people and its freedom from control and manipulation by particular interest groups.

(7) On the other hand, the SAR government (but not individual officials in the government) should as a whole also be accountable to the Central Government. Such accountability should be sufficiently discharged by the SAR government by:

(a) effectively maintaining order and stability in the SAR;

(b) duly performing its obligations towards the Central Government in accordance with the Basic Law, which include, in particular, reporting to the Central Government for the record all domestic legislation and commercial treaties or agreements with foreign countries, rendering full co-operation to the Central Government to enable it to exercise its reserved powers effectively, and refraining from transgressing the boundaries of its jurisdiction and thereby usurping the functions of the Central Government.

CRITICAL EVALUATION OF THE BASIC LAW

In the light of the above principles, it appears that the present draft of the Basic Law is blatantly deficient in the following respects:

The scope of 'the high degree of autonomy of the HKSAR' is nowhere defined in the draft, although this term appears in various articles, and is a key term in BL17 in determining the extent of the power of the Central Government to require nationwide state laws or statutes to be re-enacted in the SAR. Similarly, expressions such as 'matters which are the responsibility of the CPG' (BL169) and 'affairs which the HKSAR administers on its own in accordance with this Law' (BL21) are not defined in the text.

There is also a conspicuous absence of a general jurisdiction clause framed in the form of a list of exclusive powers delegated to the SAR government as a whole. Such a list would enable the exact scope of autonomy of the SAR to be ascertained, and all legislative, executive, and judicial powers to be freely exercised within such scope. Instead, the drafters have deliberately chosen to set out the powers to be devolved to the SAR government in different clauses, with the absurd result that the legislature, executive, and judiciary of the SAR do not apparently enjoy the same scope of power.

BL15 seeks to draw up a list of powers to be delegated to the executive of the SAR, with the implication that residual powers are to be reserved for the Central Government. On the other hand, BL16 appears to be a general delegation of power, which of course must be construed in the light of other provisions reserving power to the Central Government, such as BL12 and 13 concerning the responsibility for foreign affairs and defence. It appears as a matter of construction that BL16 operates to confer all residual powers on the SAR legislature, save and except those powers which are expressly reserved in other provisions. Similarly, the provision on the jurisdiction of the SAR judiciary in BL18 also appears in the form of a general delegation of residual power subject to expressed reservations and exceptions.

Is it the intention of the draftsmen that the respective jurisdictions of the legislature, executive, and judiciary should be different? Is there any reason why a single all-embracing article defining the exact scope of the high degree of autonomy to be enjoyed by the SAR cannot be employed? Under the Basic Law as it stands, it seems that there is no clear delineation or division of power between the central and SAR governments. Nor is the concept of exclusive jurisdiction expressly or impliedly adopted to fortify the autonomy of the SAR.

Under BL17, the NPC or its Standing Committee can direct the SAR legislature to re-enact state laws which relate to defence and foreign affairs, or which give expression to national unity and territorial integrity but are outside the scope of the high degree of autonomy of the SAR. However, this exclusionary provision serves no useful function in protecting the SAR's 'high degree of autonomy,' which remains an open concept under the Basic Law and is subject to flexible interpretation. Further, much will depend on the construction of the nebulous concepts of national unity and territorial integrity, which may extend as far as the regulation of internal security or the control of public opinion for the protection of national intergrity.

BL21 directs in clear terms that 'departments under the CPG as well as provinces, autonomous regions and municipalities directly under the Central Government shall not interfere in the affairs which the HKSAR administers on its own in accordance with this Law.' It should be noted with caution here that the NPC, its Standing Committee, and the CPG itself (which according to article 85 of the constitution means the State Council) are not subject to the same restraint. Is this an inadvertent or intentional omission? If it is an intentional omission, does it imply that any power delegated to the SAR government is liable to be over-ridden by these supreme organs of the state, and that the concept of exclusive jurisdiction has no place in the 'high degree of autonomy' of the SAR? Such fear is reinforced by BL18, which intends to take all executive acts of the Central Government, whether lawful or otherwise, completely outside the jurisdiction of the SAR courts.

BL16 and 169 seek to confer full and supreme power on the NPCSC to interpret any part of the Basic Law, and to apply it to annul or revoke any law of the SAR, whether or not such law relates exclusively to the SAR's domestic affairs, or those affairs within 'the high degree of autonomy of the HKSAR' (borrowing the term from BL17), or 'affairs which the HKSAR administers on its own' (borrowing the term from BL21). Further, as there is no distinction between justiciable provisions and non-justiciable directive policies, and no restriction on the power of the Standing Committee to interpret and apply those provisions of the Basic Law which obviously relate only to the domestic affairs of the SAR, the Standing Committee may be entitled to annul, revoke, or strike down any domestic legislation passed by the SAR in the regulation of its internal affairs. It follows that the Standing Committee may invoke this sweeping power to annul or revoke, say, a taxation ordinance, which arguably contravenes the 'low taxation policy' prescribed in BL107, or the law relating to the professional qualification of medical practitioners, which allegedly fails to 'promote the development of medical and health services and the development of Western and Chinese medicine . . .' (BL145). Consequently, the power of interpretation may in extreme cases be open to lawful abuse and misuse by Chinese officials as a political device to interfere in the internal affairs commonly understood to be within the autonomy of the SAR.

BL43 imposes a constitutional duty on the CE of the SAR to be accountable to the Central Government as well as to the SAR. The accountability of the executive, of which the CE holds the leading position, is further defined and elaborated in BL64. That article seems to suggest that by being accountable to a fully elected legislature in the manner therein prescribed, the CE would have discharged his or her accountability to the SAR. There are many controversies arising from the concepts of 'executive accountability towards the legislature' and 'a fully elected legislature,' which may be interpreted to mean the creation of a democratic order of the type practised in the West. It is not the object of this chapter to go into the substance and details of these controversies. However, it appears that the overall set-up of the power structure (disregarding for this purpose the method of selecting the CE and legislators) is designed to create an extremely powerful CE, leaving the SAR legislature in an obviously subsidiary and no more than supervisory role. Moreover, if the CE is not ultimately held accountable directly and truly to the people of the SAR through a democratic form of election based on universal suffrage, he or she will be extremely vulnerable to control and manipulation by the Central Government, which will be in a position to render to the CE another form of mandate or support, although naturally at the expense of the SAR's autonomy.

It should be noted that the manner of accountability of the CE to the Central Government is not mentioned at all in the Basic Law. Since the final power of appointment of the CE is vested in the CPG, it is possible that the appointment power will be exercised actively to ensure accountability. It is submitted that such accountability of the CE should be collectively discharged together with the principal officials and the legislature. Accountability should also be limited to the fulfilment of those obligations towards the Central Government under the Basic Law as mentioned above. Therefore, it is further submitted that the power to appoint the CE and principal officials should not be used as a political weapon by the Central Government, but should only be passively exercised as a symbol of Chinese sovereignty. However, the wide definition of principal officials in BL48(5), covering even such independent public officers as the Commissioner against Corruption and the Director of Audit, seems to suggest that this appointment power will be actively exercised to ensure that only those persons acceptable to the Central Government will be appointed. If this prerogative is exploited to the extreme, the executive of the SAR government will be no more than an extension to the SAR of the bureaucracy of the Central Government.

The method of formation of the first SAR government proposed in Annex III of the Basic Law is above all most alarming. If this method is adopted, it is conceivable the first government, including the CE and the members of the SAR legislature, will be entirely hand-picked by the Central Government. Further, if the concept of 'the grand electoral college' (which appears to be intended to function as an appointment system under disguise) is accepted as the guiding principle in chapter IV of the Basic Law for electing the CE and some of the members of the legislature of successive SAR governments, the first legislature can formulate the election laws for the grand electoral college in such a way as to favour the self-perpetuation of the first government. Then the first government will in effect determine who shall be its successors. In this case, even the highest form of devolution of power in the Basic Law will create an autonomy in name and on paper only, since the political leaders of the autonomous government will just carry out faithfully the policies and orders of their superiors who have brought them to power.

CONCLUSION

The failure and deficiency of the Basic Law in achieving the objective of conferring a high degree of autonomy on the SAR may be due to one of these three possible explanations:

(1) Inappropriate or incompetent drafting has resulted in a failure to bring out the true intention of the drafters, which is to design a constitutional system giving a high degree of genuine autonomy to the SAR.
(2) The drafters worked under the conception or misconception that a high degree of de facto autonomy might be achieved by the proposed arrangements, believing or hoping that the

Central Government would inherit the British tradition of exercising self-restraint and would not interfere with the domestic affairs of Hong Kong save in exceptional circumstances where the need to interfere for the benefit of Hong Kong and the state arose.

(3) There is a deliberate design to create several loopholes in Hong Kong's political system through which the Central Government can and will exert its political control and influence on the SAR, based on the belief that such control and influence will be beneficial both to the SAR and to the country as a whole.

If the first explanation is correct, the drafting defects can certainly be remedied by bringing in more experts to conduct a thorough review of the present draft.

The second explanation, which is the more probable one, shows the inherent conflict between sovereignty and autonomy which has remained unresolved in the minds of the Chinese drafters. It also shows that the Chinese leaders do not have sufficient confidence in the Hong Kong people to allow them to practise a high degree of autonomy without close supervision and protection by the Central Government. If this philosophy of political paternalism were to underline the framing of the Basic Law, it would not serve any useful purpose for us to dwell on the constitutional safeguards of the autonomy of the SAR. In the end, Hong Kong people will have to choose either to accept or reject the declaration of good faith made by the Chinese government. However, it seems more probable than not that Hong Kong people will prefer to rely on concrete deeds, rather than empty promises. Confidence will therefore be severely undermined if the present draft of the Basic Law is not satisfactorily amended to give sufficient constitutional safeguards to the SAR. In the absence of such safeguards, the fate of the SAR will be left entirely to the mercy of the Chinese leaders and those Chinese officials responsible for Hong Kong affairs; but those who are vested with power will be persistently subjected to the temptation, which can hardly be resisted, to use and exercise such power, whenever they think they can afford better protection for the interests of the state, or of the SAR, or of both.

If there are indeed plans and motives to exercise positive and vigorous control through the various devices mentioned above, it will be a completely futile exercise to devote further efforts to the drafting of the Basic Law on the basis of the common objectives and aspirations allegedly shared by the Chinese government and the people of Hong Kong. It is then probable that the future of

Hong Kong will witness a repetition of the same mistake persistently repeated in China in the course of the past 39 years of Communist rule, namely, a blind belief in the dictatorial rule of the Communist Party. In that case, the speedy decline in the SAR's autonomy and all its undesirable consequences would be abruptly ended by a 'glorious unification' of the two systems into one under the supreme leadership of the Communist Party ruling in the name of the sovereign state.

17 A Tale of Two Articles

MARTIN C M LEE

> It was the best of times,
>   it was the worst of times,
> it was the age of wisdom,
>   it was the age of foolishness,
> it was the epoch of belief,
>   it was the epoch of incredulity,
> it was the season of Light,
>   it was the season of Darkness,
> it was the spring of hope,
>   it was the winter of despair,
> we had everything before us,
>   we had nothing before us,
> we were all going direct to Heaven,
>   we were all going direct the other way.

from *A Tale of Two Cities* by Charles Dickens

OF ALL the articles contained in the Basic Law, two articles have attracted more criticism than any of the others. They are BL18 and 169. The object of this chapter is to give a historical account of how these two articles came to be drafted. In doing this, only material discussions on these articles will be mentioned. Except where otherwise indicated, all source materials are from official minutes kept by the staff of the Secretariat of the Basic Law Drafting Committee.

SECOND MEETING OF THE SUB-GROUP

At the second meeting of the BLDC sub-group on the relationship between the central authorities and the Special Administrative Region ('the sub-group' or 'the first sub-group') held in Shenzhen on 31 May 1986 and 1 June 1986, consensus was reached on clause 2 of chapter 9 of the Basic Law:

The power of interpretation of the Basic Law is vested in the Standing Committee of the National People's Congress. The courts of the HKSAR may interpret the provisions of the Basic Law in adjudicating cases before them.

309

It is significant to note the views expressed by individual members of the sub-group:

(a) Since the Basic Law is going to be promulgated by the NPC, it naturally has the power to interpret it. But as Hong Kong has a common law system, once a law is passed by the legislature, only the courts have the power to interpret it. Therefore, in future, the courts of the HKSAR should have the power to interpret the Basic Law while adjudicating cases. But when there is no actual case before the courts of the SAR, the NPC may interpret the Basic Law if requested to do so by the Central People's Government or the HKSAR Government.

That was my view, and there were two reasons behind it. First, under the Chinese legal system, both the NPCSC and the Supreme People's Court have the power to interpret Chinese laws, including the Chinese constitution, and also the Basic Law after 1997. And this power can be exercised by the Supreme People's Court even though there is no case before it. However, in Hong Kong, the courts can only exercise their judicial functions, including the interpretation of laws, when there are actual cases before them. Second, I suggested that the National People's Congress should interpret the Basic Law only when requested to do so by the CPG or the SAR government, in order to make sure that a litigant or a prospective litigant would not be able to gain an advantage over the other party to the action by asking the NPC or its Standing Committee to interpret a provision of the Basic Law.

(b) There should be set up under the NPC or the NPCSC a committee consisting of members from both the mainland and Hong Kong, whose task is to study and then give advice to the NPCSC in relation to the interpretation of any provision of the Basic Law before the NPCSC interprets any provision in the Basic Law. But the final decision is that of the NPCSC.

(c) The power of the courts of the SAR to interpret the Basic Law should be limited in that they shall not interpret any provision of the Basic Law relating to the rights of the CPG or to the relationship between the central authorities and the SAR.

(d) If the courts of the SAR come across any political question, then they shall listen to the Central Government's views thereon and shall not interpret such questions on their own.

(e) If the NPCSC is of the opinion that the courts of the SAR have misinterpreted any provision of the Basic Law, it should be able to interpret the same provision afresh, but without affecting the validity and effect of judgments previously rendered by the courts of the SAR. But such judgments should not be used as precedents in future.

(f)* The courts of the SAR do not have power to adjudicate on political matters or matters relating to defence and foreign affairs.

(g)* There should be set up in Hong Kong a constitutional court to try cases which involve constitutional matters.

(h)* There are some matters which are not for the courts to decide, even in England: for example, whether Great Britain had recognised the USSR in 1923. For a question such as this, the court has to accept a certificate from the Foreign Office. Therefore, in future, such a question should be decided by the CPG.

(i)* The question as to who has the final right of interpretation of the Basic Law should be decided in favour of the NPCSC because of the provisions of the Chinese constitution. There should not be any problem in this regard because even the British Government had not raised it during its negotiations with the Chinese Government on the Joint Declaration.

*(Sub-paragraphs (f) to (i) are based on my own notes taken during the meeting.)

In many ways, the second meeting was the most important meeting, because many of the views expressed at the meeting clearly influenced the subsequent drafting of BL18 and 169. One wonders whether the mainland members of the sub-group had not already formed a definite view on the matter even at that early stage. And indeed, subsequent meetings indicate that they have not made any concession.

THIRD MEETING OF THE SUB-GROUP

During the third meeting of the sub-group in Xiamen on 27 and 28 August 1986, there was a heated debate on the power of the courts of the SAR to interpret the Basic Law. On the first day of the meeting, a Hong Kong member proposed that 'the courts of the HKSAR shall only have power to interpret those provisions of the Basic Law within the scope of matters which the CPG has authorised the HKSAR government to administer.'

Later in the day, a mainland member proposed amending this clause to read: 'The courts of the HKSAR shall have power to interpret those provisions of the Basic Law relating to matters which are within the autonomy of the HKSAR.' I strongly opposed such a formulation, as well as the earlier formulation, and insisted that as the common law would continue to apply to the SAR by virtue of the Joint Declaration on the Question of Hong Kong, the courts of the Region should be given unrestricted power to interpret all the provisions of the Basic Law. However, my objection was over-ruled by the majority and BL2 of chapter 9 was then agreed (by the majority) as follows:

The power of interpretation of the Basic Law is vested in the NPCSC. The courts of the HKSAR while adjudicating cases before them may interpret those provisions of the Basic Law which are within the autonomy of the HKSAR.

If the NPCSC is of the opinion that the interpretation of a court of the HKSAR is wrong, it may interpret the relevant provision afresh, without, however, affecting the validity or effect of judgments previously rendered by the courts, but such judgments shall not be used as precedents in future.

My objection was recorded in a note set out as follows:

One member was of the view that by providing in this clause the words 'within the autonomy of the HKSAR,' it would unnecessarily restrict the power of the courts of the HKSAR, thus causing practical difficulties for the courts while adjudicating cases. The majority of members were of the view that until a better solution could be found, this clause could remain as it was. But members would be free to continue searching for a better solution.

FOURTH MEETING OF THE SUB-GROUP

The fourth meeting of the sub-group took place in Shenzhen on 10 and 11 November 1986, and, among other things, approved the report to be submitted to the next plenary session which was to take place at the end of November 1986. Clause 2 of chapter 9 was slightly amended in that the third paragraph was re-worded as follows:

If the NPCSC has interpreted any provision of the Basic Law, then the courts of the HKSAR shall adopt the same interpretation of that provision when applying it. However, judgments previously rendered shall not be affected thereby.

THIRD PLENARY SESSION

The third plenary session of the BLDC took place in Beijing from 29 November 1986 through 3 December 1986. During the meeting, I made a speech which referred 'among other things' to clause 2:

The common law applies to Hong Kong. And under the common law system, once a law is passed by the legislature, only the courts have the right to interpret it while adjudicating cases. The Joint Declaration has already laid down that the common law shall continue to apply to the SAR after 1997. If we wish to uphold the integrity of the common law, then we must let the courts of the SAR interpret all the laws of the Region, including the Basic Law.

But if the courts of the SAR only have jurisdiction to interpret those provisions of the Basic Law which are within the autonomy of the

Region, the question as to who will decide whether a particular provision of the Basic Law is within or outside the autonomy of the Region is already a difficult one to answer. If such a question is to be decided by the CPG, then many persons, particularly defendants in civil cases, will use this as a pretext to postpone the hearing of their cases, and request the NPCSC to interpret some provision in the Basic Law which falls within this category, thereby substantially delaying the trial of the actions. The NPCSC will have many cases to handle, and the courts of the SAR will not be able to deal with cases efficiently. Thus the judicial system of the SAR may be paralysed. I am therefore of the view that when the courts of the SAR are adjudicating cases, their jurisdiction to interpret the Basic Law should not be restricted to only those provisions which are within the autonomy of the Region.

SEVENTH MEETING OF THE SUB-GROUP

At the seventh meeting of the sub-group which took place from 16 through 18 February 1987 in Kunming, it was decided for the first time to look at the possibility of defining the jurisdiction of the courts of the SAR in chapter 4 of the Basic Law in order that the above-mentioned restriction on the courts of the SAR in their interpretation of the Basic Law might be removed. It was decided that all the 'legal experts' in the sub-group and in the third sub-group (on the political structure of the SAR: 'third sub-group') would hold a joint meeting on 15 March 1987 in Guangzhou. The matter was therefore deferred.

Joint meeting of legal experts

At the joint meeting of the legal experts on 15 March 1987 in Guangzhou, a number of proposals were submitted, all with the object of defining the jurisdiction of the courts of the SAR on the basis of the principle that what the courts could try under the present legal system, the courts of the future SAR could also try after 1997. A number of different formulations which were put forward sought to exclude from the jurisdiction of the SAR courts the following:

(1) 'acts of state' and 'facts of state';
(2) 'foreign and defence affairs and affairs which involve *great national interests*';
(3) 'foreign and defence affairs and affairs which relate to the sovereignty of the state'.

And my proposal was as follows:

'Acts of state' are not justiciable in the courts of the SAR; but the courts of the Region shall decide whether certain administrative acts, which include those relating to foreign and defence affairs, are or are not acts of state.

When a matter is determined by a court of the SAR to be a fact of state, the proof of that matter shall be by way of a certificate issued by the Chief Executive, which shall be binding on the courts of the SAR.

Joint meeting between the first and the third sub-group

On 8 June 1987 there was another joint meeting between the first and the third sub-group in Guangzhou. The aim then was to define the jurisdiction of the courts of the SAR by adding a provision in the section on 'Judicial Organs' in chapter 4. Altogether seven proposals were made, and whilst I put forward a proposal which avoided the use of expressions like 'acts of state' and 'facts of state' which had been objected to by the mainland members as imprecise, other members suggested the following expressions to exclude the jurisdiction of the courts of the SAR apart from defence and foreign affairs:

(1) 'the measures adopted by or responsibilities borne by the PRC in relation to foreign and defence affairs';
(2) 'sovereignty' and 'the employment and dismissal of personnel, etc';
(3) 'all matters which are the responsibility of the CPG';
(4) 'other matters which are not within the scope of autonomy of the HKSAR'; and
(5) 'the executive acts of the CPG.'

My proposal was as follows:

> An act performed, or a function exercised, by the People's Republic of China in the field of foreign or defence affairs in the course of or affecting its relationship with another state cannot be challenged, controlled or interfered with by the courts of the Hong Kong Special Administrative Region. Where any question relating to such an act or function is raised in any proceeding before the courts of the HKSAR, it shall be referred to the Chief Executive and a certificate issued by the Chief Executive with respect to such an act or function shall be binding on the courts.

I submitted this proposal in the spirit of compromise; but it was rejected. My present view is that we should not codify the common law restrictions on the jurisdiction of the courts at all.

Because of the failure to reach a consensus on any of these proposals, the joint meeting decided to leave the question to be studied further by the eight legal experts of the two sub-groups. However, at a subsequent meeting of the first sub-group held on 8 June 1987, it was decided to add the following new paragraph to the end of clause 2 of chapter 9:

> The NPCSC may consult the Basic Law Committee before giving an interpretation of this Law.

Joint meeting of legal experts

At the joint meeting of the eight legal experts of the two sub-groups in Guangzhou on 2 August 1987, the majority (with me dissenting) agreed on the text of a draft clause to be written into chapter 4 under the section 'The Judicial Organs' which sought to exclude from the jurisdiction of the courts of the SAR all cases involving defence and foreign affairs and other cases involving 'the executive acts of the CPG.' The text of this draft clause is later set out in full.

Joint meeting of the first and the third sub-group

The above draft clause in chapter 4 was then put to all the members of the first and the third sub-group at their joint meeting on 3 August 1987 and it was considered together with clause 2 of chapter 9 on the interpretation of the Basic Law.

During the meeting, some mainland members expressed the view that they did not in fact have any objection in principle to giving to the courts of the SAR unrestricted power to interpret all the provisions of the Basic Law, but they were concerned that the courts of the SAR might 'get it wrong' in their interpretation of the Basic Law in relation to defence and foreign affairs, for it might then cause great embarrassment to the CPG or even sour good relations with a friendly nation. They said that if the power of final adjudication had not been given to the SAR, they would not have insisted on restricting the jurisdiction of the courts of the SAR in their interpretation of the Basic Law. So they suggested that in a very limited number of cases involving the interpretation of the Basic Law relating to defence and foreign affairs, and possibly some other cases which might have very serious repercussions (the number being no more than one or two a year), the NPCSC should be given the power to decide, if its interpretation of any such provision of the Basic Law was different from that of the courts of the SAR, to give retrospective effect to its interpretation on judgments previously rendered. I protested strongly by saying that such a formula would seriously erode the power of final adjudication given to the SAR by the Joint Declaration, and that it would also be in breach of the Joint Declaration. I also said that if *one* case were liable to be overturned by the NPCSC, then *no* case would be immune; and that such a provision would adversely affect the confidence of overseas investors in the SAR. (This account is based on my own notes taken during the meeting.)

The joint meeting then considered the new draft provision in chapter 4 which was objected to (by the majority) on the understanding that the wording needed to be improved.

In a report prepared by the third sub-group for presentation to the fifth plenary session, the following clause in chapter 4 was set out together with a note:

> *Clause 5*: The jurisdiction of the courts of the HKSAR (to be drafted).
> *Note*: After discussions between the eight legal experts of the subject sub-group on the relationship between the central authorities and the HKSAR and the subject sub-group on the political structure of the HKSAR, a tentative draft was proposed, and was agreed to by the members of both sub-groups in principle, but the wording had still to be improved on:
> 'Apart from cases concerning defence and foreign affairs and other cases concerning the executive acts of the Central Government which are excluded from the jurisdiction of the courts by Hong Kong's previous legal system, the courts of the SAR shall have jurisdiction over all other cases within the SAR.
>
> Courts of the SAR shall, in adjudicating cases before them, seek the advice of the Chief Executive on all questions concerning defence, foreign affairs, or the executive acts of the Central Government. A statement issued by the Chief Executive regarding such questions shall be binding on the courts.
>
> Before issuing such a statement, the Chief Executive shall obtain a certificate from the NPCSC or the State Council.'
>
> With regard to the above clause, one member objected to the phrase 'the executive acts of the CPG' ... [The objection was raised by me.]

In another report prepared by the first sub-group also for presentation to the fifth plenary session, the following note appeared in relation to clause 1 of chapter 9 (the former clause 1 having been deleted):

> Regarding the question of the interpretation of the Basic Law ... , the members of this sub-group still held different views. Some members were of the view that the courts of the SAR, in adjudicating cases before them, should not be restricted in their interpretation of the Basic Law, and therefore suggested that the words 'those provisions which are within the autonomy of the HKSAR' be deleted. But some members did not agree and suggested that these words be retained .... Some members took the view that, as a general rule, the interpretation of a provision of the Basic Law by the NPCSC should not affect the result of judgments previously rendered, but asked whether it would be possible, in certain exceptional cases, to adopt a special legal procedure for resolving the question, by giving retrospective effect to the interpretation of the Basic Law by the NPCSC. If

account could be taken of these exceptional cases in this way, then the restriction imposed on the jurisdiction of the courts of the SAR to interpret the Basic Law could be lifted. But some members of this sub-group were of the view that to do this would create technical difficulties while the courts were adjudicating cases. There was also a member who held the view that if the interpretation of the Basic Law by the NPCSC were to have retrospective effect, it would adversely affect the power of final adjudication of the courts of the SAR. The members of this sub-group felt that the right to interpret the Basic Law was a very difficult question, that none of the proposals so far put forward was mature enough, and that the problem should be studied further before a solution could be found.

FIFTH PLENARY SESSION

During the fifth plenary session of the BLDC held in Beijing from 22 through 26 August 1987, I delivered a speech which referred to those particular clauses:

Re: the interpretation of the Basic Law

The present clause 1 of chapter 9 provides that the NPCSC has the power to interpret the Basic Law, but that the courts of the SAR can interpret those provisions of the Basic Law which are within the autonomy of the SAR, and further that the courts must follow the interpretation (if any) placed on any provision of the Basic Law by the NPCSC. In other words, the NPCSC has the final right of interpreting every provision of the Basic Law, though such interpretation shall not have retrospective effect. Recently a mainland member explained that the reason for the courts of the SAR not being given unrestricted power to interpret the Basic Law stemmed from the fact that the power of final adjudication had been given to the SAR, and that there was thus the concern that the courts of the SAR might be 'wrong' in their interpretation of the Basic Law, in which event the mistake could not be corrected. He therefore suggested that, should this occur, the NPCSC ought to be given power to correct the mistake by giving retrospective effect to its own interpretation on the relevant provision, thereby overturning the decision in question.

I do not agree with the present clause, and I also disagree with this mainland member that the power of final adjudication should be exchanged for the unrestricted power to interpret the Basic Law. Let me reiterate my position:

(a) The courts of the SAR must be given power to interpret all the provisions of the Basic Law.

(b) Regarding the provisions of the Basic Law which are within the limits of the autonomy of the SAR, the NPCSC should irrevocably delegate its power to the courts of the SAR to interpret them.

(c) In relation to those provisions of the Basic Law which are outside the limits of the autonomy of the SAR, if and when the NPCSC has interpreted any such provision, the courts of the SAR shall follow such interpretation, though it shall not have retrospective effect on judgments previously rendered.

Today, Hong Kong courts enjoy unrestricted power in their interpretation of every word in our constitutional documents (that is, the Letters Patent and the Royal Instructions). If in future the power of the courts of the SAR were to be restricted as suggested by the present clause, it would cause serious disruption to and would adversely affect the efficiency of the courts.

Some members take the view that the root of the problem lies in the fact that the power of final adjudication has been given to the SAR, so that if the courts were to be mistaken in their interpretation of the Basic Law, there would be no way to correct the mistake. They have therefore suggested that the power of the courts of the SAR to interpret the Basic Law should be restricted to those provisions which are within the autonomy of the SAR, or else the interpretation of the Basic Law by the NPCSC should have retrospective effect. But the truth is that this problem has nothing to do with the power of final adjudication, but has everything to do with the independence of the judiciary. For in any country where the judiciary is independent of the government, there is the possibility that some judgments handed down by the courts would not please the government and would thus be considered to be 'wrong.' But that government would not destroy the independence of its judiciary by interfering with the decisions of the courts, though it might, if necessary, change the law in question so as to ensure that there would not be similar decisions in future. With regard to the Basic Law, the NPCSC should trust the courts of the SAR and accept their interpretation of those provisions which are within the limits of the autonomy of the SAR, in order to give a high degree of autonomy to the Region. But in relation to those provisions which are outside such limits of autonomy, the NPCSC may exercise its right of final interpretation so as to avoid similar decisions from being made; and, indeed, it may even amend the relevant provisions of the Basic Law where necessary, but without affecting the result of judgments previously rendered. But if the interpretation of the Basic Law by the NPCSC were to have retrospective effect on judgments previously rendered, then the party which has lost before the Court of Final Appeal would try its best to bring the matter before the NPCSC in order to have that judgment overturned. In this way, the authority of the courts of the SAR would be eroded and the Court of Final Appeal would no longer enjoy the power of final adjudication. Further, the NPCSC would have to undertake a lot of extra work. In fact, we should not cut down the judicial power of the courts of the SAR, but should instead try to reduce to a minimum the possibility of the courts coming to a 'wrong' decision. I therefore propose a practical solution, that is, to provide by law that the Attorney General of the SAR should be informed whenever a case arises involving the interpretation of the Basic Law, so that, if necessary, he may appear and make representations to the court on behalf of the government of the SAR. In this way, the views of all parties, including the government of the SAR, will be put before the court. But it would be extremely unwise to 'drill a small hole' (in the words of a mainland member) into the power of final adjudication of the SAR in order to remedy what the CPG considers to be 'a wrong interpretation' in relation to only one or two cases — for then the price would be too great.

In conclusion, we should have confidence in the courts of the SAR, particularly the Court of Final Appeal. Otherwise we could not ensure the independence of the judiciary or fulfil the promise of giving 'a high degree of autonomy' to the SAR. And in that event, the people of Hong Kong will not have confidence in the Basic Law or the policy of 'one country, two systems' ...

Re: the jurisdiction of the courts

The explanatory note to clause 5 of section 4 of chapter 4 suggests the following: 'Apart from cases concerning defence and foreign affairs and other cases concerning executive acts of the Central Government which are excluded from the jurisdiction of the courts by Hong Kong's previous legal system, the courts of the HKSAR shall have jurisdiction over all other cases within the HKSAR.'

This clause does not effectively state in detail the present restrictions imposed by the common law on the Hong Kong courts. In particular, the words 'executive acts of the Central Government' can easily be misinterpreted or abused. Moreover, under the present legal system in Hong Kong, the unlawful acts of the British government can be challenged by any Hong Kong person who has suffered damage as a result thereof by taking proceedings under the Crown Proceedings Act. But under the present legal system in the PRC, the acts of the Central Government, even if unlawful, cannot be challenged in the courts of the PRC. And if these acts are committed in the SAR, and the courts of the Region have no jurisdiction over them, then how will the aggrieved person find redress?

In fact, under the present legal system in Hong Kong, the common law has clearly excluded the jurisdiction of courts from certain matters relating to defence and foreign affairs (such as 'acts of state') and the exercise of certain prerogative powers (such as the appointment of government officials or the dissolution of the legislature). However, it is very difficult, if not impossible, to codify these restrictions. In any event, it would be undesirable to codify them, because the common law is always developing. So it is better to leave such restrictions to the common law.

THIRTEENTH MEETING OF THE SUB-GROUP

The 13th meeting of the sub-group was held in Guangzhou on 26 and 27 October 1987. At the meeting, I proposed to amend clause 1 of chapter 9 as follows:

The power of interpretation of this Law is vested in the NPCSC. The courts of the HKSAR may interpret all the provisions of this Law.

Regarding the provisions which are within the limits of the autonomy of the HKSAR, the NPCSC will irrevocably delegate its power to the courts of the Region to interpret them when adjudicating cases.

When the NPCSC makes an interpretation of a provision of this Law which is outside the limits of the autonomy of the HKSAR, the courts of the Region, in applying such a provision, shall follow the interpretation of the NPCSC. However, cases under adjudication and judgments previously rendered shall not be affected.

The NPCSC shall consult its Committee for the Basic Law of the HKSAR before giving an interpretation of this Law.

The provisions of Chapters 3, 4, 5, 6 and 10 of this Law are or are deemed to be within the limits of the autonomy of the HKSAR. The question as to whether the provisions of the other Chapters of this Law are within the limits of the autonomy of the Region may be decided by the courts of the Region or by the NPCSC. The NPCSC will consult the Committee for the Basic Law of the HKSAR before making a decision. The decision of the NPCSC shall be final.

At the same time, a mainland member proposed to amend the same clause as follows:

The power of interpretation of the Basic Law is vested in the NPCSC.

When the NPCSC makes an interpretation of a provision of the Basic Law, the courts of the HKSAR, in applying that provision, shall follow the interpretation of the NPCSC. However, judgments previously rendered shall not be affected.

The courts of the HKSAR may interpret the provisions of the Basic Law in adjudicating cases before them. If a case involves an interpretation of the provisions of the Basic Law concerning defence, foreign affairs and other affairs administered by the Central Government, the courts of the HKSAR, before making their final judgment on the case, shall seek an interpretation of the relevant provisions from the NPCSC.

The NPCSC shall consult the Basic Law Committee of the HKSAR before giving an interpretation of this Law.

It was decided by the majority that the proposal by the mainland member be adopted as clause 1 of chapter 9, whereas my proposal would be set out as a note to it. This was duly done in the report subsequently prepared for the sixth plenary session except that it was set out as clause 168 in chapter 9. These two proposals were almost identical to the present BL169 and the note to BL169.

THIRTEENTH MEETING OF THE THIRD SUB-GROUP

At the 13th meeting of the third sub-group from 31 October 1987 through 2 November 1987 in Guangzhou, the above-mentioned tentative draft clause under chapter 4 relating to the jurisdiction of the courts of the SAR was formally adopted by the majority. However, there were other proposals, all seeking to exclude certain types of case from the jurisdiction of the courts of the SAR.

Proposal 1 used the expression 'cases concerning defence and foreign affairs and acts which are purely of a political nature [are excluded from the jurisdiction of the HKSAR courts] in the same manner as they have been excluded according to the common law and legal precedents.'

Proposal 2 sought to exclude from the jurisdiction of the courts of the SAR any cases which were formerly excluded from the Hong Kong courts under Hong Kong's previous legal system. This was my proposal.

Proposal 3 sought to exclude from the jurisdiction of the courts of the SAR all cases relating to:

(1) the relationship between the central authorities and the SAR;
(2) the validity of the executive acts of the CPG;
(3) the validity of the executive acts of the government of the SAR in implementing, in accordance with the provisions of the Basic Law, the directives of the central authorities concerning defence and foreign affairs;
(4) the validity of those executive acts of the government of the SAR in dealing with external affairs on its own as authorised by the Central Government and in accordance with the provisions of the Basic Law, which were deemed to be 'acts of state' under the laws previously in force in Hong Kong, and cases relating to the contents of the executive acts which were deemed to be 'facts of state' under the laws previously in force in Hong Kong; and
(5) the basic responsibilities of Chinese nationals towards the state (such as cases of treason and the like).

Proposal 3 is still contained in the Basic Law under the heading of 'A Collection of Opinions and Suggestions of Some Members in Regard to the Articles Drafted by their Respective Subject Sub-groups,' except that sub-paragraph (5) above is now omitted.

Proposal 4 used the expression 'defence, foreign affairs and the acts performed by the Central Government and the government of the HKSAR in the name of the state.'

SIXTH PLENARY MEETING

The sixth plenary session took place in Guangzhou from 12 through 16 December 1987. At that meeting, I made a speech which included the following comments:

The right to interpret the Basic Law (article 168)

The right to interpret the Basic Law has been the most controversial topic. Until recently, the relevant draft clause forbade the courts of the SAR from interpreting those provisions of the Basic Law which were outside the autonomy of the SAR. That draft clause was widely criticised on the ground that it would greatly reduce the efficiency of the courts of the SAR. Some members then suggested that the courts of the SAR be allowed to interpret the whole of the Basic Law, but on condition that the NPCSC would be able to review and over-rule some decisions of the Court of Final Appeal of the SAR. This attempt to 'drill a small hole' in the power of final adjudication promised in the Joint Declaration attracted even stronger criticism; and thereafter no one mentioned it again. The present draft article is yet another attempt to restrict the right of the courts of the SAR in their interpretation of the Basic Law; for while allowing, in one sentence, a court of the SAR to interpret the whole of the Basic Law, it then, in another sentence, requires it to seek from the NPCSC an interpretation on a provision of the Basic Law concerning defence, foreign affairs, or any other affair which is the responsibility of the CPG. Looking at the above three proposals, one can see a thread running through them — it shows a total lack of confidence in the courts of the SAR, and hence their right to interpret the Basic Law has to be curtailed. In the first place, the jurisdiction of the courts was restricted, so that they could not try all cases. Next came an attempt to whittle down the power of final adjudication by providing that although the courts could try all cases, their judgments in certain cases were liable to be overturned. Now, by the present draft article, although the courts of the SAR can assume jurisdiction over all cases, they must refer certain key provisions of the Basic Law to the NPCSC for an interpretation. There is really not much difference between these three proposals.

The member who has proposed the present draft article has expressed the view that the English courts also face similar restrictions, namely, if a case before the court of final appeal in England (that is, the House of Lords) involves the interpretation of a treaty of the European Economic Community, the court, before passing final judgment, has to refer the point to the Court of Justice of the European Communities for an interpretation of the relevant treaty.

But this misses the point that in relation to lower courts, the present procedure under English law is only applicable in narrowly defined circumstances; and it is always for the court itself to decide whether to refer the question or not. Now these factors have not been taken into account in the present draft article. And it is pertinent to note some of the legal principles of the English referral system as follows:

(a) The court has a full discretion in deciding whether to refer the point of construction, and the court will not refer the point unless it considers it necessary to enable it to give judgment after taking into consideration (among other things) the delay, the expense, and the effect on the trial.

(b) The point must be such that a decision on it would be conclusive of the very case before the court in England.

(c) If the same point has already been decided by the European Court in a previous case, it will not be necessary to refer it to the European Court again, and it will not be referred.

(d) If the point is reasonably clear and free from doubt, there is again no need to refer, and it will not be referred.

(e) It is only when all the essential facts have been decided that the court would consider whether it should refer the point to the European Court.

In addition, the European Court is an independent judicial body composed of experienced and renowned judges from the member states of the European Communities. The process of interpretation is regulated by judicial procedures which allow representations to be made to the European Court on behalf of the parties. Therefore, the referral procedure has not eroded the judicial independence of the English courts. However, the NPCSC is a legislative body; and the composition and the manner of operation of the Basic Law Committee, which is to advise the Standing Committee before the latter interprets the Basic Law, are not well defined. For these reasons, it is inapposite to compare our problem to the referral procedure to the European Court by the English courts.

In conclusion, I am of the view that the present draft article has not solved the problem, which requires further study and consideration. By comparison, the dissenting view set out in the note to this article is simpler and easier to operate in practice.

IN RETROSPECT

Two years have now elapsed since the BLDC first discussed this problem of interpretation of the Basic Law. There can be no doubt that it should have been settled between the Chinese and British governments during their negotiations over Hong Kong in 1984, for the feasibility of the entire Basic Law project may hinge on this single question. However that was not done, for reasons perhaps best known to the British negotiating team.

In retrospect, I regret that the result of these two years of continual debate is far from satisfactory. For in BL18, the present jurisdiction of Hong Kong courts has been substantially curtailed, despite the avowed objective of the third sub-group that whatever the Hong Kong courts could try today, the courts of the SAR ought to be able to try after 1997. As to BL169, although the courts of the SAR appear to have the power to interpret the entirety of the Basic Law, and the power of final adjudication appears to have been left intact, yet in practice, the courts of the SAR will be deprived of their *original* jurisdiction to interpret some of the key provisions of the Basic Law, that is, those concerning defence, foreign affairs, and other affairs which are the responsibility of the CPG.

Indeed, compared to the formula first introduced on 27 August 1986 to restrict the power of interpretation by the courts of the SAR only to 'those provisions of the Basic Law which are within the autonomy of the HKSAR,' the present BL18 and 169 are clearly worse. The mainland members have not made any concession at all; on the contrary, they have succeeded in making sure that the CPG will be able to exercise very firm control over the courts of the SAR.

I am glad that no lawyer in Hong Kong has supported these two articles. And it is reassuring that most of the members of the House of Lords who spoke on 9 June 1988 on the Hong Kong issue expressed serious misgivings about them. These members were Lord Cledwyn of Penrhos, Lord Bonham-Carter, Baroness Young, Lord MacLehose of Beoch, Lord Kennet, Lord Irvine of Lairg, Lord Geddes, Viscount Torrington, and Baroness Ewart-Biggs.

In a moving speech, Lord Bonham-Carter said:

> It seems that the problem which confronts the Basic Law and upon which its validity depends, is this: can one graft onto a system based on the common law, which is the system which pertains in Hong Kong today, one which has no conception, culturally or historically, of such a system? That is what we are trying to do, and it is a most ambitious and difficult project. For example, who will resolve a conflict between the HKSAR and the PRC about the interpretation of the Basic Law?
>
> Under our system we would answer quite simply by saying that it would be up to the judiciary. Articles ... 18, ... and 169 and the glosses to which I have referred, may demand interpretation. As I understand the Basic Law, that interpretation will be undertaken by the State Council of the People's Republic of China. [The reference here to 'the State Council of the PRC' is inaccurate, and it should have been 'the Standing Committee of the National People's Congress.]' Therefore, we have a situation in which our idea of law interpretation by an independent judiciary simply does not exist.
>
> Therefore, one very important question that noble Lords must consider and continue to watch is in what manner [the] Basic Law — no matter how good and how well it is drafted, and how good are its intentions — is to be interpreted, and how the differences in its interpretation between the HKSAR and the PRC are to be resolved. This is the central issue we have to confront.

And Lord Irvine had this to say:

> The Basic Law is different from any other Chinese law. It will have practical effect only in Hong Kong. It does not therefore need to be interpreted by the NPC for the benefit of courts elsewhere in China. The Basic Law is to be the foundation of Hong Kong domestic law. It should be interpreted by the Hong Kong courts and, if it is not, the Hong Kong judiciary will not be seen to be independent. There is in Hong Kong a vast amount of litigation of an international character,

which is part and parcel of Hong Kong being a great international commercial centre. The international community respects and trusts Hong Kong's independent judiciary.

And finally, Lord Kennet expressed the hope that 'that provision (BL169) will not last through the consultation period.'

THE END

How will this tale end?

It all depends on whether and to what extent BL18 and 169 as well as other defective articles not mentioned in this chapter will be amended.

As to BL18, I suggest that it be amended by simply deleting the third and fourth paragraphs and keeping only the first two paragraphs, so that it reads:

> The HKSAR is vested with independent judicial power, including that of final adjudication.
>
> The courts of the HKSAR shall have jurisdiction over all cases in the Region, except that the restrictions of their jurisdiction imposed by Hong Kong's previous legal system and principles shall be maintained.

As to BL169, my suggestion has already been set out in full above, and I will not repeat it here.

As to the other flawed articles, I would refer to a booklet entitled *The Basic Law – Some Basic Flaws* published in Hong Kong by Mr Szeto Wah and myself.

I can only hope that the people of Hong Kong will join together in unison and raise objections now to these two articles as well as the other flawed articles, so that we will have a good Basic Law for ourselves and our children.

And then, each of us can say: 'It is a far, far better thing that I do, than I have ever done....' However, it is here that the quotation will end — for unlike Sydney Carton in *A Tale of Two Cities*, the people of Hong Kong will live happily thereafter, and the SAR will enjoy a high degree of autonomy.

Appendix

The Draft Basic Law of the Hong Kong Special Administrative Region of the People's Republic of China

(For Solicitation of Opinions)

The Drafting Committee for the Basic Law of the Hong Kong Special Administrative Region of the People's Republic of China

April 1988

Preamble

Hong Kong has been part of China's territory since ancient times, but it was occupied by Britain after the Opium War in 1840. On 19 December 1984, the Chinese and British governments signed the Joint Declaration on the Question of Hong Kong, affirming that the Government of the People's Republic of China will resume the exercise of sovereignty over Hong Kong on 1 July 1997, thus fulfilling the long-cherished common aspiration of the entire Chinese people for the recovery of Hong Kong.

In order to uphold national unity and territorial integrity and to maintain Hong Kong's prosperity and stability, and taking account of the history of Hong Kong and its realities, the People's Republic of China has decided that upon China's resumption of the exercise of sovereignty over Hong Kong, a Hong Kong Special Administrative Region will be established in accordance with the provisions of Article 31 of the Constitution of the People's Republic of China and that under the principle of "one country, two systems", socialist system and policies will not be practised in Hong Kong. The basic policies of the People's Republic of China regarding Hong Kong have been elaborated by our government in the Sino-British Joint Declaration.

In accordance with the Constitution of the People's Republic of China, the National People's Congress hereby enacts the Basic Law of the Hong Kong Special Administrative Region of the People's Republic of China, prescribing the systems to be practised in the Hong Kong Special Administrative Region, in order to ensure the implementation of the basic policies of the People's Republic of China regarding Hong Kong.

Chapter 1: General Principles

Article 1 The Hong Kong Special Administrative Region is an inalienable part of the People's Republic of China.

Article 2 The National People's Congress authorizes the Hong Kong Special Administrative Region to exercise a high degree of autonomy in accordance with the provisions of this Law and to enjoy executive, legislative and independent judicial power, including that of final adjudication.

Article 3 The executive authorities and legislature of the Hong Kong Special Administrative Region shall be composed of permanent residents of Hong Kong in accordance with the relevant provisions of this Law.

Article 4 Socialist system and policies shall not be practised in the Hong Kong Special Administrative Region and the existing capitalist system and way of life shall not be changed for 50 years.

Article 5 The Hong Kong Special Administrative Region safeguards the rights and freedoms of the residents and other persons in the Region in accordance with law.

Article 6 Rights of property ownership, including those relating to acquisition, use, disposal, inheritance and compensation for lawful take over shall be protected by law. The compensation for lawful takeover shall be corresponding to the real value of the property concerned, freely convertible and paid without undue delay.

Article 7 The land and natural resources within the Hong Kong Special Administrative Region are the state property of the People's Republic of China. The government of the Hong Kong Special Administrative Region shall be responsible for their management, use and development and for their lease or grant to individuals or legal persons for use or development. The revenue derived shall be entirely at the disposal of the government of the Hong Kong Special Administrative Region.

Article 8 The laws previously in force in Hong Kong, that is, the common law, rules of equity, ordinances, subordinate legislation and customary law shall be maintained, except for those that contravene this Law or have been amended by the legislature of the Hong Kong Special Administrative Region.

Article 9 In addition to the Chinese language, the English language may also be used by the executive authorities, legislature and judicial organs of the Hong Kong Special Administrative Region.

Article 10 In accordance with Article 31 of the Constitution of the People's Republic of China, the policies and systems practised in the Hong Kong Special Administrative Region, including the social and economic systems, the system for safeguarding the fundamental rights and freedoms of its residents and the executive, legislative and judicial systems, shall be based on the provisions in this Law.

No law enacted by the legislature of the Hong Kong Special Administrative Region shall contravene this Law.

Chapter II: Relationship between the Central Authorities and the Hong Kong Special Administrative Region

Article 11   The Hong Kong Special Administrative Region is a local administrative region of the People's Republic of China, enjoying a high degree of autonomy, and comes directly under the Central People's Government.

Article 12   The Central People's Government is responsible for the foreign affairs relating to the Hong Kong Special Administrative Region.

The Central People's Government authorizes the Hong Kong Special Administrative Region to deal with relevant external affairs on its own in accordance with this Law.

The Ministry of Foreign Affairs of the People's Republic of China will establish an office in Hong Kong to deal with foreign affairs.

Article 13   The Central People's Government is responsible for the defence of the Hong Kong Special Administrative Region.

Military forces sent by the Central People's Government to be stationed in the Hong Kong Special Administrative Region for defence shall not interfere in the local affairs of the Region. The government of the Hong Kong Special Administrative Region may, in times of need, request the Central People's Government for assistance from the garrison in the maintenance of public order and disaster relief.

Apart from abiding by nation-wide laws, members of the garrison shall also abide by the laws of the Hong Kong Special Administrative Region.

All expenses for the garrison shall be borne by the Central People's Government.

Article 14   The Central People's Government appoints the Chief Executive and principal executive officials of the Hong Kong Special Administrative Region in accordance with the provisions of Chapter IV of this Law.

Article 15   The Hong Kong Special Administrative Region is vested with executive power. In accordance with the relevant provisions of this Law it shall, on its own, manage public finance, monetary matters, economy, industry and commerce, trade, taxation, postal service, civil aviation, maritime matters, traffic and transport, fishery, agriculture, personnel administration, civil affairs, labour, education, medical and health services, social welfare, culture and recreation, municipal facilities, urban planning, housing, real estate, public order, entry and exit controls, meteorology, communications, science and technology, sports and other administrative affairs.

Article 16   The Hong Kong Special Administrative Region is vested with legislative power.

Laws enacted by the legislature of the Hong Kong Special Administrative Region shall be reported to the Standing Committee of the National People's Congress for the record. The reporting for record shall not affect the entry into force of such laws.

If the Standing Committee of the National People's Congress, after consulting its Committee for the Basic Law of the Hong Kong Special Administrative Region, considers that any law of the Region is not in conformity with this Law or legal procedures, it may return the law in question for reconsideration or revoke it, but it shall not amend it. Any law returned for reconsideration or revoked by the Standing Committee of the National People's Congress shall immediately cease to have force. This cessation shall not have retroactive effect.

Article 17 The laws of the Hong Kong Special Administrative Region shall be this Law, the laws previously in force in Hong Kong as stipulated in Article 8 of this Law, and the laws enacted by the legislature of the Hong Kong Special Administrative Region.

Laws enacted by the National People's Congress or its Standing Committee will not be applied in the Hong Kong Special Administrative Region except for those stipulated in Paragraph 3 of this Article.

Laws, enacted by the National People's Congress or its Standing Committee, which relate to defence and foreign affairs as well as other laws which give expression to national unity and territorial integrity and which, in accordance with the provisions of this Law, are outside the limits of the high degree of autonomy of the Hong Kong Special Administrative Region, shall be applied locally by the government of the Hong Kong Special Administrative Region by way of promulgation or legislation on the directives of the State Council, whenever there is the need to apply any of such laws in the Region.

Except in cases of emergency, the State Council shall consult the Committee for the Basic Law of the Hong Kong Special Administrative Region and the government of the Hong Kong Special Administrative Region before issuing the above-mentioned directives.

If the government of the Hong Kong Special Administrative Region fails to act in compliance with the directives given by the State Council, the State Council may decree the application of the above-mentioned law in the Hong Kong Special Administrative Region.

Article 18 The Hong Kong Special Administrative Region is vested with independent judicial power, including that of final adjudication.

Courts of the Hong Kong [Special] Administrative Region shall have jurisdiction over all cases in the Region, except that the restrictions of their jurisdiction imposed by Hong Kong's previous legal system shall be maintained.

Courts of the Hong Kong Special Administrative Region shall have no jurisdiction over cases relating to defence and foreign affairs, which are the responsibility of the Central People's Government, and cases relating to the executive acts of the Central People's Government. Courts of the Hong Kong Special Administrative Region shall seek the advice of the Chief Executive whenever questions concerning defence, foreign affairs or the executive acts of the Central People's Government arise in any legal proceeding. A statement issued by the Chief Executive regarding such questions shall be binding on the courts.

Before issuing such a statement, the Chief Executive shall obtain a certificate from the Standing Committee of the National People's Congress or the State Council.

Article 19 The Hong Kong Special Administrative Region may enjoy other powers granted to it by the National People's Congress, the Standing Committee of the National People's Congress or the State Council.

Article 20   Residents of the Hong Kong Special Administrative Region who are Chinese nationals are entitled to participate in state affairs as prescribed by law.

In accordance with the assigned number of seats and the election procedures specified by the Standing Committee of the National People's Congress, the Chinese nationals among the Hong Kong residents shall locally elect deputies of the Hong Kong Special Administrative Region to the National People's Congress to participate in the work of the highest organ of state power.

Article 21   Departments under the Central People's Government as well as provinces, autonomous regions and municipalities directly under the Central Government shall not interfere in the affairs which the Hong Kong Special Administrative Region administers on its own in accordance with this Law.

If departments under the Central Government, provinces, autonomous regions and municipalities directly under the Central Government need to set up offices in the Hong Kong Special Administrative Region, they must have the consent of the government thereof and the approval of the Central People's Government.

All offices set up in Hong Kong by the departments under the Central Government, or by provinces, autonomous regions and municipalities directly under the Central Government and personnel of these offices shall abide by the laws of the Hong Kong Special Administrative Region.

People from other parts of China must apply for approval for entry into the Hong Kong Special Administrative Region.

The Hong Kong Special Administrative Region may establish an office in Beijing.

Article 22   The Hong Kong Special Administrative Region shall prohibit by law any act designed to undermine national unity or subvert the Central People's Government.

Chapter III: Fundamental Rights and Duties of the Residents

Article 23 Residents of the Hong Kong Special Administrative Region, or Hong Kong residents for short, include permanent residents and non-permanent residents.

Permanent residents of the Hong Kong Special Administrative Region are:

(1) Chinese nationals born in Hong Kong before or after the establishment of the Hong Kong Special Administrative Region;

(2) Chinese nationals who have ordinarily resided in Hong Kong for a continuous period of no less than seven years before or after the establishment of the Hong Kong Special Administrative Region;

(3) Persons of Chinese nationality born outside Hong Kong of those residents listed in categories (1) and (2);

(4) Persons of non-Chinese nationality who have ordinarily resided in Hong Kong for a continuous period of no less than seven years and have taken Hong Kong as their place of permanent residence before or after the establishment of the Hong Kong Special Administrative Region;

(5) Persons under 21 years of age born in Hong Kong of residents listed in category (4) before or after the establishment of the Hong Kong Special Administrative Region; and

(6) Persons other than those residents listed in categories (1) to (5), who had the right of abode only in Hong Kong before the establishment of the Hong Kong Special Administrative Region.

The above-mentioned residents have the right of abode in the Hong Kong Special Administrative Region and are qualified to obtain, in accordance with its law, permanent identity cards which state their right of abode.

Non-permanent residents of the Hong Kong Special Administrative Region are persons who, in accordance with the laws of the Hong Kong Special Administrative Region, are qualified to obtain Hong Kong identity cards but have no right of abode.

Article 24 All Hong Kong residents shall be equal before the law, regardless of their nationality, race, ethnic origin, language, sex, occupation, religious belief, political views, educational level and property status.

Article 25 Permanent residents of the Hong Kong Special Administrative Region who have reached the age of 21 shall have the right to vote and the right to stand for election as prescribed by law.

Article 26 Hong Kong residents shall have freedom of speech, of the press and of publication; freedom of association, to form and join trade unions, and to strike; and freedom of assembly and of demonstration.

Article 27 The freedom of the person of Hong Kong residents is inviolable.

Hong Kong residents shall not be unlawfully arrested, detained or imprisoned. Unlawful deprivation or restriction of the residents' freedom of the person by any means shall be prohibited. Unlawful search of the body of any resident shall be prohibited.

Article 28   The homes and other premises of Hong Kong residents shall not be violated. Unlawful search of, or intrusion into, a resident's home or other premises is prohibited.

Article 29   The freedom and privacy of communication of Hong Kong residents shall be protected by law. No department or individual may, on any ground, infringe upon the residents' freedom and privacy of communication except in cases where, to meet the needs of public security or of investigation into criminal offences, the relevant authorities may censor communication in accordance with legal procedures.

Article 30   Hong Kong residents shall have the freedom of movement within the Hong Kong Special Administrative Region and the freedom of emigration to other countries and regions. Hong Kong residents who hold valid travel documents shall have the freedom to travel and the freedom of entry and exit and, unless restrained by law, shall be free to leave the Hong Kong Special Administrative Region without special authorization.

Article 31   Hong Kong residents shall have the freedom of conscience.

Hong Kong residents shall have the freedom of religious belief and the freedom to preach and to carry out and participate in religious activities in public.

Article 32   Hong Kong residents shall have the freedom of choice of occupation.

Article 33   Hong Kong residents shall have the freedom of academic research, of literary and artistic creation, and of other cultural pursuits.

Article 34   Hong Kong residents shall have the right to confidential legal advice, access to the courts, and choice of lawyers for timely protection of their legitimate rights and interests, and for representation in the courts, and the right to judicial remedies.

Hong Kong residents shall have the right to challenge in the courts the actions of the executive organs or their personnel.

Article 35   Hong Kong residents shall have the right to social welfare; the welfare benefits of the working people shall be protected by law.

Article 36   The freedom of marriage of Hong Kong residents and their right to raise a family freely shall be protected by law.

Article 37   Hong Kong residents shall enjoy the other rights and freedoms safeguarded by the laws of the Hong Kong Special Administrative Region.

Article 38   The provisions of the "International Covenant on Civil and Political Rights" and the "International Covenant on Economic, Social and Cultural Rights" as applied to Hong Kong shall be implemented through legislation by the Hong Kong Special Administrative Region.

Article 39   The rights and freedoms enjoyed by Hong Kong residents shall not be restricted unless prescribed by law. But such restrictions shall not go beyond the necessity for the maintenance of national security, public order, public safety, public health, public morals and for the safeguarding of the rights and freedoms of other persons.

Article 40   The legitimate traditional rights and interests of the indigenous inhabitants of "New Territories" shall be protected by the Hong Kong Special Administrative Region.

Article 41 Persons in the Hong Kong Special Administrative Region other than Hong Kong residents shall, in accordance with law, enjoy the rights and freedoms of Hong Kong residents prescribed in this Chapter.
Article 42 Hong Kong residents and other persons in Hong Kong shall have the obligation to abide by the laws of the Hong Kong Special Administrative Region.

Chapter IV: Political Structure

Section 1:   The Chief Executive

Article 43   The Chief Executive of the Hong Kong Special Administrative Region is the head of the Hong Kong Special Administrative Region and represents the Region.

The Chief Executive of the Hong Kong Special Administrative Region shall be accountable to the Central People's Government and the Hong Kong Special Administrative Region in accordance with the provisions of this Law.

Article 44   The Chief Executive of the Hong Kong Special Administrative Region shall be a Chinese national of no less than 40 years of age who is a permanent resident of the Region and has ordinarily resided in Hong Kong for a continuous period of 20 years.

Article 45   The Chief Executive of the Hong Kong Special Administrative Region shall be selected by election or through consultations held locally and be appointed by the Central People's Government.

The specific method for selecting the Chief Executive is prescribed in Annex I: "Method for Selecting the Chief Executive of the Hong Kong Special Administrative Region".

The method for selecting the Chief Executive as prescribed in Annex I may be modified in the light of actual situation in the Hong Kong Special Administrative Region and in accordance with the principle of gradual and orderly progress. Such modifications shall require the endorsement of a two-thirds majority of the members of the Legislative Council of the Hong Kong Special Administrative Region and the consent of the Chief Executive, and shall be submitted to the Standing Committee of the National People's Congress for approval.

Article 46   The term of office of the Chief Executive of the Hong Kong Special Administrative Region shall be five years. He/she may serve for no more than two terms.

Article 47   The Chief Executive of the Hong Kong Special Administrative Region must be a person of integrity, dedicated to his/her duties.

The Chief Executive, on assuming office, shall declare his/her assets to the Chief Justice of the Court of Final Appeal of the Hong Kong Special Administrative Region. This declaration shall be put on record in strict confidence.

Article 48   The Chief Executive of the Hong Kong Special Administrative Region shall exercise the following powers and functions:

(1)   To lead the government of the Region;

(2)   To be responsible for the implementation of this Law and other laws which, in accordance with this Law, apply in the Hong Kong Special Administrative Region;

(3)   To sign bills passed by the Legislative Council and to promulgate laws;

To sign bills on budgets and final accounts passed by the Legislative Council and report them to the Central People's Government for the record;

(4)   To decide on government policies and to issue executive orders;

(5) To nominate and to report to the Central People's Government for appointment the following principal officials: Secretaries and Deputy Secretaries of Departments, Directors of Bureaus, Commissioner Against Corruption, Director of Audit, Commissioner of Police and Commissioner of External Affairs*3; and to propose to the Central People's Government the removal of the above-mentioned officials;

To employ advisers at or above the director level as required and subject to the approval of the Central People's Government.

(6) To appoint or remove judges of the courts at various levels in accordance with legal procedures;

(7) To appoint or remove public servants in accordance with legal procedures;

(8) To implement the directives issued by the Central People's Government in respect of the relevant matters provided for in this Law;

(9) To deal with, on behalf of the government of the Hong Kong Special Administrative Region, external affairs and other affairs authorized by the Central Authorities;

(10) To approve the introduction of motions regarding revenues or expenditure to the Legislative Council;

(11) To decide, in the light of security and public interest, whether government officials or other personnel in charge of government affairs should testify or give evidence before the Legislative Council;

(12) To pardon persons convicted of criminal offences or commute their penalties; and

(13) To handle petitions and complaints.

Article 49 If the Chief Executive considers that a bill passed by the Legislative Council is not compatible with the overall interest of the Hong Kong Special Administrative Region, he/she may return it to the Legislative Council within three months for reconsideration. If the Legislative Council passes the original bill again by no less than a two-thirds majority, the Chief Executive must sign and promulgate it within one month, or act in accordance with the provisions of Article 50 of this Law.

Article 50 If the Chief Executive refuses to sign the bill passed by the Legislative Council for a second time, or the Legislative Council refuses to pass the budget or other important bills introduced by the government and if consensus still cannot be reached after consultations, the Chief Executive may dissolve the Legislative Council.

Before dissolving the Legislative Council the Chief Executive should ask for opinions from the Executive Council. A Chief Executive can dissolve the Legislative Council only once in each term of office.

Article 51 If the Legislative Council refuses to pass the budget bill presented by the government, or if appropriation of public funds cannot be approved because the Legislative Council is already dissolved, the Chief Executive may approve temporary short-term appropriations according to the level of the previous fiscal year's expenditure prior to the election of the new Legislative Council.

Article 52   The Chief Executive shall have to resign under any of the following circumstances:

(1)   When he/she loses the ability to discharge the functions of his/her office due to serious illness or other reasons;

(2)   When, after the Legislative Council is dissolved because he/she twice refuses to sign the bill it passes, the new Legislative Council has again passed the original bill in dispute with a two-thirds majority; and

(3)   When, after the Legislative Council is dissolved because it refuses to approve the budget or any other important bill, the new Legislative Council still refuses to pass the original bill in dispute.

Article 53   If the Chief Executive of the Hong Kong Special Administrative Region is not able to discharge his/her duties for a brief period, such duties shall temporarily be assumed by Administrative Secretary, Financial Secretary, Secretary of Justice in this order of precedence.

In the event that the office of Chief Executive becomes vacant, a new Chief Executive shall be selected within six months, and during the period of vacancy, his/her duties shall be assumed according to the provisions of the preceding Paragraph.

Article 54   The Executive Council of the Hong Kong Special Administrative Region is an organ for assisting the Chief Executive in policy-making.

Article 55   Members of the Executive Council of the Hong Kong Special Administrative Region shall be appointed by the Chief Executive from among the principal officials of the executive authorities, members of the Legislative Council and public figures. Their term of office and the termination of their appointment before their term expires shall be decided by the Chief Executive. The term of office of members shall not exceed that of the Chief Executive who appoints them.

Members of the Executive Council of the Hong Kong Special Administrative Region shall be Chinese nationals who are permanent residents of the Region.

The Chief Executive may invite other persons concerned to sit in at council meetings as he/she deems necessary.

Article 56   The Executive Council of the Hong Kong Special Administrative Region shall be presided over by the Chief Executive.

Except for the appointment, removal and disciplining of public officers and the adoption of measures in emergencies, the Chief Executive shall consult the Executive Council before making important decisions, introducing a bill to the Legislative Council, enacting subsidiary legislation, or dissolving the Legislative Council.

If the Chief Executive does not adopt a majority opinion of the Executive Council, he/she must put his/her specific reasons on record.

Article 57   A Commission Against Corruption shall be established in the Hong Kong Special Administrative Region. It shall function independently and be accountable to the Chief Executive.

Article 58   A Commission of Audit shall be established in the Hong Kong Special Administrative Region. It shall function independently and be accountable to the Chief Executive.

Section 2: The Executive Authorities

Article 59 The government of the Hong Kong Special Administrative Region is the executive authorities of the Region.

Article 60 The Chief Executive of the Hong Kong Special Administrative Region is the head of the government of the Region.

Department of Administration, Department of Finance, Department of Justice, bureaus, divisions and commissions shall be established under the government of the Hong Kong Special Administrative Region.

The structure of the government of the Hong Kong Special Administrative Region shall be prescribed by law.

Article 61 The principal officials of the Hong Kong Special Administrative Region shall be Chinese nationals who are permanent residents and have ordinarily resided in Hong Kong for a continuous period of 15 years.*4

Article 62 The government of the Hong Kong Special Administrative Region shall exercise the following powers and functions:

(1) To formulate and implement policies;

(2) To manage the administrative affairs specified in Article 14 of this Law;

(3) To manage the external affairs authorized by the Central People's Government under this Law;

(4) To draw up and present budgets and final accounts; and

(5) To draft and introduce bills, motions and subsidiary legislation.

Article 63 The prosecuting authority of the Hong Kong Special Administrative Region shall institute criminal prosecutions independently, free from any interference.

Article 64 The executive authorities of the Hong Kong Special Administrative Region must abide by the law and shall be accountable to the Legislative Council of the Hong Kong Special Administrative Region in the following respects: They shall implement laws passed by the legislature and already in force; they shall present regular reports on their work to the Legislative Council; they shall answer questions raised by members of the Legislative Council; and they shall obtain approval from the Legislative Council for taxation and public expenditure.

Article 65 The establishment of advisory bodies under the executive authorities of the Hong Kong Special Administrative Region shall be maintained.

Section 3: The Legislature

Article 66 The Legislative Council of the Hong Kong Special Administrative Region*5 is the legislature of the Region.

Article 67 The Legislative Council of the Hong Kong Special Administrative Region shall be constituted by a combination of direct and indirect elections.

The specific methods for forming the Legislative Council are prescribed in Annex II: "Methods for Constituting the Legislative Council of the Hong Kong Special Administrative Region".

The methods for forming the Legislative Council provided in Annex II may be modified in the light of the actual situation in the Hong Kong

Special Administrative Region and in accordance with the principle of gradual and orderly progress. Such modifications shall require the endorsement of a two-thirds majority of the members of the Legislative Council of the Region and the consent of the Chief Executive, and shall be submitted to the Standing Committee of the National People's Congress for approval.

Article 68   The term of office of members of the Legislative Council of the Hong Kong Special Administrative Region shall be four years.

Article 69   If the Legislative Council of the Hong Kong Special Administrative Region is dissolved by the Chief Executive in accordance with the provisions of this Law, it shall be reconstituted by election within three months as prescribed by Article 67 of this Law.

Article 70   Alternative 1:

The president of the Legislative Council of the Hong Kong Special Administrative Region shall be elected from among the members of the Legislative Council.

The president of the Legislative Council of the Hong Kong Special Administrative Region shall be a Chinese national of no less than 40 years of age, who is a permanent resident of the Region and has ordinarily resided in Hong Kong for a continuous period of 20 years.

Alternative 2:

The Chief Executive shall concurrently be the president of the Legislative Council of the Hong Kong Special Administrative Region.

Article 71   The president of the Legislative Council of the Hong Kong Special Administrative Region shall exercise the following powers and functions:

(1)   To preside over meetings;

(2)   To decide on and control the agenda;

(3)   To decide on the time and duration of meetings;

(4)   To call special meetings during the recess; and

(5)   Other powers and functions as prescribed in the rules of procedure of the Legislative Council.

Article 72   The Legislative Council of the Hong Kong Special Administrative Region shall exercise the following powers and functions:

(1)   To enact, repeal or amend laws in accordance with the provisions of this Law and legal procedures;

(2)   To examine and approve budgets and final accounts submitted by the executive authorities;

(3)   To approve taxation and public expenditure;

(4)   To hear and debate on the work reports of the Chief Executive;

(5)   To raise questions on the work of the executive authorities;

(6)   To hold debates on any issue concerning public interests;

(7)   To endorse the appointment and removal of the judges of the Court of Final Appeal and the Chief Justice of the High Court;

(8)   To receive and deal with complaints from Hong Kong inhabitants; and

(9)   In the event of serious breach of law or dereliction of duty by the Chief Executive, an independent investigating committee, to be chaired by the Chief Justice of the Court of Final Appeal, on

the motion initiated jointly by one-fourth of the members of the Legislative Council and passed by the council, may be established to carry out investigations and to report its findings to the council. If the committee considers the evidence sufficient, the council may pass a motion of impeachment with a two-thirds majority and report it to the Central People's Government for decision.

Article 73   Alternative 1:
Members of the Legislative Council of the Hong Kong Special Administrative Region may, in accordance with the provisions of this Law and legal procedures, individually or jointly introduce any bills. However written consent of the Chief Executive is required before the following three kinds of bills are introduced:

(1) Bills relating to revenue and expenditure;
(2) Bills relating to government policies; and
(3) Bills relating to the structure and operation of the government.

Alternative 2:
Members of the Legislative Council of the Hong Kong Special Administrative Region may, in accordance with the provisions of this Law and legal procedures, introduce bills. Bills which do not relate to public expenditure or public policies may be introduced individually or jointly by members of the council.

Article 74   The quorum for the meeting of the Legislative Council of the Hong Kong Special Administrative Region shall be no less than half of its members.

Unless otherwise provided for in this Law, the passage of any bill or motion in the Legislative Council of the Hong Kong Special Administrative Region requires the votes of more than half of its members present.

The rules of procedure of the Legislative Council shall be established by the council on its own, but they should not contravene this Law.

Article 75   A bill passed by the Legislative Council of the Hong Kong Special Administrative Region takes effect only after it is signed and promulgated by the Chief Executive.

Article 76   Members of the Legislative Council of the Hong Kong Special Administrative Region shall not be legally liable for speeches made at meetings of the council.

Article 77   Members of the Legislative Council of the Hong Kong Special Administrative Region shall not be subject to arrest when attending or on their way to a meeting of the Legislative Council.

Article 78   The president of the Legislative Council shall declare that a member of the council is no longer qualified to serve under any of the following circumstances*6:

(1) When he/she loses the ability to discharge the functions of his/her office due to serious illness or other reasons;
(2) When he/she is absent from meeting for three consecutive months without the consent of the president of the Legislative Council;
(3) When he/she loses or renounces his/her status as a permanent resident of the Hong Kong Special Administrative Region;

(4) When he/she is bankrupt or fails to pay debts in defiance of a court ruling;

(5) When he/she is convicted and sentenced to imprisonment for one month or more for a criminal offence committed within or outside the Hong Kong Special Administrative Region and is relieved of his/her duties by a motion passed by two-thirds of the members of the Legislative Council present; and

(6) When he/she is censored for misbehaviour or breach of oath by a vote of two-thirds of the members of the Legislative Council present.

Section 4: Judicial Organs

Article 79   The courts of the Hong Kong Special Administrative Region at various levels are the judicial organs of the Region, exercising the judicial power of the Region.

Article 80   The Court of Final Appeal, the High Court, district courts, magistrates' courts and other special courts are established in the Hong Kong Special Administrative Region. The High Court comprises the Court of Appeal and the Court of the First Instance.

The judicial system previously in practice in Hong Kong shall be maintained except for those changes consequent upon the establishment of the Court of Final Appeal in the Hong Kong Special Administrative Region.

Article 81   The power of final adjudication of the Hong Kong Special Administrative Region is vested in the Court of Final Appeal in the Region, which may as required invite judges from other common law jurisdictions to sit on the Court of Final Appeal.

Article 82   The structure, powers and functions of the courts of the Hong Kong Special Administrative Region at various levels shall be prescribed by law.

Article 83   The courts of the Hong Kong Special Administrative Region decide cases in accordance with the laws applicable in the Region as prescribed in Article 17 of this Law and may refer to precedents in other common law jurisdictions.

Article 84   The courts of the Hong Kong Special Administrative Region exercise judicial power independently and free from any interference. Members of the judiciary are immune from legal action in respect of their judicial functions.

Article 85   The principle of trial by jury previously practised in Hong Kong shall be maintained.

Article 86   In criminal or civil proceedings in the Hong Kong Special Administrative Region, the principles previously applied in Hong Kong and the rights previously enjoyed by the parties to the proceedings shall be maintained.

Article 87   Judges of the courts of the Hong Kong Special Administrative Region*7 shall be appointed by the Chief Executive acting in accordance with the recommendation of an independent commission composed of local judges, persons from the legal profession and other eminent persons.

Article 88   A judge of a court of the Hong Kong Special Administrative Region may be removed for inability to discharge the functions of his/her office, or for misbehaviour, by the Chief Executive acting in accordance with the recommendation of a tribunal appointed by the Chief Justice of the Court of Final Appeal and consisting of no fewer than three local judges.

The Chief Justice of the Court of Final Appeal in the Hong Kong Special Administrative Region may be investigated for inability to discharge the functions of his/her office, or for misbehaviour, by a tribunal appointed by the Chief Executive and consisting of no fewer than five local judges and may be removed by the Chief Executive on the recommendation of the tribunal and in accordance with the procedures provided for in this Law.

Article 89   In addition to the procedures prescribed in Articles 87 and 88 of this Law, the appointment and removal of judges of the Court of Final Appeal and the Chief Justice of the High Court in the Hong Kong Special Administrative Region shall be made by the Chief Executive with the endorsement of the Legislative Council of the Region and reported to the Standing Committee of the National People's Congress for the record.

Article 90   The previous system of appointment and removal of members of the judiciary other than judges of the Hong Kong Special Administrative Region shall be maintained.

Article 91   Judges and other members of the judiciary of the Hong Kong Special Administrative Region shall be chosen by reference to their judicial and professional qualities and may be recruited from other common law jurisdictions.

Article 92   Judges and other members of the judiciary serving in Hong Kong before the establishment of the Hong Kong Special Administrative Region may all remain in employment and retain their seniority with pay, allowances, benefits and conditions of service no less favourable than before.

Article 93   The Hong Kong Special Administrative Region shall pay to judges and other members of the judiciary who retire or leave the service in compliance with regulations as well as to those who have retired or left the service before the establishment of the Hong Kong Special Administrative Region, or to their dependents, all pensions, gratuities, allowances and benefits due to them on terms no less favourable than before, and irrespective of their nationality or place of residence.

Article 94   The judicial organs of the Hong Kong Special Administrative Region may, through consultation and in accordance with law, maintain judicial relations with those of other parts of the country, and they may render assistance to each other.

Article 95   With the assistance or authorization of the Central People's Government, the government of the Hong Kong Special Administrative Region may make appropriate arrangements with foreign states for reciprocal judicial assistance.

Section 5: District Organizations

Article 96   District organizations which are not local organs of political power may be established in the Hong Kong Special Administrative Region, to be consulted by the government of the Region on district administration and other affairs, or to be responsible for providing services in such fields as culture, recreation and environmental sanitation.*8

Article 97   The powers and functions of the district organizations and their composition shall be prescribed by law.

Section 6: Public Servants

Article 98   Public servants serving in all government departments of the Hong Kong Special Administrative Region must be permanent residents of the Region, except where otherwise provided for in Article 100 of this Law and except for those below a certain salary point as prescribed by law.

Public servants must be dedicated to their duties and be responsible to the government of the Hong Kong Special Administrative Region.

Article 99   Public servants serving in all Hong Kong government departments, including the police department, before the establishment of the Hong Kong Special Administrative Region, may all remain in employment and retain their seniority with pay, allowances, benefits and conditions of service no less favourable than before.

Article 100   The government of the Hong Kong Special Administrative Region may employ British and other foreign nationals previously serving in the public service in Hong Kong, or those holding permanent identity cards of the Region to serve as public servants at various levels, but only Chinese nationals among permanent residents of the Region can fill the following posts: the Secretary and Deputy Secretaries of Departments, Directors of Bureaus, Commissioner Against Corruption, Director of Audit, Deputy Directors for Security and for Civil Service, Commissioner and Deputy Commissioners of Police, Commissioner and Deputy Commissioners of External Affairs, Commissioner of Immigration and Inspector General of Customs and Excise.

The government of the Hong Kong Special Administrative Region may also employ British and other foreign nationals as advisers to government departments and, when there is need, may recruit qualified candidates from outside the Region to professional and technical posts in government departments. These foreign nationals shall be employed only in their individual capacities and shall be responsible to the government of the Region.

Article 101   The government of the Hong Kong Special Administrative Region shall pay to public servants who retire or leave the service in compliance with regulations as well as to those who have retired or left the service in compliance with regulations before the establishment of the Hong Kong Special Administrative Region, or to their dependents, all pensions, gratuities, allowances and benefits due to them on terms no less favourable than before, and irrespective of their nationality or place of residence.

Article 102   The appointment and promotion of public servants shall be on the basis of their qualifications, experience and ability. Hong Kong's previous system of recruitment, employment, assessment, discipline, training and management for the public service, including special bodies for their appointment, pay and conditions of service, shall be maintained, except for any provisions for privileged treatment of foreign nationals.

Article 103   The Chief Executive, principal officials, members of the Executive Council and of the Legislative Council, judges of courts at all levels and other members of the judiciary in the Hong Kong Special Administrative Region must be sworn in according to law when assuming office.

Chapter V: Economy

Section 1:   Public Finance and Taxation

Article 104   The Hong Kong Special Administrative Region shall have independent finances.

The Hong Kong Special Administrative Region shall use its financial revenues exclusively for its own purposes, and they shall not be handed over to the Central People's Government.

Article 105   The government of the Hong Kong Special Administrative Region shall follow the principle of measuring expenditure by revenues in drawing up its budget.

The government of the Hong Kong Special Administrative Region shall, over a number of fiscal years taken as a whole, maintain a basic balance between total budgetary revenues and expenditure.

In principle, the rate of increase of the budgetary revenues and the expenditure of the Hong Kong Special Administrative Region shall not exceed that of the gross domestic product over a number of fiscal years taken as a whole.

Article 106   The Hong Kong Special Administrative Region shall practise an independent taxation system.

The Central People's Government shall not levy taxes in the Hong Kong Special Administrative Region.

Article 107   The Hong Kong Special Administrative Region shall continue to practise a low tax policy.

Article 108   The type of taxes, the tax rates and tax exemptions in the Hong Kong Special Administrative Region shall be prescribed by law.

Section 2:   Money and Finance

Article 109   The government of the Hong Kong Special Administrative Region shall create conditions and take measures for the maintenance of the status of the Hong Kong Special Administrative Region as an international financial centre.

Article 110   The Hong Kong Special Administrative Region shall continue to practise free and open monetary and financial policies. Its monetary and financial systems shall be governed by law.

Article 111   No exchange control policies shall be applied in the Hong Kong Special Administrative Region. Markets for foreign exchange, gold, securities and futures shall continue.

Article 112   The government of the Hong Kong Special Administrative Region shall safeguard the free flow of all capital within, into and out of the Region.

Article 113   The government of the Hong Kong Special Administrative Region shall safeguard the free operation of financial business and financial markets and shall regulate and supervise them in accordance with law.

Article 114   The Hong Kong dollar, as the legal tender in the Hong Kong Special Administrative Region, shall continue to circulate and remain freely convertible.

Article 115   The authority to issue Hong Kong currency shall be vested in the government of the Hong Kong Special Administrative Region. The system regarding the issue of Hong Kong currency shall be prescribed by law.

The issue of Hong Kong currency shall be backed up by a reserve fund of no less than 100 per cent freely convertible foreign currency.

The government of the Hong Kong Special Administrative Region may authorize designated banks to issue or continue to issue Hong Kong currency under statutory authority, after satisfying itself that any issue of currency will be soundly based and that the arrangements for such issue are consistent with the object of maintaining the stability of the currency.

Article 116   The Exchange Fund of the Hong Kong Special Administrative Region shall be managed and controlled by the government of the Region, primarily for regulating the exchange value of the Hong Kong dollar.

Section 3:   External Trade and Economic Relations

Article 117   The Hong Kong Special Administrative Region shall continue the policy of free external trade and free external economic relations.

The government of the Hong Kong Special Administrative Region shall safeguard the free movement of goods, intangible assets and capital.

Investments from outside the Region shall be protected by law.

Article 118   The Hong Kong Special Administrative Region shall remain a free port.

The Hong Kong Special Administrative Region shall not impose any tariff unless otherwise stipulated by law.

Article 119   The Hong Kong Special Administrative Region shall be a separate customs territory.

The Hong Kong Special Administrative Region may, using the name "Hong Kong, China", participate in relevant international organizations and international trade agreements, including preferential trade arrangements, such as the General Agreement on Tariffs and Trade and arrangements regarding international trade in textiles.

Article 120   Export quotas, tariff preferences and other similar arrangements, which are obtained by the Hong Kong Special Administrative Region or which were obtained and remain valid, shall be enjoyed exclusively by the Region.

Article 121   The Hong Kong Special Administrative Region may issue its own certificates of origin for products manufactured locally in accordance with prevailing rules of origin.

Section 4:   Industry, Commerce and Other Trades

Article 122   The Hong Kong Special Administrative Region shall practise free and open policies regarding industry, commerce and other trades.

Article 123   The government of the Hong Kong Special Administrative Region shall create the necessary environment and conditions for encouraging industrial investment, technological progress and the development of new industries.

Article 124   The government of the Hong Kong Special Administrative Region shall formulate appropriate policies to promote and co-ordinate the development of various trades such as commerce, tourism, real estate, transport, public utilities, services, agriculture and fishery.

Section 5: Land Leases

Article 125   The government of the Hong Kong Special Administrative Region may, on its own, formulate policies regarding the development, management and use of land.

Article 126   All leases of land granted, decided upon or renewed before the establishment of the Hong Kong Special Administrative Region which extend beyond 30 June 1997, and all rights in relation to such leases, shall continue to be recognized and protected under the law of the Region.

Article 127   As regards leases of land granted or renewed where the original leases contain no right of renewal, during the period from 27 May 1985 to 30 June 1997, which extend beyond 30 June 1997 and expire not later than 30 June 2047, the lessee is not required to pay an additional premium as from 1 July 1997, but an annual rent equivalent to 3 per cent of the rateable value of the property at that date, adjusted in step with any changes in the rateable value thereafter, shall be charged.

Article 128   In the case of old schedule lots, village lots, small houses and similar rural holdings, where the property was on 30 June 1984 held by, or, in the case of small houses granted after that date, where property is granted to, a person descended through the male line from a person who was in 1898 a resident of an established village in Hong Kong, the previous rent shall remain unchanged so long as the property is held by that person or by one of his lawful successors in the male line.

Article 129   Where leases of land without a right of renewal expire after the establishment of the Hong Kong Special Administrative Region, they shall be dealt with in accordance with laws and policies formulated by the Region on its own.

Section 6: Shipping

Article 130   The Hong Kong Special Administrative Region shall maintain Hong Kong's previous systems of shipping management and shipping regulation.

The specific functions and responsibilities of the government of the Hong Kong Special Administrative Region in respect of shipping shall be defined by it on its own.

Article 131   The Hong Kong Special Administrative Region shall be authorized by the Central People's Government to continue to maintain a shipping register and issue related certificates under its own legislation using the name "Hong Kong, China".

Article 132   With the exception of foreign warships, access for which requires the special permission of the Central People's Government, ships shall enjoy access to the ports of the Hong Kong Special Administrative Region in accordance with the laws of the Region.

Article 133 Private shipping businesses and shipping-related businesses and private container terminals in the Hong Kong Special Administrative Region may continue to operate freely.

Section 7: Civil Aviation

Article 134 The government of the Hong Kong Special Administrative Region shall create conditions and take measures for the maintenance of the status of the Region as a centre of international and regional aviation.

Article 135 The Hong Kong Special Administrative Region shall continue the previous system of civil aviation management in Hong Kong and keep its own aircraft register in accordance with provisions laid down by the Central People's Government concerning nationality marks and registration marks of aircraft.

Access of foreign military aircraft to the Hong Kong Special Administrative Region requires the special permission of the Central People's Government.

Article 136 The Hong Kong Special Administrative Region shall be responsible on its own for matters of routine business and technical management of civil aviation, including the management of airports, the provision of air traffic services within the flight information region of the Hong Kong Special Administrative Region, and the discharge of other responsibilities allocated to it under the regional air navigation procedures of the International Civil Aviation Organization.

Article 137 The Central People's Government shall, in consultation with the government of the Hong Kong Special Administrative Region, make arrangements providing for air services between the Region and other parts of the People's Republic of China for airlines incorporated in the Hong Kong Special Administrative Region and having their principal place of business in Hong Kong and other airlines of the People's Republic of China.

Article 138 All air service agreements providing for air services between other parts of the People's Republic of China and other states and regions with stops at the Hong Kong Special Administrative Region and for air services between the Hong Kong Special Administrative Region and other states and regions with stops at other parts of the People's Republic of China shall be concluded by the Central People's Government.

In concluding the international air service agreements referred to in the first Paragraph of this Article, the Central People's Government shall take account of the special conditions and economic interests of the Hong Kong Special Administrative Region and consult the government of the Region.

Representatives of the government of the Hong Kong Special Administrative Region may participate, as members of the delegations of the Government of the People's Republic of China, in air service consultations with foreign governments concerning arrangements for such services referred to in the first Paragraph of this Article.

Article 139   Acting under specific authorizations from the Central People's Government, the government of the Hong Kong Special Administrative Region may:

(1) renew or amend air service agreements and arrangements previously in force;

(2) negotiate and conclude new air service agreements providing routes for airlines incorporated in the Hong Kong Special Administrative Region and having their principal place of business in Hong Kong and rights for over-flights and technical stops; and

(3) negotiate and conclude provisional arrangements where no air service agreement with a foreign state or with another region is in force.

All scheduled air services to, from or through Hong Kong, which do not operate to, from or through the mainland of China shall be regulated by the air service agreements or provisional arrangements referred to in this Article.

Article 140   The Central People's Government shall give the government of the Hong Kong Special Administrative Region the authority to:

(1) negotiate and conclude with other authorities all arrangements concerning the implementation of the air service agreements and provisional arrangements referred to in Article 139 of this Law;

(2) issue licences to airlines incorporated in the Hong Kong Special Administrative Region and having their principal place of business in Hong Kong;

(3) designate such airlines under the air service agreements and provisional arrangements referred to in Article 139 of this Law; and

(4) issue permits to foreign airlines for services other than those to, from or through the mainland of China.

Article 141   Airlines incorporated and having their principal place of business in Hong Kong and civil aviation related businesses there before the establishment of the Hong Kong Special Administrative Region may continue to operate.

**Chapter VI: Education, Science, Culture, Sports, Religion, Labour
and Social Services**

Article 142   The Hong Kong Special Administrative Region shall
maintain the educational system previously practised in Hong Kong.
Article 143   The Government of the Hong Kong Special Administrative Region shall, on its own, formulate policies on education, including
policies regarding the educational system and its administration, the
language of instruction, the allocation of funds, the examination system,
the system of academic awards and the recognition of educational
qualifications.

Community organizations and individuals may, in accordance with
law, run educational undertakings of various kinds in the Hong Kong
Special Administrative Region.
Article 144   Educational institutions of all kinds may retain their
autonomy and enjoy academic freedom. They may continue to recruit
staff and use teaching materials from outside the Hong Kong Special
Administrative Region. Schools run by religious organizations may
continue to provide religious education, including courses on religion.

Students shall enjoy freedom to choose between educational institutions and to pursue their education outside the Hong Kong Special
Administrative Region.
Article 145   The government of the Hong Kong Special Administrative Region shall promote the development of medical and health
services and the development of Western and Chinese traditional
medicine, and encourage community organizations and individuals to
provide medical and health services of various kinds.
Article 146   The government of the Hong Kong Special Administrative Region shall, on its own, formulate policies on science and
technology. The Hong Kong Special Administrative Region shall
protect, by law, achievements in scientific and technological research,
patents, discoveries and inventions.

The government of the Hong Kong Special Administrative Region
shall, on its own, decide on the scientific and technological standards
and specifications applicable in Hong Kong.
Article 147   The government of the Hong Kong Special Administrative Region shall, on its own, formulate policies on culture and protect
the achievements and the legitimate rights and interests of authors in
their literary and artistic pursuits.
Article 148   The government of the Hong Kong Special Administrative Region shall not interfere in the internal affairs of religious
organizations and shall not restrict religious activities which do not
contravene the laws of the Region.

Religious organizations shall, in accordance with law, enjoy the rights
to acquire, use, dispose of and inherit property and the right to receive
financial assistance. Their previous property rights and interests shall be
maintained and protected.

Religious organizations may, according to their previous practice,
continue to run seminaries and other schools, hospitals and welfare
institutions and to provide other social services.

Article 149   Religious organizations and believers in the Hong Kong Special Administrative Region may maintain and develop their relations with religious organizations and believers elsewhere.

Article 150   The government of the Hong Kong Special Administrative Region shall, on its own, decide on the methods of assessing and accrediting qualifications for professional practice for the various professions. The methods of assessing and accrediting qualifications previously practised in Hong Kong may be maintained and perfected.

Persons with professional qualifications or qualifications for professional practice obtained prior to the establishment of the Hong Kong Special Administrative Region may retain their previous qualifications.

The Hong Kong Special Administrative Region shall maintain the professions and the professional organizations recognized prior to the establishment of the Region, and these organizations may, on their own, assess and accredit professional qualifications.

The government of the Hong Kong Special Administrative Region may, as required by developments in society and in consultation with the parties concerned, recognize new professions and professional organizations.

Article 151   The government of the Hong Kong Special Administrative Region shall, on its own, formulate policies on sports. Previous nongovernmental sports organizations may continue to exist and develop in accordance with law.

Article 152   The Hong Kong Special Administrative Region shall maintain the policy previously practised in Hong Kong in respect of subventions for organizations in fields such as education, medicine, culture, arts, recreation, sports, social welfare and social work. Staff previously serving in subventioned organizations in Hong Kong may remain in their employment in accordance with the previous system.

Article 153   The government of the Hong Kong Special Administrative Region shall maintain the previous social welfare system and shall formulate, on its own, policies on the development and improvement of this system in the light of the economic conditions and social needs.

Article 154   Voluntary organizations providing social services in the Hong Kong Special Administrative Region may, on their own, decide their forms of service in accordance with law.

Article 155   The Hong Kong Special Administrative Region shall, on its own, formulate labour laws and policies in the light of economic development, social needs and the specific circumstances of labour-management consultations.

Article 156   The relationship between non-governmental organizations in fields such as education, science, technology, culture, sports, the professions and social welfare as well as religious organizations in the Hong Kong Special Administrative Region and their counterparts on the mainland shall be in conformity with the principles of non-subordination, non-interference and mutual respect.

Article 157   Organizations in fields such as education, science, technology, culture, sports, health, the professions, labour, social welfare and religion in the Hong Kong Special Administrative Region may maintain and develop relations with foreign countries and other regions and with relevant international organizations. They may, as required, use the name "Hong Kong, China" in the relevant activities.

Chapter VII: External Affairs

Article 158   Representatives of the government of the Hong Kong Special Administrative Region may participate, as members of delegations of the Government of the People's Republic of China, in negotiations at the diplomatic level directly affecting the Region conducted by the Central People's Government.

Article 159   The Hong Kong Special Administrative Region may, on its own, using the name "Hong Kong, China", maintain and develop relations and conclude and implement agreements with states, regions and relevant international organizations in the appropriate fields, including the economic, trade, financial and monetary, shipping, communications, tourism, cultural and sports fields.

Article 160   Representatives of the Hong Kong Special Administrative Region may participate, as members of delegations of the Government of the People's Republic of China, in international organizations or conferences in appropriate fields limited to states and affecting the Region, or may attend in such other capacity as may be permitted by the Central People's Government and the international organization or conference concerned, and may express their views, using the name "Hong Kong, China".

The Hong Kong Special Administrative Region may, using the name "Hong Kong, China", participate in international organizations and conferences not limited to states.

The Central People's Government shall take the necessary steps to ensure that the Hong Kong Special Administrative Region shall continue to retain its status in an appropriate capacity in those international organizations of which the People's Republic of China is a member and in which Hong Kong participates in one capacity or another.

The Central People's Government shall, where necessary, facilitate the continued participation of the Hong Kong Special Administrative Region in an appropriate capacity in those international organizations in which Hong Kong is a participant in one capacity or another, but of which the People's Republic of China is not a member.

Article 161   The application to the Hong Kong Special Administrative Region of international agreements to which the People's Republic of China is or becomes a party shall be decided by the Central People's Government, in accordance with the circumstances and needs of the Region, and after seeking the views of the government of the Region.

International agreements to which the People's Republic of China is not a party but which are implemented in Hong Kong may continue to be implemented in the Hong Kong Special Administrative Region. The Central People's Government shall, as necessary, authorize or assist the government of the Region to make appropriate arrangements for the application to the Region of other relevant international agreements.

Article 162   The Central People's Government shall authorize the government of the Hong Kong Special Administrative Region to issue, in accordance with law, passports of the Hong Kong Special Administrative Region of the People's Republic of China to all Chinese nationals who hold permanent identity cards of the Region, and travel documents of the Hong Kong Special Administrative Region of the

People's Republic of China to all other persons lawfully residing in the Region. The above passports and documents shall be valid for all states and regions and shall record the holder's right to return to Hong Kong.

The government of the Hong Kong Special Administrative Region may apply immigration controls on entry into, stay in and departure from the Hong Kong Special Administrative Region by persons from foreign states and other regions.

Article 163   The Central People's Government shall assist or authorize the government of the Hong Kong Special Administrative Region to conclude visa exemption agreements with states or regions.

Article 164   The Hong Kong Special Administrative Region may, as necessary, establish official or semi-official economic and trade missions in foreign countries and shall report the establishment of such missions to the Central People's Government for the record.

Article 165   The establishment of foreign consular and other official or semi-official missions in the Hong Kong Special Administrative Region requires the approval of the Central People's Government.

Consular and other official missions established in Hong Kong by states which have formal diplomatic relations with the People's Republic of China may be maintained.

According to the circumstances of each case, consular and other official missions established in Hong Kong by states which have no formal diplomatic relations with the People's Republic of China may either be permitted to remain or be changed to semi-official missions.

States not recognized by the People's Republic of China can only establish non-governmental institutions in Hong Kong.

Chapter VIII: The Regional Flag and Regional Emblem of the Hong Kong Special Administrative Region

Article 166 Apart from displaying the national flag and national emblem, the Hong Kong Special Administrative Region may use a regional flag and regional emblem of its own (to be drafted).

Article 167 The regional flag of the Hong Kong Special Administrative Region (to be drafted).

Article 168 The regional emblem of the Hong Kong Special Administrative Region (to be drafted).

Chapter IX: Interpretation and Amendment of the Basic Law

Article 169   The power of interpretation of this Law is vested in the Standing Committee of the National People's Congress.

When the Standing Committee of the National People's Congress makes an interpretation of a provision of this Law, the courts of the Hong Kong Special Administrative Region, in applying that provision, shall follow the interpretation of the Standing Committee. However, judgments previously rendered shall not be affected.

The courts of the Hong Kong Special Administrative Region may interpret the provisions of this Law in adjudicating cases before them. If a case involves an interpretation of the provisions of this Law concerning defence, foreign affairs and other affairs which are the responsibility of the Central People's Government, the courts of the Region, before making their final judgment on the case, shall seek an interpretation of the relevant provisions from the Standing Committee of the National People's Congress.

The Standing Committee of the National People's Congress shall consult its Committee for the Basic Law of the Hong Kong Special Administrative Region before giving an interpretation of this Law.

Article 170   The power of amendment of this Law is vested in the National People's Congress.

The right to propose amendments to this Law rests with the Standing Committee of the National People's Congress, the State Council and the Hong Kong Special Administrative Region. Amendment proposals from the Hong Kong Special Administrative Region shall be submitted to the National People's Congress by the delegation of the Region to the National People's Congress after obtaining the consent of two-thirds of the deputies of the Region to the National People's Congress, two-thirds of all the members of the legislature of the Region, and the Chief Executive of the Region.

Before a proposal for an amendment to this Law is put on the agenda of the National People's Congress, the Committee for the Basic Law of the Hong Kong Special Administrative Region shall first study it and submit its views.

No amendment to this Law shall contravene the established basic policies of the People's Republic of China regarding Hong Kong.

Chapter X: Supplementary Provisions

Article 171   The first government and the first Legislative Council of the Hong Kong Special Administrative Region shall be established in accordance with the principles of national sovereignty and of smooth transition and in accordance with the stipulations of Annex III: "Method for the Formation of the First Government and the First Legislative Council of the Hong Kong Special Administrative Region".

Article 172   At the time of the establishment of the Hong Kong Special Administrative Region, the laws previously in force in Hong Kong shall be adopted as laws of the Region except for those which the Standing Committee of the National People's Congress declares to be in contravention of this Law. If any laws are later discovered to be in contravention of this Law, they can be annulled or revised according to the procedure as prescribed by this Law.

Documents, certificates, contracts, and rights and obligations valid under the laws previously in force in Hong Kong shall continue to be valid and be recognized and protected by the laws of the Hong Kong Special Administrative Region, provided that they do not contravene this Law.

Annex I   Method for Selecting the Chief Executive of the Hong Kong Special Administrative Region

Alternative 1

1. The Chief Executive of the Hong Kong Special Administrative Region shall be elected locally by a broadly representative electoral college.
2. The electoral college shall be composed of about 600 representatives from various walks of life in Hong Kong, including members of the legislature; representatives of district organizations; representatives of corporate bodies and non-corporate permanent organizations; and representatives of various functional constituencies (including industry, commerce, finance, professions, education, labour, religious communities, social services and the public servants).
3. Communities and organizations with seats in the electoral college may, according to their own rules, elect their representatives by a democratic procedure. Each elected representative must not concurrently represent several organizations and shall vote in an individual capacity. The electoral college will be dissolved after the election is completed.
4. The electoral college shall elect a nominating committee of 20 members from its own midst. The committee shall nominate three candidates for the office of the Chief Executive. Members of the nominating committee cannot run for the office of the Chief Executive, nor can they vote in the election of the Chief Executive.
5. The electoral college shall vote on the nominations by the nominating committee, and a candidate must win over half of the votes to be elected. If no one wins over half of the votes on the first ballot, a second ballot has to be taken on the two candidates with the highest number of votes. The Chief Executive elected by the electoral college shall be reported to the Central People's Government for appointment.
6. Detailed election rules shall be prescribed by the laws of the government of the Hong Kong Special Administrative Region.

Alternative 2

1. The Chief Executive of the Hong Kong Special Administrative Region shall be nominated by no less than one-tenth of the members of the legislature, and directly elected by a general election held throughout Hong Kong.
2. Each member of the legislature can nominate only one candidate for the Chief Executive.
3. The election for the Chief Executive must be genuine and held at regular intervals. The right to vote must be universal and equal. Election should be by secret ballot to ensure free expression of the will of the voters.
4. If the elected Chief Executive is a member of the legislature, the executive authorities, or the judicial organs, he/she must resign from his/her original post upon election.

5. Detailed rules for the election of the Chief Executive shall be prescribed by the laws of the Hong Kong Special Administrative Region.

Alternative 3

1. The Chief Executive shall be elected by a functional electoral college on a one-person-one-vote basis.
2. The functional electoral college shall have no more than 600 members and be composed of representatives elected from among the permanent residents of the Hong Kong Special Administrative Region, who belong to business, finance, professional, labour and other organizations which have an influence on the operation of the government and social services. The proportions of representation shall be as follows:

Business and financial organizations	25%
Professional bodies	35%
Labour organizations	10%
Religious, social welfare and philanthropic institutions	15%
Area committees and street vendors' organizations	15%

3. Any person with qualifications prescribed by Article 44 of this Law and nominated by no less than 50 permanent residents of Hong Kong can become a candidate for the Chief Executive of the Hong Kong Special Administrative Region.
4. Members of the electoral college shall not nominate or be nominated as candidates. Nominators shall not be members of the electoral college or be candidates. Candidates shall not be members of the electoral college or nominators of other candidates.

Alternative 4

1. The selection of the first Chief Executive is specified in other provisions. The second or third Chief Executives shall be selected by an advisory group through consultation.

    The advisory group shall be composed of 50–100 advisers. Candidates for advisers shall be nominated by different circles in Hong Kong, selected by the Executive Council and then appointed by the Chief Executive after approval by the Central People's Government. (These are special political advisers, different from other professional advisers.)

    Each advisory group must be formed six months before the term of office of the incumbent Chief Executive expires. But if the advisory group and the Central People's Government endorse him/her for another term, the next advisory group need not be formed.
2. Subsequent Chief Executives shall be elected by an electoral college.

    The electoral college shall be composed of former members of the Legislative Council, former members of the Executive Council, former Chief Executives, and former principal officials appointed by the Central People's Government. The first electoral college cannot be formed with less than 250 members. The number may gradually increase in the successive electoral colleges, but shall not exceed 500. Once that number is exceeded, members will have to resign in the order of their length in office. If their length in office is the same, the member elder in age shall resign first.

Three candidates for the office of the Chief Executive shall be nominated by the advisory group and, after the approval of the Central People's Government, the Chief Executive shall be voted on by the electoral college.

Alternative 5

1. The Chief Executives shall be elected by all the voters of Hong Kong on a one-person-one-vote basis. Three candidates shall be nominated, through consultation or by ballot after consultation, by the "Nominating Committee for the Election of the Chief Executive of the Hong Kong Special Administrative Region".

2. The "Nominating Committee' shall be composed of permanent residents of Hong Kong who must be broadly representative, including deputies of the Hong Kong region to the National People's Congress, members of the National Committee of the Chinese People's Political Consultative Conference from the Hong Kong region, representatives from Hong Kong's legislature and from district organizations, and from other strata and sections of society in Hong Kong.

3. The proportions of representation of the "Nominating Committee" shall be as follows:

Representatives of business and financial circles	25%
Representatives of professional bodies	25%
Representatives of labour, grass-roots and religious organizations	25%
Members of the legislature	12%
Members of district organizations	8%
Deputies to the National People's Congress and members of the National Committee of the Chinese People's Political Consultative Conference	5%

4. The "Nominating Committee" shall formulate a procedure for consultation or balloting and nominate candidates for the office of the Chief Executive. Members of the "Nominating Committee" shall not be candidates for the office of the Chief Executive.

5. Members of the "Nominating Committee" shall be elected, recommended or selected through consultation by corporate bodies or noncorporate permanent organizations in various fields. Rules of the "Nominating Committee" shall be prescribed by the laws of the Hong Kong Special Administrative Region.

6. The Hong Kong Special Administrative Region shall stipulate by law the provisions for constituency registration and voting procedures for a one-person-one-vote general election of the Chief Executive.

Annex II Method for Constituting the Legislative Council of the Hong Kong Special Administrative Region

Alternative 1

1. The legislature of the Hong Kong Special Administrative Region shall be composed of 80 persons. The proportions of representation shall be as follows:

Members elected by functional bodies	50%
Members directly elected by districts	25%
Members elected by the electoral college	25%

2. The composition of the electoral body and the nominating committee shall be the same as that prescribed in Alternative 1, "Method for Selecting the Chief Executive of the Hong Kong Special Administrative Region", and the chairman of the nominating committee shall be the Chief Executive.
3. In the above three types of election, each person can vote and stand for election only in one.
4. The term of office of the members of the legislature shall be four years, and half the members shall be elected every two years. The functional bodies shall elect half of their members to the legislature every two years. The direct election in the districts and the election by the electoral college shall be held alternately every two years, (District direct elections and elections of the Chief Executive shall take place in the same year.)
5. District direct elections: Hong Kong shall be divided into 10 constituencies, with two seats for each constituency, and the two candidates with the first and second highest number of votes shall be elected.
6. Detailed election rules shall be prescribed by the laws of the Hong Kong Special Administrative Region.

Alternative 2

1. The legislature of the Hong Kong Special Administrative Region shall be constituted as follows: No less than 50 per cent of the members shall be directly elected in a general election; no more than 25 per cent shall be elected by the functional bodies, and no more than 25 per cent shall be elected by district organizations (i.e. District Boards, Urban Council and Regional Council or other similar organizations.)
2. The direct election of the legislature must be genuine and held at regular intervals. The right to vote must be universal and equal. Election should be by secret ballot so as to ensure free expression of the will of the voters.
3. Detailed rules for the election of the legislature shall be prescribed by the laws of the Hong Kong Special Administrative Region.

Alternative 3

1. The legislature of the Hong Kong Special Administrative Region shall have 60 members.

2. Thirty per cent of the members (i.e. 18 persons) shall be elected by the advisory group from among non-advisers. At least one-third of these members (i.e. 6 persons) shall be principal officials, and the rest (around two-thirds) shall be members of the Executive Council and other public figures. (Members of the legislature elected by the advisory group must include members of the Executive Council and principal officials so as to strengthen the links between the executive and the legislature.)

3. Forty per cent of the members (i.e. 24 persons) shall be elected by functional bodies.

4. Thirty per cent of the members shall be elected directly by the districts. The members of the legislature directly elected and those elected by the advisory group shall be roughly the same in numbers and shall be elected roughly at the same time, so that balance can be maintained. (Unless the method of the election by the advisory group is accepted, direct election cannot be held.)

5. The two election methods stated above in paragraphs 3 and 4 shall be prescribed in detail by law.

Alternative 4

1. The composition of the legislature of the Hong Kong Special Administrative Region shall be as follows:

From business circles	30%
From the professions	25%
From grass-roots organizations	20%
Through district general elections	25%

2. The composition is thus divided into four major categories. The first three major categories are further divided into sub-categories according to trades or professions. The delimitation of each sub-category and the number of members it elects to the legislature shall be prescribed by the laws of the Hong Kong Special Administrative Region.

   All members of the legislature who belong to the three major categories shall be elected from corporate bodies in accordance with law.

   According to the assigned number of seats, each corporate body shall decide on its own which of the following methods to adopt for electing its members to the legislature:

   (1) Each member is directly elected on a one-person-one-vote basis;

   (2) Members from its subsidiaries are elected through indirect election on a one-unit-one-vote basis; and

   (3) The general membership conference authorizes a council to elect members through indirect election.

3. The division of the district constituencies, the voter registration, the voting procedures, and the nomination of candidate in district general elections shall be prescribed by the laws of the Hong Kong Special Administrative Region.

Notes

1. The members who put forward Alternatives 1 and 3 maintained that their proposed methods for electing members of the legislature are "package" deals, that is to say, direct district election is conditional upon the acceptance of the other two types of election.
2. Some members proposed that all the members of the legislature of the Hong Kong Special Administrative Region be elected by the functional bodies and that the method of election by the functional bodies be the same as that in Alternative 3 in Annex I.
3. A member proposed that all the members of the legislature of the Hong Kong Special Administrative Region be elected by districts through direct election on a one-person-one-vote basis. The election of the legislature must be genuine and held at regular intervals. The right to vote must be universal and equal. The election must be by secret ballot so as to ensure free expression of the will of the voters.
4. A member proposed that the method of general election on a one-person-one-vote basis should be considered together with the question of nationality, and studies must be made on the right to vote and to stand for election of Hong Kong permanent residents who have moved to a foreign country (but might not have acquired foreign nationality).

Annex III   Method for the Formation of the First Government and the First Legislative Council of the Hong Kong Special Administrative Region

1. Within the year of 1996, the National People's Congress shall establish a Preparatory Committee of the Hong Kong Special Administrative Region, which shall be responsible for the preparations of the establishment of the Region, and shall decide on the specific method for the formation of its first government. The preparatory committee shall be composed of mainland members and of Hong Kong members who shall constitute no less than 50 percent. Its chairman and members shall be appointed by the Standing Committee of the National People's Congress.

2. The Preparatory Committee for the Hong Kong Special Administrative Region shall be responsible for preparing the establishment of the "Election Committee for the First Government of the Hong Kong Special Administrative Region".

The "Election Committee" shall be composed entirely of permanent residents of Hong Kong and must be broadly representative. It shall include deputies of the Hong Kong region to the National People's Congress of the People's Republic of China, Hong Kong members of the National Committee of the Chinese People's Political Consultative Conference, experienced persons who have served in Hong Kong's administrative, legislative and advisory organizations before the establishment of the Hong Kong Special Administrative Region, as well as persons representative of all strata and sections of society.

The proportions of the composition of the "Election Committee" are tentatively proposed as follows:

Persons from business and financial circles	25%
Professionals	25%
Persons from labour, grass-roots and religious organizations	25%
Political figures of former times	20%
Deputies to the National People's Congress and members of the National Committee of the Chinese People's Political Consultative Conference	5%

3. The "Election Committee" shall formulate procedures and accordingly recommend the candidate for the first Chief Executive through local consultation or through local election after consultation, and report the recommended Chief Executive to the Central People's Government for appointment. The term of office of the first Chief Executive shall be the normal term.

4. The Chief Executive of the Hong Kong Special Administrative Region shall be responsible for preparing the election of the first government of the region according to this Law.

5. The first (or provisional) legislature of the Hong Kong Special Administrative Region shall be elected by the "Election Committee". All members of the former Hong Kong Legislative Council can be candidates for membership in the first (or provisional) legislature of the Region.

The term of office of members of the first (or provisional) legislature of the Hong Kong Special Administrative Region shall be two years.

6. The first Chief Executive of the Hong Kong Special Administrative Region shall be sworn in to office on 1 July 1997. On 1 July 1997, the first government and legislature of the Hong Kong Special Administrative Region shall be inaugurated simultaneously.

368   *Appendix*

Notes

1. The members proposed that a map showing the administrative boundaries of the Hong Kong Special Administrative Region be published by the State Council when the Basic Law is promulgated by the National People's Congress.

2. The proposal on the establishment of the Committee for the Basic Law of the Hong Kong Special Administrative Region put forward by the Sub-group on the Relationship between the Central Authorities and the Hong Kong Special Administrative Region reads as follows:

   (1) Name: To be called tentatively the Committee for the Basic Law of the Hong Kong Special Administrative Region of the Standing Committee of the National People's Congress.

   (2) Affiliation: To be a subordinate organ of the Standing Committee of the National People's Congress.

   (3) Duties: To study and submit its views to the National People's Congress or its Standing Committee on the following questions:

      (a) Questions on whether laws enacted by the legislature of the Hong Kong Special Administrative Region are in conformity with the Basic Law and legal procedures (Article 16 of the Draft Basic Law for Solicitation of Opinions);

      (b) Questions relating to the applicability of nationwide laws in the Hong Kong Special Administrative Region (Article 17);

      (c) Questions relating to the interpretation of the Basic Law (Article 169); and

      (d) Questions relating to the amendment of the Basic Law (Article 170).

   (4) Composition: To be composed of mainland members and Hong Kong members, including persons from the legal profession, appointed by the Standing Committee of the National People's Congress. The number of its members and the proportions of its composition remain to be determined.

3. The names of the different departments of the executive authorities of the Hong Kong Special Administrative Region shall tentatively be called:

   (1) The three main departments: The Department of Administration, the Department of Finance and the Department of Justice shall be called *si*, or "departments" in English, and those heading them shall be called Administrative Secretary, Financial Secretary and Secretary of Justice respectively.

   (2) Those departments with policy-making powers shall be called *ju*, or "bureaus" in English, such as the Bureau of Finance, the Bureau of Industry and Commerce, the Bureau of Transport, the Bureau of Education and Manpower and the Civil Service Bureau.

   (3) Those departments which carry out administrative duties and do not make policies shall be called *chu*, or "divisions" in English, such as the Police Division, the External Affairs Division and the Immigration Service Division.

(4) Those departments whose work is relatively independent shall be called *shu*, or "commissions" in English, such as the Commission against Corruption and the Commission of Audit.

4. The members held that in general, principal officials should be selected from among public servants. However, they can also be selected from among prominent members of society other than public servants. Principal officials of the latter type would be remunerated as public servants working on contract. They would leave the service on expiry of their terms of office. Transfers of principal officials and increase of officials of the Secretary level must be reported to the Central People's Government for approval.

5. The members agree that the English translation of (立法会议) shall continue to be "Legislative Council".

6. Whether or not members of the legislature should be required to resign after being appointed principal officials in the executive authorities remains to be studied.

7. "Judges" of the courts of the Hong Kong Special Administrative Region refers to judges of the district courts or above. Other members of the judiciary include magistrates of magistrates' courts and presiding officers at special tribunals. Other persons working in the judiciary are considered public servants.

8. The members held that if the present three-tier structure was retained, district boards should still be district consultative bodies.

Bibliography

The works included here relate in some way to the future of Hong Kong. The list is restricted to sources in the English language, and newspaper and magazine commentaries are omitted.

Adley, Robert. *All Change Hong Kong* (Poole, Dorset: Blandford Press, 1984)

Amberg, Eric M. 'Self-Determination in Hong Kong: A New Challenge to an Old Doctrine' (1985) 22 San Diego Law Review 839

Atwood, Ewin L, and Philip H Cheng. 'Public Opinion and Media Use in Hong Kong: The 1997 Question' (Occasional Papers No 15, Centre for Hong Kong Studies, Chinese University of Hong Kong; 1986)

Baker, Hugh D R. 'Life in the Cities: The Emergence of Hong Kong Man' (1983) 95 China Quarterly 469

Barry, Peter. 'A Discussion on "Separation of Church and State" in Hong Kong After 1997' (1987) 38 Tripod 63

Benton, Gregor. *The Hong Kong Crisis* (London: Pluto Press Ltd, 1983)

Berstein, Thomas P. 'China in 1984: The Year of Hong Kong' (1985) 25 Asian Survey 33

Blaustein, Albert P. 'Drafting a New Constitution for the Hong Kong SAR' in Y C Jao et al (eds), *Hong Kong and 1997* (qv) 201

Bonavia, David. *Hong Kong 1997: The Final Settlement* (Hong Kong: South China Morning Post Ltd, 1985)

Brabyn, Janice. 'Extradition and the Hong Kong SAR' (1988) 20 Case Western Reserve Journal of International Law (forthcoming)

Bucknall, Kevin B. 'Hong Kong and China: The Present and Future Relationship' (1982) 18 Asia Pacific Community 106

Bueno de Mesquita, Bruce, and others, *Forecasting Political Events: The Future of Hong Kong* (New Haven: Yale University Press, 1985)

Burns, John P. 'Immigration from China and the Future of Hong Kong' (1987) 27 Asian Survey 661

Burns, John P. 'The Process of Assimilation of Hong Kong (1997) and the Implications for Taiwan' (1986) 6 AEI Foreign Policy and Defence Review (No 3) 19

Castle, Lawrence A. 'The Reversion of Hong Kong to China: Legal and Practical Questons' (1985) 21 Willamette Law Review 327

Catholic Institute for International Relations, *The Future of Hong Kong* (Comment No 45; 1982)

Catron, Gary. 'Hong Kong and Chinese Foreign Policy, 1955–60' (1972) 51 China Quarterly 405

Cha, Louis. *On Hong Kong's Future: A Collection of Ming Pao Daily News Editorials* (Hong Kong: Ming Pao Daily News Ltd, 1984)

Chan, Johannes. 'A Bill of Rights for Hong Kong?' in Ray Wacks (qv) 72

Chan, Thomas M H. 'The Political Organisation of the HKSAR' (1988) 2 Journal of Chinese Law 115

Chang, Denis. 'Common Law in an Uncommon Setting: A Tale of Two Systems' (unpublished, 1987)

Chang, Denis. 'How China Sees It' in William McGurn (ed), *Basic Law, Basic Questions* (qv) 129

Chang, Denis. 'One Country, Two Systems' (unpublished, 1987)

Chang, Denis. 'The Basic Law of the Hong Kong SAR: Economics and Norms of Credibility' (1988) 2 Journal of Chinese Law 21

Chang, Denis. 'Towards a Jurisprudence of a Third Kind: One Country, Two Systems' (1988) 20 Case Western Reserve Journal of International Law (forthcoming)

Chang, Jaw-ling, Joanne. 'China's Hong Kong Victory: A Study of the PRC's Negotiating Style, 1982–1984' (unpublished, 1988)

Chang Pao-min. 'China, Britain and the Future of Hong Kong' (1983) 19 Asia Pacific Community 72

Chao Chien-min. 'One Country, Two Systems: A Theoretical Analysis' (1987) 14 Asian Affairs 107

Cheek-Milby, Kathleen. 'Political Representation in the Legislature' in Kathleen Cheek-Milby et al (eds), *Hong Kong: The Challenge of Transformation* (qv)

Cheek-Milby, Kathleen. 'Providing a Constitutional Framework for Legislative Power: The US and Hong Kong Experience' in *The United States Constitution: Its Birth, Growth and Influence in Asia* (Hong Kong: Hong Kong University Press, 1988)

Cheek-Milby, Kathleen. 'Redefining the Role of the Official Member of the Legislative Council' in Kathleen Cheek-Milby et al (eds), *Hong Kong: The Challenge of Transformation* (qv)

Cheek-Milby, Kathleen, David Clark, and Miron Mushkat (eds). *Hong Kong: The Challenge of Transformation* (forthcoming, 1989)

Chen, Albert H Y. '1997: The Language of the Law in Hong Kong' (1985) 15 Hong Kong Law Journal 19

Chen, Albert H Y. 'Civil Liberties in China: Some Preliminary Observations' in Ray Wacks (qv) 107

Chen, Albert H Y. 'Civil Liberties in Hong Kong: Recent Controversies, Evolving Consciousness and Future Legal Protection (1988) 2 Journal of Chinese Law 137

Chen, Albert H Y. 'Further Aspects of the Autonomy of Hong Kong under the PRC Constitution' (1984) 14 Hong Kong Law Journal 341

Chen, Albert H Y. 'Hong Kong's Legal System: Adaptations for 1997 and Beyond' in Y C Jao et al (eds), *Hong Kong and 1997* (qv) 235

Chen, Albert H Y. 'Law in a Foreign Language: The Case of Hong Kong' in Kathleen Cheek-Milby et al (eds), *Hong Kong: The Challenge of Transformation* (qv)

Cheng Chu-yuan. 'Hong Kong's Prosperity: Foundation and Prospects' (1985) 2 Journal of Chinese Studies 155

Cheng, Joseph Y S. 'Democratic Elections, Self Administration and the Future of Hong Kong' (1984) 10 Flinders Journal of History and Politics 128

Cheng, Joseph Y S. 'Hong Kong: The Challenge of the Future' (1986) 31 Asia Pacific Community 19

Cheng, Joseph Y S. 'Hong Kong: The Decline of Political Expectations and Confidence' (forthcoming in Australian Journal of Chinese Affairs in 1988)

Cheng, Joseph Y S. 'Hong Kong: The Pressure to Converge' (1987) 63 International Affairs 271

Cheng, Joseph Y S (ed). *Hong Kong in Search of a Future* (Hong Kong, Oxford, New York: Oxford University Press, 1984)

Cheng, Joseph Y S (ed). *Hong Kong in the 1980s — A Society in Transition* (Hong Kong: Summerson Eastern Publishers Ltd, 1982)

Cheng, Joseph Y S (ed). *Hong Kong in Transition* (Hong Kong: Oxford University Press, 1986)

Cheng, Joseph Y S. 'Preliminary Suggestions on the Political System of the Hong Kong Special Administrative Region' in Joseph Y S Cheng (ed), *Hong Kong in Transition* (qv) 52

Cheng, Joseph Y S. 'The 1988 District Board Elections — A Study of Political Participation in the Transitional Period' in Kathleen Cheek-Milby et al (eds), *Hong Kong: The Challenge of Transformation* (qv)

Cheng, Joseph Y S. 'The Constitutional Relationship Between the Central Government and the Future Hong Kong SAR Government' (1988) 20 Case Western Reserve Journal of International Law (forthcoming)

Cheng, Joseph Y S. 'The Future of Hong Kong: A Hong Kong Belonger's View' (1982) 58 International Affairs (London) 476

Cheng, Joseph Y S. 'The Future of Hong Kong: A Solution for Hong Kong People' (1984) 23 Asia Pacific Community 59

Cheng, Joseph Y S. 'The Future of Hong Kong: Surveys of the Hong Kong People's Attitudes' (1984) 12 Australian Journal of Chinese Affairs 113

Cheng, Loyti. 'An Economic Analysis of Capital Flight in Hong Kong' (1985) 17 New York University Journal of International Law and Politics 683

Ching, Frank. *Hong Kong and China: For Better or For Worse* (New York: China Council of the Asia Society and the Foreign Policy Association, 1985)

Ching, Frank. 'One Country, Two Nationalities?' in William McGurn (ed), *Basic Law, Basic Questions* (qv) 81

Chiu, Hungdah. 'Legal Problems with the Hong Kong Model for Unification of China and Their Implications for Taiwan' (1988) 2 Journal of Chinese Law 83

Chiu, Hungdah. 'Prospects for the Unification of China: An Analysis of the Views of the Republic of China on Taiwan' (1983) 23 Asian Survey 1081

Chiu, Hungdah. 'The 1982 Chinese Constitution and the Rule of Law' (1985) 11 Review of Socialist Law 143

Chiu, Hungdah. 'The 1984 Sino-British Agreement on Hong Kong and its Implications on China's Unification' (1985) 21 Issues and Studies (No 4) 13

Chiu, Hungdah. 'The 1984 Sino-British Settlement on Hong Kong: Problems and Analysis' in Hungdah Chiu (ed), *Hong Kong: 1997* (Maryland: School of Law, University of Maryland, Occasional Papers/Reprints Series in Contemporary Asian Studies No 3, 1984) 7

Chiu, Hungdah. 'The Hong Kong Agreement and American Foreign Policy' (1986) 22 Issues and Studies (No 6) 76

Chiu, Hungdah. 'The Re-unification of China: Perspectives from Taiwan' (unpublished, 1987)

Chiu, Hungdah, Y C Jao, and Yuan-li Wu (eds). *The Future of Hong Kong: Toward 1997 and Beyond* (New York, Westport, London: Quorum Books, 1987)

Christiansen, Kent L. 'Self-Determination for the People of Taiwan' (1984) 14 California Western International Law Journal 471

Clarke, David J. 'Autonomy Under the Basic Law' in Kathleen Cheek-Milby et al (eds), *Hong Kong: The Challenge of Transformation* (qv)

Clarke, W S. 'Hong Kong Under the Chinese Constitution' (1984) 14 Hong Kong Law Journal 71

Clarke, W S. 'The Constitution of Hong Kong and 1997' in Y C Jao et al (eds), *Hong Kong and 1997* (qv) 215

Comment: 'The Legal Regime of Hong Kong After 1997: An Examination of the Joint Declaration of the United Kingdom and the People's Republic of China' (1987) 5 International Taxation and Business Lawyers 377

Cooper, Gene. 'Hong Kong: Liberation without Liberation' (1981) 13 Bulletin of Concerned Asian Scholars 61

Copper, J, F Michael, and Y Wu. *Human Rights in Post-Mao China* (Boulder: Westview Press, 1985)

Corwin, David M. 'China's Choices: The 1984 Sino-British Joint Declaration and its Aftermath' (1987) 19 Law and Policy in International Business 505

Cuthbert, A R. 'Hong Kong 1997: The Transition to Socialism — Ideology, Discourse, and Urban Spatial Structure' (1987) 5 Environment and Planning D: Society and Space 123

Dally, Peter. *Hong Kong Time Bomb* (London: British Anti-Communist Council, 1984)

Davies, Stephen. 'The Changing Nature of Representation in Hong Kong Politics' in Kathleen Cheek-Milby et al (eds), *Hong Kong: The Challenge of Transformation* (qv)

Davis, Michael C. 'A Common Law Court in a Marxist Country: The Case for Judicial Review in the Hong Kong SAR' (1988) 16 Denver Journal of International Law and Policy (forthcoming)

Davis, Michael C. 'Anglo-American Constitutionalism with Chinese Characteristics' (1989) 37 American Journal of Comparative Law (forthcoming)

Davis, Michael C. 'Free Speech in Comparative Perspective: The Case of Hong Kong' (unpublished, 1988)

Davis, Michael C. 'The HKSAR Basic Law and the Concept of Constitutional Judicial Review' (unpublished, 1987)

Davis, Michael C. 'Where Two Legal Systems Collide: An American Constitutional Scholar in Hong Kong' (1988) 20 Case Western Reserve Journal of International Law (forthcoming)

Day, Christian C. 'The Recovery of Hong Kong by the People's Republic of China — A Fifty Year Experiment in Capitalism and Freedom' (1984) 11 Syracuse Journal of International Law and Commerce 625

Dicks, Anthony. 'Treaty, Grant, Usage or Sufferance? Some Legal Aspects of the Status of Hong Kong' (1983) 95 China Quarterly 427

Dömes, Jurgen. 'The Impact of the Hong Kong Problem and the Hong Kong Agreement on PRC Domestic Politics' (1986) 22 Issues and Studies (No 6) 31

Dömes, Jurgen, and Yu-ming Shaw. *Hong Kong: A Chinese International Concern* (Boulder: Westview Press, 1988)

Donnithorne, Audrey. 'Assimilation or Separate Identity? Observations on the Future of Hong Kong's Relations with China' in Leung Chi-keung et al (eds), *Hong Kong: Dilemmas of Growth* (qv) 619

Duncanson, Dennis. ' "Hong Kong, China" — Repossession and Penetration' (1986) 42 The World Today 104

Dunn, Lydia. 'Hong Kong after the Sino-British Declaration' (1985) 61 International Affairs 197

Dunn, Lydia. 'The Policy Role of the Non-Government Members of the Executive and Legislative Councils' in Kathleen Cheek-Milby et al (eds), *Hong Kong: The Challenge of Transformation* (qv)

Easey, Walter. *Ducking Responsibility: Britain and Hong Kong in the '80s* (Manchester: Hong Kong Research Project, 1980)

Edwards, Randle, Louis Henkin, and Andrew J Nathan. *Human Rights in Contemporary China* (New York: Columbia University Press, 1986)

Finer, S E. 'Hong Kong 1997: When the Kissing Has to Stop' (1985) 56 Political Quarterly 262

Fishburne, Benjamin P. 'Hong Kong 1997: Practical Aspects' (1988) 20 Case Western Reserve Journal of International Law (forthcoming)

Fu Jin. 'China's Recovery of Xianggang Area Fully Accords with International Law' (1983) 26 Beijing Review, 26 September, pp 14, 25

Goldstein, Jay R. 'Chinese and Western Treaty Practice: An Application to the Joint Declaration Between the People's Republic of China and Great Britain Concerning the Question of Hong Kong' (1986) 1 American University Journal of International Law and Policy 167

Greenberg, Katherine A. 'Hong Kong's Future: Can the People's Republic of China Invalidate the Treaty of Nanking as an Unequal Treaty?' (1984) 7 Fordham International Law Journal 534

Ha, Louis. 'Human and Civil Rights' in William McGurn (ed), *Basic Law, Basic Questions* (qv) 113

Harding, Harry. 'The Future of Hong Kong' (1985) 12 China Business Review (No 5) 30

Harris, P B. 'Hong Kong Confronts 1997: An Assessment of the Sino-British Agreement' (1986) 59 Pacific Affairs 45

Harris, P B. 'The International Future of Hong Kong' (1972) 48 International Affairs 60

Heilbronn, Gary. 'The Changing Face of Hong Kong's International Air Transport Relations' (1988) 20 Case Western Reserve Journal of International Law (forthcoming)

Hennessy, Peter. 'Cradock's People' [1984] New Society, 11 October, p 54

Hicks, George L. 'A New China?' (unpublished, 1987)

Hicks, George L. 'Hong Kong after the Sino-British Agreement: The Illusion of Stability' (unpublished, 1987)

Hicks, George L. 'Hong Kong on the Eve of Communist Rule' in Hungdah Chiu et al, *The Future of Hong Kong* (qv) 23

Hicks, George L. 'Red Capitalism' in William McGurn (ed), *Basic Law, Basic Questions* (qv) 97

Hicks, George L. 'The Political Economy of 1997' in Y C Jao et al (eds), *Hong Kong and 1997* (qv) 399

Hook, Brian. 'The Government of Hong Kong: Change Within Tradition' (1983) 95 China Quarterly 491

Howe, Christopher. 'Growth, Public Policy and Hong Kong's Economic Relationship with China' (1983) 95 China Quarterly 512

Hsing Kuo-ch'iang. ' "One Country, Two Systems": Theory and Practice' (1987) 23 Issues and Studies (No 3) 77

Hsiung, James C. 'The Hong Kong Settlement: Effects on Taiwan and Prospects for Peking's Reunification Bid' (1985) 12 Asian Affairs (No 2) 47

Jao, Y C. 'Hong Kong's Future as a Financial Centre' (1985) 145 Three Banks Review 35

Jao, Y C. 'Hong Kong's Future as a Free Market Economy' (1986) 22 Issues and Studies (No 6) 111

Jao, Y C. 'The 1997 Issue and Hong Kong's Financial Crisis' (1985) 2 Journal of Chinese Studies 113

Jao, Y C, Leung Chi-keung, Peter Wesley-Smith and Wong Siu-lun (eds). *Hong Kong and 1997: Strategies for the Future* (Hong Kong: Centre of Asian Studies, University of Hong Kong, 1985)

Jayawickrama, Nihal. 'Hong Kong and the International Protection of Human Rights' in Ray Wacks (qv) 31

Jayawickrama, Nihal. 'Human Rights in the Basic Law' (1988) 166 Welfare Digest (Hong Kong Council of Social Service) 3

Jayawickrama, Nihal. 'Towards a Human Rights Law in Hong Kong' in *Law Lectures for Practitioners 1987* (Hong Kong: Hong Kong Law Journal Ltd, 1987) 155

Johnson, Chalmers. 'The Mousetrapping of Hong Kong: Game in which Nobody Wins' (1984) 24 Asian Survey 887

Johnson, Graham E. '1997 and After: Will Hong Kong Survive? A Personal View' (1986) 59 Pacific Affairs 237

Jones, David A, Jr. 'A Leg to Stand On? Post-1997 Hong Kong Courts as a Constraint on PRC Abridgement of Individual Rights and Local Autonomy' (1987) 12 Yale Journal of International Law 250

Karamanian, Susan L. 'Legal Aspects of the Sino-British Draft Agreement on the Future of Hong Kong' (1985) 20 Texas International Law Journal 167

Kaul, R N. 'The Hong Kong Sino-British Accord: An Analysis' (1985) 34 Foreign Affairs Report 1

King, Ambrose Y C. 'Administrative Absorption of Politics in Hong Kong: Emphasis on the Grass Roots Level' (1975) 15 Asian Survey 422

King, Ambrose Y C. 'The Hong Kong Talks and Hong Kong Politics' (1986) 22 Issues and Studies (No 6) 52

Kuan Hsin-chi and Lau Siu-kai. 'Hong Kong's Search for a Consensus: Barriers and Prospects' in Hungdah Chiu et al (eds), *The Future of Hong Kong* (qv) 95

Kuhn, Alfred G. 'Hong Kong Now and its Future in Asia' (1985) 36 Aussenpolitik 444

Lam, C K S. 'Sovereignty over Hong Kong' (1985) 16 Cambrian Law Review 77

Lamb, H K. *A Date with Fate* (Hong Kong: Lincoln Green Publishing, 1984)

Landry, Michael D. 'Joint Declaration ... on the Question of Hong Kong, British White Paper (Sept 26, 1984)' (1985) 26 Harvard International Law Journal 249

Lasater, Martin L. 'Hong Kong's Future — and Taiwan's' (1985) Heritage Foundation Executive Memorandum No 65

Lau, Emily. 'Basic Law and the SAR Government' (1988) 166 Welfare Digest (Hong Kong Council of Social Service) 1

Lau, Emily. 'Structure of the HKSAR Government' (1988) 20 Case Western Reserve Journal of International Law (forthcoming)

Lau, Emily. 'The Right to Write' in William McGurn (ed), *Basic Law, Basic Questions* (qv) 69

Lau Siu-kai. 'Basic Law and the New Political Order of Hong Kong' (Centre for Hong Kong Studies, Chinese University of Hong Kong, 1988)

Lau Siu-kai. 'Decolonisation Without Independence: The Unfinished Political Reforms of the Hong Kong Government' (Occasional Papers No 19, Centre for Hong Kong Studies, Chinese University of Hong Kong; May 1987)

Lau Siu-kai. 'Government Intermediate Organisations and Grass-Roots Politics in Hong Kong' (1981) 21 Asian Survey 865

Lau Siu-kai. 'Local Administrative Reform in Hong Kong: Promises and Limitations' (1982) 22 Asian Survey 858

Lau Siu-kai. 'Social Change, Bureaucratic Rule, and Emergent Political Issues in Hong Kong' (1983) 35 World Politics 544

Lau Siu-kai. *Society and Politics in Hong Kong* (Hong Kong: Chinese University Press, 1982)

Lau Siu-kai and Kuan Hsin-chi. 'Hong Kong After the Sino-British Agreement: The Limits to Change' (1986) 59 Pacific Affairs 214

Lau Siu-kai and Kuan Hsin-chi. 'The 1985 District Board Election in Hong Kong: The Limits of Political Mobilisation in a Dependent Polity' (1987) 25 Journal of Commonwealth and Comparative Politics 82

Lau Siu-kai and Kuan Hsin-chi. 'The Changing Political Culture of the Hong Kong Chinese' in Joseph Y S Cheng (eds), *Hong Kong in Transition* (qv) 26

Lau Siu-kai and Kuan Hsin-chi. 'The Civic Self in a Changing Polity: The Case of Hong Kong' in Kathleen Cheek-Milby et al (eds), *Hong Kong: The Challenge of Transformation* (qv)

Lau Siu-kai and Kuan Hsin-chi. *The Ethos of the Hong Kong Chinese* (Hong Kong: Chinese University Press, forthcoming 1988)

Lawrie, Gordon. 'Hong Kong and the People's Republic of China: Past and Future' (1980) 56 International Affairs 280

Lee, Martin C M. 'How Much Autonomy?' in William McGurn (ed), *Basic Law, Basic Questions* (qv) 37

Lee, Martin C M. 'The Significance of a Written Constitution for Hong Kong' (unpublished, 1987)

Lee, Martin C M. 'The Basic Law for Hong Kong — Will it Bring About "One Country, Two Systems"?' (unpublished, 1988)

Lee, Martin C M, and Szeto Wah. *The Basic Law: Some Basic Flaws* (Hong Kong: Lee and Wah, 1988)

Lee Ta-ling. 'Hong Kong: The Human Rights Dimension' in Hungdah Chiu et al (eds), *The Future of Hong Kong* (qv) 115

Lee Ta-ling and John F Copper. *Reform in Reverse: Human Rights in the People's Republic of China, 1986/1987* (Maryland: School of Law, University of Maryland, Occasional Papers/Reprint Series in Contemporary Asian Studies, 1987)

Lee Tung-ming. 'The Sino-British Joint Declaration on the Question of Hong Kong' (unpublished PhD dissertation, University of Oklahoma, 1985)

Leong, C H. 'Professional Accreditation After 1997' (1988) 166 Welfare Digest (Hong Kong Council of Social Service) 6

Leung Chi-keung, J W Cushman and Wang Gungwu. *Hong Kong: Dilemmas of Growth* (Hong Kong: Centre of Asian Studies Occasional Papers and Monographs No 45, 1980)

Lewis, D K. *The Prospects for Hong Kong* (London: Institute for the Study of Conflict, 1982)

Li Jiaquan. 'Formula for China's Reunification' [1986] Beijing Review No 5, 3 February, p 18

Liu, William H. 'China Factor in Hong Kong Banking and Trade' (1987) 23 Issues and Studies (No 5) 83

Liu, William H. 'Hong Kong Dimensions in Post-Mao Economic Strategy' (1986) 22 Issues and Studies (No 10) 89

Liu Yiu Chu. 'Interpretation and Review of the Basic Law of the HKSAR' (1988) 2 Journal of Chinese Law 49

Macintyre, Thomas S. 'Impact of the Sino-British Agreement on Hong Kong's Economic Future' (1985) 7 Journal of Comparative Business and Capital Market Law 197

MacPherson, Kerrie L. ' "Gangren Zhi Gang": The Emergence of Local Politics' (unpublished, 1988)

McGurn, William (ed). *Basic Law, Basic Questions: The Debate Continues* (Hong Kong: Review Publishing Co Ltd, 1988)

Miners, N J. 'Alternative Governmental Structures for a Future Self-Governing Hong Kong' in Y C Jao et al (eds), *Hong Kong and 1997* (qv) 9

Miners, N J. 'Can the Colony of Hong Kong Survive 1997?' (1979) 6 Asia Pacific Community 100

Miners, N J. 'China and Hong Kong's Future' in Leung Chi-keung et al (eds), *Hong Kong: Dilemmas of Growth* (qv) 13

Miners, N J. 'Move Towards Representative Government 1984–88' in Kathleen Cheek-Milby et al (eds), *Hong Kong: The Challenge of Transformation* (qv)

Miners, N J. 'Plans for Constitutional Reform in Hong Kong, 1946–52' (1986) 107 China Quarterly 463

Miners, N J. *The Government and Politics of Hong Kong* (Hong Kong: Oxford University Press, 4th ed 1986)

Mosher, Steven W. *In Human Rights, China Remains in the Maoist Era* (1985) Heritage Foundation Asian Studies Center Backgrounder No 30

Mushkat, Miron. 'Constructing Long-Term Scenarios of the Hong Kong Economy' in Kathleen Cheek-Milby et al (eds), *Hong Kong: The Challenge of Transformation* (qv)

Mushkat, Miron. 'Environmental Change and Policy Response in Hong Kong' (1988) 17 Journal of East West Studies 55

Mushkat, Roda. 'The International Legal Status of Hong Kong Under Post-Transitional Rule' (1987) 10 Houston Journal of International Law 1

Mushkat, Roda. 'The Transition from British to Chinese Rule in Hong Kong: A Discussion of Salient International Legal Issues' (1986) 14 Denver Journal of International Law and Policy 171

Newsham, Grant. 'Rethinking Hong Kong: A Blueprint for the Future' (1982) 1 UCLA Pacific Basin Law Journal 247

O'Grady, James. 'The Legal Theory of Authority: A Source of Reassurance in the Transitional Period' in Kathleen Cheek-Milby et al (eds), *Hong Kong: The Challenge of Transformation* (qv)

Overholt, William H. 'Hong Kong after the Chinese-British Agreement' (1985) 84 Current History 256, 274

Overholt, William H. 'Hong Kong and China: A New Relationship' (1985) 84 Current History 258, 273

Overholt, William H. 'Hong Kong and the Crisis of Sovereignty' (1984) 24 Asian Survey 471

Parlin, Timothy B. 'The Nationality Crisis of Hong Kong's Non-Chinese Residents — Scholarly Myth or Harsh Reality' (1986) 12 Brooklyn Journal of International Law 369

Perry, James and Shui-yan Tang. 'Administrative Transition: Integrating Politics and Administration' in Kathleen Cheek-Milby et al (eds), *Hong Kong: The Challenge of Transformation* (qv)

Prybyla, Jan S. 'The Hong Kong Agreement and its Impact on the World Economy' (1986) 22 Issues and Studies (No 6) 92

Pye, Lucian. 'The International Position of Hong Kong' (1983) 95 China Quarterly 456

Rabushka, Alvin. 'Hong Kong's Prospects for 1997' (Standford: Hoover Institution on War, Revolution, and Peace, 1985)

Rabushka, Alvin. '*The New China: Comparative Economic Development in Mainland China, Taiwan, and Hong Kong* (Boulder, Colorado: Westview Press, 1987)

Ress, Georg. 'The Legal Status of Hong Kong after 1997: The Consequences of the Transfer of Sovereignty according to the Joint Declaration of December 19, 1984' (1986) 4 Zeitschrift fur auslandisches offentliches Recht und Volkerrecht 647

Rich, Bill. 'Hong Kong: Revolution Without Change' (unpublished, 1988)

Roff, Charles L. 'Hong Kong Property Title and the Joint Declaration' (1986) 21 Texas International Law Journal 529

Roy, S C. 'The Hong Kong Agreement: An Assessment' (1985) 21 China Report 169

Scheuer, Martin. 'Civil Liberties and Human Rights in Hong Kong and Macao — Present and Future' (unpublished, 1988)

Scobell, Andrew. 'Strung Up or Shot Down? The Death Penalty in Hong Kong and China and Implications for Post-1997' (1988) 20 Case Western Reserve Journal of International Law (forthcoming)

Scott, Ian. 'Policy-making in a Turbulent Environment: The Case of Hong Kong' (1986) 52 International Review of Administrative Sciences 447

Scott, Ian. 'The Sino-British Agreement and Political Power in Hong Kong' (1986) 31 Asia Pacific Community 1

Scott, Ian, and John P Burns (eds). *The Hong Kong Civil Service and its Future* (Hong Kong: Oxford University Press, 1988)

Shaw Yu-ming. 'An ROC View of the Hong Kong Issue' (1986) 22 Issues and Studies (No 6) 13

Simon, D F. 'Taiwan's Political Economy and the Evolving Links between the PRC, Hong Kong, and Taiwan' (1986) 6 AEI Foreign Policy and Defence Review 42

Tang Shu-hung. 'Basic Law — Its Economic Stipulations' (1988) 166 Welfare Digest (Hong Kong Council of Social Service) 4

Tsang, Iris Y L. 'Religious Freedom and the Basic Law' (1987) 38 Tripod 51

Tsang, Steve Yui-sang. *Democracy Shelved: Great Britain, China, and Attempts at Constitutional Reform in Hong Kong, 1945–1952* (Hong Kong: Oxford University Press, 1988)

Tsim, T L. '1997: Peking's Strategy for Hong Kong' (1984) 40 The World Today 37

Tsim, T L. 'One Country, Two Systems' (unpublished, 1988)

Tso, Kerrin. 'The Legal Implications of the Sino-British Treaties Regarding Hong Kong' (1981) 4 Loyola LA International and Comparative Law Journal 111

Wacks, Ray (ed). *Civil Liberties in Hong Kong* (Hong Kong, Oxford, New York: Oxford University Press, 1988)

Walden, John. 'Accountability: Past, Present and Future' in William McGurn (ed), *Basic Law, Basic Questions* (qv) 53

Walden, John. *Excellency, Your Gap is Growing!* (Hong Kong: All Noble Co Ltd, 1987)

Walden, John. *Excellency, Your Gap is Showing!* (Hong Kong: Corporate Communications Ltd, 1983)

Wang Shuwen. 'The Basic Rights and Obligations of Residents of the HKSAR' (1988) 2 Journal of Chinese Law 123

Waterson, Nigel. *Hong Kong's Future — Countdown to Communism?* (London: Bow Publications Ltd 1984)

Weng, Byron S J. 'Executive Power in the Hong Kong Basic Law' (unpublished, 1987)

Weng, Byron S J. ' "One Country, Two Systems" and the Prospects of China's Reunification' (to be published in an anthology to be released by Grinnell College in 1988)

Weng, Byron S J. 'Taiwan and Hong Kong 1987: A Review' in Anthony J Kane (ed), *China Briefing, 1988* (Boulder, Colorado: Westview Press, 1988)

Weng, Byron S J. 'The Hong Kong Model of "One Country, Two Systems": Promises and Problems' (1987–88) 14 *Asian Affairs, An American Review* (No 4) 193

Weng, Byron S J. 'The Integration of Outlying Areas: The Case of Hong Kong' in Harish Kapur (ed), *The End of an Isolation: China After Mao* (Dordrecht: Martinus Nijhoff Publications, 1985) 308.

Wesley-Smith, Peter. 'China and Hong Kong' in Ann Trotter (ed), *New Zealand and China: The Papers of the Twenty-first Foreign Policy School 1986* (University of Otago, 1986) 87

Wesley-Smith, Peter. *Constitutional and Administrative Law in Hong Kong* (Hong Kong: China and Hong Kong Law Studies Ltd, 1987), vol i

Wesley-Smith, Peter. 'Hong Kong' in Albert P Blaustein and Eric B Blaustein, *Constitutions of Dependencies and Special Sovereignties* (New York: Oceana Publications, Inc, 1985), vol v

Wesley-Smith, Peter. 'Hong Kong: The Coming Bad Years' (1983) 2 Euro-Asia Business Review (No 2) 12

Wesley-Smith, Peter. 'Hong Kong and 1997: The Options' in Joseph Y S Cheng, *Hong Kong in Search of a Future* (qv) 203

Wesley-Smith, Peter. 'Settlement of the Question of Hong Kong' (1987) 17 California Western International Law Journal 116

Wesley-Smith, Peter. 'The Hong Kong Act 1985' [1986] Public Law 122

Wesley-Smith, Peter. 'The Legal System, the Constitution, and the Future of Hong Kong' (1984) 14 Hong Kong Law Journal 137

Wesley-Smith, Peter. *Unequal Treaty 1898–1997: China, Great Britain and Hong Kong's New Territories* (Hong Kong: Oxford University Press, paperback ed 1983)

White, Robin M. 'Hong Kong: Nationality, Immigration and the Agreement with China' (1987) 36 International and Comparative Law Quarterly 483

White, Robin M. 'Nationality Aspects of the Hong Kong Settlements' (1988) 20 Case Western Reserve Journal of International Law (forthcoming)

Wilkinson, Paul. 'Hong Kong: A One-Way Ticket to an Unknown Destination' (1983) 18 Government and Opposition 442

Wilson, Dick. 'New Thoughts on the Future of Hong Kong' (1977) 8 Pacific Community 588

Wong Siu-lun. 'Modernisation and Chinese Culture in Hong Kong' (1986) 106 China Quarterly 306

Wu An-chia. 'Can the Hong Kong Settlement Serve as a Model for Taiwan?' in Hungdah Chiu et al (eds), *The Future of Hong Kong* (qv) 155

Wu An-chia. ' "One Country, Two Systems": A Model for Taiwan?' (1985) 21 Issues and Studies (No 7) 33

Wu Jianfan. 'Several Issues Concerning the Relationship Between the Central Government of the PRC and the HKSAR' (1988) 2 Journal of Chinese Law 65

Wu Yuan-li. 'In the Shadow of 1997: Interaction between Hong Kong and Its Economic Partners and Neighbours' in Hungdah Chiu et al (eds), *The Future of Hong Kong* (qv) 139

Wu Yuan-li. 'The Future of Hong Kong Before and After 1997' (1984) American Asian Review 13

Wu Yuan-li and Y C Jao. 'The Economic Consequences of 1997' (1988) 20 Case Western Reserve Journal of International Law (forthcoming)

Xiao Weiyuan. 'A Study of the Political System of the HKSAR under the Basic Law' (1988) 2 Journal of Chinese Law 95

Yan Jiaqi. 'One Country, Two Systems: Concept Points Way to Reunification' in Zhou Guo (ed), *China & the World (7)* (Beijing: Beijing Review Foreign Affairs Series, 1986) 45

Yee, Herbert S, and Wong Yiu-chung. 'Hong Kong: The Politics of the Daya Bay Nuclear Plant Debate' (1987) 63 International Affairs 617

Young, John D. 'China's Role in Two Hong Kong Disturbances: A Scenario for the Future?' (1981) 19 Journal of Oriental Studies 158

Young, John D. 'Drafting Hong Kong's Future Constitution: (II) Implications for China's Reunification' (unpublished, 1988)

Young, John D. 'Socialism versus Capitalism: Towards a Hong Kong Strategy for Absorption Without Integration' in Y C Jao et al (eds), *Hong Kong and 1997* (qv) 101

Youngson, A J (ed). *China and Hong Kong: The Economic Nexus* (Hong Kong: Oxford University Press, 1983)

Yu Teh-pei. 'An Analysis of Economic Ties Linking Hong Kong, PRC and ROC – With Special Reference to Trade' (1986) 22 Issues and Studies (No 6) 144

Zhang Youyu. 'The Reasons for and the Basic Principles in Formulating the HKSAR Basic Law, and Its Essential Contents and Mode of Expression' (1988) 2 Journal of Chinese Law 5

Zhou Guo (ed). *The Hong Kong Solution* (Beijing: Beijing Review Foreign Affairs Series, China & the World (No 6), 1985)

Index

145 int   cfra 91254

26/489